America Firsthand

EIGHTH EDITION

Volume Two
Readings from Reconstruction to the Present

Robert D. Marcus

Late of the State University
of New York College at Brockport

David Burner

State University of New York at Stony Brook

Anthony Marcus

University of Melbourne
John Jay College of Criminal Justice
of the City University of New York

BEDFORD/ST. MARTIN'S
Boston ◆ New York

FOR BEDFORD/ST. MARTIN'S

Publisher for History: Mary V. Dougherty
Executive Editor: William J. Lombardo
Senior Editor: Louise Townsend
Editorial Assistants: Katherine Flynn, Jennifer Jovin
Production Associate: Ashley Chalmers
Executive Marketing Manager: Jenna Bookin Barry
Project Management: Books By Design, Inc.
Cover Design: Billy Boardman
Cover Photo: *Duck and Cover Drill in Classroom*, February 1, 1951. Bettmann/Corbis.
Composition: Achorn International
Printing and Binding: R.R. Donnelley & Sons Company

President: Joan E. Feinberg
Editorial Director: Denise B. Wydra
Director of Marketing: Karen R. Soeltz
Director of Editing, Design, and Production: Marcia Cohen
Assistant Director of Editing, Design, and Production: Elise S. Kaiser
Manager, Publishing Services: Emily Berleth

Library of Congress Control Number: 2008933819

Manufactured in the United States of America.

4   3   2   1   0   9
f   e   d   c   b   a

For information, write: Bedford/St. Martin's, 75 Arlington Street,
Boston, MA 02116   (617-399-4000)

ISBN-10: 0-312-48907-2
ISBN-13: 978-0-312-48907-6

This book is dedicated to Robert Marcus, who died in October 2000; he was one of the two creators and coeditors of America Firsthand. *At the time of Bob's death, his doctoral sponsor Robert Wiebe — soon to pass away himself — eulogized that Bob had "a first-rate mind, was ingenious, versatile, and brimming over with fresh ideas." We remember Bob as an original thinker, a thoughtful scholar, and a true friend.*

Preface

When *America Firsthand* was launched in the late 1980s, Ronald Reagan was president; the personal computer was not yet tied to the limitless global information web we now call the Internet; educators were becoming concerned about fostering students' critical thinking skills; and U.S. history instructors were just beginning to introduce social history methods into undergraduate classes. In these last two efforts, *America Firsthand* led the way, successfully bringing the resources and tools for learning, interpreting, and writing about U.S. history to students in classrooms across the United States and Canada, while providing a uniquely personal view of how ordinary Americans lived, witnessed, and made history.

Now, more than twenty years later, we live in what is commonly called the Information Age. Students and instructors are confronted by a staggering array of historical sources, resources, and images, available on millions of Web sites put up by community groups, political organizations, governments, universities, and just about anybody willing to manage a blog. The sources one can draw on are increasingly diverse, fragmented, particular, and de-contextualized. It is for this reason that *America Firsthand* remains more than ever a crucial classroom resource. Whether used as a companion to a survey text or as a stand-alone, this collection, covering the broad sweep of U.S. history from new world encounters to the twenty-first century, provides a common ground where students can ponder and debate key historical moments and topics and test their ideas against other ideas in the classroom and in the world beyond. The editors of *America Firsthand* are proud to provide the intellectual space in which students can discover the pleasures and challenges of primary documents while developing the critical skills necessary to read, interpret, and understand America's past.

The eighth edition continues *America Firsthand*'s emphasis on individuals making and living history, adding newly uncovered and rediscovered documents with more of the voices and topics that reviewers have asked for: more from Asian Americans and Native Americans, and more on religion, popular and political culture, technology, and the environment. In Volume One, students read the words of Pueblo Indians in revolt against the Spanish empire and those of a Scots-Iroquois leader fighting for the British; they learn about the experiences of Jews in colonial America and of deists and revivalists in the nineteenth century; and they experience the back and forth mudslinging of political propaganda through revolutionary era cartoons; in Volume Two, they encounter naturalist

John Muir fighting to preserve his beloved American wilderness; they learn what it was like to move to a single-family home for the first time in a place called "the suburbs" in the 1940s; and they read an account by a fledgling dot.com-er who risks it all in the 1990s high-tech boom. This is but a small sampling from the rich array of new documents and old favorites contained in this edition.

The eighth edition retains our popular Points of View, part-opening features that juxtapose readings on a specific event or topic, providing students with opportunities for critical thinking and analysis of different perspectives from the past. For instance, in Volume One, students encounter contrasting views of the conquest of Mexico by conquistador Hernando Cortés and Nahua natives, and in Volume Two multiple perspectives on the creation and dropping of the atomic bomb on Hiroshima and Nagasaki during World War II. Critical thinking questions at the close of the documents help students sift through the evidence, make connections, and analyze the readings in relation to one another.

Volume One offers two new Points of View, one contrasting the experiences of colonial women, the other juxtaposing the views of Frederick Douglass and a Southern slaveholder at the close of the Civil War, as both men contemplate the future. Volume Two also contains two new Points of View, one featuring accounts of the Battle of Little Bighorn by Native Americans and by an Italian American soldier of fortune who was present at "Custer's last stand," the other featuring witnesses to the Guantánamo Bay Detention Center and their public battle over the legacy of George W. Bush's war on terror.

This edition also includes one new visual portfolio in each volume, with commentary, background information, and critical-thinking questions to help students engage in meaningful analysis of the images. The first volume features a set of patriot and loyalist propaganda cartoons, exposing students to the kind of visual propaganda and powerful imagery that was and remains an important means of influencing the public. The second volume includes a new portfolio on "The Peopling of the West" with broadsides, photographs, and cartoons that convey the incredible ethnic diversity that characterized the West during the second half of the nineteenth century.

In addition to the visual portfolios that appear in each volume, we include stand-alone visual documents throughout, sources that are treated the same as the textual documents, with headnotes and questions to help students make sense of these images as evidence. Volume One, for example, gives students the opportunity to analyze an early French map that suggests the relationship between mapmaking and colonialism, while Volume Two features photographs, both provocative and challenging, of the 1992 Los Angeles riots in the wake of the Rodney King verdict.

Throughout, we retain sources that users have said they wanted and dropped less successful ones. New selections in the first volume include Mary Rowlandson's captivity narrative (the first example of a colonial woman's autobiographical writing); the views of Elihu Palmer, often described as America's first atheist; and a description of the events that led Henry "Box" Brown, once a relatively well-off urban slave, to abandon everything and mail himself to freedom in a box. Fresh selections in the second volume include tales of life on the road during the Great Depression, inside views of the feminist and Puerto Rican ethnic rights movements of the 1960s, and Al Gore's speech on global warming when he accepted the Nobel Prize in 2007.

As in previous editions, carefully written headnotes preceding the selections prepare students for each reading and help locate personalities in their times and places. Questions to Consider immediately following the headnotes offer points to reflect on when reading and encourage in-depth analysis. This time around we have added even more gloss notes at the base of the page within the accounts to identify unfamiliar names and terms.

To better equip students with the tools for working with all the sources in this collection—visual as well as textual—we have revised and expanded the student introduction on Studying and Writing History. And to ensure that instructors get the support *they* need, the *Instructor's Resource Manual* has been thoroughly revised and updated by Margaret Rung of Roosevelt University. Available online at bedfordstmartins.com/marcusburner, this manual includes discussion of the main themes and topics in each part, references to and summaries of relevant books and articles, strategies for teaching with the documents including in-class learning activities and Suggestions for Collaborative Learning Exercises for each Points of View feature, as well as ample discussion and essay questions.

America Firsthand, Eighth Edition, presents the American experience through the perspectives of diverse people who have in common a vivid record of the world they inhabited and of the events they experienced. We hope that this collection will continue to provide a rich and rewarding intellectual space for students, one in which they can develop their own interest in firsthand sources to further their own historical knowledge, bringing that knowledge to bear in the classroom, in their lives, and in the world beyond.

ABOUT THE AUTHORS

The eighth edition of *America Firsthand* has been brought to press by Anthony Marcus, who replaced his father, Robert Marcus, after his untimely death in October 2000, joining co-author David Burner. Burner, a Guggenheim Fellow and emeritus scholar at the State University of New York at Stony Brook, together with his longtime friend and collaborator Robert Marcus brought *America Firsthand* into the world and nurtured it over several successful editions. Anthony Marcus is an historian and anthropologist who has taught college students for over fifteen years and published on race, ethnicity, and public policy in the United States, Latin America, Australia, and Indonesia. With the eighth edition, he seeks to continue *America Firsthand*'s tradition of pedagogical excellence and to uphold his father's oft-stated commitment to "include people from many groups whose experience has been, until recently, largely lost in mainstream history."

ACKNOWLEDGMENTS

We would like to thank all the instructors who graciously provided helpful comments for improving *America Firsthand*: Lesley Gordon, University of Akron; John Wigger, University of Missouri; Richard Meixsel, James Madison University; Sharon Anderson, Tennessee Tech University; Jennifer Helgren, University of the Pacific; Martha K. Robinson, Clarion University; Steven Kite, Fort Hays State University; Tim Lehman, Rocky Mountain College; Kathleen Clark, University of Georgia; Deborah Blackwell, Texas A&M International University; Sharon Rubin, Ramapo College of New Jersey; Craig Smith, Missouri State University; Margaret Rung, Roosevelt University; Nikki Taylor, University of Cincinnati; Mary Ann Bodayla, Southwest Tennessee Community College; Wendy Castro, University of Central Arkansas; Melinda Barr, Oklahoma City Community College; Joyce Goldberg, University of Texas–Arlington; Scott Newman, Loyola University–Chicago; and Laurie Chin, California State University–Long Beach. And finally, thanks to Gerald Sider, whose 2003 book *Between History and Tomorrow: Making and Breaking Everyday Life in Rural Newfoundland* provided the inspiration for the title of Chapter 7 of Volume Two.

We are also grateful to all the members of the Bedford/St. Martin's staff who have been involved with the development of the reader from start to finish and have made this edition of *America Firsthand* the best that it can be. Thanks to Katherine Flynn and Jennifer Jovin for helping with numerous tasks on this project; to photo researcher Lisa Jelly Smith for help with the expanded visual component; to Donna Dennison and Billy Boardman for creating the new book covers; to Emily Berleth and Nancy Benjamin for turning the manuscript into a book; to Joan Feinberg and Denise Wydra for agreeing to bring out another edition and making sure that it happened; to Mary Dougherty and William Lombardo, who oversaw the business and logistical side; to Jane Knetzger, who oversaw the editorial development of the project; and to Louise Townsend, whose tireless efforts and ability to be maddeningly picky about details, while still getting the big picture, made her exactly the navigator that this project needed at this time.

Introduction: Using Sources to Study the Past

The study of history offers us a way of knowing who we are, where we have come from, and where we are headed. Perhaps because we live in the present it is sometimes easy to assume that people in the past were basically like us, just with different clothing, as is the case in most Hollywood history movies, where protagonists are made sympathetic to contemporary audiences by giving them modern goals and desires. In such "historical dramas" people fight for their nation, even if neither it nor the very idea of a nation exists yet; they make great sacrifices for romantic love, even if this concept has not yet been invented; struggle to protect the innocence of children, even if there is not yet a concept of childhood; and demand personal freedom, in societies where the greatest goal is to have a defined place in the social order. These uses of dramatic license to place modern motivations and values into the past is called historical anachronism, and it usually leads to good movies, but rather poor understanding of how our ancestors made decisions and took actions. History is a systematic attempt to study the differences and similarities between the past and the present, in order to understand how we got from there to here and how we may craft our future.

How, then, do we as students of history or historians approach the study of our past? The first step is to pose a research question about the past. For example:

- What was social life like between African Americans and white Americans in colonial Virginia?

Asking this question is important because so much of our vision of race relations before the civil rights movement of the 1940s–1960s is built on visions of the hardened institutionalized slavery of the mid-nineteenth century and the Jim Crow segregation that followed. Some historians, like Edmund Morgan, have argued that relations between whites and blacks were more fluid and equal in the first century of the British colonization of North America, when slavery was not hereditary or restricted to African Americans, who could still testify in court, cohabit with white women, buy their own freedom, and even own slaves, all providing that they converted to Christianity.

Knowing something about how the nineteenth-century horrors of industrial scale slavery, laws against literacy among slaves, and finally segregation emerged from an earlier, and perhaps less harsh, time can help us understand the nature of race relations in America and tell us something about the potential for changes in the future. Whatever our motivation is for posing questions such as the one above, the first step in trying to address them is to find relevant sources that may provide answers. These come in two broad categories: *primary sources* and *secondary sources*.

PRIMARY SOURCES

Primary sources are documents and artifacts directly produced by the individuals and groups that participated in or witnessed the situation, event, or topic being researched. They are a lot like the evidence and testimony that lawyers use in a courtroom to present different versions of what happened and why. Often answering the question "why" is just as important as figuring out what actually happened. For example, if it is known that a defendant shoved his brother off a roof to his death, it matters to the judge, jury, and district attorney whether the action was self-defense, an accident, or occurred in the heat of anger. If the court can establish that the killer invited his brother to the roof two days after learning that his brother had named him as sole beneficiary in a life insurance policy, the results are likely to be very different than if we discover that it was the dead brother who set up the meeting on the roof and neither stood to benefit from the death.

All the sources included in *America Firsthand* are primary ones, but this is only a small sample of what is possible in primary source research. The types of primary sources are as limitless as the imagination of the historian. Human records of all kinds leave useful information for scholars and students. From a drawing done by an eighteenth-century child showing what was taught to young elites to DNA suggesting that Thomas Jefferson had children with his African American slave, Sally Hemings, or a colonial New York candlestick holder made by a Portuguese Jew with designs borrowed from Native Americans to oral history interviews, every primary source leaves behind clues for the historian. The problem is often sorting out which clues are useful and which are not. This may change depending on what questions are being asked and what techniques are available at the time of research.

Not only can science and technology make old primary sources newly important; social and political changes also open up new possibilities for asking different *kinds* of questions of the evidence. Obviously, Thomas Jefferson's DNA had little value before modern advances in genetics but also, until the study of slavery and sexual relations between whites and blacks had advanced to a certain stage, few historians would have dared ask questions about Jefferson's potential fathering of children by a slave woman. Similarly, historian James Lockhart probably never would have crossed the globe to bring together Nahua descriptions of the conquest of Mexico (Volume One, Document 2) if there had not been an indigenous civil rights movement when he was in school in the 1960s and 1970s that drew attention to the native point of view. There would have been far less interest before September 11, 2001, in why Shams Alwujude

(Volume Two, Document 42) chooses to wear a traditional Middle Eastern head covering. Instead, it probably would have been ignored as an old-fashioned cultural tradition soon to disappear, as did the Italian, Greek, and Jewish female head coverings in the United States during the early twentieth century. Prompted by events of the present, historians are now busy looking for new primary sources to answer research questions pertaining to such questions as whether or not the prevalence and use of Muslim head coverings in the United States has increased over time and if so, why. What type of visual or written primary sources might help historians to answer this question?

Returning to our first question about the social life between African Americans and white Americans in colonial Virginia, the relationship between Sally Hemings and Thomas Jefferson might tell us something important. Although Hemings was born at the very end of the colonial period, the world that she and Jefferson inhabited may have been as much like the seventeenth century as the nineteenth century. Now that it is widely accepted, thanks to DNA testing, that Hemings bore Jefferson a child, much of the controversy revolves around how equal, unequal, voluntary, or coerced the sexual relationship was between an aged former president and the teenage girl who was his legal property. For some the inequality of race and age and the fact that Jefferson owned Hemings is decisive proof that it was a highly coercive relationship. For others, who argue that men and women of every race had legally unequal marriages at that time, the fact that Hemings signed legal documents for Jefferson, traveled with him, and chose to remain with him, even though they lived for a time in France, where she was legally a free woman and may have had many offers of marriage from eligible Frenchmen is proof that this relationship was somewhat mutual.

What kind of evidence do you think would show that this relationship was coercive and unequal? What kind of evidence would show that Hemings was her own woman? Does the fact that she was the half sister of Jefferson's deceased wife say anything about the mixing of races among the elites in colonial America? For some commentators, "the bottom line" is that Jefferson never married Hemings and could not, by law. However, the existence of such key primary sources as laws allow a variety of interpretations. The mere fact that courts started to pass miscegenation (intermarriage between people of different racial background) laws in the eighteenth century is a good sign that a) there were such interracial marriages; b) blacks and whites were increasingly being allocated different positions in society; and c) inequality was becoming increasingly fixed. The historian may find clues in primary sources as complex as philosophic essays and autobiographies and as simple as shopping lists, photographs, and Hemings' signature on Jefferson household payments for animal feed.

SECONDARY SOURCES

Secondary sources are books and articles in scholarly journals that bring together collections of evidence in order to interpret and build arguments around what happened. They offer answers to research questions and provide stories that link together all the evidence into coherent and interesting narratives. Secondary sources provide background about a particular subject, include important references to primary sources through footnotes and bibliographies, and raise questions, topics, and debates that form the foundation for further research. To take the courtroom analogy a step further, it is the lawyer's job, like the historian's, to take the evidence (primary sources) and build a case (secondary source). It is impossible to build a case unless you have some idea of what the other lawyers are saying, what their evidence is, and how they plan to structure their case. This is why courts have a "discovery" process that requires lawyers to share their evidence with opposing counsel before trial. And it is why history teachers send students off to the library to read secondary sources before allowing them to plunge into the difficult task of going through birth records or ship manifests looking for new evidence, trying to rearrange the old evidence, or combining the two to create a new understanding of what happened. The exciting part of history is when you come up with your own questions about the past and find answers that create knowledge and spark new ways of understanding the past, present, and even the future.

APPROACHING SOURCES CRITICALLY

In any courtroom trial, opposing lawyers try many ways to poke holes in each other's argument, but at the end of the day, the jury must decide what evidence is most relevant, whose testimony is the most reliable, and which argument is most convincing. The same standard applies to historical sources. In determining if slavery was economically inefficient, do we trust the tax office's records or the plantation owner's financial records, his complaints to his congressman about how much tax he was paying, or his boastful letters to his sister about cheating on his taxes? Is there a good reason why some or all of these sources may be lying, stretching the truth, or simply misleading? Who is a more reliable witness to slavery, the slave or the slaveholder; the Northern abolitionist or the Southern politician; the poor white farmer who hates the slaveholders or the English gentleman visiting his Georgia cousins? Every person has a unique point of view, set of beliefs, way of seeing things, and reason for giving testimony, and we must critically analyze and evaluate everything and assume nothing. This point of view constitutes the bias of the source. Because all sources are biased, it is important that you develop a set of questions for interrogating primary sources. Some useful questions to ask are these:

- What is the historical context for the document? When was it produced, and how does it relate to important events of the period? (Note: The headnotes for the sources included in this book provide you with background information.)
- Who is the author? What can you tell about that person's background, social status, and so on?
- What can you infer about the purpose of the document? Who was its intended audience?

- What does the style and tone of the document tell you about the author's purpose?
- What main points does the author seek to communicate or express?
- What does the document suggest about the author's point of view and biases? Consider whether the author misunderstood what he or she is relating or had reason to falsify the account on purpose.
- What can you infer about how typical for the period the views expressed in the document are?

Additional thought must be given to visual sources. When working with visual sources, ask the following questions in addition to those above:

- How is the image framed or drawn? What was included? What might have been excluded? What does this tell you about the event, person, or place you are analyzing?
- What medium (drawing, painting, or photograph, etc.) did the creator employ? What constraints did the medium impose on the creator? For example, photographic technology in the nineteenth century was very rudimentary and involved large, bulky cameras with very slow shutter speeds. This tells us something about why people often posed stiffly, without smiles on their faces, for early photographs. Likewise, while there are numerous Civil War photographs, most were posed or created after battles because the camera's shutter speeds did not allow for action photography.
- Do you know if the work was expensive or cheap to produce? What might this suggest about the event, person, or place you are analyzing?

Historians strive not to use the standards of the present to make judgments on the past. When working with both primary and secondary sources, the question of historical context must always be considered. For example, the decision to drop atomic bombs on Hiroshima and Nagasaki is often said to have been made without the same taboos, socio-political fears, and ecological concerns that are today tied to atomic energy and atomic weapons. It was largely assumed, during the entire process of developing atomic weapons, that they would be used. At the time, there was little serious discussion of not using this new war technology to hasten the end of the war with Japan, beyond a few last-minute letters and petitions from the very atomic scientists who had spent years and vast sums of money working to develop this new weapon. This was the historical context in which the decision to drop the atomic bomb was made. To bring in more modern concerns such as nuclear proliferation and environmental impact would be moving beyond this decision's historical context.

However, you should be wary of simply absolving those who made the bomb, gave the orders, and carried out the mission by reducing history to "the way people viewed things back then." It is difficult enough to figure out today's social context or how people view things now; the past is even more uncertain and filled with dissenting views. Many respected and important people during the prewar years had argued passionately against the dropping of bombs on civilian populations. They claimed that it was ethically unforgivable and not a particularly useful or effective practice of war that might strengthen a civilian population's will to fight, rather than soften them up for conquest. These people might have had no knowledge of the devastation of atomic weapons, but they were living at the time that Hiroshima and Nagasaki were bombed, and they certainly would not have viewed it as an acceptable act of warfare. Several international conventions attempted to eliminate bombing of civilians from modern warfare and thousands of journals, letters, autobiographies, movies, novels, and popular songs suggest that throughout the twentieth century many politicians, generals, and bomber pilots were uncomfortable with this peculiarly abstract and violent form of warfare against civilians.

There are, therefore, no easy answers to the question, "How did people view things back then?" Like the present, the past contains a multitude of contested and contradictory norms, values, and perspectives held by a variety of people with different understandings of the context in which people took action and made history. This is the most complicated aspect of historical inquiry and interpretation, taking evidence, finding the right context, and telling a story about the similarities and differences between past and present. Returning to the first question in this introduction, we cannot know whether blacks and whites were once equal in seventeenth-century Virginia, unless we know something about the contemporary values, rules, and social expectations of the time. What did it mean to be equal? If being a member of the Church of England was the key marker of belonging in seventeenth-century Virginia, it may be that African converts to Christianity had more rights than Irish, Jews, and Native Americans. Such a situation would suggest that a fully formed code of caste/color inequality had not yet developed, and we might look for clues a bit later in colonial history.

Because all sources, firsthand primary accounts and secondary works by historians, have unique points of view and reasons for seeing things the way they do, you need to question and critically analyze everything. Read all historical documents with skepticism, taking into account how their authors' points of view fit into the context of the time, the voices of contemporaries, and the way they might have imagined themselves being remembered historically. This last consideration, people's own sense of how they make history, has always been important. But it may have become even more important in the contemporary world that Andy Warhol characterized as providing everybody with "fifteen minutes of fame." Ultimately, the craft of history is as subjective as a trial verdict. We can never know what actually happened. We can establish a fair trial, one with relevant evidence, good witnesses, and brilliant lawyers. This will get us closer to the truth, but never fully beyond a shadow of a doubt. Historians, after all, are asking big and highly charged political questions that go beyond the innocence or guilt of one person to attempt to understand society's most deeply held values, intimate behaviors, and strongly protected interests. Fortunately, we have the ability to reopen any case at any time and work to overturn a verdict that just does not sit right with us. It is just a matter of getting in there, studying the sources, and researching and writing history.

Contents

PART FIVE
"The American Century": War, Affluence, and Uncertainty

189

Part Six

Contested Boundaries: Moral Dilemmas
at Home and Abroad   243

PART SEVEN
Between History and Tomorrow: After the Cold War

PART ONE

After the Civil War

New South and New West

"I have vowed that if I should have children—the first ingredient of the first principle of their education shall be uncompromising hatred & contempt of the Yankee," declared a white Southerner toward the end of the Civil War. "I'm free as a frog!" exulted one former slave. You will read similar responses from both white Southerners like Caleb Forshey and black Southerners like Felix Haywood facing the future after the war. High hopes or extreme bitterness promised a painful future for the South.

While slavery had effectively met its end, victory for the Union did not resolve questions about the roles that African American men and women would play in American life. The first attempts to secure rights for the former slaves, known as Reconstruction, produced three new amendments to the Constitution, which initiated a movement toward equality that today, nearly a century and a half later, still remains incomplete. Despite federal laws mandating economic freedom for African Americans, determined opposition from white Southerners largely defeated Reconstruction. In part, this resistance took legal forms such as marshaling public opinion, applying economic power, and organizing politically. But the resort to terror came early and continued in various forms for generations. The Ku Klux Klan, arising soon after the war, quickly became an armed conspiracy intimidating, whipping, and killing African Americans like Rosy Williams's husband Jim and their white allies.

In the end, three institutions replaced slavery in the postwar South—Jim Crow or segregation in social affairs, a whites-only Democratic Party in politics, and sharecropping in economics. Southern farmers developed arrangements such as the Grimes family's sharecrop contract, which offered neither slavery nor full freedom to work where one chose, while in the North parallel restrictions on free labor like the Swindell Brothers' contract appeared.

At the same time that the former slaves' hopes for freedom were being dashed in the South, the West—with its vast opportunities and awesome landscape—drew capital and population and stirred the American imagination (as illustrated in the Visual Portfolio "The Peopling of the West," pages 47–55). However, the completion of the first transcontinental railroad link in 1869, the renewed movement westward that it generated, and the collapse of the buffalo herds that fed and sheltered the Plains Indians helped to decimate the remaining independent Native American peoples. The Battle of Little Bighorn (1876), remembered here in accounts by Italian soldier-for-hire Charles DeRudio and by She Walks with Her Shawl and other Indians, was the last Native American victory in centuries of sporadic warfare between Indians and settlers. As Native Americans were shunted to reservations often far distant from their ancestral homes, their young people were placed in boarding schools to educate them in the ways of the settler society. The struggles of Zitkala-Ša, a Sioux from the Yankton reservation in South Dakota, to find her place in both the Sioux and the white worlds indicate the complexities lurking behind the stereotypes.

POINTS OF VIEW

The Battle of Little Bighorn (1876)

1

Victory at Greasy Grass

She Walks with Her Shawl and One Bull

Americans vividly remember the Plains Indians, whose last great victory came at the Little Bighorn in 1876, the "feather-streaming, buffalo-chasing, wild-riding, recklessly fighting Indian of the plains," as one historian describes their young male warriors. In most American imaginations, they are the archetype of the American Indian.

The reality is far more complex, however. The religion, elaborate warrior code, fierce grief for the dead, and stunning rituals and visions of other worlds were largely borrowed from the many Indian cultures these nomads briefly conquered as they swept across the Plains in the eighteenth and nineteenth centuries on horses first brought to the Americas by the Spanish conquistadors. The rifle, acquired from French, English, and, later, American traders, was one of their most cherished cultural symbols, though, as noted in this account, the less expensive and easily crafted tomahawk was also employed in battle. And their beads were all from Europe. Anthropologists use the term syncretic

Jerome A. Greene, ed., *Lakota and Cheyenne: Indian Views of the Great Sioux War, 1876–1877* (Norman: University of Oklahoma Press, 1994), 42–46, 54–59.

to describe the culture of nomadic Plains Indians like the Lakota Sioux: a magnificent amalgam of all the peoples they had encountered. Indigenous, surely, but in this they were also quintessentially American.

The horse and rifle brought wealth and military might. The Plains became a terrain of ritual hunting and warfare, and prosperity permitted extensive trade and the elaboration of Indian cultures. For about a century, competing powers hindered conquest of the Plains Indians. But over time, emigrants to the West Coast, wasteful white buffalo hunters, the miners, the railroads, rushes of settlers, and a determined U.S. Army all disrupted Indian life. A series of Indian wars, beginning during the Civil War, rapidly resulted in all but a few Plains Indians being pushed onto reservations.

By 1876 the great Western saga appeared about over. But thousands of Sioux and Northern Cheyenne, still off of or escaping from the reservations, gathered briefly at the Little Bighorn River, which they called the Greasy Grass, to enjoy religious rituals, hunting, and their defiance of the U.S. Army. General George Armstrong Custer and his premier Indian fighters, the Seventh Cavalry, found them there and promptly attacked.

We see the ensuing battle through the eyes of a Hunkpapa Lakota woman, She Walks with Her Shawl, and a Minneconjou Lakota man, One Bull, the adopted son of Sitting Bull. Keep in mind that both accounts are filtered through white interviewers.

QUESTIONS TO CONSIDER

1. Observe in each account how these informants reacted to the battle. What role did each assume? What can you learn about Lakota culture from their actions?
2. What can you infer about Sitting Bull's role from One Bull's account?
3. On the basis of these accounts, does the usual characterization of the battle as a "massacre" seem accurate? Why or why not?

SHE WALKS WITH HER SHAWL
(HUNKPAPA LAKOTA)

Account given to Walter S. Campbell in 1931

I was born seventy-seven winters ago, near Grand River, [in present] South Dakota. My father, Slohan, was the bravest man among our people. Fifty-five years ago we packed our tents and went with other Indians to Peji-slawakpa (Greasy Grass). We were then living on the Standing Rock Indian reservation [Great Sioux Reservation, Standing Rock Agency]. I belonged to Sitting Bull's band. They were great fighters. We called ourselves Hunkpapa. This means confederated bands. When I was still a young girl (about seventeen) I accompanied a Sioux war party which made war against the Crow Indians in Montana. My father went to war 70 times. He was wounded nearly a dozen times.

But I am going to tell you of the greatest battle. This was a fight against Pehin-hanska (General Custer). I was several miles from the Hunkpapa camp when I saw a cloud of dust rise beyond a ridge of bluffs in the east. The morning was hot and sultry. Several of us Indian girls were digging wild turnips. I was then 23 years old. We girls looked towards the camp and saw a warrior ride swiftly, shouting that the soldiers were only a few miles away and that the women and children including old men should run for the hills in an opposite direction.

I dropped the pointed ash stick which I had used in digging turnips and ran towards my tipi. I saw my father running towards the horses. When I got to my tent, mother told me that news was brought to her that my brother had been killed by the soldiers. My brother had gone early that morning in search for a horse that strayed from our herd. In a few moments we saw soldiers on horseback on a bluff just across the Greasy Grass (Little Big Horn) river. I knew that there would be a battle because I saw warriors getting their horses and tomahawks.

I heard Hawkman shout, Ho-ka-he! Ho-ka-he! (Charge.) The soldiers began firing into our camp. Then they ceased firing. I saw my father preparing to go to battle. I sang a death song for my brother who had been killed.

My heart was bad. Revenge! Revenge! For my brother's death. I thought of the death of my young brother, One Hawk. Brown Eagle, my brother's companion on that morning, had escaped and gave the alarm to the camp that the soldiers were coming. I ran to a nearby thicket and got my black horse. I painted my face with crimson and unbraided my black hair. I was mourning. I was a woman, but I was not afraid.

By this time the soldiers (Reno's men) were forming a battle line in the bottom about a half mile away. In another moment I heard a terrific volley of carbines. The bullets shattered the tipi poles. Women and children were running away from the gunfire. In the tumult I heard old men and women singing death songs for their warriors who were now ready to attack the soldiers. The chanting of death songs made me brave, although I was a woman. I saw a warrior adjusting his quiver and grasping his tomahawk. He started running towards his horse when he suddenly recoiled and dropped dead. He was killed near his tipi.

Warriors were given orders by Hawkman to mount their horses and follow the fringe of a forest and wait until commands were given to charge. The soldiers kept on firing. Some women were also killed. Horses and dogs too! The camp was in great commotion.

Father led my black horse up to me and I mounted. We galloped towards the soldiers. Other warriors joined in with us. When we were nearing the fringe of the woods an order was given by Hawkman to charge. Ho-ka-he! Ho-ka-he! Charge! Charge! The warriors were now near the soldiers. The troopers were all on foot. They shot straight, because I saw our leader killed as he rode with his warriors.

The charge was so stubborn that the soldiers ran to their horses and, mounting them, rode swiftly towards the river. The Greasy Grass river was very deep. Their horses had to swim to get across. Some of the warriors rode into the water and tomahawked the soldiers. In the charge the Indians rode among the troopers and with tomahawks unhorsed several of them. The soldiers were very excited. Some of them shot into the air. The Indians chased the soldiers across the river and up over a bluff.

Then the warriors returned to the bottom where the first battle took place. We heard a commotion far down the valley. The warriors rode in a column of fives. They sang a victory song. Someone said that another body of soldiers were attacking the lower end of the village. I heard afterwards that the soldiers were under the command of Long Hair (Custer). With my father and other youthful warriors I rode in that direction.

We crossed the Greasy Grass below a beaver dam (the water is not so deep there) and came upon many horses. One soldier was holding the reins of eight or ten horses. An Indian waved his blanket and scared all the horses. They got away from the men (troopers). On the ridge just north of us I saw blue-clad men running up a ravine, firing as they ran.

The dust created from the stampeding horses and powder smoke made everything dark and black. Flashes from carbines could be seen. The valley was dense with powder smoke. I never heard such whooping and shouting. "There was never a better day to die," shouted Red Horse. In the battle I heard cries from troopers, but could not understand what they were saying. I do not speak English.

Long Hair's troopers were trapped in an enclosure. There were Indians everywhere. The Cheyennes attacked the soldiers from the north and Crow King from the South. The Sioux Indians encircled the troopers. Not one got away! The Sioux used tomahawks. It was not a massacre, but [a] hotly contested battle between two armed forces. Very few soldiers were mutilated, as oft has been said by the whites. Not a single soldier was burned at the stake. Sioux Indians do not torture their victims.

After the battle the Indians took all the equipment and horses belonging to the soldiers. The brave men who came to punish us that morning were defeated; but in the end, the Indians lost. We saw the body of Long Hair. Of course, we did not know who the soldiers were until an interpreter told us that the men came from Fort Lincoln, then [in] Dakota Territory. On the saddle blankets were the cross saber insignia and the letter seven.

The victorious warriors returned to the camp, as did the women and children who could see the battle from where they took refuge. Over sixty Indians were killed and they were also brought back to the camp for scaffold-burial. The Indians did not stage a victory dance that night. They were mourning for their own dead. . . .

ONE BULL (MINNECONJOU LAKOTA)

Account given to John P. Everett in the 1920s

I was in Sitting Bull's camp on [Little] Big Horn River, One Horn Band Hinkowoji [Minneconjou] Tepee. They were called that because they planted their gardens near the river. Itazipco (Without Bow [Sans Arc]) was another band. Ogalala [Oglala] was the Red Cloud band. Another band, Schiyeio means Cheyenne. They were a different tribe, not Lakota. They were friends of Lakota.

Pizi (Gall) had another band. All the different bands camped together. There were many other chiefs with their bands. Four Horn and Two Moon and many others. Whenever the chiefs held a council they went to Sitting Bull's camp because he was a good medicine man.

Lakota and Cheyennes had gone to this camp to look after their buffalo and so young men and women could get acquainted. White men had driven our buffalo away from Lakota land. So we went where buffalo were to take care of them and keep white men away.

I was a strong young man 22 years old. On the day of the fight I was sitting in my tepee combing my hair. I don't know what time it was. About this time maybe. (Two P.M.) Lakota had no watches in those days. I had just been out and picketed my horses and was back in my tepee. I saw a man named Fat Bear come running into camp and he said soldiers were coming on the other side of the river and had killed a boy named Deeds who went out to picket a horse. Then I came out of my tepee and saw soldiers running their horses toward our camp on same side of the river. We could hear lots of shooting. I went to tepee of my uncle, Sitting Bull, and said I was going to go take part in the battle. He said, "Go ahead, they have already fired."

I had a rifle and plenty of shells, but I took that off and gave it to Sitting Bull and he gave me a shield. Then I took the shield and my tomahawk and got on my horse and rode up to where the soldiers were attacking us. They were firing pretty heavy. They were all down near the river in the timber. Lakota were riding around fast and shooting at them. I rode up to some Lakota and said, "Let's all charge at once." I raised my tomahawk and said, "Wakontanka help me so I do not sin but fight my battle." I started to charge. There were five Lakota riding behind me. We charged for some soldiers that were still fighting and they ran to where their horses were in the timber. Then the soldiers all started for the river. I turned my horse and started that way too and there was a man named Mato Washte (Pretty Bear) right behind me and he and his horse were shot down. I followed the soldiers. They were running for the river. I killed two with my tomahawk. Then the soldiers got across the river. I came back to where Pretty Bear was and got him up on my horse. He was wounded and covered with blood. I started my horse toward the river where the soldiers were trying to get across.

Then I let Pretty Bear get off my horse and I went across the river after the soldiers. I killed one more of them with my tomahawk.

Then I saw four soldiers ahead of me running up the hill. I was just about to charge them when someone rode along beside me and said, "You better not go any farther. You are wounded." That was Sitting Bull. I was not wounded but I was all covered with blood that got on me when I had Pretty Bear on my horse. So I did what Sitting Bull told me. Then Sitting Bull rode back but I went on. Another Lakota went after these four soldiers. He had a rifle and shot one of them off his horse. One of the soldiers kept shooting back but without hitting us. The man that was with me was a Lakota but I did not know who he was. Now the soldiers were getting together up on the hill and we could see the other soldiers coming with the pack mules a long way off.

Then I went back across the river and rode down it a way, then I rode with the man who was shooting at the four soldiers and we crossed the river again just east of Sitting Bull's camp. We saw a bunch of horsemen up on a hill to the north and they were Lakotas. We rode up to them and I told them I had killed a lot of soldiers and showed them my tomahawk. Then I said I was going up and help kill Custer's soldiers, but Sitting Bull told me not to go so I didn't go but we rode up where we could see the Lakotas and Cheyennes killing Custer's men. They had been shooting heavy but the Indians charged them straight from the west and then some rode around them shooting and the Indians were knocking them off their horses and killing them with tomahawks and clubs. THEY WERE ALL KILLED. There were a lot of Sioux killed. The others were picking them up on their horses and taking them back to camp.

Then we had a war dance all night and in the morning we heard that the soldiers with the pack mules were up on the hill and the Sioux started up after them. I went with Sitting Bull and volunteered to go help kill these soldiers but Sitting Bull said no. So we watched the fight from a hill. I didn't have my rifle with me then, just my tomahawk. The Sioux surrounded them and they fought that way all day. The soldiers had ditches dug all around the hill. Then along towards sundown the Sioux broke camp and went [south] to the mountains.

The Sioux did not take any prisoners that I know of. I didn't see any. I don't know how many Indians there were, but it was a very big band. Many bands together. The Indians had rifles with little short cartridges. I didn't use mine.

After the fight we all stayed in the Big Horn Mountains about ten days. After that they broke camp and went north following along the Tongue River. Then we went to the Little Missouri, and we found a place where there must have been some soldiers for we found a lot of sacks of yellow corn piled up. Then some of the bands went one way and some went another. One little band went to Slim Buttes and they were all killed by soldiers.

I was with Sitting Bull all the time we were in camp on the [Little] Big Horn and saw him during the battle. He was telling his men what to do. The first I knew of any soldiers was when they killed the boy who went to picket his horse across the river from Sitting Bull's camp. Before we broke camp that night we saw the walking soldiers coming from down the river but my uncle said, "We won't fight them. We have killed enough. We will go. . . ."

2

Witness to Custer's Last Stand
Charles DeRudio

The Battle of Little Bighorn was not the U.S. Army's biggest defeat at the hands of Native Americans, but it was the most famous. On June 25, 1876, the Seventh U.S. Cavalry rode into battle in Eastern Montana Territory, led by Civil War general George Armstrong Custer. When the smoke had cleared the next day, 268 members of the U.S. Army were dead, including Custer and his entire battalion. Though it is known histori-cally as Custer's Last Stand, Little Bighorn (or Greasy Grass, as the Plains Indians called it) was, in many ways, the last stand for Native Americans on the Great Plains. It would be the last time that Native Americans posed a significant threat to the U.S. military.

Historians have long argued about the legacy of Little Bighorn. There are thou-sands of works debating what happened on that summer day in Montana, what went wrong, whether it was Custer's fault, and how it was that the battle had ended so disas-trously for the U.S. military. Nearly every person connected to Little Bighorn, either for profit or politics, published an account, including Custer's widow. The account that follows was written and sent to the New York Herald *by Charles DeRudio, one of the men who witnessed the activities of Lakota women described by She Walks with Her Shawl.*

Born in Northern Italy in 1832, Count Carlo Camillo di Rudio or Charles DeRu-dio, as he called himself in the United States, was one of the many foreign-born soldiers who fought under Custer. He began his strange journey to Little Bighorn as an anti-monarchist who fought for a unified and free Italy (then under the control of Austria). After the antimonarchists were defeated, DeRudio went into exile in London, where he became involved in a failed plot to kill Emperor Napoleon III at the opera in Paris. Sentenced to life imprisonment at the French penal colony on Devil's Island, DeRudio escaped and found his way to New York City on the eve of the Civil War, joining the army and becoming an officer for an all-black regiment, owing to his swarthy complex-ion. DeRudio continued in the army after the war and was assigned as a lieutenant in the Seventh Cavalry, under Custer. Perhaps because of his radical politics, Custer dis-liked DeRudio, who, at forty-four, was the oldest officer under his command. Just before the attack, Custer moved DeRudio to another company. This saved DeRudio's life and enabled him to write his account of the Battle of Little Bighorn.

The Custer Myth: A Source Book of Custerania, written and compiled by Colonel W. A. Graham (Harrisburg, Penn.: The Stackpole Co., 1953), 76–78.

QUESTIONS TO CONSIDER

1. What personal considerations might have gone into DeRudio's account of the battle?
2. What might have motivated Lakota women to act in the way that DeRudio describes?
3. In what ways does DeRudio's account contribute to determining what went wrong for the U.S. Army at Little Bighorn?

Camp on N. side Yellowstone, July 5, '76

I had a narrow escape at the battle of the Little Bighorn on the 25 & 26 of June and I will endeavor to give you my experience of Indian fighting. At about 10 A.M. on the 25th June, Gen. Custer's scouts returned and reported that they had discovered an Indian village about 15 miles distant, on the Little Bighorn, and that from what they had seen, they supposed the Indians to be retreating before our advance. We continued our march two or three miles farther when a halt was ordered and Gen. Custer began preparations for attacking the enemy. He detailed Co's. H, D & K, under the command of Col. F. W. Benteen to take the left of our route, with orders, so I hear, to sweep everything in his way: Co's. M, A, & G were put under the command of Col. Reno; and being temporarily attached to Co. A, I found myself with this division. Gen. Custer took Co's. E, I, F, L & C, and occupied the right of the line of attack. The remaining Company, B, was left to guard the packtrain. After marching two or three miles, our command, the center, was ordered to trot and hold the gait until we reached the river, six or seven miles distant. Having reached the river, we forded, and on reaching the plain beyond the opposite bank, we were ordered into line of battle.

Everything being as was ordered, we started on a gallop and for two miles pursued on the verge of an immense and blinding cloud of dust raised by the madly flying savages ahead of us. The dust cloud was so dense that we could distinguish nothing, so Col. Reno halted the battalion and after dismounting, formed a skirmish line—the right flank resting on the edge of a dry thickly wooded creek. While the horses were being led to shelter in the wood, the Indians opened a galling fire on us which was immediately responded to, the skirmish continuing for about one-half hour. It was now discovered that on the other side of the creek, in a park-like clearing, there were a few lodges, and the whole line crossed the creek to find the lodges deserted, and be received by about two hundred yelping, yelling redskins. The fire from the numerically superior force necessitated a retreat which was almost impossible, as we were now surrounded by warriors. When we entered the engagement we were only 100 strong and the fire of the enemy had made havoc in our little band. When we were half way over the creek, I, being in the rear, noticed a guidon[1] planted on the side we had left and returned to take it. When coming through the wood, the guidon entangled itself in the branches and slipped out of my hand. I dismounted to

---

1. **guidon:** A military flag or battle standard.

pick it up and led my horse to the south bank of the creek. As I was about to mount, my horse was struck with a bullet, and becoming frightened, he ran into the Indians, leaving me dismounted in the company of about 300 Sioux not more than 50 yards distant. They poured a whistling volley at me, but I was not wounded, and managed to escape to the thicket near by, where I would have an opportunity of defending myself and selling my life at a good high figure. In the thicket I found Mr. Girard [Fred Gerard], the interpreter; a half-breed Indian; and Private O'Neill [Private Thomas F. O'Neill], of Co. "G", 7th Cav. The first two of the quartet had their horses, while O'Neill like myself, was dismounted. I told the owners of the horses that the presence of the animals would betray us, suggesting at the same time that they be stampeded. They declined to act on the suggestion and I left them and crawled through the thick underwood into the deep dry bottom of the creek, where I could not easily be discovered, and from whence I hoped to be able under cover of darkness to steal out and re-join the command. I had not been in this hiding place more than 10 minutes when I heard several pistol shots fired in my immediate vicinity, and shortly thereafter came the silvery, but to me diabolical voices of several squaws. I raised my head with great caution to see what the women were at and to discover their exact location. I found the women at the revolting work of scalping a soldier who was perhaps not yet dead. Two of the ladies were cutting away, while two others performed a sort of war dance around the body and its mutilators. I will not attempt to describe to you my feelings at witnessing the disgusting performance. Finally the squaws went away, probably to hunt for more victims and I employed the time thinking of my perilous position.

While thus engaged, I heard a crackling noise near me, which upon investigation I found proceeded from burning wood, the Indians having ignited a fire. The wood being very dry, the fire made rapid headway, and I was forced from my hiding place. I crawled out of the creek bottom the same way I had approached, and as I was about to ascend the bank, I heard a voice calling "Lieutenant, Lieutenant." I could see no one, but the call was repeated, and advancing a few yards in the direction from which it proceeded, I found all three of the party I had left a short time before, hidden in the bottom of the creek. Mr. Girard told me he had left the horses tied together, where I had seen them, and followed down after me. I found that the party, like myself, was afraid of the progress of the fire; but fortunately for us, the wind subsided, and a little rain fell which, thank God, was sufficient to arrest the flames and revive our hope that we might be able to remain there until night. It was now 3 o'clock P.M.: six more hours to wait, and you may imagine how immensely long we found them. During this time we could hear and often see Indians around us and could hear them talk quite near us. I cannot find words sufficiently expressive to describe my many thoughts during those hours of suspense. Finally the time came when under the protection of night (it was very cloudy) we were able to come out of our hiding places and take the direction of the ford, which was two miles to the south, through an open plain. Mr. Girard and the scout mounted their horses and the soldier and myself took hold, each one, of a horses tail, and followed them. Mr. Girard proposed that, in case he should be obliged to run and leave us, and succeeded in joining the command, he would notify Col. Reno the commander, of my position. During our transit through the open plain we passed many Indians returning to their village and could hear but not see them as the night was very dark. We reached the wood near what we took to be the ford we had passed in the morning, but we were mistaken and had to hunt for the crossing. Once we forded the stream but found it was at a bend and that we would have to ford it again. When we re-crossed the river, we ran full into a band of eight savages. The two mounted men ran for their lives, the soldier and myself jumped into the bushes near us. I cocked my revolver and in a kneeling position was ready to fire at the savages if they should approach me. They evidently thought, from the precipitate retreat of the two mounted men, that all of us had decamped; and began to talk among themselves. In a few minutes to my surprise they continued their course, and soon after went out of hearing. I raised up from my position, approached the bank of the river and called to the soldier, who immediately answered. We then saw that all the fords were well guarded by the savages, and it would be very dangerous to attempt to cross any part of the river. The night passed and in the dim dawn of day we heard an immense tramping, as of a large cavalry command, and the splashing of the water convinced us that some troops were crossing the river. I imagined it was our command, as I could distinctly hear the sound of the horses shoes striking the stones. I cautiously stepped to the edge of the bushes to look out (I was then no more than three yards from the bank of the river), and thought I recognized some gray horses mounted by men in military blouses, and some of them in white hats. They were, I thought, going out of the valley, and those that had already crossed the river were going up a very steep bluff, while others were crossing after them. I saw one man with a buckskin jacket, pants, top boots and white hat, and felt quite sure I recognized him as Capt. Tom Custer which convinced me that the cavalrymen were of our command.

With this conviction I stepped boldly out on the bank and called to Capt. Custer, "Tom, don't leave us here." The distance was only a few yards and my call was answered by an infernal yell and a discharge of 300 or 400 shots. I then discovered my mistake and found the savages were clad in clothes and mounted on horses which they had captured from our men. Myself and the soldier jumped into the bushes (the bullets mowing down the branches at every volley), and crawled off to get out of range of the fire. In doing so we moved the top branches of the undergrowth, and the Indians on the top of the bluff fired where they saw the commotion and thus covered us with their rifles. We now decided to cross a clearing of about twenty yards and gain another wood; but before doing this, I took the precaution to look out. The prospect was terribly discouraging for on our immediate right, not more than fifty yards distant, I saw four or five Indians galloping toward us. Near by me there were two cottonwood stumps nearly touching each other, and behind this slender barricade myself and the soldier knelt down, he with his carbine and I with my revolver, ready to do for a few of the savages before they could kill us. They had not seen us and when the foremost man was just abreast of me and about ten yards distant, I fired. They came in Indian file, and at my fire they turned a right-about and were making off when Pvt. O'Neill fired his carbine at the second savage, who at that moment was reining his pony to turn him back. The private's eye was true, and his carbine trusty, for Mr. Indian dropped his rein, threw up his paws and laid down on the grass to sleep his long sleep. The gentleman I greeted rode a short distance and then did likewise. The rest of the party rode on, turned the corner of the wood and disappeared. During all this time the fire from the bluffs continued, but after we had fired our shots, it ceased, and we retired to the thicket. From our position we could see the Indians on the bluffs, their horses picketed under cover of the hill, and a line of sharpshooters, all lying flat on their stomachs. We could hear the battle going on above us on the hills, the continued rattle of the musketry, the cheering of our command, and the shouting of the savages. Our hopes revived when we heard the familiar cheer of our comrades, but despondency followed fast for we discovered that our wood was on fire and we had to shift our position. We crawled almost to the edge of the wood, when we discovered that the fiends had fired both sides. We moved around until we found a thick cluster of what they call bulberry trees, under which we crept. The grass on the edge of this place was very green, as it had been raining a little while before, and there was no wind. When the fire approached our hiding place it ran very slowly so that I was enabled to smother it with my gauntlet gloves. The fire consumed all the underwood around us and was almost expended by this time. There we were in a little oasis, surrounded by fire, but comparatively safe from the elements, and with the advantage of seeing almost everything around us without being seen. We could see savages going backward and forward, and one standing on picket not more than 70 or 80 yards from us, evidently put there to watch the progress of the fire. At about 4 o'clock P.M. this picket fired 4 pistol shots in the air at regular intervals from each other and which I interpreted as a signal of some kind. Soon after this fire we heard the powerful voice of a savage crying out, making the same sound four times, and after these two signals, we saw 200 or more savages leave the bluffs and ford the river, evidently leaving the ground. About one hour after, the same double signals were again repeated, and many mounted Indians left at a gallop. Soon the remainder of those left on the bluffs also retired.

Hope now revived, the musketry rattle ceased and only now and then we could hear a far off shot. By 6 o'clock everything around us was apparently quiet and no evidence or signs of any Indians were near us. We supposed the regiment had left the field, and all that remained for us to do was to wait for the night and then pass the river and take the route for the Yellowstone River, and there construct a raft and descend to the mouth of the Powder River, our supply camp. Of course during the 36 hours that we were in suspense, we had neither water nor food. At 8 P.M. we dropped ourselves into the river, the water reaching our waists, crossed it twice and then carefully crawled up the bluffs, took our direction and slowly and cautiously proceeded southward.

After marching two miles, I thought I would go up on a very high hill to look around and see if I could discover any sign of our command; and on looking around I saw a fire on my left and in the direction where we supposed the command was fighting during the day, probably two miles from us. Of course we made two conjectures on this fire: it might be an Indian fire and it might be from our command. The only way to ascertain was to approach it cautiously and trust to chance. Accordingly we descended the hill, and took the direction of the fire. Climbing another and another hill, we listened a while and then proceeded on for a mile or more, when on the top of a hill we again stopped and listened. We could hear voices, but not distinctly enough to tell whether they were savages or our command.

We proceeded a little farther and heard the bray of a mule, and soon after, the distinct voice of a sentry challenging with the familiar words "Halt; Who goes there?" The challenge was not directed to us, as we were too far off to be seen by the picket, and it was too dark; but this gave us courage to continue our course and approach, though carefully, lest we should run into some Indians again. We were about 200 yards from the fire and I cried out: "Picket, don't fire; it is Lt. DeRudio and Pvt. O'Neill," and started to run. We received an answer in a loud cheer from all the members of the picket and Lt. Varnum. This officer, one of our bravest and most efficient, came at once to me and was very happy to see me again, after having counted me among the dead.

My first question was about the condition of the regiment. I was in hopes that we were the only sufferers, but I was not long allowed to remain in doubt. Lt. Varnum said he knew nothing of the five companies under Custer and that our command had sustained a loss in Lts. McIntosh and Hodgson. It was about 2 A.M. when I got into camp, and I soon after tried to go to sleep; but though I had not slept for two nights, I could not close my eyes. I talked with Lt. Varnum about the battle and narrated to him adventures and narrow escapes I had had. Morning soon came and I went to see the officers, and told them that the Indians had left.

At 8 o'clock we saw cavalry approaching, first a few scouts and then a dense column and soon learned it was Gen. Brisbin's command coming up to our relief. Presently a long line of infantry appeared on the plain and Gen. Gibbon came up. Ah! who that was there will ever forget how our hearts thrilled at sight of those blue coats! And when Gens. Gibbon and Terry rode into our camp, men wept like children.

Yours truly,
CHARLES C. DeRUDIO

P.S. I should do injustice to my feelings if I should omit to mention the fidelity and bravery of Private O'Neill. He faithfully obeyed me and stood by me like a brother. I shall never cease to remember him and his service to me during our dangerous companionship. This brave soldier is highly thought of by his company commander, and of course ever will be by me and mine.

CHAS. DeRUDIO.

FOR CRITICAL THINKING

1. The U.S. Army lost many battles to Native Americans. Why did the Battle of Little Bighorn catch people's imagination?
2. From reading the preceding accounts what do you think were Custer's key mistakes?

3

African Americans during Reconstruction

Felix Haywood et al.

Wherever travelers went in the months following Appomattox, they saw abandoned fields, twisted rails, burned buildings, white men hobbling about on one leg or dangling an empty sleeve, and former slaves exploring their new freedom or searching for food, shelter, and work. The war had settled some things: secession and slavery were dead. The South was desperately impoverished, its prewar economy gone with the wind.

All else was confusion. Freedmen struggled to define their freedom. Some left the plantations to which they had been bound and found their families separated by slavery and war. Many — perhaps most — saw freedom in the ownership of land, a dream encouraged by a field order issued by General William Tecumseh Sherman in January 1865 that assigned some vacant lands to former slaves. As a black soldier told his white officer: "Every colored man will be a slave and feel himself a slave until he could raise his own bale of cotton and put his own mark upon it and say, 'Dis is mine!'"

Yet soon after the first jubilee of freedom, the Andrew Johnson administration, falling under the influence of former Confederates, revoked Sherman's order assigning land to former slaves and stood by as white Southerners began to force the freedmen back into old patterns — assigning them work under coercive labor contracts and allowing states to govern their daily activities by "black codes" that denied them their civil rights. When these policies provoked a political reaction in the North, Republicans in Congress took control of Southern policy through a series of Reconstruction acts. While restoring civil rights and providing military protection, these acts failed to provide land to the freedmen. The Thirteenth (1865), Fourteenth (1868), and Fifteenth Amendments (1870) to the U.S. Constitution decreed an equality between the races that did not become a reality in African Americans' daily lives in either the North or the South. For about a decade the federal government made vigorous efforts to help freedmen gain education, legal and medical services, reasonable employment contracts, and a measure of political power. But those efforts were abandoned once the Northern public, tired of disorder in the South and wary of government intervention, abandoned the former slaves to their old masters. African Americans were soon left to respond however they could to the social revolution brought about by emancipation, the war's impoverishment of the South, and the violence of groups like the Ku Klux Klan.

Historians have pieced together the story of the freedmen's actions from a multiplicity of sources. Interviews with former slaves collected in the 1930s, a sample of which

"African Americans React to Reconstruction," from B. A. Botkin, ed., *Lay My Burden Down: A Folk History of Slavery* (Chicago: University of Chicago Press, 1945), 65–70, 223–24, 241–42, 246–47.

you will read here, are an important source for comprehending the lives of those freed, and then abandoned, after the Civil War.

QUESTIONS TO CONSIDER

1. Judging from these accounts, what were the major problems that former slaves faced after the war?
2. What did these former slaves expect of freedom?
3. Why did some freedmen continue to work for their former masters?

FELIX HAYWOOD

San Antonio, Texas. Born in Raleigh, North Carolina. Age at interview: 88.

The end of the war, it come just like that—like you snap your fingers. . . . How did we know it! Hallelujah broke out—. . .

Everybody went wild. We felt like heroes, and nobody had made us that way but ourselves. We was free. Just like that, we was free. It didn't seem to make the whites mad, either. They went right on giving us food just the same. Nobody took our homes away, but right off colored folks started on the move. They seemed to want to get closer to freedom, so they'd know what it was—like it was a place or a city. Me and my father stuck, stuck close as a lean tick to a sick kitten. The Gudlows started us out on a ranch. My father, he'd round up cattle—unbranded cattle—for the whites. They was cattle that they belonged to, all right; they had gone to find water 'long the San Antonio River and the Guadalupe. Then the whites gave me and my father some cattle for our own. My father had his own brand—7 B)—and we had a herd to start out with of seventy.

We knowed freedom was on us, but we didn't know what was to come with it. We thought we was going to get rich like the white folks. We thought we was going to be richer than the white folks, 'cause we was stronger and knowed how to work, and the whites didn't, and they didn't have us to work for them any more. But it didn't turn out that way. We soon found out that freedom could make folks proud, but it didn't make 'em rich.

Did you ever stop to think that thinking don't do any good when you do it too late? Well, that's how it was with us. If every mother's son of a black had thrown 'way his hoe and took up a gun to fight for his own freedom along with the Yankees, the war'd been over before it began. But we didn't do it. We couldn't help stick to our masters. We couldn't no more shoot 'em than we could fly. My father and me used to talk 'bout it. We decided we was too soft and freedom wasn't going to be much to our good even if we had a education.

WARREN MCKINNEY

Hazen, Arkansas. Born in South Carolina. Age at interview: 85.

I was born in Edgefield County, South Carolina. I am eighty-five years old. I was born a slave of George Strauter. I remembers hearing them say, "Thank

God, I's free as a jay bird." My ma was a slave in the field. I was eleven years old when freedom was declared. When I was little, Mr. Strauter whipped my ma. It hurt me bad as it did her. I hated him. She was crying. I chunked him with rocks. He run after me, but he didn't catch me. There was twenty-five or thirty hands that worked in the field. They raised wheat, corn, oats, barley, and cotton. All the children that couldn't work stayed at one house. Aunt Mat kept the babies and small children that couldn't go to the field. He had a gin and a shop. The shop was at the fork of the roads. When the war come on, my papa went to built forts. He quit Ma and took another woman. When the war close, Ma took her four children, bundled 'em up and went to Augusta. The government give out rations there. My ma washed and ironed. People died in piles. I don't know till yet what was the matter. They said it was the change of living. I seen five or six wooden, painted coffins piled up on wagons pass by our house. Loads passed every day like you see cotton pass here. Some said it was cholera and some . . . consumption [tuberculosis]. Lots of the colored people nearly starved. Not much to get to do and not much houseroom. Several families had to live in one house. Lots of the colored folks went up North and froze to death. They couldn't stand the cold. They wrote back about them dying. No, they never sent them back. I heard some sent for money to come back. I heard plenty 'bout the Ku Klux. They scared the folks to death. People left Augusta in droves. About a thousand would all meet and walk going to hunt work and new homes. Some of them died. I had a sister and brother lost that way. I had another sister come to Louisiana that way. She wrote back.

I don't think the colored folks looked for a share of land. They never got nothing 'cause the white folks didn't have nothing but barren hills left. About all the mules was wore out hauling provisions in the army. Some folks say they ought to done more for the colored folks when they left, but they say they was broke. Freeing all the slaves left 'em broke.

That reconstruction was a mighty hard pull. Me and Ma couldn't live. A man paid our ways to Carlisle, Arkansas, and we come. We started working for Mr. Emenson. He had a big store, teams, and land. We liked it fine, and I been here fifty-six years now. There was so much wild game, living was not so hard. If a fellow could get a little bread and a place to stay, he was all right. After I come to this state, I voted some. I have farmed and worked at odd jobs. I farmed mostly. Ma went back to her old master. He persuaded her to come back home. Me and her went back and run a farm four or five years before she died. Then I come back here.

LEE GUIDON

South Carolina. Born in South Carolina. Age at interview: 89.

Yes, ma'am, I sure was in the Civil War. I plowed all day, and me and my sister helped take care of the baby at night. It would cry, and me bumping it [in a straight chair, rocking]. Time I git it to the bed where its mama was, it wake up and start crying all over again. I be so sleepy. It was a puny sort of baby. Its papa was off at war. His name was Jim Cowan, and his wife Miss Margaret Brown 'fore she married him. Miss Lucy Smith give me and my sister to them. Then she married Mr. Abe Moore. Jim Smith was Miss Lucy's boy. He lay out in the woods all time. He say no need in him gitting shot up and killed. He say let the slaves be free. We lived, seemed like, on 'bout the line of York and Union counties. He lay out in the woods over in York County. Mr. Jim say all the fighting 'bout was jealousy. They caught him several times, but every time he got away from 'em. After they come home Mr. Jim say they never win no war. They stole and starved out the South. . . .

After freedom a heap of people say they was going to name theirselves over. They named theirselves big names, then went roaming round like wild, hunting cities. They changed up so it was hard to tell who or where anybody was. Heap of 'em died, and you didn't know when you hear about it if he was your folks hardly. Some of the names was Abraham, and some called theirselves Lincum. Any big name 'cepting their master's name. It was the fashion. I heard 'em talking 'bout it one evening, and my pa say, "Fine folks raise us and we gonna hold to our own names." That settled it with all of us. . . .

I reckon I do know 'bout the Ku Kluck. I knowed a man named Alfred Owens. He seemed all right, but he was a Republican. He said he was not afraid. He run a tanyard and kept a heap of guns in a big room. They all loaded. He married a Southern woman. Her husband either died or was killed. She had a son living with them. The Ku Kluck was called Upper League. They get this boy to unload all the guns. Then the white men went there. The white man give up and said, "I ain't got no gun to defend myself with. The guns all unloaded, and I ain't got no powder and shot." But the Ku Kluck shot in the houses and shot him up like lacework. He sold fine harness, saddles, bridles— all sorts of leather things. The Ku Kluck sure run them outen their country. They say they not going to have them round, and they sure run them out, back where they came from. . . .

For them what stayed on like they were, Reconstruction times 'bout like times before that 'cepting the Yankee stole out and tore up a scandalous heap. They tell the black folks to do something, and then come white folks you live with and say Ku Kluck whup you. They say leave, and white folks say better not listen to them old yankees. They'll git you too far off to come back, and you freeze. They done give you all the use they got for you. . . .

TOBY JONES

Madisonville, Texas. Born in South Carolina. Age at interview: 87.

I worked for Massa 'bout four years after freedom, 'cause he forced me to, said he couldn't 'ford to let me go. His place was near ruint, the fences burnt, and the house would have been, but it was rock. There was a battle fought near his place, and I taken Missy to a hideout in the mountains to where her father was, 'cause there was bullets flying everywhere. When the war was over, Massa come home and says, "You son of a gun, you's supposed to be free, but you ain't, 'cause I ain't gwine give you freedom." So I goes on working for him till I gits the chance to steal a hoss from him. The woman I wanted to marry, Govie, she 'cides to come to Texas with me. Me and Govie, we rides the hoss 'most a hundred miles, then we turned him a-loose and give him a scare back to his house, and come on foot the rest the way to Texas.

All we had to eat was what we could beg, and sometimes we went three days without a bite to eat. Sometimes we'd pick a few berries. When we got cold we'd crawl in a brushpile and hug up close together to keep warm. Once in a while we'd come to a farmhouse, and the man let us sleep on cottonseed in his barn, but they was far and few between, 'cause they wasn't many houses in the country them days like now.

When we gits to Texas, we gits married, but all they was to our wedding am we just 'grees to live together as man and wife. I settled on some land, and we cut some trees and split them open and stood them on end with the tops together for our house. Then we deadened some trees, and the land was ready to farm. There was some wild cattle and hogs, and that's the way we got our start, caught some of them and tamed them.

I don't know as I 'spected nothing from freedom, but they turned us out like a bunch of stray dogs, no homes, no clothing, no nothing, not 'nough food to last us one meal. After we settles on that place, I never seed man or woman, 'cept Govie, for six years, 'cause it was a long ways to anywhere. All we had to farm with was sharp sticks. We'd stick holes and plant corn, and when it come up we'd punch up the dirt round it. We didn't plant cotton, 'cause we couldn't eat that. I made bows and arrows to kill wild game with, and we never went to a store for nothing. We made our clothes out of animal skins.

4

White Southerners' Reactions to Reconstruction

Caleb G. Forshey and the Reverend James Sinclair

Like their former slaves, white Southerners at the end of the Civil War exhibited a wide variety of attitudes. Granted generous surrender terms that protected them from charges of treason and allowed them to keep horses and mules "to put in a crop," returning Confederate soldiers at first were more resigned to the outcome of the war than those who stayed at home and had less opportunity to discharge their anger during the war. Although many in the South had initially been ready to accept peace on the conqueror's terms, Northern uncertainty as to what these terms should be made those Southerners waver and encouraged those who were already angry. The president called for one policy and Congress for another. Northerners elected a Republican Congress that demanded freedom, civil rights, even the franchise for former slaves living in the South, and yet the same Northerners tolerated the denial of civil rights to African Americans living in the North. In the fall of 1865, three Republican states—Connecticut, Wisconsin, and Minnesota—voted down amendments to their constitutions that would have enfranchised blacks. This fueled resistance to Republican demands among white Southerners.

Assembled to examine Southern representation in Congress, the Congressional Joint Committee of Fifteen was part of the Republican Congress's opposition to President Andrew Johnson's plan of Reconstruction. In 1866, the committee held hearings as part of its effort to develop the Fourteenth Amendment. Despite the president's veto, Congress had already enlarged the scope of the Freedmen's Bureau to care for displaced former slaves and to try by military commission those accused of depriving freedmen of civil rights.

Of the two white Southerners whose interviews with the committee are included here, Caleb Forshey had supported secession while James Sinclair, although a slaveholder, had opposed it. A Scottish-born minister who had moved to North Carolina in 1857, Sinclair expressed Unionist sentiments that led to the loss of his church and then to his arrest during the war. In 1865, he was working with the Freedmen's Bureau.

The Report of the Committees of the House of Representatives Made during the First Session, Thirty-Ninth Congress, 1865–1866, vol. 2 (Washington, D.C.: Government Printing Office, 1866); Forshey: 129–32; Sinclair: 168–71.

QUESTIONS TO CONSIDER

1. What did Caleb Forshey think of Union efforts to protect former slaves through military occupation and the Freedmen's Bureau?
2. What were Forshey's beliefs about African Americans?
3. What was the plight of former slaves and white Unionists according to James Sinclair?

CALEB G. FORSHEY

Washington, D.C., March 28, 1866

Question: Where do you reside?

Answer: I reside in the State of Texas.

Question: How long have you been a resident of Texas?

Answer: I have resided in Texas and been a citizen of that State for nearly thirteen years.

Question: What opportunities have you had for ascertaining the temper and disposition of the people of Texas towards the government and authority of the United States?

Answer: For ten years I have been superintendent of the Texas Military Institute, as its founder and conductor. I have been in the confederate service in various parts of the confederacy; but chiefly in the trans-Mississippi department, in Louisiana and Texas, as an officer of engineers. I have had occasion to see and know very extensively the condition of affairs in Texas, and also to a considerable extent in Louisiana. I think I am pretty well-informed, as well as anybody, perhaps, of the present state of affairs in Texas.

Question: What are the feelings and views of the people of Texas as to the late rebellion, and the future condition and circumstances of the State, and its relations to the federal government?

Answer: After our army had given up its arms and gone home, the surrender of all matters in controversy was complete, and as nearly universal, perhaps, as anything could be. Assuming the matters in controversy to have been the right to secede, and the right to hold slaves, I think they were given up tee-totally, to use a strong Americanism. When you speak of feeling, I should discriminate a little. The feeling was that of any party who had been cast in a suit he had staked all upon. They did not return from feeling, but from a sense of necessity, and from a judgment that it was the only and necessary thing to be done, to give up the contest. But when they gave it up, it was without reservation; with a view to look forward, and not back. That is my impression of the manner in which the thing was done. There was a public expectation that in some very limited time there would be a restoration to former relations. . . . It was the expectation of the people that, as soon as the State was organized as proposed by the President, they would be restored to their former relations, and things would go on as before.

Question: What is your opinion of a military force under the authority of the federal government to preserve order in Texas and to protect those who have been loyal, both white and black, from the aggressions of those who have been in the rebellion?

Answer: My judgment is well founded on that subject: that wherever such military force is and has been, it has excited the very feeling it was intended to prevent; that so far from being necessary it is very pernicious everywhere, and without exception. The local authorities and public sentiment are ample for protection. I think no occasion would occur, unless some individual case that our laws would not reach. We had an opportunity to test this after the surrender and before any authority was there. The military authorities, or the military officers, declared that we were without laws, and it was a long time before the governor appointed arrived there, and then it was sometime before we could effect anything in the way of organization. We were a people without law, order, or anything; and it was a time for violence if it would occur. I think it is a great credit to our civilization that, in that state of affairs, there was nowhere any instance of violence. I am proud of it, for I expected the contrary; I expected that our soldiers on coming home, many of them, would be dissolute, and that many of them would oppress the class of men you speak of; but it did not occur. But afterwards, wherever soldiers have been sent, there have been little troubles, none of them large; but personal collisions between soldiers and citizens.

Question: What is your opinion as to the necessity and advantages of the Freedmen's Bureau, or an agency of that kind, in Texas?

Answer: My opinion is that it is not needed; my opinion is stronger than that—that the effect of it is to irritate, if nothing else. While in New York city recently I had a conversation with some friends from Texas, from five distant points in the State. We met together and compared opinions; and the opinion of each was the same, that the negroes had generally gone to work since January; that except where the Freedmen's Bureau had interfered, or rather encouraged troubles, such as little complaints, especially between negro and negro, the negro's disposition was very good, and they had generally gone to work, a vast majority of them with their former masters. . . . The impression in Texas at present is that the negroes under the influence of the Freedmen's Bureau do worse than without it.

I want to state that I believe all our former owners of negroes are the friends of the negroes; and that the antagonism paraded in the papers of the north does not exist at all. I know the fact is the very converse of that; and good feeling always prevails between the masters and the slaves. But the negroes went off and left them in the lurch; my own family was an instance of it. But they came back after a time, saying they had been free enough and wanted a home.

Question: Do you think those who employ the negroes there are willing to make contracts with them, so that they shall have fair wages for their labor?

Answer: I think so; I think they are paid liberally, more than the white men in this country get; the average compensation to negroes there is greater than the average compensation of free laboring white men in this country. It seems to have regulated itself in a great measure by what each neighborhood was doing; the negroes saying, "I can get thus and so at such a place." Men have hired from eight to fifteen dollars per month during the year, and women at about two dollars less a month; house-servants at a great deal more.

Question: Do the men who employ the negroes claim to exercise the right to enforce their contract by physical force?

Answer: Not at all; that is totally abandoned; not a single instance of it has occurred. I think they still chastise children, though. The negro parents often neglect that, and the children are still switched as we switch our own children. I know it is done in my own house; we have little house-servants that we switch just as I do our own little fellows.

Question: What is your opinion as to the respective advantages to the white and black races, of the present free system of labor and the institution of slavery?

Answer: I think freedom is very unfortunate for the negro; I think it is sad; his present helpless condition touches my heart more than anything else I ever contemplated, and I think that is the common sentiment of our slaveholders. I have seen it on the largest plantations, where the negro men had all left, and where only women and children remained, and the owners had to keep them and feed them. The beginning certainly presents a touching and sad spectacle. The poor negro is dying at a rate fearful to relate.

I have some ethnological theories that may perhaps warp my judgment; but my judgment is that the highest condition the black race has ever reached or can reach, is one where he is provided for by a master race. That is the result of a great deal of scientific investigation and observation of the negro character by me ever since I was a man. The labor question had become a most momentous one, and I was studying it. I undertook to investigate the condition of the negro from statistics under various circumstances, to treat it purely as a matter of statistics from the census tables of this country of ours. I found that the free blacks of the north decreased 8 per cent.; the free blacks of the south increased 7 or 8 per cent., while the slaves by their sides increased 34 per cent. I inferred from the doctrines of political economy that the race is in the best condition when it procreates the fastest; that, other things being equal, slavery is of vast advantage to the negro. I will mention one or two things in connexion with this as explanatory of that result. The negro will not take care of his offspring unless required to do it, as compared with the whites. The little children will die; they do die, and hence the necessity of very rigorous regulations on our plantations which we have adopted in our nursery system.

Another cause is that there is no continence among the negroes.[1] All the continence I have ever seen among the negroes has been enforced upon plantations, where it is generally assumed there is none. For the sake of procreation, if nothing else, we compel men to live with their wives. The discipline of the plantation was more rigorous, perhaps, in regard to men staying with their wives, than in regard to anything else; and I think the procreative results, as shown by the census tables, is due in a great measure to that discipline. . . .

Question: What is the prevailing inclination among the people of Texas in regard to giving the negroes civil or political rights and privileges?

Answer: I think they are all opposed to it. There are some men—I am not among them—who think that the basis of intelligence might be a good basis for the elective franchise. But a much larger class, perhaps nine-tenths of our

---

1. **"no continence among the negroes":** By this, Forshey means that they did not rein in their sexual impulses.

people, believe that the distinctions between the races should not be broken down by any such community of interests in the management of the affairs of the State. I think there is a very common sentiment that the negro, even with education, has not a mind capable of appreciating the political institutions of the country to such an extent as would make him a good associate for the white man in the administration of the government. I think if the vote was taken on the question of admitting him to the right of suffrage there would be a very small vote in favor of it—scarcely respectable: that is my judgment.

THE REVEREND JAMES SINCLAIR

Washington, D.C., January 29, 1866

Question: What is generally the state of feeling among the white people of North Carolina towards the government of the United States?

Answer: That is a difficult question to answer, but I will answer it as far as my own knowledge goes. In my opinion, there is generally among the white people not much love for the government. Though they are willing, and I believe determined, to acquiesce in what is inevitable, yet so far as love and affection for the government is concerned, I do not believe that they have any of it at all, outside of their personal respect and regard for President Johnson.

Question: How do they feel towards the mass of the northern people—that is, the people of what were known formerly as the free States?

Answer: They feel in this way: that they have been ruined by them. You can imagine the feelings of a person towards one whom he regards as having ruined him. They regard the northern people as having destroyed their property or taken it from them, and brought all the calamities of this war upon them.

Question: How do they feel in regard to what is called the right of secession?

Answer: They think that it was right. . . . that there was no wrong in it. They are willing now to accept the decision of the question that has been made by the sword, but they are not by any means converted from their old opinion that they had a right to secede. It is true that there have always been Union men in our State, but not Union men without slavery, except perhaps among Quakers. Slavery was the central idea even of the Unionist. The only difference between them and the others upon that question was, that they desired to have that institution under the aegis of the Constitution, and protected by it. The secessionists wanted to get away from the north altogether. When the secessionists precipitated our State into rebellion, the Unionists and secessionists went together, because the great object with both was the preservation of slavery by the preservation of State sovereignty. There was another class of Unionists who did not care anything at all about slavery, but they were driven by the other whites into the rebellion for the purpose of preserving slavery. The poor whites are to-day very much opposed to conferring upon the negro the right of suffrage; as much so as the other classes of the whites. They believe it is the intention of government to give the negro rights at their expense. They cannot see it in any other light than that as the negro is elevated they must proportionately go down. While they are glad that slavery is done away with, they are bitterly opposed to conferring the right of suffrage on the negro as the most prominent secessionists; but it is for the reason I have stated, that they think rights conferred on the negro must necessarily be taken from them, particularly the ballot, which was the only bulwark guarding their superiority to the negro race.

Question: In your judgment, what proportion of the white people of North Carolina are really, and truly, and cordially attached to the government of the United States?

Answer: Very few, sir; very few. . . .

Question: Is the Freedmen's Bureau acceptable to the great mass of the white people in North Carolina?

Answer: No, sir; I do not think it is; I think the most of the whites wish the bureau to be taken away.

Question: Why do they wish that?

Answer: They think that they can manage the negro for themselves: that they understand him better than northern men do. They say, "Let us understand what you want us to do with [the] negro—what you desire of us; lay down your conditions for our readmission into the Union, and then we will know what we have to do, and if you will do that we will enact laws for the government of these negroes. They have lived among us, and they are all with us, and we can manage them better than you can." They think it is interfering with the rights of the State for a bureau, the agent and representative of the federal government, to overslaugh the State entirely, and interfere with the regulations and administration of justice before their courts.

Question: Is there generally a willingness on the part of the whites to allow the freedmen to enjoy the right of acquiring land and personal property?

Answer: I think they are very willing to let them do that, for this reason; to get rid of some portion of the taxes imposed upon their property by the government. For instance, a white man will agree to sell a negro some of his land on condition of his paying so much a year on it, promising to give him a deed of it when the whole payment is made, taking his note in the mean time. This relieves that much of the land from taxes to be paid by the white man. All I am afraid of is, that the negro is too eager to go into this thing; that he will ruin himself, get himself into debt to the white man, and be forever bound to him for the debt and never get the land. I have often warned them to be careful what they did about these things.

Question: There is no repugnance on the part of the whites to the negro owning land and personal property?

Answer: I think not.

Question: Have they any objection to the legal establishment of the domestic relations among the blacks, such as the relation of husband and wife, of parent and child, and the securing by law to the negro the rights of those relations?

Answer: That is a matter of ridicule with the whites. They do not believe the negroes will ever respect those relations more than the brutes. I suppose I have married more than two hundred couples of negroes since the war, but the whites laugh at the very idea of the thing. . . .

Question: What, in general, has been the treatment of the blacks by the whites since the close of hostilities?

Answer: It has not generally been of the kindest character, I must say that; I am compelled to say that.

Question: Are you aware of any instance of personal ill treatment towards the blacks by the whites?

Answer: Yes, sir.

Question: Give some instances that have occurred since the war.

Answer: [Sinclair describes the beating of a young woman across her buttocks in graphic detail.]

Question: What was the provocation, if any?

Answer: Something in regard to some work, which is generally the provocation.

Question: Was there no law in North Carolina at that time to punish such an outrage?

Answer: No, sir; only the regulations of the Freedmen's Bureau; we took cognizance of the case. In old times that was quite allowable; it is what was called "paddling."

Question: Did you deal with the master?

Answer: I immediately sent a letter to him to come to my office, but he did not come, and I have never seen him in regard to the matter since. I had no soldiers to enforce compliance, and I was obliged to let the matter drop.

Question: Have you any reason to suppose that such instances of cruelty are frequent in North Carolina at this time—instances of whipping and striking?

Answer: I think they are; it was only a few days before I left that a woman came there with her head all bandaged up, having been cut and bruised by her employer. They think nothing of striking them.

Question: And the negro has practically no redress?

Answer: Only what he can get from the Freedmen's Bureau.

Question: Can you say anything further in regard to the political condition of North Carolina—the feeling of the people towards the government of the United States?

Answer: I for one would not wish to be left there in the hands of those men; I could not live there just now. But perhaps my case is an isolated one from the position I was compelled to take in that State. I was persecuted, arrested, and they tried to get me into their service; they tried everything to accomplish their purpose, and of course I have rendered myself still more obnoxious by accepting an appointment under the Freedmen's Bureau. . . .

Question: Suppose the military pressure of the government of the United States should be withdrawn from North Carolina, would northern men and true Unionists be safe in that State?

Answer: A northern man going there would perhaps present nothing obnoxious to the people of the State. But men who were born there, who have been true to the Union, and who have fought against the rebellion, are worse off than northern men.

5

The Murder of Jim Williams

Rosy Williams et al.

There have been three distinct Ku Klux Klans: they flourished in the 1860s and 1870s, from the 1920s to the early 1940s, and from the 1950s through to the present. The first, which concerns us here, began as a loosely bound fraternity in Tennessee in 1866 but soon turned into a violent organization dedicated to defeating Republican Reconstruction governments in the South and intimidating and controlling African Americans. In rural counties in many parts of the region, the Klan and its allies, sworn to secrecy on penalty of "death, death, death," controlled regions for months or even years, destroying the property of blacks or their white allies, driving people away, assaulting, and killing. Local governments and law enforcement agencies, dominated by or simply intimidated by the Klan, failed to stop these activities. Nationally, Republicans demanded action against the Klan while Democrats discounted its activities. In 1871, the Republicans, who then controlled both houses of Congress, established a joint House-Senate committee chaired by Senator John Scott of Pennsylvania to investigate the Klan. Its twelve-volume report is our main source of knowledge of the first Klan.

The climax of Klan activity came in 1871 with a reign of terror in a number of South Carolina counties. President Ulysses S. Grant, who since taking office had been reluctant to intervene in the South, requested from Congress a bill to put down the mounting atrocities in South Carolina and elsewhere. The result was the Ku Klux Act of 1871. It allowed the president to suspend the writ of habeas corpus, *which in turn enabled federal military authorities to arrest Klansmen when local authorities refused to do so. This was not, as some alleged, martial law, since all such prisoners were eventually tried in federal courts.*

The lynching on March 6, 1871, of Jim Williams, an outspoken enemy of the Klan and the captain of a black militia unit, became the single most famous event in the history of the South Carolina Klan. One of Yorkville's most prominent citizens, Dr. J. Rufus Bratton, was called to testify before the Committee and was later accused of leading the raid. As soon as the suspension of habeas corpus *threatened his arrest, he fled to Canada, where he lived in exile until 1877, when President Rutherford B. Hayes, as part of the many deals that finally ended Reconstruction, dropped all charges against*

U.S. Congress, *Testimony Taken by the Joint Select Committee to Inquire into the Condition of Affairs in the Late Insurrectionary States, South Carolina* [usually referred to as the *KKK Report*] (Washington, DC: Government Printing Office, 1872), vol. 3, 1720–21; *KKK Report, South Carolina*, vol. 3, 1724–27; *KKK Report, South Carolina*, vol. 3, 1342–59 passim.

him. Bratton returned to Yorkville as something of a local hero. The Klan's day had ended, but few Klansmen were ever punished for their actions.

QUESTIONS TO CONSIDER

1. What happened on the night that Jim Williams was hanged? Piece together an account of events from the testimony. Whose testimony do you find most persuasive and why?
2. What does this terrible event tell you about relations between blacks and whites in this part of South Carolina?
3. What was James Bratton's opinion on blacks' voting and participation in the political process?

TESTIMONY OF MRS. ROSY WILLIAMS

Mrs. Rosy Williams, (colored,) widow of Jim Williams, was the eighth witness called for the prosecution. She was sworn, and testified as follows:

Direct Examination by Mr. Corbin:

Question: Are you the wife of Jim Williams?

Answer: Yes, sir.

Question: Where do you live; where did you live when Jim Williams was living?

Answer: On Bratton's place.

Question: In what county, York County?

Answer: Yes, sir.

Question: When was Jim Williams killed—your husband?

Answer: The 7th of March.

Question: Tell the court and jury all about it—all you know about it.

Answer: They came to my house about two o'clock in the night; came in the house and called him.

Question: Who came?

Answer: Disguised men. I can't tell who it was. I don't know any of them.

Question: What do you call them?

Answer: I call them Ku-Klux.

Question: How many came?

Answer: I don't know how many there was.

Question: How many do you think?

Answer: I reckon about nine or ten came into the house, as nigh as I can guess it.

Question: What did they do?

Answer: He went under the house before they came, and after they came in he came up in the house and gave them the guns; there were but two in the house, and then they asked him for the others, and cussed, and told him to come out. He told them he had never had any of the guns. He went with them, and after they had took him out-doors they came in the house after me, and said there were some guns hid. I told them there was not; and after I told them that they went out, and after they had went out there I heard him make a fuss like he was strangling.

Question: Who?

Answer: Williams. Then I went to the door and pulled the door open, and allowed to go down and beg them not to hurt him. They told me not to go out there. Well, I didn't go out. Then they told me to shut the door and take my children and go to bed. I shut the door but didn't go to bed. I looked out of the crack after them until they got under the shadows of the trees. I couldn't see them then.

Question: Did they take Jim Williams?

Answer: Yes, sir; but I couldn't tell him from the rest.

Question: Was that the last you ever saw him alive?

Answer: Yes, sir.

Question: Or did you see him again?

Answer: No, sir; the next morning I went and looked for him, but I didn't find him. I was scared, too. Then I went for my people, to get some one to go help me look for him; and I met an old man who told me they had found him, and said he was dead. They had hung him; but I didn't go out there until 12 o'clock.

Question: Did you go out there then — did you see him?

Answer: Yes, sir.

Question: What was his condition?

Answer: He was hung on a pine tree.

Question: With a rope around his neck?

Answer: Yes, sir.

Question: Dead?

Answer: Yes, sir; he was dead.

TESTIMONY OF JOHN CALDWELL

John Caldwell was the next witness called, who, being duly sworn, testified as follows:

Direct Examination by Mr. Corbin:

Question: What is your name?

Answer: John Caldwell. . . .

Question: How long have you resided in York County?

Answer: Twenty-seven years. I was born and raised there.

Question: How old are you?

Answer: About twenty-seven years.

Question: In what portion of York County do you reside?

Answer: In the western portion.

Question: Have you ever been a member of the Ku-Klux organization in York County?

Answer: Yes, sir; I have.

Question: When did you join the order?

Answer: In 1868.

Question: Where was that?

Answer: At Yorkville.

Question: Who initiated you?

Answer: Major J. W. Avery.

Question: What was his relation to the order at that time?

Answer: He just came to me and asked me to walk up to his store. He took me into a room and said he wanted me to join an order. I asked him what he was getting it up for. He said it was in self-defense.

Question: Were you initiated by him then? Did he administer the oath? Can you tell us about what that oath was?

Answer: I cannot remember.

Question: Can you tell us the substance of it?

Answer: Only the last portion of it.

Question: What was that?

Answer: I understood that any person who divulged the secrets of the organization should "suffer death, death, death."

Question: Do you think you would recognize the oath were you to hear it again?

Answer: No, sir; only that portion of it. . . .

Question: Commence at the beginning and describe the raid on Jim Williams; when you got the order to go; where you went to muster; who took command of the men, and what road you traveled; what you did when you got to Jim Williams's house, and all about the matter.

Answer: The first I heard of it was at Yorkville; I was told there by Dr. Bratton that they were going down to McConnellsville; I asked him what he was going after; he said he was going for some guns; he asked me if I would go, and I said I would have nothing to do with it; I had never been on a raid; he asked me the name of the chief man in our county; I told him I understood it was William Johnson or Alonzo Brown was the leading man in our county.

Question: Do you mean in your portion of the county?

Answer: Yes, sir.

Question: Go on and tell all you know.

Answer: Johnson came to me and told me to meet him at the muster-patch; that was William Johnson.

Question: What is his relation to the order?

Answer: He was chief.

Question: Of what Klan?

Answer: Of the Rattlesnake Klan. I went out to the muster-ground that night; it is called the brier-patch; I met several men there. . . . Dr. Bratton came there, and Lindsay Brown and Rufus McLain.

Question: Did you put on your disguise at the brier-patch?

Answer: Yes, sir.

Question: What sort of disguises are they?

Answer: Most of them were black gowns, with heads and false-faces.

Question: What sort of heads were they?

Answer: They were made out of black cloth, or dark cloth.

Question: How were they ornamented?

Answer: Some had horns, and some had not.

Question: Had you horses there?

Answer: Yes, sir.

Question: Were the men armed?

Answer: No, sir. I don't believe I saw a gun in the party.

Question: Had they pistols?

Answer: I didn't see any pistols.

Question: Now tell us where they went.

Answer: We went down to the Pinckney road, and there we met another party of men. . . .

Question: What did they do there?

Answer: We stopped then, and there were four men initiated there. . . .

Question: Who was in command of the party?

Answer: Bratton was at the head of the party. He was riding in front.

Question: What Bratton was that?

Answer: Dr. J. Rufus Bratton, of Yorkville.

Question: Go on with what you had to say.

Answer: We went on then to McConnellsville; and about 200 or 300 yards from there we halted; and they said there were some guns down at that place, and they sent a party to search and get them. A man then came from the party that went forward and said, bring up the horses; and they took them down. They said there was a gun at Mr. Moore's; and they went up there for a black man; but I don't know who he was.

Question: At whose place was this?

Answer: They said it was Mr. Moore's place.

Question: What did they do with the black man?

Answer: They asked him about Jim Williams; how far away he lived. They asked him if he knew if Williams had any guns. He said he thought there were twelve or fifteen guns there. Then they took this black-masked man and mounted him on a horse or mule, and carried him a piece; then they halted and turned the black man loose, and he went back home. Then they went on from there about three miles, and stopped in a thicket, and a party of ten went off—I don't know whether there were more than ten—and were gone probably an hour.

Question: Can you describe the place?

Answer: It was in an old piney thicket on the side of a hill.

Question: What did you do?

Answer: I remained there with the horses. I was not well, and I just remained there with the horses.

Question: Did the party go forward?

Answer: Yes, sir. Before I got off my horse I heard some one call for ten men, and that party then went off. I saw them go off; and they were gone probably one hour when they returned.

Question: Did you hear anything of them while they were gone?

Answer: Not a word.

Question: Did the same crowd return?

Answer: Yes, sir.

Question: What was said by any of them as to what they had done?

Answer: I asked if they had found the black man Jim Williams, and if they saw him. I got no answer, and they just got on their horses to leave.

Question: Who ordered them?

Answer: I heard some man say, "Mount your horses," and then they mounted and took across over the fence, and I got up forward to the foremost man—Dr. Bratton. I asked him if he had found the negro. He said yes. Said I, "Where, where is he?" Said he, "He is in hell, I expect."

Question: What further was said?

Answer: I asked him, "You didn't kill him?" He said, "We hung him." I said, "Dr. Bratton, you ought not to have done that." He then pulled out his watch, and said, "We have no time to spare; we have to call on one or two more."

TESTIMONY OF DR. JAMES R. BRATTON

James R. Bratton sworn and examined.

By the Chairman:

Question: Do you reside in this place?

Answer: Yes, sir, and have been residing here for twenty-five years.

Question: Are you a native of this State?

Answer: Yes, sir; of this county.

Question: What is your occupation?

Answer: I have been practicing medicine here for twenty-five years.

Question: Have you had an opportunity of becoming acquainted with the people of this county generally?

Answer: Yes, sir, I think I have.

Question: Does your practice extend through the county?

Answer: Through the different sections of the county.

Question: Our purpose is to inquire into the security of life, person, and property through this county, and the manner in which the laws are executed. Have you any knowledge of any offenses against the law, or against the security of person and property, that have not been redressed in the ordinary courts of justice?

Answer: I have no personal knowledge of anything of the kind. I merely hear rumors and reports. Personally, I know nothing about it.

Question: Have you been called upon, as a physician, to either testify before, or certify upon, any inquests on the bodies of dead men?

Answer: I have not. I have only heard these reports from the coroner's inquests; that is the way I get my information about these cases.

Question: How many persons have you heard of who have been killed in this county within the last six or eight months?

Answer: There was a man up here named Tom Black, or Roundtree, that they say was killed—I cannot tell when. One report says he was killed by negroes for his money; another, that it was by white men in disguise. He had been to Charlotte a few days before that, to sell his cotton, and, when killed, his money could not be found; but who killed him I cannot tell. . . .

Question: Any others?

Answer: Yes, sir; a negro was hung about twelve miles below by some persons, who I cannot tell.

Question: What was his name?

Answer: Williams.

Question: Was he a militia captain?

Answer: He was.

Question: When was that?

Answer: That was some time in this year, in February or March; in the latter part of February or the first of March; I do not remember the date exactly.

Question: Do you recollect the day of the week?

Answer: No, sir, I do not remember it.

Question: Do you recollect the day you heard it?

Answer: No, sir; nor the day it was done; it was some time in the latter part of February or the first of March.

Question: Was that done by men in disguise?

Answer: Yes, sir, it was so reported; that was the testimony at the coroner's inquest.

Question: Were you at that inquest?

Answer: I was not; but it was so reported to me by the coroner.

Question: Was that in February or March?

Answer: Yes, sir.

Question: Are those the only cases you have known of?

Answer: I do not know any other cases that I can think of now. I have not fixed any other cases upon my mind. Let me see, there may have been other cases.

Question: Those are cases of actual death about which I am inquiring now?

Answer: What do you mean by that?

Question: Persons killed.

Answer: Those three are negroes killed. I do not know any other cases to my knowledge. . . .

Question: Do you discredit the statements of negroes who say they were whipped?

Answer: In many cases I do.

Question: Do you think the men who disguise themselves could be easily told?

Answer: I do not say that, but a great many of these people dislike to work, and if they can get the protection of the State or the United States to relieve them from work they will do it, and I have no faith in their testimony.

Question: In negro testimony?

Answer: I have not.

Question: Is there any concerted arrangement here for the purpose of intimidating the negroes either with regard to their political rights or their making complaints against those who have whipped them or otherwise committed violence upon them?

Answer: I know nothing of the kind. The truth is this, I think it is just the reverse. If ever our people were earnest in anything it is to teach the negro his duty to be quiet and passive and attend to his duty; to let public meetings alone; to go and vote as he pleases, allowing no man to interfere with him. I do not know any cases where a darkey has been interfered with at the polls.

Question: Is attendance at a political meeting considered imprudent or wrong in them?

Answer: When they attend in large numbers they create great confusion and annoyance; but I do not know a procession that has been interfered with.

Question: Is that the light in which the white people view that subject, that the negroes had better stay away altogether from political meetings?

Answer: Yes, sir. Our advice is "have as little to do with politics as possible; if you want to vote, vote, but vote for no dishonest, vicious, ignorant, and wicked man; vote for whom you please, so he is honest, whether a radical or a democrat." That has been my advice to them all.

Question: Do you know of no organization in this county intended to prevent negroes from voting as they saw proper?

Answer: I don't; and that has not been the case.

Question: Do you know anything of this organization commonly called Ku-Klux?

Answer: I am no member of the Ku-Klux, and know nothing of their proceedings. . . .

Question: Have you any knowledge of the men who participated in the hanging of Captain Williams?

Answer: I have no knowledge of that fact.

Question: Has no man said anything to you about it?

Answer: No, sir; no man has said, "I did it," or "he did." I know nothing about it as to who hung him.

Question: Either from those who participated in it or from any other person?

Answer: No, sir.

Question: Did you learn that he was hanged?

Answer: Yes, sir.

Question: That that was the mode of his killing—that he was hung?

Answer: Yes, sir.

Question: Were you upon the inquest of any one of these men who were murdered by violence in this county?

Answer: No, sir. I was engaged all the time in other business. Generally in these cases in the country they take the nearest physician. . . .

Question: What, in your opinion, have been the causes of whatever disturbances have occurred in this county within a year; what are the principal leading causes of any troubles that may have existed, whether breaking out by Ku-Klux acts or any other mode of proceeding?

Answer: Why, sir, my opinion is this: that these burnings of people's houses and barns and gin-houses produced this disturbance.

Question: Was that last summer?

Answer: That was last fall and winter, and this spring. I do not know that there were any burnings last summer that I remember. I think it was all this winter.

Question: You have given an estimate of the number of the whippings of negroes, whether by Ku-Klux or other negroes, or somebody else for private reasons, at twelve or fifteen. What is the probable number of burnings of gin-houses in this county in the last year?

Answer: I will have to count them up. Thomason, stables and barn; Warren, gin-houses; Miller, gin-house; Crosby, gin-house; Preacher Castle, barn; my brother's thrashing-house was burnt the other night. A boy confessed it afterward. He simply did it because my brother had told him not to go into his select orchard. He had a large orchard and told him that he and the rest of the colored people might go in there, but not in the garden. He did go into the garden. He caught him there and cursed him a little, and, in a few days, this fire took place. . . .

Question: Out of these six cases [of arson], is there any evidence to connect the negroes, as a class, with the burning?

Answer: No, sir.

Question: Yet you give these burnings as the outrages against the negroes?

Answer: That is the general impression among the people.

Question: What justice is there in charging the negroes, as a class, with burning, any more than the murderers who are operating through the country?

Answer: Let me tell you. These people are easily excited to action, and when we had the candidates last fall, strange to say, one candidate actually made this speech: "You have to succeed in this county if you have to burn every blade of grass," or something to that effect.

Question: Did you hear it?

Answer: No, sir.

Question: Who reported it to you?

Answer: I do not know.

Question: Who made the speech?

Answer: Doctor Neagle.

Question: Who heard it?

Answer: Almost any citizen you can take up.

Question: You cannot swear that he said it?

Answer: No, sir.

Question: You are willing to believe it?

Answer: Yes, sir.

Question: And that the negroes did these burnings, incited by that?

Answer: I am more disposed to think that the negroes did it than that white persons did it.

Question: And yet you have no opinion as to the murderers in this county?

Answer: No, sir.

6

Work under Sharecropper and Labor Contracts

Grimes Family and Swindell Brothers

The end of slavery and the impoverishment of the South in the aftermath of the Civil War seriously disrupted Southern agriculture. Five years after the war's end, Southern cotton production was still only about half of what it had been in the 1850s. The large plantations, no longer tended by gangs of slaves or hired freedmen, were broken up into smaller holdings, but the capital required for profitable agriculture meant that control of farming remained centralized in a limited elite of merchants and large landholders.

Various mechanisms arose to finance Southern agriculture. Tenants worked on leased land, and small landowners gave liens on their crops to get financing. But the most common method of financing agriculture was sharecropping. Agreements like the Grimes family's sharecrop contract determined the economic life of thousands of poor rural families in the southern United States after the Civil War. Families, both African American and white, lacking capital for agriculture were furnished seed, implements, and a line of credit for food and other necessities to keep them through the growing season. Accounts were settled in the winter after crops were in. Under these conditions a small number of farmers managed to make money and eventually became landowners, but the larger part found themselves in ever deeper debt at the end of the year, with no choice but to contract again for the next year.

Another form of labor contract was the agreement, like that of the Swindell Brothers' firm, to pay the passage to America for immigrants with needed skills in return for their agreeing to work for a fixed period of time. Under pressure from labor organizations, this form of recruitment, legalized during the Civil War, was banned in 1885.

QUESTIONS TO CONSIDER

1. What restrictions on the freedom of sharecroppers were built into the contract?
2. Which restrictions might have been the most significant in preventing sharecroppers from achieving independence?

From the Grimes Family Papers (#3357), 1882, held in the Southern Historical Collection, University of North Carolina, Chapel Hill; Wayne Moquin, ed., *Makers of America*, vol. 4, *Seekers after Wealth* (Chicago: Encyclopaedia Britannica Educational Corp., 1971).

3. Why would labor organizations object to agreements like the Swindell contract?

4. What would motivate workers to enter into such contracts?

GRIMES FAMILY PAPERS

To every one applying to rent land upon shares, the following conditions must be read, and *agreed to.*

To every 30 or 35 acres, I agree to furnish the team, plow, and farming implements, except cotton planters, and I *do not* agree to furnish a cart to every cropper. The croppers are to have half of the cotton, corn and fodder (and peas and pumpkins and potatoes if any are planted) if the following conditions are complied with, but—if not—they are to have only two fifths (2/5). Croppers are to have no part or interest in the cotton seed raised from the crop planted and worked by them. No vine crops of any description, that is, no watermelons, muskmelons, . . . squashes or anything of that kind, except peas and pumpkins, and potatoes, are to be planted in the cotton or corn. All must work under my direction. All plantation work to be done by the croppers. My part of the crop to be *housed* by them, and the fodder and oats to be hauled and put in the house. All the cotton must be topped about 1st August. If any cropper fails from any cause to save all the fodder from his crop, I am to have enough fodder to make it equal to one half of the whole if the whole amount of fodder had been saved.

For every mule or horse furnished by me there must be 1000 good sized rails . . . hauled, and the fence repaired as far as they will go, the fence to be torn down and put up from the bottom if I so direct. All croppers to haul rails and work on fence whenever I may order. Rails to be split when I may say. Each cropper to clean out every ditch in his crop, and where a ditch runs between two croppers, the cleaning out of that ditch is to be divided equally between them. Every ditch bank in the crop must be shrubbed down and cleaned off before the crop is planted and must be cut down every time the land is worked with his hoe and when the crop is "laid by," the ditch banks must be left clean of bushes, weeds, and seeds. The cleaning out of all ditches must be done by the first of October. The rails must be split and the fence repaired before corn is planted.

Each cropper must keep in good repair all bridges in his crop or over ditches that he has to clean out and when a bridge needs repairing that is outside of all their crops, then any one that I call on must repair it.

Fence jams to be done as ditch banks. If any cotton is planted on the land outside of the plantation fence, I am to have *three fourths* of all the cotton made in those patches, that is to say, no cotton must be planted by croppers in their home patches.

All croppers must clean out stables and fill them with straw, and haul straw in front of stables whenever I direct. All the cotton must be manured, and enough fertilizer must be brought to manure each crop highly, the croppers to pay for one half of all manure bought, the quantity to be purchased for each crop must be left to me.

No cropper to work off the plantation when there is any work to be done on the land he has rented, or when his work is needed by me or other croppers. Trees to be cut down on Orchard, House field & Evanson fences, leaving such as I may designate.

Road field to be planted from the *very edge of the ditch to the fence*, and all the land to be planted close up to the ditches and fences. *No stock of any kind* belonging to croppers to run in the plantation after crops are gathered.

If the fence should be blown down, or if trees should fall on the fence outside of the land planted by any of the croppers, any one or all that I may call upon must put it up and repair it. Every cropper must feed, or have fed, the team he works, Saturday nights, Sundays, and every morning before going to work, beginning to feed his team (morning, noon, and night *every day* in the week) on the day he rents and feeding it to and including the 31st day of December. If any cropper shall from any cause fail to repair his fence as far as 1000 rails will go, or shall fail to clean out any part of his ditches, or shall fail to leave his ditch banks, any part of them, well shrubbed and clean when his crop is laid by, or shall fail to clean out stables, fill them up and haul straw in front of them whenever he is told, he shall have only two-fifths (2/5) of the cotton, corn, fodder, peas and pumpkins made on the land he cultivates.

If any cropper shall fail to feed his team Saturday nights, all day Sunday and all the rest of the week, morning/noon, and night, for every time he so fails he must pay me five cents.

No corn nor cotton stalks must be burned, but must be cut down, cut up and plowed in. Nothing must be burned off the land except when it is *impossible* to plow it in.

Every cropper must be responsible for all gear and farming implements placed in his hands, and if not returned must be paid for unless it is worn out by use.

Croppers must sow & plow in oats and haul them to the crib, but *must have no part of them*. Nothing to be sold from their crops, nor fodder nor corn to be carried out of the fields until my rent is all paid, and all amounts they owe me and for which I am responsible are paid in full.

I am to gin & pack all the cotton and charge every cropper an eighteenth of his part, the cropper to furnish his part of the bagging, ties, & twine.

The sale of every cropper's part of the cotton to be made by me when and where I choose to sell, and after deducting all they owe me and all sums that I may be responsible for on their accounts, to pay them their half of the net proceeds. Work of every description, particularly the work on fences and ditches, to be done to my satisfaction, and must be done over until I am satisfied that it is done as it should be.

No wood to burn, nor light wood, nor poles, nor timber for boards, nor wood for any purpose whatever must be gotten above the house occupied by Henry Beasley—nor must any trees be cut down nor any wood used for any purpose, except for firewood, without my permission.

SWINDELL BROTHERS CONTRACT

Antwerp, Dec. 15, 1882

Agreement between the firm of Swindell Bros. of the first part, and John Schmidt, gatherer, and Carl Wagner, blower, of the second part.

The undersigned, of the second part, covenants and agrees with the party of the first part that they will for two consecutive years, beginning January 1, 1882, work and duly perform such duties as instructed by the party of the first part or his superintendents. The party of the first part covenants and agrees to pay the undersigned, who may duly perform their duties, the price generally paid by Baltimore manufacturers for the size of 16 by 24 inches, and all sheets shall be estimated at eight sheet of 36 by 54 inches for 100 square feet. The party of the first part covenants and agrees that the wages of each glassblower shall be an average of $80 per calendar month, on condition that he makes 180 boxes of 100 square feet per calendar month.

The gatherer shall receive 65 percent of the sum paid the blower for wages per calendar month for actual work performed during the fire. It is agreed that the party of the first part shall retain 10 percent of the wages of each and every workman until the expiration of this contract as a guarantee of the faithful performance of the provisions of this contract. The aforesaid 10 percent shall be forfeited by each and every workman who shall fail to comply with the provisions of this contract.

It is further agreed that the party of the first part shall advance the passage money for the parties of the second part.

It is further agreed that the party of the first part have the right to discharge any of the workmen for drunkenness or neglect of duty, or for disturbing the peace, or creating dissatisfaction among them, or for joining any association of American workmen.

The said Swindell Bros., their heirs, and assigns, shall be considered the parties of the first part, and they agree to pay each blower $12 per week and the gatherer $9.00 per week, on condition that each perform his work faithfully at every blowing. The parties of the first part agrees to make monthly settlements for the parties of the second part, after the advances for the passage, etc., shall have been repaid. Provided you faithfully perform your work for the term of contract (two years), we will pay back the passage money from Europe to America.

Swindell Bros.
Yohonn Schmidt, *Gatherer*
Carl Wagener, *Blower*

7

School Days of an Indian Girl
Zitkala-Ša (Gertrude Simmons Bonnin)

From the mid-1880s to the 1930s, the thrust of American Indian policy was to assimilate Native Americans into the larger society. Boarding schools for Native American children became a common strategy for inducting promising young Native Americans into white culture. Officials were particularly eager to educate girls, hoping to alter the domestic culture of the Indians.

Zitkala-Ša, or Red Bird (1876–1938), a Sioux from the Yankton reservation in South Dakota, described in a series of articles in the Atlantic Monthly *in 1900 her experiences at a Quaker missionary school for Native Americans in Wabash, Indiana, which she attended from age eight to eleven. She returned to the school four years later to complete the course of study and then attended Earlham College in Richmond, Indiana, somehow acquiring the capacity to succeed in the white world without losing her Native American heritage. After returning to the Sioux country, she married a Sioux and began a lifetime of work to improve the status and condition of Indian peoples. In a long career that ended with her death in 1938, she played an influential role in the organization of Native American communities, which led to major though not thoroughly satisfying federal reforms in the late 1920s and 1930s.*

QUESTIONS TO CONSIDER

1. What did Zitkala-Ša mean when she said she returned to the reservation "neither a wild Indian nor a tame one"? What did she reject about her education, and what did she accept?
2. Given the pain of her school experience, what reasons can you suggest for Zitkala-Ša's return to school?
3. What did Zitkala-Ša mean by her final comment about the Indian schools: "[F]ew there are who have paused to question whether real life or long-lasting death lies beneath this semblance of civilization"?

The first turning away from the easy, natural flow of my life occurred in an early spring. It was in my eighth year; in the month of March, I afterward learned. At this age I knew but one language, and that was my mother's native tongue. . . .

Zitkala-Ša (Gertrude Simmons Bonnin), "The School Days of an Indian Girl," *Atlantic Monthly* 89 (January–March 1900): 45–47, 190, 192–94.

"Mother, my friend Judéwin is going home with the missionaries. She is going to a more beautiful country than ours; the palefaces told her so!" I said wistfully, wishing in my heart that I too might go.

Mother sat in a chair, and I was hanging on her knee. Within the last two seasons my big brother Dawée had returned from a three years' education in the East, and his coming back influenced my mother to take a farther step from her native way of living. First it was a change from the buffalo skin to the white man's canvas that covered our wigwam. Now she had given up her wigwam of slender poles, to live, a foreigner, in a home of clumsy logs.

"Yes, my child, several others besides Judéwin are going away with the palefaces. Your brother said the missionaries had inquired about his little sister," she said, watching my face very closely.

My heart thumped so hard against my breast, I wondered if she could hear it.

"Did he tell them to take me, mother?" I asked, fearing lest Dawée had forbidden the palefaces to see me, and that my hope of going to the Wonderland would be entirely blighted.

With a sad, slow smile, she answered: "There! I knew you were wishing to go, because Judéwin has filled your ears with the white men's lies. Don't believe a word they say! Their words are sweet, but, my child, their deeds are bitter. You will cry for me, but they will not even soothe you. Stay with me, my little one! Your brother Dawée says that going East, away from your mother, is too hard an experience for his baby sister."

Thus my mother discouraged my curiosity about the lands beyond our eastern horizon; for it was not yet an ambition for Letters that was stirring me. But on the following day the missionaries did come to our very house. I spied them coming up the footpath leading to our cottage. A third man was with them, but he was not my brother Dawée. It was another, a young interpreter, a paleface who had a smattering of the Indian language. I was ready to run out to meet them, but I did not dare to displease my mother. With great glee, I jumped up and down on our ground floor. I begged my mother to open the door, that they would be sure to come to us. Alas! They came, they saw, and they conquered!

Judéwin had told me of the great tree where grew red, red apples; and how we could reach out our hands and pick all the red apples we could eat. I had never seen apple trees. I had never tasted more than a dozen red apples in my life; and when I heard of the orchards of the East, I was eager to roam among them. The missionaries smiled into my eyes, and patted my head. I wondered how mother could say such hard words against them.

"Mother, ask them if little girls may have all the red apples they want, when they go East," I whispered aloud in my excitement.

The interpreter heard me, and answered: "Yes, little girl, the nice red apples are for those who pick them; and you will have a ride on the iron horse if you go with these good people."

I had never seen a train, and he knew it.

"Mother, I'm going East! I like big red apples, and I want to ride on the iron horse! Mother, say yes!" I pleaded.

My mother said nothing. The missionaries waited in silence; and my eyes began to blur with tears, though I struggled to choke them back. The corners of my mouth twitched, and my mother saw me.

"I am not ready to give you any word," she said to them. "Tomorrow I shall send you my answer by my son." . . .

[The next day] my brother Dawée came for mother's decision. I dropped my play, and crept close to my aunt.

"Yes, Dawée, my daughter, though she does not understand what it all means, is anxious to go. She will need an education when she is grown, for then there will be fewer real Dakotas, and many more palefaces: This tearing her away, so young, from her mother is necessary, if I would have her an educated woman. The palefaces, who owe us a large debt for stolen lands, have begun to pay a tardy justice in offering some education to our children. But I know my daughter must suffer keenly in this experiment. For her sake, I dread to tell you my reply to the missionaries. Go, tell them that they may take my little daughter, and that the Great Spirit shall not fail to reward them according to their hearts." . . .

THE CUTTING OF MY LONG HAIR

The first day in the land of apples was a bitter-cold one; for the snow still covered the ground, and the trees were bare. A large bell rang for breakfast, its loud metallic voice crashing through the belfry overhead and into our sensitive ears. The annoying clatter of shoes on bare floors gave us no peace. The constant clash of harsh noises, with an undercurrent of many voices murmuring an unknown tongue, made a bedlam within which I was securely tied. And though my spirit tore itself in struggling for its lost freedom, all was useless.

A paleface woman, with white hair, came up after us. We were placed in a line of girls who were marching into the dining room. These were Indian girls, in stiff shoes and closely clinging dresses. The small girls wore sleeved aprons and shingled hair. As I walked noiselessly in my soft moccasins, I felt like sinking to the floor, for my blanket had been stripped from my shoulders. I looked hard at the Indian girls, who seemed not to care that they were even more immodestly dressed than I, in their tightly fitting clothes. While we marched in, the boys entered at an opposite door. I watched for the three young braves who came in our party. I spied them in the rear ranks, looking as uncomfortable as I felt.

A small bell was tapped, and each of the pupils drew a chair from under the table. Supposing this act meant they were to be seated, I pulled out mine and at once slipped into it from one side. But when I turned my head, I saw that I was the only one seated, and all the rest at our table remained standing. Just as I began to rise, looking shyly around to see how chairs were to be used, a second bell was sounded. All were seated at last, and I had to crawl back into my chair again. I heard a man's voice at one end of the hall, and I looked around to see him. But all the others hung their heads over their plates. As I glanced at the long chain of tables, I caught the eyes of a paleface woman upon me. Immediately

I dropped my eyes, wondering why I was so keenly watched by the strange woman. The man ceased his mutterings, and then a third bell was tapped. Every one picked up his knife and fork and began eating. I began crying instead, for by this time I was afraid to venture anything more.

But this eating by formula was not the hardest trial in that first day. Late in the morning, my friend Judéwin gave me a terrible warning. Judéwin knew a few words of English; and she had overheard the paleface woman talk about cutting our long, heavy hair. Our mothers had taught us that only un-skilled warriors who were captured had their hair shingled by the enemy. Among our people, short hair was worn by mourners, and shingled hair by cowards!

We discussed our fate some moments, and when Judéwin said, "We have to submit, because they are strong," I rebelled.

"No, I will not submit! I will struggle first!" I answered.

I watched my chance, and when no one noticed I disappeared. I crept up the stairs as quietly as I could in my squeaking shoes,—my moccasins had been exchanged for shoes. Along the hall I passed, without knowing whither I was going. Turning aside to an open door, I found a large room with three white beds in it. The windows were covered with dark green curtains, which made the room very dim. Thankful that no one was there, I directed my steps toward the corner farthest from the door. On my hands and knees I crawled under the bed, and cuddled myself in the dark corner.

From my hiding place I peered out, shuddering with fear whenever I heard footsteps near by. Though in the hall loud voices were calling my name, and I knew that even Judéwin was searching for me, I did not open my mouth to an-swer. Then the steps were quickened and the voices became excited. The sounds came nearer and nearer. Women and girls entered the room. I held my breath and watched them open closet doors and peep behind large trunks. Some one threw up the curtains, and the room was filled with sudden light. What caused them to stoop and look under the bed I do not know. I remember being dragged out, though I resisted by kicking and scratching wildly. In spite of myself, I was carried downstairs and tied fast in a chair.

I cried aloud, shaking my head all the while until I felt the cold blades of the scissors against my neck, and heard them gnaw off one of my thick braids. Then I lost my spirit. Since the day I was taken from my mother I had suffered extreme indignities. People had stared at me. I had been tossed about in the air like a wooden puppet. And now my long hair was shingled like a coward's! In my anguish I moaned for my mother, but no one came to comfort me. Not a soul reasoned quietly with me, as my own mother used to do; for now I was only one of many little animals driven by a herder.

IRON ROUTINE

A loud-clamoring bell awakened us at half past six in the cold winter mornings. From happy dreams of Western rolling lands and unlassoed freedom we tumbled out upon chilly bare floors back again into a paleface day. We had short time to jump into our shoes and clothes, and wet our eyes with icy water, before a small hand bell was vigorously rung for roll call. . . .

A paleface woman, with a yellow-covered roll book open on her arm and a gnawed pencil in her hand, appeared at the door. Her small, tired face was coldly lighted with a pair of large gray eyes. . . .

Relentlessly her pencil black-marked our daily records if we were not present to respond to our names, and no chum of ours had done it successfully for us. No matter if a dull headache or the painful cough of slow consumption had delayed the absentee, there was only time enough to mark the tardiness. It was next to impossible to leave the iron routine after the civilizing machine had once begun its day's buzzing; and as it was inbred in me to suffer in silence rather than to appeal to the ears of one whose open eyes could not see my pain, I have many times trudged in the day's harness heavy-footed, like a dumb sick brute. . . .

I grew bitter, and censured the woman for cruel neglect of our physical ills. I despised the pencils that moved automatically, and the one teaspoon which dealt out, from a large bottle, healing to a row of variously ailing Indian children. I blamed the hard-working, well-meaning, ignorant woman who was inculcating in our hearts her superstitious ideas. Though I was sullen in all my little troubles, as soon as I felt better I was ready again to smile upon the cruel woman. Within a week I was again actively testing the chains which tightly bound my individuality like a mummy for burial. . . .

INCURRING MY MOTHER'S DISPLEASURE

In the second journey to the East I had not come without some precautions. I had a secret interview with one of our best medicine men, and when I left his wigwam I carried securely in my sleeve a tiny bunch of magic roots. This possession assured me of friends wherever I should go. So absolutely did I believe in its charms that I wore it through all the school routine for more than a year. Then, before I lost my faith in the dead roots, I lost the little buckskin bag containing all my good luck.

At the close of this second term of three years I was the proud owner of my first diploma. The following autumn I ventured upon a college career against my mother's will.

I had written for her approval, but in her reply I found no encouragement. She called my notice to her neighbors' children, who had completed their education in three years. They had returned to their homes, and were then talking English with the frontier settlers. Her few words hinted that I had better give up my slow attempt to learn the white man's ways, and be content to roam over the prairies and find my living upon wild roots. I silenced her by deliberate disobedience.

Thus, homeless and heavy-hearted, I began anew my life among strangers.

As I hid myself in my little room in the college dormitory, away from the scornful and yet curious eyes of the students, I pined for sympathy. Often I wept in secret, wishing I had gone West, to be nourished by my mother's love, instead of remaining among a cold race whose hearts were frozen hard with prejudice.

During the fall and winter seasons I scarcely had a real friend, though by that time several of my classmates were courteous to me at a safe distance. . . .

. . . I appeared as the college representative in [an oratorical] contest. This time the competition was among orators from different colleges in our state. It was held at the state capital, in one of the largest opera houses.

Here again was a strong prejudice against my people. In the evening, as the great audience filled the house, the student bodies began warring among themselves. Fortunately, I was spared witnessing any of the noisy wrangling before the contest began. The slurs against the Indian that stained the lips of our opponents were already burning like a dry fever within my breast.

But after the orations were delivered a deeper burn awaited me. There, before that vast ocean of eyes, some college rowdies threw out a large white flag, with a drawing of a most forlorn Indian girl on it. Under this they had printed in bold black letters words that ridiculed the college which was represented by a "squaw." Such worse than barbarian rudeness embittered me. While we waited for the verdict of the judges, I gleamed fiercely upon the throngs of palefaces. My teeth were hard set, as I saw the white flag still floating insolently in the air.

Then anxiously we watched the man carry toward the stage the envelope containing the final decision.

There were two prizes given, that night, and one of them was mine!

The evil spirit laughed within me when the white flag dropped out of sight, and the hands which furled it hung limp in defeat.

Leaving the crowd as quickly as possible, I was soon in my room. The rest of the night I sat in an armchair and gazed into the crackling fire. I laughed no more in triumph when thus alone. The little taste of victory did not satisfy a hunger in my heart. In my mind I saw my mother far away on the Western plains, and she was holding a charge against me.

RETROSPECTION

. . . At this stage of my own evolution, I was ready to curse men of small capacity for being the dwarfs their God had made them. In the process of my education I had lost all consciousness of the nature world about me. Thus, when a hidden rage took me to the small white-walled prison which I then called my room, I unknowingly turned away from my one salvation.

Alone in my room, I sat like the petrified Indian woman of whom my mother used to tell me. I wished my heart's burdens would turn me to unfeeling stone. But alive, in my tomb, I was destitute!

For the white man's papers I had given up my faith in the Great Spirit. For these same papers I had forgotten the healing in trees and brooks. On account of my mother's simple view of life, and my lack of any, I gave her up, also. I made no friends among the race of people I loathed. Like a slender tree, I had been uprooted from my mother, nature, and God. I was shorn of my branches, which had waved in sympathy and love for home and friends. The natural coat of bark which had protected my oversensitive nature was scraped off to the very quick.

Now a cold bare pole I seemed to be planted in a strange earth. Still, I seemed to hope a day would come when my mute aching head, reared upward to the sky, would flash a zigzag lightning across the heavens. With this dream of vent for a long-pent consciousness, I walked again amid the crowds.

At last, one weary day in the schoolroom, a new idea presented itself to me. It was a new way of solving the problem of my inner self. I liked it. Thus I resigned my position as teacher; and now I am in an Eastern city, following the long course of study I have set for myself. Now, as I look back upon the recent past, I see it from a distance, as a whole. I remember how, from morning till evening, many specimens of civilized peoples visited the Indian school. The city folks with canes and eyeglasses, the countrymen with sunburnt cheeks and clumsy feet, forgot their relative social ranks in an ignorant curiosity. Both sorts of these Christian palefaces were alike astounded at seeing the children of savage warriors so docile and industrious.

As answers to their shallow inquiries they received the students' sample work to look upon. Examining the neatly figured pages, and gazing upon the Indian girls and boys bending over their books, the white visitors walked out of the schoolhouse well satisfied: they were educating the children of the red man! They were paying a liberal fee to the government employees in whose able hands lay the small forest of Indian timber.

In this fashion many have passed idly through the Indian schools during the last decade, afterward to boast of their charity to the North American Indian. But few there are who have paused to question whether real life or long-lasting death lies beneath this semblance of civilization.

The Peopling of the West

The phrase "manifest destiny" was first made popular by journalist John L. O'Sullivan in 1845, when he argued that it is "our manifest destiny to overspread and to possess the whole of the continent which Providence has given us for the development of the great experiment of liberty." Shortly thereafter, the United States took much of the Southwest from Mexico. However, the Civil War and struggles over slavery, freedom, and the future development of the West prevented the nation from doing much "overspreading and possessing" during the following two decades.

When the Civil War ended, the nation turned its full attention to the West, finally making good on the countless economic development schemes that had been promoted since the Louisiana Purchase of 1803. The transcontinental railroad and the Homestead Act defined this great shift westward. The Homestead Act of 1862 guaranteed 160 acres of public land to any family that had not taken up arms against the U.S. government during the Civil War, on the condition that they "improve" or farm the land. The news of this act spread throughout Europe and brought millions of people from crowded cities, towns, and agricultural regions—with the poorest and most agricultural countries losing large percentages of their national population.

Second only to Ireland in population lost to American migration, Norway had whole regions stripped of population in the nineteenth century. The Norwegian families pictured in Figure 1 are an example of some of the 800,000 Norwegians—a third of the population—who left Norway between 1825 and 1925, many to take up homesteads. The photo was obviously carefully posed. What do you notice about the choices that were made in placement within the frame of people, clothing, and objects? What do you think these choices tell us about this time and place and the lives of these migrants?

Not all migrants to the West were escaping agrarian crisis in Europe. The eastern United States was also crowded with land-hungry farmers, impoverished city dwellers looking for opportunity, and adventurers who had read the many stories about western overnight fortunes, gunfighters, and wide-open spaces that were popular at the time. Some came West in organized migrations, like the Mormons and other religious minorities and utopian communities. However, most families and individuals simply trickled across the Mississippi in ones and twos, numbers of whom would eventually add up to millions.

Figure 1. Norwegian immigrant family in Dakota Territory, 1898.

The experience of African Americans was, as usual, somewhat different. Reconstruction brought new opportunity to many former slaves, who built schools, farms, and community institutions, and elected black senators and members of Congress. At various times during Reconstruction blacks were the majority of elected officials in South Carolina, Louisiana, and Mississippi. However, with little unclaimed land, the tiny Southern industrial economy was devastated by war and poor transportation networks. Financiers were afraid to invest in a region where big questions of land ownership, citizenship rights, and control of the military were still unresolved.

When President Rutherford B. Hayes removed the federal troops from the South in 1877, the balance permanently tilted back toward the plantation owners, who reclaimed title to their land and control over the government, often using violence and torture to deny freedmen their new rights. The final result was the sharecropping system, in which ex-slaves were forced to pay a share of the crop to former owners in exchange for the right to farm. Driven by poverty and rumors of a restoration of slavery, a mass movement of ex-slaves, known as "exodusters," migrated west to Kansas, where they tried to set up utopian communities without masters or slaves.

Benjamin "Pap" Singleton, pictured in Figure 2, was a former slave turned political activist and entrepreneur who printed thousands of posters urging

Figure 2. Benjamin "Pap" Singleton's "Ho for Kansas!" flyer, 1878.

African Americans to abandon the old South and take up homestead land in Kansas, the state that had made John Brown famous for fighting slavery. He found suitable land and helped organize passage for tens of thousands of African Americans. Singleton called his organization the Homestead Association. How do you think the politicians who passed this act felt about Singleton's use of the name and the land offer?

Despite vigilante efforts by armed whites attempting to drive back the exodusters, more than 50,000 made it to the Western states. Some prospered and stayed, but many arrived with few resources and little support from such well-organized groups as Singleton's Homestead Association. Some of these refugees from slavery were forced further West and some returned home to the South. The families in Figure 3 are waiting for a ferry on their journey to Kansas. What do you think the photographer wanted to communicate with this photograph? What do you notice about the possessions of these migrants?

For some of the roughly 200,000 black soldiers who had served in the Union Army, the political conflicts of Reconstruction had held no appeal from the start. They preferred to remain in the U.S. Army and become "Buffalo Soldiers" fighting Indian wars to make the Western territories and states safe for homesteaders. They became some of the most feared and effective Indian fighters, eventually providing support to "manifest destiny" in Cuba and the Philippines during the Spanish American War of 1898. The nine men pictured in Figure 4 are posed in a very different way from most nineteenth-century photos, especially

Figure 3. Exodusters going West, late 1870s.

military ones, where people stand stiffly in beautifully starched and cleaned uniforms. How would you explain the choices made by this photographer? Why do you think the soldiers took up such informal, almost modern, poses?

Finally, it is always tempting to identify African American history with economic compulsion, political struggle, and racial tension, but blacks also numbered among the landless agricultural workers known as cowboys, who provided much of the romance of life in the old West. Young African Americans joined the world of rodeos, shooting, and wild horseback competitions, and they took up the often dangerous and poorly paid work of cattle herders. Figure 5 features Nat Love, the most famous black cowboy, known as Deadwood Dick for his shooting prowess.

Figure 4. Buffalo soldiers, 1880s.

Figure 5. Nat Love, 1870s.

Born a slave, he had been freed by the Union Army at the age of fifteen and remade himself out West as a popular rodeo performer. In his later years he became a Pullman porter and, like many famous cowboys, wrote an autobiography. How does this image correspond to your vision of a cowboy? Famous cowboys in the old West were known to be masters of self-promotion. In what ways does Nat Love seem to be marketing himself in this photo? Photos of Deadwood Dick were common in the nineteenth century. Why do you think that contemporary Americans might be surprised to know that there were African American cowboys?

But the Western states were not only settled by those migrating from the eastern United States and western Europe. The phrase "go West young man" conjures up images of a long, dangerous, and romantic journey across the continent or many weeks at sea from New York around the tip of South America up to San Francisco. This vision of the settlement of the West by displaced New Yorkers; African Americans escaping sharecropping; and Irish, Germans, and Norwegians escaping nineteenth-century European rural poverty misses one of the crucial foundations of the fabulous wealth that continues to draw people from across the United States and around the world to the Western states: the Pacific. Many of those nineteenth-century settlers made a relatively short boat trip up the coast from Chile, Colombia, or Mexico and many others came via well-traveled routes across the Pacific by boat from China, Japan, India, the Philippines, and Australia.

Among the many peoples who populated the West from the countries of the East, there was no group more important to the development of American life out West than the Chinese. The first of the forty-niners who discovered gold in California, tens of thousands of Chinese migrated to California in the three decades after gold was discovered. Some struck it rich prospecting for gold, others found gold, but not enough to make up the high prospecting taxes that were unfairly levied on Chinese, and many built commercial enterprises connected to the growing wealth and Pacific trade that were developing in California. The transcontinental railroad, completed in 1869, brought thousands of Chinese to the Western states to blast away mountains, build bridges, and lay track. It was dangerous, sometimes fatal, low-paid work for migrants, but it provided many opportunities that were not available in the declining agricultural regions of China.

By the 1870s there were roughly 75,000 Chinese in California, almost 10 percent of the state's population, and with the end of the gold rush and the disappearance of jobs building the railroad, the Chinese became the victims of probably the most well orchestrated anti-immigrant campaign in American history. Politicians like Denis Kearney organized anti-Chinese political parties and violent anti-Chinese riots that killed many migrants and diverted attention away from the problems of rising inequality and unemployment in the Western states. Finally, in 1882 Congress passed the Chinese Exclusion Act, which took the remarkable step of barring people of Chinese descent from entering the United States regardless of their citizenship. Figure 6 suggests some of the open hostility that had become acceptable in Western states where Chinese were typically not allowed to vote, work in dozens of occupations, or testify in court in their own defense. What do you think O'Donnell means in connecting "the bosses" and the Chinese? What do you think his slogan "The Best Coroner . . . will make the Best Mayor" says about the role of a mayor?

But not all white Americans were anti-Chinese. Figure 7, from the progressive magazine *Harper's*, suggests the degree to which many people around the

Figure 6. Anti-Chinese campaign ad, 1888.

PACIFIC CHIVALRY.
Encouragement to Chinese Immigration.

Figure 7. *Harper's* cartoon, 1869.

United States did not approve of the anti-Chinese politics and were shocked by the violence against this hard-working migrant group. What do you think is meant by the writing on the wall behind the main image? What do you think the editors of *Harper's* were trying to say by putting a caption below that reads "Encouragement to Chinese Immigration"?

The West, like all economically developing regions, needed far more labor than could be provided domestically. The exclusion of the Chinese forced employers in the West to reach out to other countries across the Pacific for migrants. Japan filled some of the gap created by Chinese exclusion, but this migration slowed because of expanding economic opportunities in Japan, which were connected to its rise as an industrial power with its own overseas empire. The Japanese who stayed in California often imported brides and started families and their own farms.

The Indian subcontinent, then a British colony, also filled some of the labor demand in the Western states. Sikhs, in particular, came in the late-nineteenth and early-twentieth centuries and were employed in agriculture and other jobs requiring heavy manual labor, as shown in Figure 8. As was the case with many of the sojourner migrant laborers in the nineteenth century, nearly all of them were male and most expected to return to their native land. However, many Sikhs stayed, built their own temples, and either imported wives from South Asia or married into the large Mexican community.

Finally, not everybody journeyed West or sailed East. The West had been populated for many thousands of years by Native Americans. The Hollywood movies that stereotyped the West may have missed what the West was really

Figure 8. Sikh workers building the railroad, 1908.

about. Nearly everywhere that settlers arrived they found ordinary Native Americans who did not easily fit with the big plans for economic development, rigid racial and ethnic categories, and romantic stereotypes, and who had only a tenuous connection to a federal government thousands of miles away in Washington.

Once the Plains Indians had been defeated in the late-nineteenth century, governments across the West were forced to confront the far more difficult task of fitting these original residents into the new society that was emerging. Though there were some small successes, for the most part federal and state government policy was both brutal and stupid in its various attempts to "civilize," "pacify," "Christianize," "Anglicize," segregate, integrate, or simply ignore this group of Americans who, by virtue of their birth into a group defined by its continuing connection to the land, typically had fewer choices than did the poorest newly arriving migrant. Figure 9 shows one example of how Native Americans were made to fit into the new West. The image depicts little girls praying at the foot of their beds at the Phoenix Indian School in Arizona in 1900. Such American Indian schools where native languages were forbidden and native culture was denigrated were common. Though they are now understood to be a form of cultural genocide, ironically these schools also had the effect of providing a common language, a shared experience, and the broad social networks that were later used to build a national Native American political movement in the twentieth century. Based on your reading of Zitkala-Ša's account of her experience (Document 7) and this photograph, what conclusions might you be able to reach about how these students' lives would change once they came to the Phoenix Indian School?

Figure 9. Indian children praying at Phoenix Indian School, 1900.

FOR CRITICAL THINKING

1. Why did people immigrate West? What factors—social, political, economic, cultural—seemed to be the most important and for which groups of immigrants?
2. What can you glean about gender roles from these images? How do you think women's experiences might have been changed by the trip West (or East, as the case may be)?
3. Compare and contrast Figures 1 and 3.
4. Do the images in this portfolio challenge traditional notions about the U.S. West in history? If so, how?

PART TWO

The Gilded Age

Industrial Growth and Crisis

Remarkable economic growth affected virtually all of America outside of the South during and after the Civil War. In 1882, when the Senate Committee on Education and Labor held hearings on the increasingly bitter conflict between labor and capital, it heard much on both the hardships and opportunities of this new economy. Brass worker Joseph T. Finnerty detailed the uncomfortable changes for industrial workers as enterprises grew, while the piano manufacturer William Steinway extolled the opportunities and higher standards of living created by vast manufactures. George Rice learned that it was not just workers who were threatened by the new economy when he was driven out of business by Standard Oil. His fight against monopolies as a plaintiff in a famous case against John D. Rockefeller would eventually spur the passage of antitrust laws.

The upward and outward expansion of cities matched the growth of industry. Both immigrants and Americans leaving farms and small towns swelled the raw, booming cities. Corrupt political organizations, usually called "machines," often managed the political needs of these new urbanites. Full-time politicians, like George Washington Plunkitt, who rewarded their constituents in return for their votes, ran these organizations. In the process, such amenities as public buildings, sewers, and water were provided but, reformers complained, often at too high a price or too low a quality.

Cities generally were violent places, but Southern cities like Memphis, Tennessee, shared with the Southern countryside a particularly horrendous form of violence: lynching, which swept through the South in the 1880s. The journalist Ida B. Wells-Barnett's account of the first lynchings in Memphis details how she became a leader in the battle against this method of terrorizing African Americans. For most of its long history, this battle was led by women who recognized that using false accusations of rape, specifically the rape of white women by black men, was a means of subjugating women as well as African Americans.

But the Gilded Age was far more than bankers and industrialists enriching themselves while African Americans and small businessmen and workers struggled to avoid being left behind. On the West Coast environmentalists like John Muir founded a new social movement that successfully protected vast sections of the American wilderness from economic development.

POINTS OF VIEW
Industrialism and Progress (1882)

8
The Decline of the Independent Craftsman
Joseph T. Finnerty

By 1860, the United States was already among the richest of nations, its prosperity based on producing food and raw materials for its own people and for consumers elsewhere in the Atlantic world. In the half century that followed, it became the world's largest industrial power. While agriculture continued to grow, vast expansion of industry gave the era its particular character. In 1859, 140,000 establishments might have been called factories, most of them tiny undertakings with one owner and four or five workers. In 1914, the United States had 268,000 factories, many of them large firms with hundreds of workers.

Americans who lived through the half century of growth did not need to see statistics to understand what had taken place. Lying over the valleys of eastern Pennsylvania and Ohio, layers of smog covered steel and glass mills. For many working people, time was marked off by the rude blast of factory whistles summoning employees to work early in the morning and signaling an end to the day. Everywhere new cities and towns sprang up to shelter people at the newly opened mines and factories.

Industrial workers experienced these changes in a poignant way. As late as 1870, few Americans worked for wages. Those who did usually labored side by side with their employers. Joseph T. Finnerty recalls here how labor and management worked closely together in the years after the Civil War. Many city artisans still worked in jobs like that of silversmith or cabinetmaker, cobblers made shoes by hand, and chandlers dipped tapers in hot wax one at a time. Individuals often took enormous pride in their work. By 1900, however, about two-thirds of the labor force consisted of wage earners

---

Testimony of Joseph T. Finnerty, *Report of the Committee of the Senate upon the Relations between Labor and Capital*, 5 vols. (Washington, DC: Government Printing Office, 1885), vol. 1, 740–46.

rather than self-employed people, and conditions between management and labor had deteriorated as firms grew larger. "The employer," one laborer observed, "has pretty much the same feeling toward the men that he has toward his machinery."

The rising number of industrial workers, increasingly frequent strikes occasioned by swings in the economy, and growing friction between labor and management became issues for national political debate. Arguments raged over whether workers were prospering or suffering in the new economy and whether their living and working conditions had deteriorated. In 1882, the U.S. Senate unanimously adopted a resolution directing its Committee on Education and Labor to conduct a broad investigation into "the relations between labor and capital, the wages and hours of labor, the condition of the laboring classes in the United States, and their relative condition and wages as compared with similar classes abroad, and to inquire into the division of labor and capital of their joint productions in the United States; also, the subject of labor strikes." In hearings held across the country the following year, the committee collected testimony from an unusually wide array of witnesses: industrialists, reformers, union leaders, workers, clergymen, and an assortment of unclassifiable crackpots. The senators on the panel were remarkable in their unfailing courtesy to witnesses, avoidance of partisan bickering, and welcoming stance to ordinary workers like Joseph T. Finnerty, giving the testimony permanent value in considering the impact of industrialism on working people.

Questions to Consider
1. To what extent should Joseph T. Finnerty's testimony be read as that of a worker and to what extent as that of a representative of the Central Labor Union of New York?
2. What, according to Finnerty, were the main changes in the life of bronze workers over the previous fifteen years?
3. What were the effects of doing bronze work on the workers? Why did they tend to drink heavily?

TESTIMONY INTRODUCED BY THE CENTRAL LABOR UNION OF NEW YORK

New York, August 28, 1883

Joseph T. Finnerty sworn and examined.

By Mr. George:

Question. Please state your age and occupation—*Answer.* I am thirty-two years old; I am a brass worker.

Q. How long have you been a brass worker?—*A.* Fourteen years.

Q. What were the wages that you received, say, fourteen years ago—I mean brass workers generally?

Decreased Wages

A. The wages paid in the trade fourteen years ago were from $18 to $21 a week.

Q. What are the wages now of the same class of workmen, with the same skill, and working the same number of hours—if they do work the same number of hours now?—*A.* From $12 to $18 a week; on an average $15 a week.

Q. Do you think $15 a week is a fair statement of the average now?—*A.* Yes, sir; it is rather above than below the average.

Division of Labor in the Trades

Q. Has there been any change in the last fourteen or fifteen years in the mode of working brass, as to the part that the brass worker performs in the business of production in that industry? If so, state what that change is?—*A.* There has been a change. Fourteen years ago the workman was supposed to finish all his own work right through, with a very small exception. To-day the trade is so broken up that it takes eight men to finish the same job.

Q. What do you call a "job"? Explain that?—*A.* Well, to make a water-cock or a chandelier, or a steam-valve, all such things as those are "jobs." The making of a water-cock is broken up now into twelve different parts.

Q. You say that fifteen years ago each man did one of these jobs complete?—*A.* Yes, sir; a man who was making a chandelier made it right through, a valve-maker made his work right through, and a cock-maker made his work right through.

Q. But now I understand you to say that in making a chandelier a man does but one-tenth of the work?—*A.* Yes; one-tenth or one-twelfth, and in making a brass cock or steam-valve he does only about one-fourth of it.

Q. How has that change been brought about?—*A.* Principally by the introduction of machinery for turning out the work faster and cheaper. A man now being employed on the machine gets no chance of learning the trade beyond the particular branch that he works at, and, being kept constantly at that one branch, he becomes very expert and turns that part of the work out quicker and cheaper than it could be done on the old plan.

Q. You say it takes twelve men now to make a brass cock; are there four different machines that are used in making a thing of that kind?—*A.* There are four different operations and machines; three lathes and a polishing machine. Fourteen years ago there was only one lathe used to do that job but now there are four besides the polishing machine.

Q. How is it in making a chandelier?—*A.* There are polishers, dippers, buffers, chasers, filers, and all of these have their own special branches and do nothing else.

Q. And each one of them, I suppose, does his part by the aid of a machine?—*A.* Yes, sir; with the exception of the dipper or bronzer, the man that gives the color. He puts it on by hand. All the others do their parts by machinery.

Q. The man's principal business, then, is to adjust the machine to the piece of brass, or the brass to the machine, and to keep it there till the work is done?—*A.* Yes, sir; but he has got to exercise a little skill, of course.

Q. Yes; of course, he must have sense enough to adjust it properly, but his principal duty is to keep the brass in the proper position with reference to the machine, and then the machine will do the work; is that correct?—*A.* That is correct as to one man, the dipper. The others have the machine running and it does the work. Formerly it was all done by hand.

Q. Then the result is that a man who works in brass now with this machinery never becomes a perfect workman—that is, he never learns to turn out a job complete? — *A.* No, sir.

Q. In other words he learns to do only one-tenth or one-fourth of a job, as the case may be. He does not learn the other parts of the trade? —*A.* No, sir; he does not.

Q. Of course, this subdivision of labor and this introduction of machinery has added very much to the production of brass work? —*A.* Yes, sir.

Production Increased—Quality Deteriorated

Q. Explain to the committee, in your own way, the difference in amount between the production of one man, say fifteen years ago, and what one man can now produce with the aid of machinery? Or, take a group of men, four, or five, or six, and explain to us how much value each man can impart to this work by the aid of machinery? — *A.* I think the best way I can explain that to the committee is to take some one article for an illustration? I will take a chandelier for instance. Fourteen years ago a man working one week at $21 a week would finish a chandelier and it could be sold for $300. Today, with all the machinery and all the branches of the business combined, eight or ten men can turn out thirty-six chandeliers, which can be sold at $150 apiece; making in the neighborhood of $4,000, for the week's work of the eight men.

Q. You say that formerly one man in a week would make a chandelier worth about $300? —*A.* Yes.

Q. And that now eight men working the one week and using machinery can make thirty-six chandeliers worth each $150? —*A.* Well, worth from $100 to $150.

Q. Would $125 be the average selling price of those chandeliers? — *A.* Yes, sir.

Q. So that one man fifteen years ago produced in a week a manufactured article worth $300? —*A.* Yes, sir.

Q. And now eight men working the same time produce articles worth about $4,350, which makes an average of about $540 for each man's work. Is that about correct? —*A.* Well, say $450. The other figure might be a little too high. I want to keep right down to the bottom facts.

Q. What was the value of the raw material put into a chandelier fifteen years ago? —*A.* The chandelier that was made fourteen or fifteen years ago was all solid bronze work—genuine work. The chandeliers that are made to-day are nothing but a mere hollow shell. There is considerable less bronze used in all bronze work now than there was fourteen years ago. Things were made solid and reliable at that time and intended to last, but now it is not so. . . .

The Social Condition of the Men Getting Worse

Q. Tell us now, if you can, about the social condition of the bronze workers as compared with their condition fourteen or fifteen years ago, and whether it has grown better or worse. —*A.* Well, I remember that fourteen years ago the workmen and the foremen and the boss were all as one family; it was just as easy and as free to speak to the boss as any one else, but now the boss is superior, and the men all go to the superintendent or to the foreman; but we would not think of looking the foreman in the face now any more than we would the boss.

Q. Is that so when you are off duty as well as when you are on?—A. Off duty as well as on duty, we would not dream of speaking to him on the street, unless he was a personal acquaintance or some old reliable hand in the shop that might have grown up there. The average hand growing up in the shop now would not think of speaking to the boss, would not presume to recognize him, nor the boss would not recognize him either.

Q. By the "boss" I suppose you mean the owner of the factory?— A. Yes, sir.

Q. You have told us that the wages have been reduced. How is it as to the style of living of the workmen now compared with how they lived fourteen or fifteen years ago?—A. That appears to be about the same as far as house rent is concerned. There was a reduction of house rents some years ago, but they have reached up again.

Q. Are other things about equal?—A. About equal.

Q. Let me see if I understand you fully. You get less wages than you did fifteen years ago?—A. Yes.

Q. Now, do you mean to say that the wages which you receive at present will buy as much of the comforts of life as the wages which you received then would?—A. By no means. I say that the rents are the same as they were fourteen years ago, but the man who had apartments of four or five rooms at that time is confining himself to perhaps three rooms now.

Q. How are the social surroundings of the workingmen now, as to the character of the neighborhoods in which they live; for I have noticed that there are some very fine neighborhoods in this city and some others that are very poor.— A. The bronze workers as a rule live in tenement houses. They are surrounded by the poorest class, the cheapest class; the cheapest element of the laboring people, and they are no better than anybody else.

Q. Was that so fifteen years ago, or is there a difference since that time?— A. It was different then. A mechanic was considered somebody, and he felt that he was somebody; he was a skilled mechanic, and he was considered above the poor laborer on the street.

Q. How is it as to the neighborhoods where they live and the character of their dwellings at present as compared with fifteen years ago; are they better or worse than they were then?—A. If there is any change, it is for the worse; the tendency is to get worse.

Q. Are you a married man?—A. Yes.

Q. How long have you been married?—A. Six years.

Q. State now what opportunities you have of supporting your family comfortably and giving your children such social privileges and enjoyments as are necessary for their comfort and happiness.—A. I have not any other facilities beyond the average workingmen's opportunity to train up their children; that is, to send them to the public schools. We cannot go any further than that on our wages.

Q. Is that about the average condition of the bronze workers in this city? — *A.* The average is a little worse than my case; the average of the brass workers could not live as well as I do, because their average wages is only $15 a week, while my wages is $20 a week.

Impossibility of Saving from Present Wages

Q. Do the bronze workers who are married men lay up anything, as a general rule? — *A.* No, sir; they do not. If they happen to be able to make both ends meet at the end of the year they are doing wonders. Of course in every class of people there may be one or two in a hundred that would get rich, no matter what wages they received, but the bronze worker generally saves no money, and if he can keep his family in food and clothes and pay his rent he feels that he is doing wonders.

Q. Before the introduction of this machinery, by which the man has been reduced to being one-tenth or one-fourth of a complete tradesman, how much capital did it take to become a brass worker on one's own account?

Increased Difficulty of Starting in Business

A. At that time a man that had $300 or $400 could start a brass shop himself and make a living out of it, but to-day no man who understands the condition of the trade would start with less than $5,000. He would need that much to supply machinery and start his shop, and then he would have a hard road to travel.

Q. At that time, if a man had a room large enough to work in, and had his tools and a little money to buy the raw material, he could become an independent workman, you say, making his brass work himself and selling it to the public? — *A.* Yes, sir.

Q. But now the conditions have changed so much that it would take $5,000 even to start a shop and fit it up with the necessary machinery? — *A.* Yes, sir. There is one thing about brass shops that you had better understand, and that is that almost every brass shop has special patents and its own special line of business, and one does not compete with the others in their lines. In chandeliers, for instance, some make high-priced chandeliers, while others make a specialty of the cheap chandelier, and the regular brass shops each make a specialty of one department. John Mathews, for example, makes soda-water fountains; another shop makes a specialty of injectors, and another of pumps. So that, to a certain extent, each of these shops has got a monopoly of its own line of business. At the same time they may have the facilities for making anything that comes in their line, but their prices are so high for anything outside of their regular work, their specialty, that a man who wants any article will go to some shop that make a specialty of the kind of work he wants; a man who wants a pump will go to a pump factory, or a man who wants a soda-water fountain will go to a soda-fountain factory.

Q. Fourteen years ago, as I understand you, a brass worker might hope, by prudence and economy, to become an independent worker for himself? — *A.* Yes, sir; but now the trade is controlled by the larger companies. They have their drummers or agents in different parts of the country, and it takes capital to carry on the business in that way; and in order to establish an independent brass shop you have to have your connections made all through the country, something which a poor man cannot do.

Q. So you consider that it is about hopeless for a brass worker now to aspire to the condition of brass manufacturer? —*A.* Yes, sir; it is hopeless, and I think they will not try it any more.

Q. Has that change any effect on the habits of saving of the working men? —*A.* No, sir; I cannot say that it has any effect. They are living up to the way they are accustomed to live, and the minute you undertake to drive them down any lower than that there is a row.

Q. What I mean is this: Has the stimulus, the inducement to save by close living, and all that sort of thing been lessened in any degree by the fact that there is now no hope of a workman ever becoming a boss or having an independent establishment of his own? —*A.* All the brass worker cares about now is to hold his job, and he will put up with any kind of abuse as long as he is not discharged.

Q. But fourteen years ago you say it was different. —*A.* Yes, sir. He would not stand any abuse at all then, and no abuse would be offered to him then; he was treated as a skilled workman.

Q. Did many of the workers in brass fourteen years ago actually get into the position of independent brass manufacturers? —*A.* Oh, yes, sir. There are some of our leading firms to-day that started under the different condition that existed fourteen or fifteen years ago.

Q. Were these men more provident or economical or stingy at that time, as a rule, than the workmen are now, when they have no hope of becoming independent workers? —*A.* The men who are bosses now, and who were workmen at that time, were not saving or stingy, and while they were merely getting journeymen's wages they did not save anything; but when they got to be foremen, then they commenced to save, and when they became superintendents they made enough money to start for themselves.

The Brass Workers' Organization

Q. Is there a labor organization of the brass workers? —*A.* There is.

Q. Do you belong to it? —*A.* I do.

Q. Have they ever made a strike? —*A.* Only once—for eight hours—and they failed to get it. They have never struck for higher wages.

Q. Have you any rule in your organization limiting the number of apprentices that shall be taken into the shops? —*A.* No, sir. The organization does not attempt at all to interfere with the rights of the shop; we could not do it. In the first place the boss has entire power to hire whoever he pleases—boys or men; he can put in forty or fifty boys, and there is nobody going to object.

Brass Working Unhealthy

There is one thing that I want to say a word about, and that is the health of the men in the trade. Brass working is very injurious to the health. The polishers and the molders are all the time breathing the vapors or the particles that are floating around in the air, and the average life is only about thirty-five years among the molders, and out of every forty molders thirty are compelled to drink strong drink to drown this breathing of the vapors.

By the Chairman:

Q. Do you mean that they have to take it medicinally?—*A.* Yes, sir; either beer or whisky; in order to cure the effects of the fumes. Before they pour the metal they go out and take a drink; the fumes flow up and around slowly, and the men have to keep in the fumes until they have all their metals poured. Then they are perspiring, and they go out and have another drink; so that they are generally hard drinkers, and the trade makes them so.

Q. Your idea is that the alcohol in the drinks operates as a medicine to counteract the poisonous effects of the fumes that you speak of?—*A.* Yes, sir; they take it to drown the effects of the fumes. Polishers are always breathing the particles that float in the atmosphere. Polishing and molding are two branches of the trade that are very hard and laborious.

Q. How long have you worked at the business?—*A.* Fourteen years.

Q. What is your age?—*A.* Thirty-two years.

Q. How old is the oldest man in your employment that you are acquainted with who has pursued the business continually?—*A.* The oldest man I know is sixty years of age. There are only very few old men in the trade, which numbers about 4,000 men. I do not suppose you could raise a dozen old men in the trade. As soon as they get up to be a certain age they drop the trade or there is fault found with their work.

Q. Do you expect to follow the business for the remainder of your life?—*A.* No, sir; I expect to get out of it as soon as I can.

Q. Do you think you would live to be forty-five years old if you continued at your business?—*A.* I might.

Q. You are a pretty strong, healthy man naturally?—*A.* Yes, sir. . . .

9

Workers Prosper as Industry Grows

William Steinway

The national wealth of the United States increased in the last half of the nineteenth century from about $4.5 billion to nearly $64 billion. This enormous growth materially benefited most of the American people, including wage workers, whose real wages rose substantially. Nonetheless, workers gave much evidence of what one official described as

Testimony of William Steinway, *Report of the Committee of the Senate upon the Relations between Labor and Capital*, 5 vols. (Washington, DC: Government Printing Office, 1885), vol. 2, 1085–95.

"the feeling of bitterness which so frequently manifests itself in their utterances." And workers showed their discontent not only in utterances: labor disturbances formed a regular part of the landscape of the Gilded Age. Some—like the great railroad strike of 1877, the Homestead walkout of 1892, and the Pullman strike of 1894—made dramatic national headlines. Less remembered are the smaller strikes occurring each year by the hundreds and then thousands in the last quarter of the nineteenth century.

Those who were socially conscious worried especially about the many working people in the great cities who lived in flimsy overcrowded housing with inadequate sanitation that quickly degenerated into disease-ridden slums. In these substandard environments, crime and immorality flourished. People in such circumstances had no protection against dips in the economy, nor could they afford to educate their children, whose labor was too soon needed for family survival. "If a man has not got a boy to act as 'back boy' [earning wages]," a Massachusetts textile worker asserted, "it is very hard for him to get along."

Contemporaries struggled to explain—or explain away—such problems. The Senate Committee on the Relations between Labor and Capital of 1883 (see Selection 8) heard many theories about the sources of labor discontent. The explanations offered by the piano manufacturer William Steinway, excerpted here, were characteristic of the beliefs of successful businessmen. Social mobility, he argued, was not only still possible but was increasingly available with industrial growth; Steinway pointed to his own experience of rising from apprentice to industrialist as proof. Educational improvements and other practical reforms would render workers prosperous and content within the current economic system. He especially urged apprenticeships and industrial schooling as well as the dispersal of industry from downtown locations into suburbs where workers could secure good housing at reasonable prices.

Yet much of Steinway's experience was atypical of American industrial development. The Steinway piano was an exotic bloom in nineteenth-century America. The nation had risen to industrial preeminence by supplying materials like steel and oil for industry and by creating inexpensive goods like Kodak cameras or cheap brass chandeliers for mass markets. It is hard to think of another nineteenth-century American product like the Steinway, a luxury good that competed against the finest European products. In fact, it can be argued that the Steinway was a German product made in the United States. The Steinway family had learned to manufacture great pianos in Germany, almost all Steinway's skilled employees in America had learned their trade in Germany, and Steinway paid for German instruction in the public schools his workers attended in Queens. Nonetheless, nothing could have been more American than his testimony to the senators about his unaided rise to the apex of piano manufacturing, his faith in education, or his optimism that all social conflict could be resolved and that every worthy citizen could prosper.

QUESTIONS TO CONSIDER

1. What is William Steinway's view of labor unions?
2. What is Steinway's view of the condition of labor in the United States?

3. How does Steinway think the conditions of workers in the United States compare with conditions in Europe? In what areas is the United States ahead? In what areas is Europe ahead?
4. What does he think is needed to improve the conditions of workers in the United States?

New York, September 27, 1883

William Steinway examined.

By Mr. Call:

Question. Have you seen the resolution under which the committee is conducting this examination? —*Answer.* Yes, sir.

Mr. Call. The committee will be glad to hear from you any facts or opinions you may have to present on the several subjects mentioned in the resolution, first stating your residence and occupation and your connection with labor in this country and abroad.

The Witness. I was born in Brunswick, Germany, in 1836, and came to the city of New York in the spring of 1850, when fourteen years of age, with my father, mother, and the rest of our family. We worked for three years in the factories here, learning the language and the customs of the people, and in March, 1853, started the business of Steinway & Sons—my father, my two brothers, and myself—which has now become the most extensive establishment of its kind in existence. We have three distinct establishments, manufactories rather, our New York factory, at Fourth avenue and Fifty-second and Fifty-third streets; a large establishment at Astoria, N.Y., opposite One hundred and twentieth street, where we employ over 400 men, and where we have carried out our ideas of improving the condition of the workingmen by giving them light and air and good houses to live in, building them public baths, and laying out a public park, keeping up at our own expense in the public school a teacher who teaches German and music free of charge, and various other advantages. We employ about 1,000 workmen, a great majority of whom are skilled workmen. I will remark that in the first three years when I worked as an apprentice and journeyman, and in the first few years when our business was small, I had ample opportunities of studying the lot of the workingman by actual experience, also the way that workingmen worked, and I can say that skilled artisans to-day are far better off than they were a third of a century ago. At that time but very few people, even skilled laborers, were able to save money and put it in bank. To-day the skilled laborers, more especially in the piano-forte trade, and the wood-working establishments, have wages double what they were in those times; and from my experience also as director in savings banks, &c., I find that a great many skilled artisans, those blessed with health, have constituted a great portion of the depositors in banks. The wages in the piano-forte trade, that is to say, the skilled laborers, have averaged $20 per week (ranging from $15 to $30).

We ourselves have a branch establishment in Hamburg, and from my travels in Europe and my study of the condition of the workingmen in both hemispheres, especially in the piano-forte trade, I will say here that of my own personal knowledge the wages of skilled artisans in the piano-forte trade in the cities of New York, Boston, Baltimore, and Philadelphia, where they are most densely congregated, average precisely three times the amount that the skilled artisans of Europe do in the same trade.

The introduction of machinery in our business, and in the wood-working establishments, has been of great benefit by doing the hard work which formerly imperiled the health and lives of the skilled artisans. I will further state that of the about one hundred piano-forte manufacturers of the United States, which are chiefly concentrated in the four cities I have named, nearly all have been workingmen themselves.

Labor Ought to Organize

The relations between ourselves and our men have always been very good until lately disturbed by the entrance of the socialistic and the communistic element in the labor unions. I myself think that labor ought to organize, as it has organized. I am not opposed to labor unions, and any labor union that is carried on in a sensible way can do a great deal, not only toward bettering their own condition in the way of wages, but also in equalizing wages in the various cities, and in resisting in times of depression the great deterioration and fall of wages. We have gone through very hard strikes. We have been singled out. Our house being the strongest and largest, has been made the target of strikes. It is just about a year ago now that one of the most senseless strikes was inaugurated during my absence in Europe by the socialistic and communistic element inducing our men to strike against an honest, faithful bookkeeper, against whom they were unable to allege the slightest grievance, except that they did not want him, and that their union had so ordered. They were unsuccessful, however. . . . [B]ut, as I said . . . I am not opposed to labor unions; but on the contrary will here give it as my opinion that strikes are a necessity and should not be legislated against, and cannot be legislated against. . . .

Manufacturers Miscalled Capitalists

A great mistake is also made by the workingmen and the professional agitators, who foment strikes, by calling manufacturers capitalists.

Of about 100 piano-forte manufacturers in the United States known throughout the world to make the best pianos in existence, and conceded so by musical talent and authority in Europe, there are but four wealthy houses— about 20 to 25 people of moderate means—and the rest, that is, 60 or 70 manufacturers in the piano-forte trade, just manage to eke out a hand-to-mouth existence. These are hard words, but they are literally true.

The Horrors of the Tenement House System

. . . I consider one of the greatest evils under which workingmen live, especially in the city of New York, is the horrors of the tenement houses—the terrible rents that they have to pay. The average workingman's family has one room in which they cook, wash, iron, and live, and one or two, or possibly three, bed rooms, of which generally one or two are dark rooms, without any windows, or without admitting God's pure air. This is a terrible evil, which is, however, chiefly caused by the insular position of the city of New York, where, in winter, in times of ice and fog, it is impossible that workingmen should come long distances and be in time for their work.

The horrors of the tenement houses are having a very baneful effect upon the morals and character of the coming generation; in fact, I may say a terrible effect. But I do not see what legislation can do. Capitalists consider tenement houses a poor investment, paying poor returns. The only thing that I can imagine is to do as *we* have done, remove the very large factories requiring much room and many men from out of the city of New York into the suburbs.

Want of an Apprentice Law

A second great evil under which we are suffering, and it seems to me it is an evil that has been increasing from year to year, is, that in no country of the wide world, as I have found during my experience and my extensive travels, are there so many young men growing up without learning a trade or any particular calling, as in the United States. We have no apprentice law. In our own business, as well as the wood-working business, everybody is unwilling to take an apprentice, for the simple reason that it is a well known fact that the first year or two when a boy is learning a trade he will produce nothing, and will spoil a great deal, and will take up the time of a skilled man to teach him, and yet the moment he has learned one little branch of the trade he leaves, shifts for himself. He has not learned the business properly, and the consequence is that he is dependent, and, in times of great depression, cannot find employment. Hence we have no supply of skilled artisans growing up, and have to draw for our extra skilled labor on Europe. When I came to this country, in 1850, the majority, indeed I might say seven-eighths, of the journeyman piano makers were Americans, skilled workmen. Through our apprentice law, or rather through the total want of one, the entire native element has been thrown out of the piano business, and to-day seven-eighths of the workingmen in the piano shops, and over one-half in the New England States, are Germans.

By the Chairman:

Q. Is that for lack of an apprentice law as much as it is from the fact that skilled labor already trained has found its way here from abroad and has entered into competition, and made the employment of apprentices by employers a thing undesirable on their part? —*A.* No, sir; I attribute it entirely, or chiefly, to the lack of a proper apprentice law.

Industrial Schools

The total want of industrial schools in this city is a very great evil. There ought to be industrial schools all over each city where boys can go and find for what business they have aptitude and talent. Then, under regular apprentice laws, under which a boy could be bound for, say, five years at rising wages, commencing at $3 a week for the first year, getting $3.50 the second year, $4 a week the third year, and so on, they would learn a trade well. During the last two or three years the employer could have the advantage, since during the first one or two years he lost. . . .

Compulsory Education

I would also advocate a law compelling every child between the ages of six and fourteen to go to school. I have found in my experience as an employer and executor, and as worker in benevolent enterprises in which I have been engaged, that there is a great deal more ignorance in reading and writing among young men and women growing up in this city—mostly children of foreigners—than anybody has any idea of. During the war we raised a fund to assist the wives of men that went to the war, and I found that one-half of those who had grown up in this country, or had come here when they were little children, were unable to sign their names. I never would have believed it possible if I had not myself experienced it. Hence I think that a compulsory law compelling every child between the ages of six and fourteen years to be sent to school should be enacted, and that parents should be punished if they did not enforce it. . . .

Independence of Skilled Artisans

Having gone through the panics of 1861, 1867, and 1873, I know that skilled artisans are absolutely independent of bad times, for a skilled workman will always find employment. It is so in the piano-forte trade and in the kindred trade in wood. . . . I found that all the skilled piano-forte manufacturers and those in the wood-working trades readily retained and found employment at remunerative wages; whereas the half skilled men who knew only one little branch of a trade were thrown out of employment. Hence the necessity of educating our young men who wish to learn trades to make them thorough skilled workingmen. In other words, do away with the curse of the American mechanics—young men learning only one portion of a skilled trade, and being then absolutely dependent upon that because they do not know anything else. . . .

Relative Condition of Workingmen in Europe and America

The Chairman. The resolution calls attention to the relative conditions of all working people abroad, and working people in America, specific and general classes. What is your observation in that respect?

A. I have paid a great deal of attention to the condition of the workingmen, and, as I before stated, in our own business and kindred trades I find that first-class skilled artisans in this country earn from double to three times as much as skilled artisans of the same rank do in Europe. In unskilled labor I find the proportion is not so favorable to the American laborer. It is true that they earn more money here, but the cost of living, especially rents, is so much enhanced that they are not much better off in a pecuniary way than the workingman in Europe. But their social position here is much higher than that in Europe, and they have a much better chance here to get along than they have in Europe where every thing is more limited. But the skilled artisans are far better off in this country; they wear better clothing, have better food, and have a chance to live better, move in better society, and in fact their condition is in every way far superior. Still there remains a great deal to be done, and a great deal could be done to improve their condition in this country in the way I have indicated. . . .

Merchants, Manufacturers, etc. — Their Relative Conditions in Europe and America

Q. How in regard to the relative condition of merchants, of manufacturers, of the ordinary class of business men on this side of the ocean and the corresponding class on the other side of the ocean—those who manage the business affairs of communities?—*A.* The manufacturers of Europe do not work nearly as hard as our Americans do, who are on their feet from morning to night, and on whom the rack and tear of business wears very fast. The manufacturers in Europe have this advantage: they have much cheaper money than manufacturers in America, who have to depend upon outside help, and who have to borrow money for that purpose. And I think that, as a general thing, the European manufacturers are just as well off as our own. . . .

I found that in Europe there are a great many more manufacturing establishments where the business has been handed down from father to son—they are long established trades—whereas, in this country, manufacturers have generally worked their own way up from nothing, through their own energy, and have, after awhile, accumulated a competence. . . .

Operative Classes— Their Wages and Conditions in Europe and America Contrasted

Q. Have you any general information as to the condition of the laboring classes employed in manufacturing—as to their food, and their dwelling places, as compared with the same classes in this country?—*A.* I made a special study of that. At Mulhausen, in Alsace, in the city of Crefeld, in Rhenish Prussia, a great silk center, and several other places, I found that they have wretched habitations, and are very poorly clad and ill-fed, not nearly so well as the operatives in this country.

Q. How is it as to the wages that those classes receive there and here?— *A.* From what I observed I found that the wages are considerably less in Europe than those paid here, even setting aside our own business.

Q. The skilled laborers are paid less there—how about the labor that is not so much skilled?—*A.* Unskilled labor is also paid less. In other words, it is very rare to see a workingman in Europe whose family can lay by anything, whereas here thrifty, skilled mechanics, blessed with health, and not meeting with sickness or other misfortune, have a chance to save money and do save money.

Q. Then you say that in this country the laborer is much better off in his social and pecuniary conditions, and in the means of enjoying the comforts of life?—*A.* Undoubtedly. . . .

Education of the Working Classes
in Europe and America

By the Chairman:

Q. How do they compare with our own working people in the matter of education? —*A.* In Germany, where, since 1818, school attendance has been compulsory, there is hardly a person to be found who cannot read and write. Every child between the age of five and fourteen must attend school, and if not attending school the parents would be punished. The result is, that a person unable to read and write, unless they are very old people, is unknown.

By Mr. Call:

Q. That is true throughout Germany generally, is it? —*A.* Yes. In France and England it is not so favorable, nor in Belgium, because up to a few years ago there was no law compelling children to go to school.

By the Chairman:

Q. Do you think that education is improving the condition of the laboring people in those countries? —*A.* It undoubtedly has done so. It has given them greater intelligence and better knowledge of their trades.

Industrial Schools in Germany

By Mr. Call:

Q. How about industrial schools there? —Are they extensive? —*A.* Yes; they are. I have seen several myself.

Q. People are taught their trades in the public schools, are they? —*A.* Yes; boys of fourteen to fifteen years of age are taken, and it is ascertained what trades they have aptitudes for, thus preparing them for learning their trades. One of the greatest boons that education could bestow upon boys here would be to give them a similar opportunity.

Q. For that reason you find skilled labor far more abundant there than here? —*A.* Yes. Here, in good times, there is a great want of skilled labor, and there there is always a greater supply than demand. Hence the great immigration of skilled artisans to this country. . . .

Q. I understood you to say that you worked as a journeyman yourself in this country? —*A.* Yes.

Q. Had you greater opportunities outside your own knowledge and capacity for building up the vast business that you have built up — greater opportunities than many others who were your contemporaries? —*A.* To be just, I think that, being father and sons, we were possessed of some greater advantages when we came here — we had great advantages over one single individual. I am modest enough to say that I personally could not have done so but for the harmony and good management that prevailed in our firm by reason of our relationship.

Q. Any other family with the same advantages would have had the same results? —*A.* Yes.

Q. The point I wanted to get at was that it was not due to any adventitious aid of capital, but to yourselves as workingmen and economists? —*A.* Yes.

Q. You do not consider that you owe this success to anything outside of yourselves, do you?—*A.* No; I think not. But it was simply because we were all skilled artisans and had learned the trade thoroughly, and had special talents. We had no outside help at all. We worked our way up, and I know dozens of others who have done the same thing.

Q. Do you know anything in the relations of capital, as it is called (as a general name for an economical cause), anything in the relations of capital and labor unfriendly to the success of the workingman in becoming a director of labor, and of a great combination of labor in this country?—*A.* Not at all. I think, under the institutions of our country, if an individual has the talent, the energy, and the industry he has as good a chance to-day as ever to work himself up.

Legislative Measures; Child Labor; Industrial Schools, etc.

Q. Is there anything in the shape of public legislation or voluntary action that you would suggest that will improve that opportunity?—*A.* I think that is one of the greatest problems, and I do not see that legislation can do much more than it has done now, with the exception of what I have indicated. There should be an apprentice law and a stringent law against child-labor, so as to give the children of the poor people a chance to perfect their education, and the industrial schools could be established and every effort made toward giving artisans and laboring people healthy, happy homes.

Q. With those things supplied, either by public law or voluntary action, would you consider the relations now existing under our institutions as favorable as they could be made?—*A.* As favorable as it is possible to make them, in my opinion. Anything further would simply help one class in opposition to another. In this country it must be left to individual talent and industry. I think in this country a young man has a better chance to work up in the world than anywhere else that I have seen. . . .

Removal of City Factories

By Mr. Pugh:

Q. I understood you to condemn the presence of those large manufacturing establishments in our cities, and to charge the discomfort of the operatives in them to the fact largely of the presence of such establishments in cities?—*A.* Yes; I think every effort ought to be directed to having the large establishments go out to the suburbs of the city, in order to give the workingmen a chance to live as human beings ought to live. . . .

Q. Your factory, I understand you to say, is removed from New York?—*A.* We still have a large factory, which we call our "finishing" factory, in New York. It is the case-making factory. The iron and steel works for making the hardware, &c., has been removed over to Astoria, and one department after another has been added thereto, and within a few years the entire establishment will be removed from New York to Astoria.

Q. Do your artisans there live in rented houses?—*A.* Some of our artisans have already acquired homes of their own, but others of them live in rented houses, and not more than two families in one house, where they have gas, water, free baths, free schools, and every advantage. We have upwards of four hundred men there.

Q. At Astoria? —A. At Astoria.

Q. And you have found them able to improve their condition there? —A. Oh, yes; very much so. There is no sickness or anything of that kind there, and they are all feeling comfortable and happy, and I think the large wealthy manufacturers should also remove their factories from the cities and establish them somewhere in the suburbs, and do something for their workingmen in that way.

Q. You think that that would be a solution of a great part of the trouble arising between labor and capital? —A. Certainly a solution of the tenement-house trouble.

Q. And that, you think, is a large part of the cause of distress and dissatisfaction among the people? —A. Yes; I think it is a great cause of dissatisfaction among the workingmen—the bad places that they have to live in, and the high rents they have to pay. Yet tenement houses are considered a very poor investment by capitalists.

FOR CRITICAL THINKING

1. How is it possible for Joseph T. Finnerty to see a decline in the situation of working people at the same time that William Steinway sees their lot as improving? Is one person right and the other wrong, or are they talking about different things?
2. How would Finnerty respond to the proposals for improvement put forward by William Steinway? Are Steinway's suggestions responsive to the problems in bronze workers' lives that Finnerty outlines?
3. If you were one of the senators on the Committee on the Relations between Labor and Capital, what, if any, legislation would you suggest to improve the situation of workers based on the testimonies of Finnerty and Steinway?
4. Do Finnerty and Steinway agree on anything? If so, what?

10

Losing Out to Standard Oil
George Rice

Even the optimistic Andrew Carnegie noted in his lecture to young men that "as business gravitates more and more to immense concerns," opportunity might be threatened. George Rice (1835–1905) did all that Carnegie would have suggested. Entering the oil business early, he kept, as Carnegie advised, all his eggs in one basket and watched the basket closely. What he saw was the Standard Oil Company under John D. Rockefeller undercut his operation and eventually drive him out of business.

Rice's legal and intellectual counterattack on Standard Oil led the charge against "the trusts." He supplied information to two of the major reporters on that corporation, Henry Demerest Lloyd and Ida Tarbell, whose books and articles encouraged antitrust legislation. And he spent considerable time in legal pursuit of Standard Oil, a quest that never met with success during his lifetime but that eventually inspired efforts that led to the breakup of the giant corporation in 1911.

After a dramatic personal encounter in 1898 with John D. Rockefeller during depositions for one of Rice's many suits against Standard Oil, Rice was interviewed by a reporter for the New York World. *Here is his explanation of how Standard Oil operated.*

QUESTIONS TO CONSIDER
1. How, according to George Rice, did Standard Oil undercut its competitors?
2. Do you agree with Rice that this constituted unfair competition?
3. What was Rice's attitude toward large corporations, and how did it reflect popular feelings?

"I have been twenty years fighting John D. Rockefeller and the Standard Oil Trust, and I am not through yet."

The man who said this was George Rice, of Marietta, O. He is the man who told John D. Rockefeller to his face last Wednesday in the New Netherland Hotel, where Mr. Rockefeller had been testifying before the State Commission sent from Ohio to get evidence in proceedings intended to prove him guilty of contempt of the Ohio Supreme Court, that his great wealth was built on wrecks of other men's business.

New York World, October 16, 1898, 25.

It was a dramatic scene. Mr. Rockefeller and Mr. Rice have known each other well for a generation. In a twenty-year fight men are apt to get well acquainted.

But when the great multi-millionaire walked across the parlor, and, extending his hand—which was not taken—said to George Rice in a suave tenor voice:

"HOW ARE YOU, GEORGE! WE ARE GETTING TO BE GRAY-HAIRED MEN NOW, AIN'T WE? DON'T YOU WISH YOU HAD TAKEN MY ADVICE YEARS AGO?" the group of onlookers were not prepared for what followed.

George Rice drew himself up to his full height, which is about 6 feet 2 inches, his bright gray eyes flashed fire, and his massive frame visibly vibrated with suppressed anger, as he looked the great oil magnate straight in the face and said: "Perhaps it would have been better for me if I had. YOU HAVE CERTAINLY RUINED MY BUSINESS, AS YOU SAID YOU WOULD."

Mr. Rockefeller recoiled and his face showed a shade of pallor. The words of Rice had evidently stung him. Quickly recovering himself he turned from his accuser, saying, "Oh, pshaw, that isn't so, George!"

"But I say it is so," was the instant rejoinder of George Rice, and, raising his voice so that everybody in the room could hear him, he pointed his index finger at the Oil King, and added: "You know well that by the power of your great wealth you have ruined my business, and you cannot deny it."

MR. RICE TELLS HIS EXPERIENCE TO THE WORLD

This ended the episode in the hotel parlor. A few hours later, sitting in his private room, Mr. Rice gave to a *World* representative the full story of how he was ruined as an oil refiner by the machinations of the great Standard Oil Laocoon[1] in whose coils an uncounted multitude of competitors have been crushed to death.

"I am but one of many victims of Rockefeller's colossal combination," said Mr. Rice, "and my story is not essentially different from the rest. You ask me to tell you what I meant by telling Mr. Rockefeller, as I did publicly to-day, that he had ruined my business. The whole story, with all its inside details of intrigue and conspiracy, would require a volume to tell. I will tell you as much of it as you choose to ask me for. What particular phase of my experience do you care to have me relate?"

"Give me your personal story, Mr. Rice—just what happened to you in your own business."

"Well, I went into the oil-producing business in West Virginia in 1872, and in 1876 I went into the oil-refining business. Immediately I did that my fight with the Standard Oil people began. I established what was known as the

1. **Laocoon:** Refers to the El Greco painting of the ancient Trojan priest Laocoon and his sons being crushed to death by serpents sent by the gods.

Ohio Oil Works, which had a capacity of about 100,000 barrels of crude oil per annum. I found to my surprise at first, though I afterward understood it perfectly, that the Standard Oil Company was offering the same quality of oil at much lower prices than I could do—from one to three cents a gallon less than I could possibly sell it for.

"I sought for the reason and found that the railroads were in league with the Standard Oil concern at every point, giving it discriminating rates and privileges of all kinds as against myself and all outside competitors.

"For instance, I found that the railroads would not furnish tank-cars to any competitors, while the Standard combination was able by its immense wealth to buy its own cars. It owns from 8,000 to 10,000 tank-cars, and the railroads pay them sufficient mileage on the use of those Standard Oil cars to pay for the first cost of the cars inside of three years. A tank-car, when it comes back empty, cannot bring any goods. The transcontinental lines charge $105 to return an empty cylinder tank-car from the Pacific coast to the Missouri River, while they charge the trust nothing at all for the return of their own exclusive box tank-cars. This gives the trust an advantage of over $100 a car.

"Again, the independent competitor, like myself, was obliged to ship his oil in box-cars and pay 25 per cent more freight on the weight of the wooden barrels, while no charge at all was made to the Standard Oil Trust on the weight of the iron cylinders.

"Again, the railroads deduct 63 gallons (or over 400 pounds) from the filled capacity of each Standard Oil tank-car, which is the same as carrying 1 1/4 per cent of their rail products entirely free of cost. This went on up to March 15, 1890, and was one of the things that helped to wreck my business. Yet another thing helped to ruin me. The railroads allowed the trust to deliver its oils in less than carload quantities at the same rates as for full carloads. They allowed the trust to stop its cars, whether carrying oil in bulk or barrels, at different stations and take it off in small quantities without paying the higher rates which independent competitors were always charged for small quantities thus delivered. Of course, against such discriminations as these the independent competitor of moderate capital could not contend. He was driven to the wall every time, as I was."

MIGHT HAVE BEEN WORTH A MILLION

"My refinery," continued Mr. Rice, "has been shut down for two years. If I had had a fair and equal show with the railroads my refinery plant to-day would have been easily worth a million dollars and would have been growing all the time. As it is, I am out of the business, my plant is worthless and the men whom it would have employed are either idle or finding other work. These discriminations of which I have spoken are as bad to-day as they have ever been. The public needs to understand that the railroads and Standard Oil monopoly are really one and the same thing. The officers and directors of the Oil Trust are also the presidents and directors of one-fifth of the total railroad mileage of the United States. This is no mere statement of mine. It is proved by *Poor's Manual*.

"The trust was formed in January, 1882, and from that time the lines were drawn tighter and tighter to oppress and strangle every competitor. It was the highwayman's policy of 'stand and deliver.' I had my choice offered me to either give up my business at a price far less than I knew it to be worth, or to be robbed of it under forms of law. I chose not to accept the price and my business was destroyed. The threat of the trust was made good, and I suppose that is what John D. Rockefeller must have meant when he asked me if I didn't wish I had been wiser and listened to him years ago."

"Well, do you now wish, Mr. Rice, that you had knuckled to the trust and saved your money?"

"Not a bit of it," replied the "ruined" but plucky oil refiner of Marietta. "I have made a fight for principle, and I am neither sorry for it nor ashamed of it. I have been before the courts many times; I have been before Congressional committees; and I have appeared time and time again before the Interstate Commerce Commission, all the time trying to get relief from these gross discriminations. I confess I have made very little headway as yet. I shall go on with the fight as long as I live, and it may be that I shall never win. But, sooner or later, in my lifetime or afterward, the people of this country will surely take up this fight as their own and settle the question of whether they will rule the railroads and the trusts or be ruled by them."

LAWS NOT ENFORCED

"I have made a mistake, apparently, in supposing that the laws of our country could and would be enforced. I supposed the courts and the other authorities of the land would support me in my right to a free and equal chance in business with all my fellow-citizens, John D. Rockefeller included. But I have learned by long years of conflict and trial and tribulation, which have cost me untold worry and a lot of money, that this is not so; that I have no business rights which the railroads and this great trust can be made to respect.

"The Interstate Commerce Commission is all right in theory, but it does not have the courage of its powers; it suffers from the paralysis of political influences. The laws are neither feared nor respected by the men of many millions."

"Tell me just how the shoe was made to pinch you personally. How did the trust manage to close your refinery at Marietta?"

"Why, that's easy to tell. Every car of oil that I sent into any part of the United States the trust would jump on it and cut the life out of it. I mean to say that as soon as my oil arrived at the point to which it was shipped the trust would cut the price, so that the man who bought my oil lost money on the sale of it. They would not cut the prices to the whole town, but only to my one customer, and the whole town knew of this man's having lost money by trading with me. From that time forward, of course, I could get no orders in that town. . . .

"In 1872, the trunk lines of railroads made a contract with a corporation called 'The South Improvement Company,' which was only another name for the Standard Oil Company, under which the Standard Oil Company was allowed the most outrageous discriminating freight rates. It seems incredible that these contracts should have been made. They not only gave the Standard Oil Company heavy rebates on their own shipments of oil, but gave them rebates on the shipments of their competitors. At that time the Standard Oil Company only had 10 per cent of the petroleum industry of the country, while their competitors had 90 per cent. The rebates allowed to the Standard people were from 40 cents to $1.06 per barrel on crude petroleum, and from 50 cents to $1.32 per barrel on refined petroleum. Thus the Standard Oil Company received nine times as much for rebates on the shipments of its competitors than it did on its own.

"In 1874," continued Mr. Rice, "the railroads forced the independent pipe lines of the country to sell out their plants to the Standard Oil Company at the price of old junk, and gave to the latter, besides, still further discriminating rebates on freight. A circular was issued on Sept. 9, 1874, known as 'The Rutter Circular,' from the freight office of the New York Central and Hudson River Railroad Company, establishing new rates on refined and crude oil. Under this circular the Standard Oil Company was given an advantage of 20 cents a barrel in the freight charges on crude oil connected with its pipe-line system, which the independent refineries did not have. In that same year the Standard company secured the railroad terminal oil facilities of all the trunk lines centering in New York City. Many fortunes invested in the independent pipe lines were wrecked by that move, through no fault of their managers and no lack of business skill, but simply because the Standard Oil officials, acting in collusion with the railroad officials, had established these unfair discriminations in freight rates between the oil that came through the Standard pipes and that which came through other pipes.

"To show you how the rebate system worked in my own case, let me say that in 1885, I was charged 25 cents a barrel for carrying oil from Macksburg to Marietta, a distance of twenty-five miles, while the Standard Oil Company only paid 10 cents a barrel for the same distance. More than this, out of the 35 cents a barrel that I paid the trust actually received 25 cents. In other words, the trust received about two-thirds of all the money I paid for freight."

TRUST "GREATER" THAN THE COURTS OR THE COUNTRY

"You spoke of your having fought the trust for twenty years. Give me a general outline of your encounter with it."

"Well, about 1879 or 1880 I, with others, brought about a public investigation by the Legislature of Ohio as to the discriminations by the railroads of which I have spoken. Nothing came of that investigation except that we proved any number of facts on which further agitation and action was based. I have gone before the Interstate Commerce Commission in many cases trying to get these discriminations stopped. I brought an action through the Attorney-General of Ohio in 1887 to forfeit the charters of two railroads for gross discrimination, and I proved my case. The courts decided, clear up to the highest court, that these two railroads could not make those discriminating charges.

"I obtained at great cost a decree of the Court to that effect. Apparently it was a conclusive victory. In reality it was of no account. The discriminating rates went on as before, and they are still going on to-day. There is no use in trying to stop it. In March, 1892, the Ohio Supreme Court rendered a judgment against the Standard Oil Company, of Ohio, ordering it to discontinue all business relations with the trust.

"The company has pretended to comply with the decree. In fact the trust still exists and the Standard Oil Company, of Ohio, is still a part of it. The way they have got around it is this: On March 21, 1892, the trust resolved on paper to wind up its affairs, and trustees were appointed for that purpose. Then they issued another kind of trust certificate, called an 'Assignment of Legal Title,' which they made marketable and allowed to be transferred from one holder to another on their trust transfer books, which makes this certificate just as negotiable and salable as the old original trust certificate."

$140,060,000 PROFITS IN SIX YEARS

"In this way the trust is still kept intact. In proof of this fact the trust is known to have declared and paid since March, 1892, up to September of this year, 26 regular quarterly dividends of 3 per cent., and 59 per cent. besides in special dividends, or a total of 137 per cent. — dividends, which, based on their reported capitalization of $102,230,700, amounts to $140,060,000 paid in dividends since its pretended dissolution. No more proof is required that the trust has not been dissolved and that the decree of the Supreme Court of Ohio has been treated with contempt."

"But while you have been ruined, Mr. Rice, it is said, you know, that the mass of consumers have gained — that the price of oil is cheaper, because of the trust. What do you say to this suggestion that you, and others like you, have been crushed for the general good?"

"It is a trust lie," replied Mr. Rice warmly. "There is not the least truth in it. Refined oil for general consumption is as much higher in price as these gross rebates and discriminations amount to, because it is fair to assume, on general principles, that the railroads are making money on the transportation of Standard oil. It only costs three-eighths of a cent a gallon to refine oil. The Standard Oil Trust may possibly save one-eighth of a cent on that, but not more. How much does that amount to in the problem of the cost of oil to the retail consumer?

"Refined oil would certainly have been cheaper right along for the last twenty years but for the Standard combination. If the railroad rates had been honest, and the allowances for rebate had been fair and square to all oil producers and refiners, the mass of the people must and would have got the benefit of it. There is no question that the people have paid millions more for oil than they would have done if the laws against conspiracies and combinations in restriction of fair trade could have been enforced. The price of refined oil is notoriously high to-day compared with the low price of crude oil. There is a difference of from 100 to 300 per cent between crude and refined oil prices, when we all know that crude oil can be turned into refined oil and sold all within thirty days."

"Do you see no remedy ahead for the condition of things which ruined your business as a refiner?"

THE REMEDY—ENFORCE THE LAW

"No, I see no remedy, so long as the railroads are under their present management. I have myself tried every known avenue of relief, and my experience has satisfied me that Blackstone[2] did not foresee the conditions of law and justice now prevailing in this country when he wrote his famous maxim, "There is no wrong without a legal remedy." There is no relief for present conditions in this country except by the Government's acquiring ownership of the railroads. There is plenty of law existing now, but it cannot be enforced. It is a dead letter. The Interstate Commerce act has been law for ten years, and the penalty for the violation of it is a fine of $500 and two years in the State prison. It is violated every day, and it has been violated every day for ten years past, but I observe that no one has yet been sent to prison, and I do not believe that any violator of this law ever expects to be."

Speaking of Mr. Rockefeller, the man who said to him at the public hearing at the New Netherland Hotel, Thursday: "We are getting to be gray-haired men now, aren't we, George? Don't you wish you had taken my advice years ago?" Mr. Rice said: "There is no doubt whatever that Mr. Rockefeller, through the operations of the Standard Oil Trust, is the richest man in the world to-day. I know their business, because it is also mine, and I believe that the Rockefellers are now worth $200,000,000.

"John D. Rockefeller's personal income from the trust and other sources has for several years exceeded $12,000,000 per annum."

---

2. **Blackstone:** Sir William Blackstone was an eighteenth-century English jurist who wrote the four-volume *Commentaries on the Laws of England.*

11

Honest and Dishonest Graft
George Washington Plunkitt

Reformers such as Lincoln Steffens, whose series of articles "The Shame of the Cities" ex-
posed municipal corruption across the United States, blamed most of the ills of large cities
on the political organizations or "machines" that often ran them. In New York City, the
most powerful machine was the Democratic Party's Tammany Hall. The following selec-
tion, by Tammany politician George Washington Plunkitt (1843–1924), offers a view of
the political machine that differs significantly from that of reformers.

Plunkitt's reflections of his political experience were published, edited, and perhaps
embroidered on by newspaperman William L. Riordon in 1905. Plunkitt's view of
American politics directly contravened the opinions typical of the Progressive Era.
While the thrust of reformers, through civil service laws and other programs, was to
limit the power of political parties and their machines, Plunkitt argued that parties and
political machines performed vital functions. "Honest graft" was, he said, the oil that
kept the machines, and government, in motion.

QUESTIONS TO CONSIDER

1. What, according to George Washington Plunkitt, is the distinction between honest graft and dishonest graft? Why does he consider this distinction important? Is it considered important today?
2. What is Plunkitt's argument against civil service reform? Why does it
   not benefit his particular constituents?
3. What, according to Plunkitt, is the basis for his political success?

HONEST GRAFT AND DISHONEST GRAFT

"Everybody is talkin' these days about Tammany men growin' rich on graft, but
nobody thinks of drawin' the distinction between honest graft and dishonest
graft. There's all the difference in the world between the two. Yes, many of our
men have grown rich in politics. I have myself. I've made a big fortune out of
the game, and I'm gettin' richer every day, but I've not gone in for dishonest
graft—blackmailin' gamblers, saloon-keepers, disorderly people, etc.—and
neither has any of the men who have made big fortunes in politics.

William L. Riordon, *Plunkitt of Tammany Hall* (New York: McClure, Phillips, 1905), 3–10, 19–28,
46–55.

"There's an honest graft, and I'm an example of how it works. I might sum up the whole thing by sayin': 'I seen my opportunities and I took 'em.'

"Just let me explain by examples. My party's in power in the city, and it's goin' to undertake a lot of public improvements. Well, I'm tipped off, say, that they're going to lay out a new park at a certain place.

"I see my opportunity and I take it. I go to that place and I buy up all the land I can in the neighborhood. Then the board of this or that makes its plan public, and there is a rush to get my land, which nobody cared particular for before.

"Ain't it perfectly honest to charge a good price and make a profit on my investment and foresight? Of course, it is. Well, that's honest graft.

"Or, supposin' it's a new bridge they're goin' to build. I get tipped off and I buy as much property as I can that has to be taken for approaches. I sell at my own price later on and drop some more money in the bank.

"Wouldn't you? It's just like lookin' ahead in Wall Street or in the coffee or cotton market. It's honest graft, and I'm lookin' for it every day in the year. I will tell you frankly that I've got a good lot of it, too. . . .

"Up in the watershed I made some money, too. I bought up several bits of land there some years ago and made a pretty good guess that they would be bought up for water purposes later by the city.

"Somehow, I always guessed about right, and shouldn't I enjoy the profit of my foresight? It was rather amusin' when the condemnation commissioners came along and found piece after piece of the land in the name of George Plunkitt of the Fifteenth Assembly District, New York City. They wondered how I knew just what to buy. The answer is—I seen my opportunity and I took it. I haven't confined myself to land; anything that pays is in my line. . . .

"I've told you how I got rich by honest graft. Now, let me tell you that most politicians who are accused of robbin' the city get rich the same way.

"They didn't steal a dollar from the city treasury. They just seen their opportunities and took them. That is why, when a reform administration comes in and spends a half million dollars in tryin' to find the public robberies they talked about in the campaign, they don't find them.

"The books are always all right. The money in the city treasury is all right. Everything is all right. All they can show is that the Tammany heads of departments looked after their friends, within the law, and gave them what opportunities they could to make honest graft. Now, let me tell you that's never goin' to hurt Tammany with the people. Every good man looks after his friends, and any man who doesn't isn't likely to be popular. If I have a good thing to hand out in private life, I give it to a friend. Why shouldn't I do the same in public life?

"Another kind of honest graft. Tammany has raised a good many salaries. There was an awful howl by the reformers, but don't you know that Tammany gains ten votes for every one it lost by salary raisin'?

"The Wall Street banker thinks it shameful to raise a department clerk's salary from $1500 to $1800 a year, but every man who draws a salary himself says: 'That's all right. I wish it was me.' And he feels very much like votin' the Tammany ticket on election day, just out of sympathy.

"Tammany was beat in 1901 because the people were deceived into believin' that it worked dishonest graft. They didn't draw a distinction between dishonest and honest graft, but they saw that some Tammany men grew rich, and supposed they had been robbin' the city treasury or levyin' blackmail on disorderly houses, or workin' in with the gamblers and lawbreakers.

"As a matter of policy, if nothing else, why should the Tammany leaders go into such dirty business, when there is so much honest graft lyin' around when they are in power? Did you ever consider that?

"Now, in conclusion, I want to say that I don't own a dishonest dollar. If my worst enemy was given the job of writin' my epitaph when I'm gone, he couldn't do more than write:

"'George W. Plunkitt. He Seen His Opportunities, and He Took 'Em.'"

THE CURSE OF CIVIL SERVICE REFORM

"This civil service law is the biggest fraud of the age. It is the curse of the nation. There can't be no real patriotism while it lasts. How are you goin' to interest our young men in their country if you have no offices to give them when they work for their party? Just look at things in this city to-day. There are ten thousand good offices, but we can't get at more than a few hundred of them. How are we goin' to provide for the thousands of men who worked for the Tammany ticket? It can't be done. These men were full of patriotism a short time ago. They expected to be servin' their city, but when we tell them that we can't place them, do you think their patriotism is goin' to last? Not much. They say: 'What's the use of workin' for your country anyhow? There's nothin' in the game.' And what can they do? I don't know, but I'll tell you what I do know. I know more than one young man in past years who worked for the ticket and was just overflowin' with patriotism, but when he was knocked out by the civil service humbug he got to hate his country and became an Anarchist.

"This ain't no exaggeration. I have good reason for sayin' that most of the Anarchists in this city to-day are men who ran up against civil service examinations. Isn't it enough to make a man sour on his country when he wants to serve it and won't be allowed unless he answers a lot of fool questions about the number of cubic inches of water in the Atlantic and the quality of sand in the Sahara desert? There was once a bright young man in my district who tackled one of these examinations. The next I heard of him he had settled down in Herr Most's saloon smokin' and drinkin' beer and talkin' socialism all day. Before that time he had never drank anything but whisky. I knew what was comin' when a young Irishman drops whisky and takes to beer and long pipes in a German saloon. That young man is to-day one of the wildest Anarchists in town. And just to think! He might be a patriot but for that cussed civil service. . . .

"When the people elected Tammany, they knew just what they were doin'. We didn't put up any false pretenses. We didn't go in for humbug civil service and all that rot. We stood as we have always stood, for rewardin' the men that won the victory. They call that the spoils system. All right; Tammany is for the spoils system, and when we go in we fire every anti-Tammany man from office that can be fired under the law. It's an elastic sort of law and you can bet it will be stretched to the limit. Of course the Republican State Civil Service Board will stand in the way of our local Civil Service Commission all it can; but say!—suppose we carry the State some time won't we fire the up-State Board all right? Or we'll make it work in harmony with the local board, and that means that Tammany will get everything in sight. I know that the civil service humbug is stuck into the constitution, too, but, as Tim Campbell[1] said: 'What's the constitution among friends?'

"Say, the people's voice is smothered by the cursed civil service law; it is the root of all evil in our government. You hear of this thing or that thing goin' wrong in the nation, the State or the city. Look down beneath the surface and you can trace everything wrong to civil service. I have studied the subject and I know. The civil service humbug is underminin' our institutions and if a halt ain't called soon this great republic will tumble down like a Park-avenue house when they were buildin' the subway, and on its ruins will rise another Russian government.

"This is an awful serious proposition. Free silver and the tariff and imperialism and the Panama Canal are triflin' issues when compared to it. We could worry along without any of these things, but civil service is sappin' the foundation of the whole shootin' match. Let me argue it out for you. I ain't up on sillygisms, but I can give you some arguments that nobody can answer.

"First, this great and glorious country was built up by political parties; second, parties can't hold together if their workers don't get the offices when they win; third, if the parties go to pieces, the government they built up must go to pieces, too; fourth, then there'll be h_ _ _ to pay.

"Could anything be clearer than that? Say, honest now; can you answer that argument? Of course you won't deny that the government was built up by the great parties. That's history, and you can't go back of the returns. As to my second proposition, you can't deny that either. When parties can't get offices, they'll bust. They ain't far from the bustin' point now, with all this civil service business keepin' most of the good things from them. How are you goin' to keep up patriotism if this thing goes on? You can't do it. Let me tell you that patriotism has been dying out fast for the last twenty years. Before then when a party won, its workers got everything in sight. That was somethin' to make a man patriotic. Now, when a party wins and its men come forward and ask for their reward, the reply is, 'Nothin' doin', unless you can answer a list of questions about Egyptian mummies and how many years it will take for a bird to wear out a mass of iron as big as the earth by steppin' on it once in a century?'

"I have studied politics and men for forty-five years, and I see how things are driftin'. Sad indeed is the change that has come over the young men, even in my district, where I try to keep up the fire of patriotism by gettin' a lot of jobs for my constituents, whether Tammany is in or out. The boys and men don't

---

1. **Tim Campbell:** Timothy J. Campbell was an Irish-born New York City Democratic politician elected to Congress twice, between 1885 and 1895.

get excited any more when they see a United States flag or hear the 'Star Spangled Banner.' They don't care no more for fire-crackers on the Fourth of July. And why should they? What is there in it for them? They know that no matter how hard they work for their country in a campaign, the jobs will go to fellows who can tell about the mummies and the bird steppin' on the iron. Are you surprised then that the young men of the country are beginnin' to look coldly on the flag and don't care to put up a nickel for fire-crackers? . . .

"Now, what is goin' to happen when civil service crushes out patriotism? Only one thing can happen: the republic will go to pieces. Then a czar or a sultan will turn up, which brings me to the fourthly of my argument—that is, there will be h_ _ _ to pay. And that ain't no lie."

TO HOLD YOUR DISTRICT—STUDY HUMAN NATURE AND ACT ACCORDIN'

"There's only one way to hold a district; you must study human nature and act accordin'. You can't study human nature in books. Books is a hindrance more than anything else. If you have been to college, so much the worse for you. You'll have to unlearn all you learned before you can get right down to human nature, and unlearnin' takes a lot of time. Some men can never forget what they learned at college. Such men may get to be district leaders by a fluke, but they never last.

"To learn real human nature you have to go among the people, see them and be seen. I know every man, woman, and child in the Fifteenth District, except them that's been born this summer—and I know some of them, too. I know what they like and what they don't like, what they are strong at and what they are weak in, and I reach them by approachin' at the right side.

"For instance, here's how I gather in the young men. I hear of a young feller that's proud of his voice, thinks that he can sing fine. I ask him to come around to Washington Hall and join our Glee Club. He comes and sings, and he's a follower of Plunkitt for life. Another young feller gains a reputation as a baseball player in a vacant lot. I bring him into our baseball club. That fixes him. You'll find him workin' for my ticket at the polls next election day. Then there's the feller that likes rowin' on the river, the young feller that makes a name as a waltzer on his block, the young feller that's handy with his dukes—I rope them all in by givin' them opportunities to show themselves off. I don't trouble them with political arguments. I just study human nature and act accordin'.

"But you may say this game won't work with the high-toned fellers, the fellers that go through college and then join the Citizens' Union. Of course it wouldn't work. I have a special treatment for them. I ain't like the patent medicine man that gives the same medicine for all diseases. The Citizens' Union kind of a young man! I love him! He's the daintiest morsel of the lot, and he don't often escape me.

"Before telling you how I catch him, let me mention that before the election last year, the Citizens' Union said they had four hundred or five hundred enrolled voters in my district. They had a lovely headquarters, too, beautiful roll-top desks and the cutest rugs in the world. If I was accused of havin' contributed to fix up the nest for them, I wouldn't deny it under oath. What do I mean by that? Never mind. You can guess from the sequel, if you're sharp.

"Well, election day came. The Citizens' Union's[2] candidate for Senator, who ran against me, just polled five votes in the district, while I polled something more than 14,000 votes. What became of the 400 or 500 Citizens' Union enrolled voters in my district? Some people guessed that many of them were good Plunkitt men all along and worked with the Cits just to bring them into the Plunkitt camp by election day. You can guess that way, too, if you want to. I never contradict stories about me, especially in hot weather. I just call your attention to the fact that on last election day 395 Citizens' Union enrolled voters in my district were missin' and unaccounted for. . . .

"As to the older voters, I reach them, too. No, I don't send them campaign literature. That's rot. People can get all the political stuff they want to read—and a good deal more, too—in the papers. Who reads speeches, nowadays, anyhow? It's bad enough to listen to them. You ain't goin' to gain any votes by stuffin' their letter-boxes with campaign documents. Like as not you'll lose votes, for there's nothin' a man hates more than to hear the letter-carrier ring his bell and go to the letter-box expectin' to find a letter he was lookin' for, and find only a lot of printed politics. I met a man this very mornin' who told me he voted the Democratic State ticket last year just because the Republicans kept crammin' his letter-box with campaign documents.

"What tells in holdin' your grip on your district is to go right down among the poor families and help them in the different ways they need help. I've got a regular system for this. If there's a fire in Ninth, Tenth, or Eleventh Avenue, for example, any hour of the day or night, I'm usually there with some of my election district captains as soon as the fire-engines. If a family is burned out I don't ask whether they are Republicans or Democrats, and I don't refer them to the Charity Organization Society, which would investigate their case in a month or two and decide they were worthy of help about the time they are dead from starvation. I just get quarters for them, buy clothes for them if their clothes were burned up, and fix them up till they get things runnin' again. It's philanthropy, but it's politics, too—mighty good politics. Who can tell how many votes one of the fires bring me? The poor are the most grateful people in the world, and, let me tell you, they have more friends in their neighborhoods than the rich have in theirs.

"If there's a family in my district in want I know it before the charitable societies do, and me and my men are first on the ground. I have a special corps to look up such cases. The consequence is that the poor look up to George W. Plunkitt as a father, come to him in trouble—and don't forget him on election day.

---

2. **Citizens' Union:** The Citizens Union was a nonpartisan organization founded in 1897 to fight the corruption of Tammany Hall. It elected Seth Low, New York's first reform mayor, in 1901.

"Another thing, I can always get a job for a deservin' man. I make it a point to keep on the track of jobs, and it seldom happens that I don't have a few up my sleeve ready for use. I know every big employer in the district and in the whole city, for that matter, and they ain't in the habit of sayin' no to me when I ask them for a job.

"And the children—the little roses of the district! Do I forget them? Oh, no! They know me, every one of them, and they know that a sight of Uncle George and candy means the same thing. Some of them are the best kind of vote-getters. I'll tell you a case. Last year a little Eleventh Avenue rosebud whose father is a Republican, caught hold of his whiskers on election day and said she wouldn't let go till he'd promise to vote for me. And she didn't."

ON *THE SHAME OF THE CITIES*

"I've been readin' a book by Lincoln Steffens on *The Shame of the Cities*. Steffens means well but, like all reformers, he don't know how to make distinctions. He can't see no difference between honest graft and dishonest graft and, consequent, he gets things all mixed up. There's the biggest kind of a difference between political looters and politicians who make a fortune out of politics by keepin' their eyes wide open. The looter goes in for himself alone without considerin' his organization or his city. The politician looks after his own interests, the organization's interests, and the city's interests all at the same time. See the distinction? For instance, I ain't no looter. The looter hogs it. I never hogged. I made my pile in politics, but, at the same time, I served the organization and got more big improvements for New York City than any other livin' man." . . .

Antilynching Campaign in Tennessee
Ida B. Wells-Barnett

Lynching—the murder, especially by hanging, of a person accused of some offense, real or imagined, by a mob—is an old crime in the United States. The word can be traced back to the way Colonel Charles Lynch and his fellow patriots in revolutionary Virginia dealt with suspected Tories. Lynchings, especially of blacks, began to increase in the 1880s and peaked in 1892, the worst year in American history for this brutal crime.

Thomas Moss, Calvin McDowell, and Henry Stewart, friends of Ida B. Wells-Barnett (1864–1931) and respectable and successful members of the Memphis African American community, were among the approximately 250 Americans whose lynchings were recorded in 1892. (There were doubtless more of which no record was made.) The murder of her friends changed Wells-Barnett's entire life. Already well known as a leading African American journalist and reformer—she had sued a railroad company in 1883 for forcing her to leave a "whites-only" car—she left Memphis after her angry editorial on the lynchings put her life in danger, and she became a tireless activist against the crime. Her campaign helped make opposition to lynching a leading cause among African American activists until World War II, when lynchings largely—but not completely—ceased.

In answering the accusation that lynching was the response to "the new Negro crime"—the propensity of black men to rape white women—Wells-Barnett researched in detail the circumstances of the 728 lynchings of the previous ten years that she was able to authenticate. Her evidence refuted the excuse that the victims had committed rape. Only a third of black lynching victims were even accused of rape. Many died for crimes like "race prejudice," "making threats," or "quarreling with whites." Some of the victims were women and even children.

QUESTIONS TO CONSIDER

1. How does Ida B. Wells-Barnett explain the lynchings of her friends and others? Do you agree with her?
2. What is Wells-Barnett's strategy for Memphis's African Americans to respond to the lynchings? What do you think of it?
3. Do you agree with Wells-Barnett that "every white man in Memphis who consented" to the lynchings and rioting "is as guilty as those who fired the guns"?

Alfreda M. Duster, ed., *Crusade for Justice: The Autobiography of Ida B. Wells* (Chicago: University of Chicago Press, 1970), 47–52.

While I was thus carrying on the work of my newspaper, happy in the thought that our influence was helpful and that I was doing the work I loved and had proved that I could make a living out of it, there came the lynching in Memphis which changed the whole course of my life. . . .

Thomas Moss, Calvin McDowell, and Henry Stewart owned and operated a grocery store in a thickly populated suburb [of Memphis]. Moss was a letter carrier and could only be at the store at night. Everybody in town knew and loved Tommie. An exemplary young man, he was married and the father of one little girl, Maurine, whose godmother I was. He and his wife Betty were the best friends I had in town. And he believed, with me, that we should defend the cause of right and fight wrong wherever we saw it.

He delivered mail at the office of the *Free Speech*, and whatever Tommie knew in the way of news we got first. He owned his little home, and having saved his money he went into the grocery business with the same ambition that a young white man would have had. He was the president of the company. His partners ran the business in the daytime.

They had located their grocery in the district known as the "Curve" because the streetcar line curved sharply at that point. There was already a grocery owned and operated by a white man who hitherto had had a monopoly on the trade of this thickly populated colored suburb. Thomas's grocery changed all that, and he and his associates were made to feel that they were not welcome by the white grocer. The district being mostly colored and many of the residents belonging either to Thomas's church or to his lodge, he was not worried by the white grocer's hostility.

One day some colored and white boys quarreled over a game of marbles and the colored boys got the better of the fight which followed. The father of the white boys whipped the victorious colored boy, whose father and friends pitched in to avenge the grown white man's flogging of a colored boy. The colored men won the fight, whereupon the white father and grocery keeper swore out a warrant for the arrest of the colored victors. Of course the colored grocery keepers had been drawn into the dispute. But the case was dismissed with nominal fines. Then the challenge was issued that the vanquished whites were coming on Saturday night to clean out the People's Grocery Company.

Knowing this, the owners of the company consulted a lawyer and were told that as they were outside the city limits and beyond police protection, they would be justified in protecting themselves if attacked. Accordingly the grocery company armed several men and stationed them in the rear of the store on that fatal Saturday night, not to attack but to repel a threatened attack. And Saturday night was the time when men of both races congregated in their respective groceries.

About ten o'clock that night, when Thomas was posting his books for the week and Calvin McDowell and his clerk were waiting on customers preparatory to closing, shots rang out in the back room of the store. The men stationed there had seen several white men stealing through the rear door and fired on them without a moment's pause. Three of these men were wounded, and others fled and gave the alarm.

Sunday morning's paper came out with lurid headlines telling how officers of the law had been wounded while in the discharge of their duties, hunting up criminals whom they had been told were harbored in the People's Grocery Company, this being "a low dive in which drinking and gambling were carried on: a resort of thieves and thugs." So ran the description in the leading white journals of Memphis of this successful effort of decent black men to carry on a legitimate business. The same newspaper told of the arrest and jailing of the proprietor of the store and many of the colored people. They predicted that it would go hard with the ringleaders if these "officers" should die. The tale of how the peaceful homes of that suburb were raided on that quiet Sunday morning by police pretending to be looking for others who were implicated in what the papers had called a conspiracy, has been often told. Over a hundred colored men were dragged from their homes and put in jail on suspicion.

All day long on that fateful Sunday white men were permitted in the jail to look over the imprisoned black men. Frenzied descriptions and hearsays were detailed in the papers, which fed the fires of sensationalism. Groups of white men gathered on the street corners and meeting places to discuss the awful crime of Negroes shooting white men.

There had been no lynchings in Memphis since the Civil War, but the colored people felt that anything might happen during the excitement. Many of them were in business there. Several times they had elected a member of their race to represent them in the legislature in Nashville. And a Negro, Lymus Wallace, had been elected several times as a member of the city council and we had had representation on the school board several times. Mr. Fred Savage was then our representative on the board of education.

The manhood which these Negroes represented went to the county jail and kept watch Sunday night. This they did also on Monday night, guarding the jail to see that nothing happened to the colored men during this time of race prejudice, while it was thought that the wounded white men would die. On Tuesday following, the newspapers which had fanned the flame of race prejudice announced that the wounded men were out of danger and would recover. The colored men who had guarded the jail for two nights felt that the crisis was past and that they need not guard the jail the third night.

While they slept a body of picked men was admitted to the jail, which was a modern Bastille. This mob took out of their cells Thomas Moss, Calvin McDowell, and Henry Stewart, the three officials of the People's Grocery Company. They were loaded on a switch engine of the railroad which ran back of the jail, carried a mile north of the city limits, and horribly shot to death. One of the morning papers held back its edition in order to supply its readers with the details of that lynching.

From its columns was gleaned the above information, together with details which told that "It is said that Tom Moss begged for his life for the sake of his wife and child and his unborn baby"; that when asked if he had anything to say, told them to "tell my people to go West—there is no justice for them here"; that Calvin McDowell got hold of one of the guns of the lynchers and because they could not loosen his grip a shot was fired into his closed fist.

When the three bodies were found, the fingers of McDowell's right hand had been shot to pieces and his eyes were gouged out. This proved that the one who wrote that news report was either an eyewitness or got the facts from someone who was.

The shock to the colored people who knew and loved both Moss and McDowell was beyond description. Groups of them went to the grocery and elsewhere and vented their feelings in talking among themselves, but they offered no violence. Word was brought to the city hall that Negroes were massing at the "Curve" where the grocery had been located. Immediately an order was issued by the judge of the criminal court sitting on the bench, who told the sheriff to "take a hundred men, go out to the Curve at once, and shoot down on sight any Negro who appears to be making trouble."

The loafers around the courts quickly spread the news, and gangs of them rushed into the hardware stores, armed themselves, boarded the cars and rushed out to the Curve. They obeyed the judge's orders literally and shot into any group of Negroes they saw with as little compunction as if they had been on a hunting trip. The only reason hundreds of Negroes were not killed on that day by the mobs was because of the forebearance of the colored men. They realized their helplessness and submitted to outrages and insults for the sake of those depending upon them.

This mob took possession of the People's Grocery Company, helping themselves to food and drink, and destroyed what they could not eat or steal. The creditors had the place closed and a few days later what remained of the stock was sold at auction. Thus, with the aid of the city and county authorities and the daily papers, that white grocer had indeed put an end to his rival Negro grocer as well as to his business.

As said before, I was in Natchez, Mississippi, when the worst of this horrible event was taking place. Thomas Moss had already been buried before I reached home. Although stunned by the events of that hectic week, the *Free Speech* felt that it must carry on. Its leader for that week said:

> The city of Memphis has demonstrated that neither character nor standing avails the Negro if he dares to protect himself against the white man or become his rival. There is nothing we can do about the lynching now, as we are outnumbered and without arms. The white mob could help itself to ammunition without pay, but the order was rigidly enforced against the selling of guns to Negroes. There is therefore only one thing left that we can do; save our money and leave a town which will neither protect our lives and property, nor give us a fair trial in the courts, but takes us out and murders us in cold blood when accused by white persons.

This advice of the *Free Speech*, coupled with the last words of Thomas Moss, was taken up and reechoed among our people throughout Memphis. Hundreds disposed of their property and left. Rev. R. N. Countee and Rev. W. A. Brinkley, both leading pastors, took their whole congregations with them as they, too, went West. Memphis had never seen such an upheaval among colored people. Business was practically at a standstill, for the Negro was famous then, as now, for spending his money for fine clothes, furniture, jewelry, and pianos and other musical instruments, to say nothing of good things to eat. Music houses had more musical instruments, sold on the installment plan, thrown back on their hands than they could find storage for.

Six weeks after the lynching the superintendent and treasurer of the City Railway Company came into the office of the *Free Speech* and asked us to use our influence with the colored people to get them to ride on the streetcars again. When I asked why they came to us the reply was that colored people had been their best patrons, but that there had been a marked falling off of their patronage. There were no jim crow[1] streetcars in Memphis then. I asked what they thought was the cause. They said they didn't know. They had heard Negroes were afraid of electricity, for Memphis already had streetcars run by electricity in 1892. They wanted us to assure our people that there was no danger and to tell them that any discourtesy toward them would be punished severely.

But I said that I couldn't believe it, because "electricity has been the motive power here for over six months and you are just now noticing the slump. How long since you have observed the change?" "About six weeks," said one of them. "You see it's a matter of dollars and cents with us. If we don't look after the loss and remedy the cause the company will get somebody else who will."

"So your own job then depends on Negro patronage?" I asked. And although their faces flushed over the question they made no direct reply. "You see it is like this," said the superintendent. "When the company installed electricity at a cost of thousands of dollars last fall, Negro labor got a large share of it in wages in relaying tracks, grading the streets, etc. And so we think it is only fair that they should give us their patronage in return."

Said I, "They were doing so until six weeks ago, yet you say you don't know the cause of the falling off. Why, it was just six weeks ago that the lynching took place." "But the streetcar company had nothing to do with the lynching," said one of the men. "It is owned by northern capitalists." "And run by southern lynchers," I retorted. "We have learned that every white man of any standing in town knew of the plan and consented to the lynching of our boys. Did you know Tom Moss, the letter carrier?" "Yes," he replied.

"A finer, cleaner man than he never walked the streets of Memphis," I said. "He was well liked, a favorite with everybody; yet he was murdered with no more consideration than if he had been a dog, because he as a man defended his property from attack. The colored people feel that every white man in Memphis who consented to his death is as guilty as those who fired the guns which took his life, and they want to get away from this town.

"We told them the week after the lynching to save their nickels and dimes so that they could do so. We had no way of knowing that they were doing so before this, as I have walked more than I ever did in my life before. No one has been arrested or punished about that terrible affair nor will they be because all are equally guilty."

---

1. **jim crow:** Discrimination against African Americans in public places, such as streetcars.

"Why don't the colored people find the guilty ones?" asked one of them.

"As if they could. There is strong belief among us that the criminal court judge himself was one of the lynchers. Suppose we had the evidence; could we get it before that judge? Or a grand jury of white men who had permitted it to be? Or force the reporter of the *Appeal* to tell what he saw and knows about that night? You know very well that we are powerless to do any of these things."

"Well we hope you will do what you can for us and if you know of any discourtesy on the part of our employees let us know and we will be glad to remedy it."

When they left the office I wrote this interview for the next issue of the *Free Speech* and in the article told the people to keep up the good work. Not only that, I went to the two largest churches in the city the next Sunday, before the paper came out, and told them all about it. I urged them to keep on staying off the cars.

Every time word came of people leaving Memphis, we who were left behind rejoiced. Oklahoma was about to be opened up, and scores sold or gave away property, shook Memphis dust off their feet, and went out West as Tom Moss had said for us to do.

13

Protecting Yosemite

John Muir

Preservationist John Muir was probably the most important individual in the founding of the modern environmental movement. Famous for books about his adventures in nature and essays and speeches about the philosophy of natural preservation, Muir was the founder of the Sierra Club and the primary influence behind the creation of Yosemite National Park in 1890.

Born in 1838 in Scotland, Muir came with his family to Wisconsin in 1849. Interested in nature from a young age, Muir briefly studied botany at the University of Wisconsin, but dropped out to wander in what he would later call the "university of the wilderness." Muir finally found his calling when he moved to California in 1868, taking up residence in the Yosemite Valley and working as a ferry operator, sheepherder, bronco buster, and saw mill operator. Muir spent his spare time climbing mountains, walking Indian trails, and studying the natural environment. Though largely self-taught, Muir developed important theories about the geological formation of the Yosemite Valley and recorded important discoveries about the interconnections of the local ecosystem.

After a brief period of farming, Muir threw himself into environmental activism. In 1890 he became nationally famous, writing two articles for Century Magazine *that led Congress to designate Yosemite the country's second national park, after Yellowstone. Unimpressed by his victory, which had left the Yosemite Valley under California state administration, Muir founded the Sierra Club in 1892 to continue the fight to extend the zone of federal protection and monitor the Calforina state authorities, who he believed were too concerned with economic development to have the park's best interests at heart. The Sierra Club went on to be the most important environmentalist organization in the United States and Muir came to be an influential, national figure, befriending such famous and powerful men as President Theodore Roosevelt and railroad executive E. H. Harriman, both of whom he took on camping trips into the heart of Yosemite.*

Roosevelt, pictured here (see photo on page 96) with Muir at Yosemite's Glacier Point, was already a passionate environmentalist. He had banned Christmas trees in the White House and would eventually designate tens of millions of acres as protected national forests. However, he, like many of the most important environmentalists of the time, believed in

John Muir, "Proceedings of the Meeting of the Sierra Club Held November 23, 1895." Published in *Sierra Club Bulletin*, 1896.

President Theodore Roosevelt and John Muir hiking at Glacier Point, California, 1903.

"conservationism," or the efficient and sustainable commercial use of lands and natural resources. This was in sharp contrast to Muir's belief in "preservation of nature," which meant protecting the natural environment as something important, spiritual, and joyous for its own sake.

QUESTIONS TO CONSIDER

1. Many critics have argued that Muir's preservationist philosophy was elitist and exclusionary. What evidence do you find for or against this criticism in the reading?
2. Muir lost his last great battle, to protect the Hetch Hetchy Valley from a dam project designed to provide water for San Francisco. Why do you think he was more successful in protecting Yosemite?
3. What do Muir's descriptions and the language he uses reveal about his views of nature?
4. How do Muir's views of nature and preservation fit with contemporary perspectives on environmentalism? How do they differ?
5. As the photograph of President Roosevelt and John Muir reveals, Roosevelt loved the outdoors. During their time in Yosemite hiking and

camping together, the two men engaged in much discussion of nature and managing the environment. What might some of Muir's arguments to Roosevelt have been during this precious time with such a powerful national figure? How might Roosevelt have responded to Muir and justified his position?

This last summer I wanted to go to Alaska to explore some fine busy glaciers that are working on the flanks of Mt. St. Elias and the mountains about Cook's Inlet and Prince William's Sound. But I could not get away early enough for such extended explorations as would be required there; and so I just rambled off for an easy six weeks' saunter in the Sierra above Yosemite, and about the head-waters of the Tuolumne, and down the Grand Cañon of the Tuolumne to Hetch Hetchy and the sugar pine woods of the main forest belt. On this ramble I was careful to note the results of the four years of protection the region had enjoyed as a park under the care of the Federal Government, and I found them altogether delightful and encouraging. When I had last seen the Yosemite National Park region, the face of the landscape in general was broken and wasted, like a beautiful countenance destroyed by some dreadful disease. Now it is blooming again as one general garden, in which beauty for ashes has been granted in fine wild measure. The flowers and grasses are back again in their places as if they had never been away, and every tree in the park is waving its arms for joy. Only the few spots held as cattle ranches under private ownership continue to look frowzy and wasted; but the condition of even these has been greatly improved under protection from the sheep scourge. Lilies now swing and ring their bells around the margins of the forest meadows and along the banks of the streams throughout the lower and middle portions of the park. The broad tangles and beds of chaparral have put forth new shoots and leaves, and are now blooming again in all their shaggy beauty and fragrance. The open spaces on the slopes are covered with beds of gilias of many species and purple spraquea, monardella, etc.; while on the steeper slopes the driest friable soil, that was most deeply raked and dibbled by the hoofs of the sheep, has been replanted, mostly by a delicate species of gymnophytum, whose winged seeds were the first to reach those desolate places. Soon, however, they will be followed by other plants to enrich the bloom; for in the work of beauty Nature never stops.

In the highlands of the park the tough sod of the glacier meadows was never wholly destroyed, but their delicate grasses were not allowed to bloom beneath the feet of the trampling sheep, and all the bright flowers that so charmingly enameled the close, smooth sod—gentians, daisies, ivesias, orthocarpus, bryanthus, etc.—vanished as if not a root or seed had been spared. This year, I am happy to say, I found these blessed flowers blooming again in their places in all the fineness of wildness—three species of gentians, in patches acres in extent, blue as the sky, blending their celestial color with the purple panicles of the grasses, and the daisies and bossy, rosy spikes of the varied species of orthocarpus and bryanthus—nearly every trace of the sad sheep years of repression and destruction having vanished. Blessings on Uncle Sam's blue-coats! In what we may call homeopathic doses, the quiet, orderly soldiers have done this fine job, without any apparent friction or weak noise, in the still calm way that the United States troops do their duty. Uncle Sam has only to say: "There is your duty," and it is done. . . .

So Uncle Sam's soldiers, in attending to those marauding shepherds and their flocks, tried to gather in two at a blow. A very suggestive flock, not of sheep, but of shepherd and their dogs, was seen this summer crossing the Yosemite National Park. Nine Portuguese shepherds and eighteen shepherd dogs were marched across the park from the extreme northern boundary, across the Tuolumne Cañon and the rugged topography of the Merced basin to the southern boundary at Wawona, and presented as prisoners before Captain Rodgers, who had charge of the troop guarding the park. These shepherds submitted to being driven along over hill and dale day after day as peacefully as sheep, notwithstanding they had a little previously been boasting of their fighting qualities and the surprising excellence of their guns, and with what deadly effect they would use them if interfered with in their divine right of stealing pasturage. But when they were calmly confronted with a soldier, armed with the authority of the United States and a gun of much surer fire than theirs, they always behaved well, and became suddenly unbelligerent. Occasionally a flock would be found in some remote, hidden valley of the park, attended by three or four shepherds, so that a watch could be kept on the movements of the soldiers from the heights around the camp. But, sooner or later, they would be caught and made to obey the laws;—for every year the whole park is faithfully policed.

In my wanderings this summer I met small squads of mounted soldiers in all kinds of out-of-the-way places, fording roaring, bowlder-choked streams, crossing rugged cañons, ever alert and watchful; and knowing, as we do, the extreme roughness of the topography of the park in general, our thanks are due these quiet soldiers for unweariedly facing and overcoming every difficulty in the way of duty. And always it is refreshing to know that in our changeful Government there is one arm that is permanent and ever to be depended on.

The Yosemite National Park was made October 1, 1890. For many years I had been crying in the wilderness, "Save the forests!" but, so far as I know, nothing effective was done in the matter until shortly before the park was organized. In the summer of 1889, I took one of the editors of the *Century Magazine* out for a walk in Yosemite and in the woods and bowlder-choked cañons around it; and when we were camped one day at the Big Tuolumne Meadows, my friend said, "Where are all those wonderful flower gardens you write so much about?" And I had to confess—woe's me!—that uncountable sheep had eaten and trampled them out of existence. Then he said, "Can't something be done to restore and preserve so wonderful a region as this? Surely the people of California are not going to allow these magnificent forests, on which the welfare of the whole State depends, to be destroyed?" Then a National Park was proposed, and I was requested to write some articles about the region to help call attention to it, while the *Century* was freely used for the same purpose, and every friend that could be found was called on to write or speak a good word for it. The California Academy of Sciences became interested, and began to work, and so did the State University. Even the soulless Southern Pacific R.R. Co., never counted on for anything good, helped nobly in pushing the bill for this park through Congress. Mr. Stow in particular charged our members of Congress that whatever they neglected they must see that the bill for a National Park around Yosemite Valley went through. And in a little over a year from the time of our first talk beside that Tuolumne camp-fire the bill organizing the park passed Congress, and a troop of cavalry was guarding it.

But no sooner were the boundaries of the park established, then interested parties began to try to break through them. Last winter a determined effort was made to have the area of the park cut down nearly one-half. But the Sierra Club and other good friends of the forests on both sides of the continent made a good defense, and to-day the original boundaries are still unbroken.

The battle we have fought, and are still fighting, for the forests is a part of the eternal conflict between right and wrong, and we cannot expect to see the end of it. I trust, however that our Club will not weary in this forest well-doing. The fight for the Yosemite Park and other forest parks and reserves is by no means over; nor would the fighting cease, however much the boundaries were contracted. Every good thing, great and small, needs defense. The smallest forest reserve, and the first I ever heard of, was in the Garden of Eden; and though its boundaries were drawn by the Lord, and embraced only one tree, yet even so moderate a reserve as this was attacked. And I doubt not, if only one of our grand trees in the Sierra were reserved as an example and type of all that is most noble and glorious in mountain trees, it would not be long before you would find a lumberman and a lawyer at the foot of it, eagerly proving by every law terrestrial and celestial that that tree must come down. So we must count on watching and striving for these trees, and should always be glad to find anything so surely good and noble to strive for. . . .

When I first saw Yosemite, and read the notices posted by the State Commissioners, forbidding the cutting or marring the beauty in any way of the trees and shrubs, etc., I said, "How fine it is that this grand valley has been made a park, for the enjoyment of all the world! Here we shall have a section of the wonderful flora of the mountains of California, with most of its wild inhabitants preserved, when all about it has been injured or destroyed." But instead of enjoying special protection, on account of its marvelous grandeur, it has suffered special destruction, for lack of the extraordinary care that so much trampling travel in it required. Therefore, now, instead of being most preciously cared for as the finest of all the park-gardens, it looks like a frowzy, neglected backwoods pasture. The best meadows are enclosed for hay-fields by unsightly fences, and all the rest of the floor of the valley is given up to the destructive pasturage of horses belonging to campers and those kept for the use of tourists. Each year the number of campers increases, and of course, destructive trampling and hacking becomes heavier from season to season. Camping parties, on their arrival in the valley, are required to report to the Guardian, to register and have camp-grounds assigned to them, and their attention is called to the rules and regulations prohibiting the cutting of trees and underbrush, etc.; but as the Guardian has no power to enforce the rules — has not a single policeman under his orders, — they are of non-effect, or nearly so. Most campers and tourists appreciate their privileges, but some, I am sorry to say, need the services of a soldier as much as the sheep-owners who break over the boundaries of the park. Not a single horse or cow should be allowed to trample the Yosemite garden. It was given to the State for a higher use than pasturage. Hay and grain in abundance may be hauled into the valley and sold to the owners of saddle-trains and campers, at moderate prices, at stables and corrals provided by the Commission. Then, of course, every disfiguring fence would be useless, and the wild vegetation would be gradually restored.

Since the fires that formerly swept through the valley have been prevented, the underbrush requires much expensive attention, that will call for the services of a skilled landscape artist. The wasting banks of the river also require treatment of the same kind, and so, indeed, does the whole wasted floor of the valley. As far as the hotel and saddle-train service is concerned, little fault can be found; but good management of the valley in general by a Board of Commissioners appointed by the Governor, whole terms of office depend on ever-changing politics, must, I think, be always difficult or impossible as long as the people of California remain lukewarm and apathetic in the matter. The solution of the whole question, it seems to me, is recession of the valley to the Federal government, to form a part of the Yosemite National Park, which naturally it is. One management for both is enough; and management by the unchanging War Department must be better than State management, ever changing and wavering with the political pulse. Anyhow, people usually get what they deserve; and Californians can obtain immensely better results, even from a State Commission, if they really care enough. Golden Gate Park, under State Commissioners, is well managed. Emerson says: "Things refuse to be mismanaged long," and now, when Yosemite affairs seem at their worst, there are hopeful signs in sight. . . .

This year, nearly as many campers as tourists visited the valley, and their stay was much longer. It is encouraging to learn that so many of the young men and women growing up in California are going to the mountains every summer and becoming good mountaineers, and, of course, good defenders of the Sierra forests and of all the reviving beauty that belongs to them. For every one that I found mountaineering back of Yosemite in the High Sierra, ten years ago, I this year met more than a hundred. Many of these young mountaineers were girls, in parties of ten or fifteen, making bright pictures as they tramped merrily along through the forest aisles, with the sparkle and exhilaration of the mountains in their eyes—a fine, hopeful sign of the times. . . .

The Sierra forests are growing just where they do the most good and where their removal would be followed by the greatest number of evils. The welfare of the people in the valleys of California and the welfare of the trees on the mountains are so closely related that the farmers might say that oranges grow on pine-trees, and wheat, and grass.

Now any kind of forest on the flank of the Sierra would be of inestimable value as a cover for the irrigating streams. But in our forests we have not only a perfect cover, but also the most attractive and interesting trees in every way, and of the highest value, spiritual and material, so that even the angels of heaven might well be eager to come down and camp in their leafy temples.

Mr. Camminetti[1] said last winter that there were seventy-five actual farms included in the Yosemite National Park whose owners were all praying to have the boundaries so changed as to leave their farms out. But this is not so. On the contrary, there is little or nothing in the park that can properly be called a farm, but only garden-patches, small hay-meadows, and cattle-ranches; and all the owners, as far as I know, are rejoicing in their protection from the sheep scourge.

The two Sequoia National Parks are also protected by a troop of cavalry; but the grand Sierra Forest Reservation, extending from the south boundary of the Yosemite Park to the Kern river, is not yet protected. Many Government notices were nailed on trees along the trails as warnings to trespassers; but as there was no one on the ground to enforce obedience to the rules, cattle and sheep-owners have paid little or no attention to them.

Now, Mr. Runcie,[2] who is familiar with army affairs, and last summer spent some time with the troops guarding the sequoia parks, says that the troops stationed every summer in the sequoia parks could also effectually guard the great forest reserve at the same time, if only the military authority were extended over it. This we hope will be done. But we must remember that after all trespassers are kept off the parks and reservations and running fires prevented, much more will remain to be done. The underbrush and young trees will grow up as they are growing in Yosemite, and unless they are kept under control the danger from some chance fire, from lightning, if from no other source, will become greater from year to year. The larger trees will then be in danger. Forest management must be put on a rational, permanent scientific basis, as in every other civilized country.

1. **Mr. Camminetti:** California congressman who introduced a bill in 1893 to reduce the boundaries of Yosemite National Park.
2. **Mr. Runcie:** Member of the Sierra Club committee.

PART THREE

An Age of Reform

Responses to Industrial America

While the middle class flourished at the turn of the twentieth century, the labor movement grew on the recognition that "once a worker" most likely meant "always a worker," particularly for women, children, immigrants, and members of other groups for whom opportunities for a better life would not often materialize. Working conditions at the Triangle Shirtwaist Company offered a warning of the uneven effects of industrial growth. By the time the Triangle fire occurred, American society was only beginning to recognize the new workers in their midst and the peculiar dangers they faced. As they sewed garments that defined middle-class style in new but uninspected high-rise factory buildings, young immigrant women were risking their lives in unsafe conditions for low wages.

Nowhere were the perils and promises of the time more inextricably mixed than in the lives of new immigrants like those who wrote to the "Bintel Brief" advice column of the *Jewish Daily Forward* with questions about their attempts to adjust to and succeed in a new and often bewildering society. During this age of uncertainty and social insecurity, reformers of every variety emerged across the country. Led by young muckraking journalists like Jacob Riis and Ida M. Tarbell, who waged a moral campaign to bring order to the chaos of modern life, this movement also had its strange outsiders like Carrie Nation, whose reign of terror against saloon owners may have contributed to the passing of the Eighteenth Amendment, banning alcohol in 1919.

World War I multiplied both the perils and promises of American life. This war, like the Korean and Vietnam wars later on, stirred social discontent. The war exacerbated tensions between older Americans and immigrants, raising questions of who was an American (or an Irish American, a German American, and so on), who was loyal, and who was not; hundreds of socialists and antiwar activists like Kate Richards O'Hare were imprisoned for opposing the war—a stark contrast to the light punishments imposed on Nation for her "hatchetations."

Another major change wrought by the war was the movement of African Americans to Northern cities. As the letters assembled by Emmett J. Scott reveal, fresh opportunities in war industries combined with the depredations of the boll weevil on cotton crops stimulated a great folk migration. Further fueled by the next great war and the ensuing era of cold war prosperity, this population shift would transform race relations and the nature of American cities for generations to come.

The images in the Visual Portfolio "Urban Industrial America" (pages 139–46) illuminate this rich and frightening land of contrasts and show how photographers struggled to understand a new world in the making.

POINTS OF VIEW

The Triangle Shirtwaist Fire (1911)

14

Conditions at the Triangle Shirtwaist Company

Pauline Newman et al.

"I think if you want to go into the . . . twelve-, fourteen- or fifteen-story buildings they call workshops," New York City's fire chief testified in 1910, "you will find it very interesting to see the number of people in one of these buildings with absolutely not one fire protection, without any means of escape in case of fire." At the time, over half a million New Yorkers worked eight or more floors above ground level, beyond the eighty-five-foot reach of the firefighters' ladders. When the shirtwaist makers struck in 1909, they demanded improved safety and sanitary conditions as well as better wages. The strikers did not win most of their demands, and fire safety in particular did not improve.

On Saturday, March 25, 1911, the issues of the strike received renewed significance when fire broke out in the shop of the Triangle Shirtwaist Company on the eighth, ninth, and tenth floors of a modern, fireproof loft building in lower Manhattan. The number of exits was inadequate, doors were locked to prevent pilfering, other doors opened inward, and the stairwell had no exit to the roof. Hundreds of workers were trapped; within half an hour, 146 of them, mostly young immigrant women, had died. The owners of the Triangle Shirtwaist Company were later tried for manslaughter, found not guilty, and collected insurance to replace their factory.

Barbara Mayer Wertheimer, *We Were There: The Story of Working Women in America* (New York: Pantheon, 1977), 294–95; Leon Stein, *The Triangle Fire* (Philadelphia: Lippincott, 1962), 55–56, 59–60, 144–45, 191–92.

The fire evoked a public cry for labor reform. More than 120,000 people attended a funeral for the unclaimed dead. The International Ladies Garment Workers Union and the Women's Trade Union League, both supporters of previous strikes and safety protests, were now joined by New York City's leading civic organizations in protest meetings and demands—eventually heeded by the state legislature—for factory safety legislation.

In a speech many years later to a group of trade union women, Pauline Newman, who became the first woman organizer for the International Ladies Garment Workers Union, recounts what it was like to work at the Triangle Company. Kate Alterman, Anna Gullo, and Ida Nelson testified at the company owners' trial about their experience during that terrible half hour. Rose Schneiderman's speech at the elite memorial meeting held at the Metropolitan Opera House on April 2, 1911, to commemorate the victims created a sensation and began the twenty-nine-year-old Schneiderman's career in labor reform.

QUESTIONS TO CONSIDER

1. What were the main abuses that Pauline Newman reported?
2. How did Kate Alterman, Anna Gullo, and Ida Nelson manage to survive the fire?
3. Would a speech like Rose Schneiderman's help the cause of factory safety, or would it alienate potential supporters?

PAULINE NEWMAN

I'd like to tell you about the kind of world we lived in 75 years ago because all of you probably weren't even born then. Seventy-five years is a long time, but I'd like to give you at least a glimpse of that world because it has no resemblance to the world we live in today, in any respect.

That world 75 years ago was a world of incredible exploitation of men, women, and children. I went to work for the Triangle Shirtwaist Company in 1901. The corner of a shop would resemble a kindergarten because we were young, eight, nine, ten years old. It was a world of greed; the human being didn't mean anything. The hours were from 7:30 in the morning to 6:30 at night when it wasn't busy. When the season was on we worked until 9 o'clock. No overtime pay, not even supper money. There was a bakery in the garment center that produced little apple pies the size of this ashtray [*holding up ashtray for group to see*] and that was what we got for our overtime instead of money.

My wages as a youngster were $1.50 for a seven-day week. I know it sounds exaggerated, but it isn't; it's true. If you worked there long enough and you were satisfactory you got 50 cents a week increase every year. So by the time I left the Triangle Waist Company in 1909, my wages went up to $5.50, and that was quite a wage in those days.

All shops were as bad as the Triangle Waist Company. When you were told Saturday afternoon, through a sign on the elevator, "If you don't come in on Sunday, you needn't come in on Monday," what choice did you have? You had no choice.

I worked on the 9th floor with a lot of youngsters like myself. Our work was not difficult. When the operators were through with sewing shirtwaists, there was a little thread left, and we youngsters would get a little scissors and trim the threads off.

And when the inspectors came around, do you know what happened? The supervisors made all the children climb into one of those crates that they ship material in, and they covered us over with finished shirtwaists until the inspector had left, because of course we were too young to be working in the factory legally.

The Triangle Waist Company was a family affair, all relatives of the owner running the place, watching to see that you did your work, watching when you went into the toilet. And if you were two or three minutes longer than foremen or foreladies thought you should be, it was deducted from your pay. If you came five minutes late in the morning because the freight elevator didn't come down to take you up in time, you were sent home for half a day without pay.

Rubber heels came into use around that time and our employers were the first to use them; you never knew when they would sneak up on you, spying, to be sure you did not talk to each other during working hours.

Most of the women rarely took more than $6.00 a week home, most less. The early sweatshops were usually so dark that gas jets (for light) burned day and night. There was no insulation in the winter, only a pot-bellied stove in the middle of the factory. If you were a finisher and could take your work with you (finishing is a hand operation) you could sit next to the stove in winter. But if you were an operator or a trimmer it was very cold indeed. Of course in the summer you suffocated with practically no ventilation.

There was no drinking water, maybe a tap in the hall, warm, dirty. What were you going to do? Drink this water or none at all. Well, in those days there were vendors who came in with bottles of pop for 2 cents, and much as you disliked to spend the two pennies you got the pop instead of the filthy water in the hall.

The condition was no better and no worse than the tenements where we lived. You got out of the workshop, dark and cold in winter, hot in summer, dirty unswept floors, no ventilation, and you would go home. What kind of home did you go to? You won't find the tenements *we* lived in. Some of the rooms didn't have any windows. I lived in a two-room tenement with my mother and two sisters and the bedroom had no windows, the facilities were down in the yard, but that's the way it was in the factories too. In the summer the sidewalk, fire escapes, and the roof of the tenements became bedrooms just to get a breath of air.

We wore cheap clothes, lived in cheap tenements, ate cheap food. There was nothing to look forward to, nothing to expect the next day to be better.

Someone once asked me, "How did you survive?" And I told him, what alternative did we have? You stayed and you survived, that's all.

KATE ALTERMAN

At the Fire

Then I went to the toilet room. Margaret [Schwartz] disappeared from me and I wanted to go up Greene Street side, but the whole door was in flames, so I went and hid myself in the toilet rooms and bent my face over the sink, and then

I ran to the Washington side elevator, but there was a big crowd and I couldn't pass through there. Then I noticed someone, a whole crowd around the door and I saw Bernstein, the manager's brother, trying to open the door, and there was Margaret near him. Bernstein tried the door, he couldn't open it.

And then Margaret began to open the door. I take her on one side—I pushed her on the side and I said, "Wait, I will open that door." I tried, pulled the handle in and out, all ways and I couldn't open it. She pushed me on the other side, got hold of the handle and then she tried. And then I saw her bending down on her knees, and her hair was loose, and the trail of her dress was a little far from her, and then a big smoke came and I couldn't see.

I just know it was Margaret, and I said, "Margaret," and she didn't reply. I left Margaret, I turned my head on the side and I noticed the trail of her dress and the ends of her hair begin to burn. Then I ran in, in a small dressing room that was on the Washington side, there was a big crowd and I went out from there, stood in the center of the room, between the machines and between the examining tables.

I noticed afterwards on the other side, near the Washington side windows, Bernstein, the manager's brother throwing around like a wildcat at the window, and he was chasing his head out of the window, and pull himself back in—he wanted to jump, I suppose, but he was afraid. And then I saw the flames cover him. I noticed on the Greene Street side someone else fell down on the floor and the flames cover him.

And then I stood in the center of the room, and I just turned my coat on the left side with the fur to my face, the lining on the outside, got hold of a bunch of dresses that was lying on the examining table not burned yet, covered my head and tried to run through the flames on the Greene Street side. The whole door was a red curtain of fire, but a young lady came and she wouldn't let me in. I kicked her with my foot and I don't know what became of her.

I ran out through the Greene Street side door, right through the flames on to the roof.

ANNA GULLO

At the Fire

[T]he flames came up higher. I looked back into the shop and saw the flames were bubbling on the machines. I turned back to the window and made the sign of the cross. I went to jump out of the window. But I had no courage to do it. . . .

. . . I had on my fur coat and my hat with two feathers. I pulled my woolen skirt over my head. Somebody had hit me with water from a pail. I was soaked.

At the vestibule door there was a big barrel of oil. I went through the staircase door. As I was going down I heard a loud noise. Maybe the barrel of oil exploded. I remember when I passed the eighth floor all I could see was a mass of flames. The wind was blowing up the staircase.

When I got to the bottom I was cold and wet. I was crying for my sister. I remember a man came over to me. I was sitting on the curb. He lifted my head and looked into my face. It must have been all black from the smoke of the fire. He wiped my face with a handkerchief. He said, "I thought you were my sister." He gave me his coat.

I don't know who he was. I never again found my sister alive. I hope he found his.

IDA NELSON

At the Fire

I don't know what made me do it but I bent over and pushed my pay into the top of my stocking. Then I ran to the Greene Street side and tried to get into the staircase. . . .

[But where Anna Gullo had just exited, there was now a wall of fire.] I couldn't get through. The heat was too intense.

I ran back into the shop and found part of a roll of piece goods. I think it was lawn;[1] it was on the bookkeeper's desk. I wrapped it around and around me until only my face showed.

Then I ran right into the fire on the stairway and up toward the roof. I couldn't breathe. The lawn caught fire. As I ran, I tried to keep peeling off the burning lawn, twisting and turning as I ran. By the time I passed the tenth floor and got to the roof, I had left most of the lawn in ashes behind me. But I still had one end of it under my arm. That was the arm that got burned.

ROSE SCHNEIDERMAN

At the Memorial Meeting
at the Metropolitan Opera House

I would be a traitor to those poor burned bodies if I were to come here to talk good fellowship. We have tried you good people of the public—and we have found you wanting.

The old Inquisition had its rack and its thumbscrews and its instruments of torture with iron teeth. We know what these things are today: the iron teeth are our necessities, the thumbscrews are the high-powered and swift machinery close to which we must work, and the rack is here in the firetrap structures that will destroy us the minute they catch fire.

This is not the first time girls have been burned alive in this city. Every week I must learn of the untimely death of one of my sister workers. Every year thousands of us are maimed. The life of men and women is so cheap and property is so sacred! There are so many of us for one job, it matters little if 140-odd are burned to death.

We have tried you, citizens! We are trying you now and you have a couple of dollars for the sorrowing mothers and brothers and sisters by way of a charity gift. But every time the workers come out in the only way they know to protest against conditions which are unbearable, the strong hand of the law is allowed to press down heavily upon us.

---

1. **lawn:** A thin cotton or linen fabric.

Public officials have only words of warning for us—warning that we must be intensely orderly and must be intensely peaceable, and they have the workhouse just back of all their warnings. The strong hand of the law beats us back when we rise—back into the conditions that make life unbearable.

I can't talk fellowship to you who are gathered here. Too much blood has been spilled. I know from experience it is up to the working people to save themselves. And the only way is through a strong working-class movement.

15

A Fire Trap
William Gunn Shepherd

On the afternoon of March 25, 1911, when fire broke out in the loft building at Washington Place and Greene Street in lower Manhattan that housed the Triangle Shirtwaist Company, New York World *reporter William Gunn Shepherd (1878–1933) happened to be in the vicinity. Finding a telephone in a store across the street, he reported the scene before him to a relay of four men at the newspaper. Then the exhausted Shepherd returned to the* World *building further downtown at Park Row to rewrite his dispatches. Accompanying his story were pictures, diagrams of the scene, reports from other journalists, and a list of the dead. The first six pages of the newspaper's next edition were wholly given over to the fire.*

This article is a remarkably complete eyewitness account of a great public disaster. Given that it appeared in a conservative and respected newspaper, it suggests—both by what it says and what it does not—a great deal about how respectable people of the period thought about the victims and heroes of such an event.

QUESTIONS TO CONSIDER
1. What relationship does William Gunn Shepherd see between the fire and the earlier strike?
2. How did Shepherd deal with the issue of criminal liability?
3. Who does Shepherd believe are the victims, heroes, and villains in this tragedy, and why?

At 4.35 o'clock yesterday afternoon fire springing from a source that may never be positively identified was discovered in the rear of the eighth floor of the ten-story building at the northwest corner of Washington place and Greene street, the first of three floors occupied as a factory of the Triangle Waist Company.

At 11.30 o'clock Chief Croker made this statement:

New York World, March 26, 1911.

Every body has been removed. The number taken out, which includes those who jumped from the windows, is 141. The number of those that have died so far in the hospitals is seven, which makes the total number of deaths at this time 148.

At 2 o'clock this morning Chief Croker estimated the total dead as one hundred and fifty-four. He said further: "I expected something of this kind to happen in these so-called fire-proof buildings, which are without adequate protection as far as fire-escapes are concerned."

More than a third of those who lost their lives did so in jumping from windows. The firemen who answered the first of the four alarms turned in found 30 bodies on the pavements of Washington place and Greene street. Almost all of these were girls, as were the great majority of them all.

A single fire escape, a single stairway, one working passenger elevator and one working freight elevator offered the only means of escape from the building. A loft building under the specifications of the law, no other ways of egress were required, and to this fact, which also permitted the use of the building as a factory, the dreadful toll may be traced. Two other elevators were there, but were not in operation.

The property damage resulting from the fire did not exceed $100,000.

To accommodate the unprecedented number of bodies, the Charities pier at the foot of East Twenty-sixth street was opened, for the first time since the Slocum disaster,[1] with which this will rank, for no fire in a building in New York ever claimed so many lives before.

Inspection by Acting Superintendent of Buildings Ludwig will be made the basis for charges of criminal negligence on the ground that the fire-proof doors leading to one of the enclosed tower stairways were locked.

The list of dead and injured will be found on page 4.

STREETS LITTERED WITH BODIES
OF MEN AND WOMEN

It was the most appalling horror since the Slocum disaster and the Iroquois Theatre fire in Chicago. Every available ambulance in Manhattan was called upon to cart the dead to the Morgue—bodies charred to unrecognizable blackness or reddened to a sickly hue—as was to be seen by shoulders or limbs protruding through flame eaten clothing. Men and women, boys and girls were of the dead that littered the street; that is actually the condition—the streets were littered.

The fire began in the eighth story. The flames licked and shot their way up through the other two stories. All three floors were occupied by the Triangle Waist Company. The estimate of the number of the employees at work is made by Chief Croker at about 1,000. The proprietors of the company say 700 men and girls were in their place.

Whatever the number, they had no chance of escape. Before smoke or flame gave signs from the windows the loss of life was fully under way. The first

---

1. **Slocum disaster:** The *General Slocum*, an excursion steamship, caught fire in the East River in 1904, killing more than a thousand of its passengers and crew.

signs that persons in the street knew that these three top stories had turned into red furnaces in which human creatures were being caught and incinerated was when screaming men and women and boys and girls crowded out on the many window ledges and threw themselves into the streets far below.

They jumped with their clothing ablaze. The hair of some of the girls streamed up of flame as they leaped. Thud after thud sounded on the pavements. It is the ghastly fact that on both the Greene street and the Washington place sides of the building there grew mounds of the dead and dying.

And the worst horror of all was that in this heap of the dead now and then there stirred a limb or sounded a moan.

Within the three flaming floors it was as frightful. There flames enveloped many so that they died instantly. When Fire Chief Croker could make his way into the three floors he found sights that utterly staggered him—that sent him, a man used to viewing horrors, back and down into the street with quivering lips.

The floors were black with smoke. And then he saw as the smoke drifted away bodies burned to bare bones. There were skeletons bending over sewing machines.

The elevator boys saved hundreds. They each made twenty trips from the time of the alarm until twenty minutes later when they could do no more. Fire was streaming into the shaft, flames biting at the cables. They fled for their own lives.

Some—about seventy—chose a successful avenue of escape. They clambered up a ladder to the roof. A few remembered the fire escape. Many may have thought of it, but only as they uttered cries of dismay.

Wretchedly inadequate was this fire escape—a lone ladder running down a rear narrow court, which was smoke filled as the fire raged, one narrow door giving access to the ladder. By the scores they fought and struggled and breathed fire and died trying to make that needle-eye road to self-preservation.

Those who got the roof—got life. Young men of the University of New York Commercial and Law School, studious young fellows who had chosen to spend their Saturday afternoon in study, answered the yells for aid that came from the smoking roof by thrusting ladders from the upper windows of their class rooms to the frantic men and women on the roofs.

None of the fire-besieged hesitated an instant. In going down on all fours and struggling across these slender bridges—eighty feet above the paved court—to the out-thrust arms of the students. It is a fact that none of the men on the roof, wild with excitement as they were, made a movement toward the ladder till the girls had crossed to safety.

Those who did make the fire escape—and these were but the few who had, in spite of panic, first thought of it—huddled themselves into what appeared as bad a trap as the one from which they had escaped. They found themselves let down into an absolutely closed court; and when through the cellar of the Asch Building they sought to make their way to the street, they encountered on the ground floor iron shutters securely clamped into place.

For a time they stood around or knelt in prayer, not knowing when the burning building might crash in upon them. Some of these dashed back and screamed, in the hope of attracting the attention of the law students in the university building. But there were so many agonized cries ringing in the air that the youths never heard the shouts from below.

Those who had got down the fire escape and found themselves cut off from the street by the iron shutters rushed frantically back to the court and ran around distraught, until firemen putting their implements to the iron shutters rushed through the Greene street entrance. They herded the wild-eyed group to the street.

Shivering at the chasm below them, scorched by the fire behind, there were some that still held positions on the window sills when the first squad of the firemen arrived.

The nets were spread below with all promptness. Citizens were commandeered into the service—as the firemen necessarily gave their attention to the one engine and hose of the force that first arrived.

The catapult force that the bodies gathered in the long plunges made the nets utterly without avail. Screaming girls and men, as they fell, tore the nets from the grasp of the holders and the bodies struck the sidewalks and lay just as they fell. Some of the bodies ripped big holes through the life-nets.

The curious, uncanny feature about this deadly fire is that it was not spectacular from flame and smoke. The city had no sign of the disaster that was happening. The smoke of the fire scarcely blackened the sky. No big, definite clouds arose to blot out the sunshine and the springtime brightness of the blue above.

Concentrated, the fire burned within. The flames caught all the flimsy lace stuff and linens that go into the making of spring and summer shirt-waists and fed eagerly upon the rolls of silk.

The cutting room was laden with the stuff on long tables. The employees were toiling over such material at the rows and rows of machines. Sinisterly the spring day gave aid to the fire. Many of the window panes facing south and east were drawn down. Draughts had full play.

It was the first fire with heavy loss of life in a skyscraper factory building in this city, but it bore out Fire Chief Croker's predictions of several years' standing. These were that such a fire would absolutely mean disaster! The walls of such buildings are fireproof, but the contents of the buildings—as in this case—are highly inflammable. The fire, having no manner of eating into the walls, concentrates on all the food it can find in the interior. The result is a furnace, with the flames fighting upward till they strike the roof. Then the fire mushrooms and starts back down the walls.

This is what happened in the Asch Building yesterday. Before a curl of smoke sifted outward through the windows the flames had swept and swirled around the rooms and mercilessly killed.

FOUR THOUSAND OUT BEFORE THE FIRE

Four thousand workers most fortunately had left the building about an hour and a half before—had tripped along toward the east side laughingly, buoyantly. For this was their fine day—pay day. These were the girls and boys and men and women from the factories and waterooms on the seven lower floors and the shipping departments in the basement.

All the places except the Triangle Waist Company's factory closed down at 3 o'clock yesterday. The Triangle Waist Company does not recognize the union. Around their big shop a strike centered not long ago. The delay in the filling of orders caused by the strike had made it necessary for the toilers to work overtime. That was why they sat bent over their machines and otherwise were busy at their tasks yesterday afternoon.

Those of the Triangle factory had, many of them, drawn their pay. Detectives were placed on guard over the bodies till they were taken to the Morgue, lest vandals should seek to rob. But no such creature appeared on the scene of the disaster. When darkness came upon the rows of bodies huddled under brown tarpaulins the vigilance was renewed. But no ghoul attempted to prowl among the dead.

So swift and unwarningly did the fire come that the first man on the street aware of it saw no smoke at all. He saw only a girl standing on a window ledge on the ninth floor of the building, waving her arms and shrieking that she was going to jump. He yelled back at her to stand where she was. And then as he stared, wonderingly, he saw a mere puff of smoke, such as a man might blow from a cigarette.

This man, John Maron of No. 116 Waverly Place, suddenly took panic as he saw the girl lean far over the sill and come tumbling down, with a flutter of her skirts. He saw her fall past floor after floor and strike the pavement on her head.

A man who later gave his name as R. Garner, but would not tell his address, had seen Maron and heard him shout, without realizing what it meant until the girl's body on the pavement came across his vision. Then he too looked upward.

What he saw made him rush for the nearest fire box at an opposite corner, about one hundred feet away. He had seen countless windows crowded with white faces and he had heard a frantic, swelling call for help.

He tore at the key of the fire box. And he said last night that somehow before he turned he became conscious that there was a frightful rain of bodies from the windows.

The first fireman to arrive took but a single glance at the tall building, saw with a gasp the heap of bodies and rushed to summon all the help available. Police whistles began to shrill their calls, and from opposite buildings hundreds were leaning out of windows, shouting insanely in their agony at the sight.

It seemed a long time to the helpless watchers before wailing sirens of many fire engines, the rattling bells of patrol wagons and ambulances sounded near by. Reserve after reserve squad of police from everywhere in the city were shunted to the neighborhood. Fifteen ambulances took stations along Washington Place. Calls for more ambulances went out.

In less than half an hour ten thousand persons were pressing the swiftly constructed police lines. Thousands ran down the side streets from Broadway. A huge crowd lined along the lawns of Washington Square, peering down Washington Place. For the most part the crowd could barely see the evidence of the horror that had happened—could make out but vaguely the black objects on the water blackened sidewalks.

WOMEN GOT FIRST CHANCE
AT THE WINDOWS

From all that could be learned it appears that the men among these shirt waist workers were really men—pallid faced weaklings as they might have appeared as they threaded their way to the shop early yesterday morning. It appears that even the boys acted in fine, manly fashion.

Eye witnesses of those who saw the wild leaps from the windows declared that the girls were given first chance at even this miserable prospect of saving their lives. Men could be seen in the reddening rooms helping the girls to the window sills for a final breath of life sustaining air.

On the ledge of a ninth story window two girls stood silently watching the arrival of the first fire apparatus. Twice one of the girls made a move to jump. The other restrained her, tottering in her foothold as she did so. They watched firemen rig the ladders up against the wall. They saw the last ladder lifted and pushed into place. They saw that it reached only the seventh floor.

For the third time the more frightened girl tried to leap. The bells of arriving fire wagons must have risen to them. The other girl gesticulated in the direction of the sounds. But she talked to ears that could no longer hear. Scarcely turning, her companion dived head first into the street.

The other girl drew herself erect. The crowd in the street were stretching their arms up at her shouting and imploring her not to leap. She made a steady gesture, looking down as if to assure them she would remain brave.

But a thin flame shot out of the window at her back and touched her hair. In an instant her head was aflame. She tore at her burning hair, lost her balance and came shooting down upon the mound of bodies below.

ELEVATOR BOYS MADE TWENTY TRIPS

If it had not been for the courage of the elevator boys the disaster might have been doubly if not trebly appalling. These young men, John Vito and Joseph Gasper, ran their cars up and down until the shafts were ablaze. Each made no less than twenty trips up and down after the first alarm was given.

And Vito attributes fine heroism to Maurice Blanck and Isaac Harris, the owners of the Triangle Waist Company. He says the partners stood by the shafts, holding back men who would have pressed forward and calling to him to take only the women down. Vito showed bloody hands to indicate how he had fought back the few cowardly men who had tried to overrun the women.

Blanck's two little children and their governess were with him when the alarm came. He had just ordered a taxicab and was awaiting its arrival before starting for his home. Blanck and his children and his partner, Harris, managed afterward to make their way to the roof and the men handed the governess and the children over the ladder to the students of the University Law School and then themselves crawled to safety.

FOR CRITICAL THINKING

1. In 1991 twenty-five workers were killed at the Imperial Foods chicken processing plant in Hamlet, North Carolina, under nearly identical circumstances as those eighty years earlier in the Triangle Shirtwaist fire. While the owner of the plant received heavy punishment for locked fire doors and no safety inspection, relatively few people remember the event. What elements, besides the body count, made the Triangle fire such an important historic event?
2. Compare and contrast contemporary views with those of 1911 concerning the balance between the importance of government inspecting and regulating working conditions at privately owned enterprises and the importance of not hindering economic growth.
3. How does Shepherd's report compare with the survivors' accounts?

16

A Bintel Brief

Abraham Cahan

Years before Ann Landers, Dear Abby, Ask Amy, and other contemporary advice colum-
nists, there was "A Bintel Brief." In 1906 the Jewish Daily Forward, *a Yiddish-lan-*
guage newspaper addressing the more than half a million Jewish immigrants in New
York City, began running an advice column under a title that translates as "a bundle of
letters." The column spoke to Jews from Russia, Hungary, Poland, Romania, and the
Middle East, with different traditions and dialects as well as skills and opportunities,
struggling with one another as well as their new circumstances in some of the most crowded
urban neighborhoods in the world. These immigrants and their neighborhoods were
among the subjects of reform journalist Jacob Riis, whose images of poverty so influenced
Americans' vision of the cities. (See the Visual Portfolio "Urban Industrial America" on
pages 139–46.)

The editor of the Jewish Daily Forward *was Abraham Cahan (1860–1951),*
who also wrote several novels about immigrant life. Cahan contributed some of the let-
ters as well as the responses. "A Bintel Brief" gave advice on all kinds of personal prob-
lems. These excerpts from the early years of the column offer fascinating glimpses into
Jewish immigrant life at the turn of the century and speak of issues central to the expe-
riences of most immigrants.

QUESTIONS TO CONSIDER

1. What are the major tensions of immigrant life as revealed in the letters?
2. What values did Abraham Cahan represent in his answers?
3. How does Cahan's advice compare to that given today in similar newspaper columns and on daytime talk shows?

Worthy Editor,

We are a small family who recently came to the "Golden Land." My husband,
my boy and I are together, and our daughter lives in another city.

I had opened a grocery store here, but soon lost all my money. In Europe
we were in business; we had people working for us and paid them well. In short,
there we made a good living but here we are badly off.

Isaac Metzker, *A Bintel Brief: Sixty Years of Letters from the Lower East Side to the* JEWISH DAILY FOR-
WARD (New York: Doubleday, 1971), 42–44, 49–51, 54–55, 58–59, 63–64, 68–70, 109–10, 117–18.

My husband became a peddler. The "pleasure" of knocking on doors and ringing bells cannot be known by anyone but a peddler. If anybody does buy anything "on time," a lot of the money is lost, because there are some people who never intend to pay. In addition, my husband has trouble because he has a beard, and because of the beard he gets beaten up by the hoodlums.

Also we have problems with our boy, who throws money around. He works every day till late at night in a grocery for three dollars a week. I watch over him and give him the best because I'm sorry that he has to work so hard. But he costs me plenty and he borrows money from everybody. He has many friends and owes them all money. I get more and more worried as he takes here and borrows there. All my talking doesn't help. I am afraid to chase him away from home because he might get worse among strangers. I want to point out that he is well versed in Russian and Hebrew and he is not a child any more, but his behavior is not that of an intelligent adult.

I don't know what to do. My husband argues that he doesn't want to continue peddling. He doesn't want to shave off his beard, and it's not fitting for such a man to do so. The boy wants to go to his sister, but that's a twenty-five-dollar fare. What can I do? I beg you for a suggestion.

> Your Constant reader,
> F. L.

Answer:

Since her husband doesn't earn a living anyway, it would be advisable for all three of them to move to the city where the daughter is living. As for the beard, we feel that if the man is religious and the beard is dear to him because the Jewish law does not allow him to shave it off, it's up to him to decide. But if he is not religious, and the beard interferes with his earnings, it should be sacrificed.

Dear Editor,

For a long time I worked in a shop with a Gentile girl, and we began to go out together and fell in love. We agreed that I would remain a Jew and she a Christian. But after we had been married for a year, I realized that it would not work.

I began to notice that whenever one of my Jewish friends comes to the house, she is displeased. Worse yet, when she sees me reading a Jewish newspaper her face changes color. She says nothing, but I can see that she has changed. I feel that she is very unhappy with me, though I know she loves me. She will soon become a mother, and she is more dependent on me than ever.

She used to be quite liberal, but lately she is being drawn back to the Christian religion. She gets up early Sunday mornings, runs to church and comes home with eyes swollen from crying. When we pass a church now and then, she trembles.

Dear Editor, advise me what to do now. I could never convert, and there's no hope for me to keep her from going to church. What can we do now?

> Thankfully,
> A Reader

Answer:

Unfortunately, we often hear of such tragedies, which stem from marriages between people of different worlds. It's possible that if this couple were to move to a Jewish neighborhood, the young man might have more influence on his wife.

Dear Editor,

I am a girl from Galicia and in the shop where I work I sit near a Russian Jew with whom I was always on good terms. Why should one worker resent another?

But once, in a short debate, he stated that all Galicians were no good. When I asked him to repeat it, he answered that he wouldn't retract a word, and that he wished all Galician Jews dead.

I was naturally not silent in the face of such a nasty expression. He maintained that only Russian Jews are fine and intelligent. According to him, the *Galitzianer* are inhuman savages, and he had the right to speak of them so badly.

Dear Editor, does he really have a right to say this? Have the Galician Jews not sent enough money for the unfortunate sufferers of the pogroms in Russia? When a Gentile speaks badly of Jews, it's immediately printed in the newspapers and discussed hotly everywhere. But that a Jew should express himself so about his own brothers is nothing? Does he have a right? Are Galicians really so bad? And does he, the Russian, remain fine and intelligent in spite of such expressions?

As a reader of your worthy newspaper, I hope you will print my letter and give your opinion.

With thanks in advance,
B. M.

Answer:

The Galician Jews are just as good and bad as people from other lands. If the Galicians must be ashamed of the foolish and evil ones among them, then the Russians, too, must hide their heads in shame because among them there is such an idiot as the acquaintance of our letter writer.

Worthy Editor,

I am eighteen years old and a machinist by trade. During the past year I suffered a great deal, just because I am a Jew.

It is common knowledge that my trade is run mainly by the Gentiles and, working among the Gentiles, I have seen things that cast a dark shadow on the American labor scene. Just listen:

I worked in a shop in a small town in New Jersey, with twenty Gentiles. There was one other Jew besides me, and both of us endured the greatest hardships. That we were insulted goes without saying. At times we were even beaten up. We work in an area where there are many factories, and once, when we were leaving the shop, a group of workers fell on us like hoodlums and beat us. To top it off, we and one of our attackers were arrested. The hoodlum was let out on bail, but we, beaten and bleeding, had to stay in jail. At the trial, they fined the hoodlum eight dollars and let him go free.

After that I went to work on a job in Brooklyn. As soon as they found out that I was a Jew they began to torment me so that I had to leave the place. I have already worked at many places, and I either have to leave, voluntarily, or they fire me because I am a Jew.

Till now, I was alone and didn't care. At this trade you can make good wages, and I had enough. But now I've brought my parents over, and of course I have to support them.

Lately I've been working on one job for three months and I would be satisfied, but the worm of anti-Semitism is beginning to eat at my bones again. I go to work in the morning as to Gehenna,[1] and I run away at night as from a fire. It's impossible to talk to them because they are common boors, so-called "American sports." I have already tried in various ways, but the only way to deal with them is with a strong fist. But I am too weak and there are too many.

Perhaps you can help me in this matter. I know it is not an easy problem.

> Your reader,
> E. H.

Answer:

In the answer, the Jewish machinist is advised to appeal to the United Hebrew Trades and ask them to intercede for him and bring up charges before the Machinists Union about this persecution. His attention is also drawn to the fact that there are Gentile factories where Jews and Gentiles work together and get along well with each other.

Finally it is noted that people will have to work long and hard before this senseless racial hatred can be completely uprooted.

Worthy Editor,

I was born in America and my parents gave me a good education. I studied Yiddish and Hebrew, finished high school, completed a course in bookkeeping and got a good job. I have many friends, and several boys have already proposed to me.

Recently I went to visit my parents' home in Russian Poland. My mother's family in Europe had invited my parents to a wedding, but instead of going themselves, they sent me. I stayed at my grandmother's with an aunt and uncle and had a good time. Our European family, like my parents, are quite well off and they treated me well. They indulged me in everything and I stayed with them six months.

---

1. **Gehenna:** Hell.

It was lively in the town. There were many organizations and clubs and they all accepted me warmly, looked up to me—after all, I was a citizen of the free land, America. Among the social leaders of the community was an intelligent young man, a friend of my uncle's, who took me to various gatherings and affairs.

He was very attentive, and after a short while he declared his love for me in a long letter. I had noticed that he was not indifferent to me, and I liked him as well. I looked up to him and respected him, as did all the townsfolk. My family became aware of it, and when they spoke to me about him, I could see they thought it was a good match.

He was handsome, clever, educated, a good talker and charmed me, but I didn't give him a definite answer. As my love for him grew, however, I wrote to my parents about him, and then we became officially engaged.

A few months later we both went to my parents in the States and they received him like their own son. My bridegroom immediately began to learn English and tried to adjust to the new life. Yet when I introduced him to my friends they looked at him with disappointment. "This 'greenhorn'[2] is your fiancé?" they asked. I told them what a big role he played in his town, how everyone respected him, but they looked at me as if I were crazy and scoffed at my words.

At first I thought, Let them laugh, when they get better acquainted with him they'll talk differently. In time, though, I was affected by their talk and began to think, like them, that he really was a "greenhorn" and acted like one.

In short, my love for him is cooling off gradually. I'm suffering terribly because my feelings for him are changing. In Europe, where everyone admired him and all the girls envied me, he looked different. But, here, I see before me another person.

I haven't the courage to tell him, and I can't even talk about it to my parents. He still loves me with all his heart, and I don't know what to do. I choke it all up inside myself, and I beg you to help me with advice in my desperate situation.

> Respectfully,
> A Worried Reader

Answer:

The writer would make a grave mistake if she were to separate from her bridegroom now. She must not lose her common sense and be influenced by the foolish opinions of her friends who divided the world into "greenhorns" and real Americans.

We can assure the writer that her bridegroom will learn English quickly. He will know American history and literature as well as her friends do, and be a better American than they. She should be proud of his love and laugh at those who call him "greenhorn."

---

2. **greenhorn:** Newly arrived immigrant.

Dear Editor,

Since I do not want my conscience to bother me, I ask you to decide whether a married woman has the right to go to school two evenings a week. My husband thinks I have no right to do this.

I admit that I cannot be satisfied to be just a wife and mother. I am still young and I want to learn and enjoy life. My children and my house are not neglected, but I go to evening high school twice a week. My husband is not pleased and when I come home at night and ring the bell, he lets me stand outside a long time intentionally, and doesn't hurry to open the door.

Now he has announced a new decision. Because I send out the laundry to be done, it seems to him that I have too much time for myself, even enough to go to school. So from now on he will count out every penny for anything I have to buy for the house, so I will not be able to send out the laundry any more. And when I have to do the work myself there won't be any time left for such "foolishness" as going to school. I told him that I'm willing to do my own washing but that I would still be able to find time for study.

When I am alone with my thoughts, I feel I may not be right. Perhaps I should not go to school. I want to say that my husband is an intelligent man and he wanted to marry a woman who was educated. The fact that he is intelligent makes me more annoyed with him. He is in favor of the emancipation of women, yet in real life he acts contrary to his beliefs.

Awaiting your opinion on this, I remain,

> Your reader,
> The Discontented Wife

Answer:

Since this man is intelligent and an adherent of the women's emancipation movement, he is scolded severely in the answer for wanting to keep his wife so enslaved. Also the opinion is expressed that the wife absolutely has the right to go to school two evenings a week.

Dear Editor,

I plead with you to open your illustrious newspaper and take in my "Bintel Brief" in which I write about my great suffering.

A long gloomy year, three hundred and sixty-five days, have gone by since I left my home and am alone on the lonely road of life. Oh, my poor dear parents, how saddened they were at my leaving. The leave-taking, their seeing me on my way, was like a silent funeral.

There was no shaking of the alms box, there was no grave digging and no sawing of boards, but I, myself, put on the white shirt that was wet with my mother's tears, took my pillow, and climbed into the wagon. Accompanying me was a quiet choked wail from my parents and friends.

The wheels of the wagon rolled farther and farther away. My mother and father wept for their son, then turned with heavy hearts to the empty house. They did not sit shive[3] even though they had lost a child.

I came to America and became a painter. My great love for Hebrew, for Russian, all of my other knowledge was smeared with paint. During the year that I have been here I have had some good periods, but I am not happy, because I have no interest in anything. My homesickness and loneliness darken my life.

Ah, home, my beloved home. My heart is heavy for my parents whom I left behind. I want to run back, but I am powerless. I am a coward, because I know that I have to serve under *"Fonie"*[4] for three years. I am lonely in my homesickness and I beg you to be my counsel as to how to act.

Respectfully,
V. A.

Answer:

The answer states that almost all immigrants yearn deeply for dear ones and home at first. They are compared with plants that are transplanted to new ground. At first it seems that they are withering, but in time most of them revive and take root in the new earth.

The advice to this young man is that he must not consider going home, but try to take root here. He should try to overcome all these emotions and strive to make something of himself so that in time he will be able to bring his parents here.

---

3. **shive:** Period of mourning.
4. *"Fonie":* The czar.

17

Letters from the Great Migration

Emmett J. Scott et al.

These letters to the newspaper the Chicago Defender, *collected by the distinguished African American educator and editor Emmett J. Scott (1873–1957), reflect one of the most important events of American social history, the "great migration" of about half a million African Americans largely from the rural South to Northern cities early in the twentieth century. World War I, both by stimulating business and by cutting off immigration from Europe, created opportunities such as had never before existed for African Americans. The widespread circulation of Chicago newspapers throughout the South, particularly the* Defender, *gave African Americans in the South a picture of the thriving economies and available jobs in Chicago and other Northern cities.*

There were numerous reasons why African Americans sought to escape the South: Jim Crow, political disenfranchisement, lynching and other forms of mob violence, and more immediately, injury to the rural economy from floods and boll weevil infestations. The migration northward was a great, leaderless folk movement—the individual decisions of hundreds of thousands to flee the South by whatever means they could find in search of a world offering better schools, greater personal safety and dignity, and the chance for economic improvement.

The migration had enormous long-term effects. In the next half century, six million African Americans left the South, most moving to cities. The migration brought political power and cultural authority to black America and moved many blacks into the American middle class. It also provoked race riots, created vast ghettos, and influenced white movement to segregated suburbs.

QUESTIONS TO CONSIDER

1. What were the main purposes of the letters to the *Defender*?
2. What were the hopes of these letter writers?
3. To what extent do you think these hopes were realistic?

Sherman, Ga., Nov. 28, 1916

Dear Sir: This letter comes to ask for all infirmations concerning employment in your connection in the warmest climate. Now I am in a family of (11) eleven

Emmett J. Scott, "Letters of Negro Migrants of 1916–1918," *Journal of Negro History* (July 1919): 177–80.

more or less boys and girls (men and women) mixed sizes who want to go north as soon as arrangements can be made and employment given places for shelter and so on (etc) now this are farming people they were raised on the farm and are good farm hands I of course have some experience and qualefication as a coman school teacher and hotel waiter and along few other lines.

I wish you would write me at your first chance and tell me if you can give us employment at what time and about what wages will you pay and what kind of arrangement can be made for our shelter. Tell me when can you best use us now or later.

Will you send us tickets if so on what terms and at what price what is the cost per head and by what route should we come. We are Negroes and try to show ourselves worthy of all we may get from any friendly source we endeavor to be true to all good causes, if you can we thank you to help us to come north as soon as you can.

Anniston, Ala., April 23, 1917

Dear Sir: Please gave me some infamation about coming north i can do any kind of work from a truck gardin[1] to farming i would like to leave here and i cant make no money to leave I ust make enough to live one please let me here from you at once i want to get where i can put my children in schol.

Brookhaven, Miss., April 24, 1917

Gents: The cane growers of Louisiana have stopped the exodus from New Orleans, claiming shortage of labor which will result in a sugar famine.

Now these laborers thus employed receive only 85 cents a day and the high cost of living makes it a serious question to live.

There is a great many race people around here who desires to come north but have waited rather late to avoid car fare, which they have not got. isnt there some way to get the concerns who wants labor, to send passes here or elsewhere so they can come even if they have to pay out of the first months wages? Please done publish this letter but do what you can towards helping them to get away. If the R. R. Co. would run a low rate excursion they could leave that way. Please ans.

Savannah, Ga., April 24, 1917

Sir: I saw an advertisement in the Chicago Ledger where you would send tickets to any one desireing to come up there. I am a married man with a wife only, and I am 38 years of age, and both of us have so far splendid health, and would like very much to come out there provided we could get good employment regarding the advertisement.

Fullerton, La., April 28, 1917

Dear sir: I was reading about you was neading labor ninety miles of Chicago what is the name of the place and what R R extends ther i wants to come north

---

1. **truck gardin:** "Truck garden," i.e., a garden given over to producing vegetables for the market.

and i wants a stedy employment ther what doe you pay per day i dont no anything about molding works but have been working around machinery for 10 years. Let me no what doe you pay for such work and can you give me a job of that kind or a job at common labor and let me no your prices and how many hours for a day.

Atlanta, Ga., April 30, 1917

Dear Sir: In reading the Chicago Defender I find that there are many jobs open for workmen, I wish that you would or can secure me a position in some of the northern cities; as a workman and not as a loafer. One who is willing to do any kind of hard in side or public work, have had broad experience in machinery and other work of the kind. A some what alround man can also cook, well trained devuloped man; have travel extensively through the western and southern states; A good strong *morial religious* man no habits. I will accept transportation on advance and deducted from my wages later. It does not matter where, that is; as to city, country, town or state since you secure the positions. I am quite sure you will be delighted in securing a position for a man of this description. I'll assure you will not regret of so doing. Hoping to hear from you soon.

Houston, Tx., April 30, 1917

Dear Sir: wanted to leave the South and Go any Place where a man will be any thing Except a Ker I thought would write you for Advise as where would be a Good Place for a Comporedly young man That want to Better his Standing who has a very Promising young Family.

I am 30 years old and have Good Experience in Freight Handler and Can fill Position from Truck to Agt.

would like Chicago or Philadelphia But I dont Care where so long as I Go where a man is a man.

Beaumont, Texas, May 7, 1917

Dear Sir: I see in one of your recent issue of collored men woanted in the North I wish you would help me to get a position in the North I have no trade I have been working for one company eight years and there is no advancement here for me and I would like to come where I can better my condition I woant work and not affraid to work all I wish is a chance to make good. I believe I would like machinist helper or Molder helper. If you can help me in any way it will be highly appreciate hoping to hear from you soon

18

The Trial of Kate Richards O'Hare
Kate Richards O'Hare et al.

In 1917 and 1918, the U.S. Congress passed Woodrow Wilson's Espionage and Sedition Acts, providing up to twenty years in prison to all who would "willfully obstruct the recruiting or enlistment service of the United States" or use seditious language about the form of government. These acts, passed during World War I, were directed primarily at the Socialist Party of America, which in recent years had become a third national party, garnering almost a million votes in the 1912 presidential election. In 1917 its membership voted to oppose the war, declaring it of benefit to capitalists, not workers, a stand which led to the imprisonment of hundreds of militants and party leaders.

Kate Richards O'Hare, known as "red Kate," was a fiery leader of the Socialist Party whose evangelical rhetoric had converted poor farmers across the Plains states to socialism. Committed to ending what she believed to be an immoral war, O'Hare had already given dozens of speeches in small towns across America by the time the Espionage Act was passed. Not until July 17, 1917, when she spoke at Bowman, North Dakota, did the law catch up with her. North Dakota was at the time a center of socialism and populism. In 1915 the Nonpartisan League, a broad farmers' movement that included many socialists, swept into power in the state. Though not explicitly antiwar, the Nonpartisan League had gained popularity partially through its intense criticism of war profiteering. The league's major party enemies, the Democrats, seeking to identify the league with O'Hare's "unpatriotic" opposition to the war, made an issue of her speech, leading to her arrest for obstructing recruitment and enlistments in the armed forces.

At her trial O'Hare faced a judge who had made public statements against both socialism and women who were active in public life. Her jury, selected from a county populated by impoverished farmers, was composed of twelve conservative businessmen. She was found guilty and sentenced to five years in prison. Her appeal was rejected by a higher court and she served fourteen months in prison before her sentence was commuted by the Department of Justice in accordance with a nationwide amnesty.

Upon release she helped lead the 1920 presidential campaign of fellow Espionage Act prisoner Eugene V. Debs, who garnered over 900,000 votes from his prison cell. O'Hare's incarceration had made her an ardent advocate of prison reform, a cause she

---

The Trial of Kate Richards O'Hare for Disloyalty, Bismarck, North Dakota, 1917, Hon. Martin J. Wade, Judge, reprinted in Robert Marcus and Anthony Marcus, eds., *On Trial: American History through Court Proceedings and Hearings*, Vol. 2 (St. James, N.Y.: Brandywine Press, 1998), 96–98, 100–104.

remained active in until her death in 1948. She also founded a school for workers' education and campaigned for her fellow socialist Upton Sinclair in his 1934 race for governor of California.

QUESTIONS TO CONSIDER

1. Why did Kate Richards O'Hare oppose America's involvement in World War I?
2. What was O'Hare's defense at her trial?
3. Did O'Hare believe that she was serving her country?
4. Do you think O'Hare received a fair trial?

Mr. Hildreth.[1] Gentlemen of the jury: The Congress of the United States declared war on Germany on the 6th day of April, 1917. The purposes of that war are known to all men. It is to settle the great question as to whether democracy shall rule the world or autocracy. Our soldiers are now crossing the seas. Back of the men who go into the line of entrenchments to do or die must rest the great reserve forces of the Nation.

Our government has called to the colors under the draft act young men between the ages of 21 and 31 years. The man power of the Nation not only is involved, the resources of the Nation are not only involved, but greater than all of these elements of national strength is the spirit of our people. Whatever tends to destroy the spirit of the people, the patriotism of the people, to lessen it here at home while our troops are fighting the battles of the Nation in Europe, lessens our strength as a Nation, minimizes the patriotism of our people, and contributes in no small degree to strengthening the armies of the Central Powers.

One of the methods that have been used in the past in the wars of the Republic to injure the patriotism of the people has been the abuse of free speech. In every war we have been engaged in we have been confronted with the propagandist, the agitator, and the corruptionist. These forces have made it difficult for us to win battles, have prolonged wars, injured the unity of the Nation and been destructive of complete success on the battlefield. It was true of the Revolutionary War, the War of 1812, the Mexican War, and the great Rebellion; and it is true today that in this country, where we have a written Constitution, trial by jury, freedom of the press, and liberty of speech, we are met with a hostility on our own shores far more dangerous than the guns of our European foes.

This great evil was known to all men. Therefore Congress, on the 15th day of June, 1917, passed this Espionage act, and the defendant is charged in this indictment with having violated that act.

She went to Bowman and before an audience of from 100 to 150 people made a speech which, in some respects, has no parallel in the English language. She said: "Any person who enlists in the army of the United States of America

---

1. **Mr. Hildreth:** Melvin Hildreth, the prosecuting attorney.

will be used for fertilizer, and that is all that he is good for; and the women of the United States are nothing more or less than brood sows to raise children to get into the army and be made into fertilizer." Search the annals of history and you will find no parallel in any country in the world. It was a direct blow at the spirit of the people, at the patriotism of the people. It was made intentionally and for the purpose charged. It was made to willfully obstruct the enlistment service of the United States, to the injury of the service of the United States, and to obstruct the recruiting service of the United States. . . .

This lecture, this speech, stirred this Commonwealth as no other speech. Why? Because this woman had gone upon the rostrum and, before the people of a great country, had instilled in their hearts and minds that this was [the financier J. P.] Morgan's war and not the war of the United States; that this was a war to protect the investments of financiers and not the democracy of the world; that this was a war that was brought about by moneyed interests; that this was a war not intended to break down the autocracy of Europe, but to build up the moneyed interests of the country; that this war was unjust and was being waged for that purpose and that alone, when she knew that the United States had suffered injury after injury at the hands of the German Government, when she knew that its ships that had a right to sail upon the seas had been sunk and the bodies of thousands of men, women, and children consigned to a watery grave under circumstances of the greatest atrocity and in violation of every principle of the laws of nations and of humanity. And yet she was telling the people that this was a war not in the defense of the American people on the sea and on the land, but that it was a war for the benefit of the moneyed interests of the country. False and pernicious doctrine! A doctrine that, if instilled in the minds of the people of this country, would prevent us from raising armies and navies and would be more potential in behalf of the Central Powers than the soldiers that are across the seas to fight the battles of the Republic. That was her attitude; that was her position; and that is her position here today. She rather justifies her position. She declares that it was a war in behalf of special interests, and not one for the cause of the people of the earth.

Gentlemen of the jury, we are not concerned with the politics of this defendant. We are indifferent as to whether she is a Socialist, a Democrat, or a Republican. But we are not indifferent to her violation of this statute which forbade her efforts upon the rostrum to carry out the evil intentions which this statute was aimed to prevent. . . .

Gentlemen of the jury, this case is one of the most important that has ever been tried in the United States. The defendant made her speech on the 17th of July, 1917. She has repeated that speech in many places throughout this Commonwealth. Here in this State, where its men and women have been taught to love the land of their adoption, where men and women have been taught that under our system of free schools, universities, and where a million church spires point to heaven, she would instill in the minds of the young, not the patriotism of the fathers of this Republic but the zeal of those who would destroy this Government, destroy its institutions, and drag this flag in the dust of Socialism.

Take the case. Render such a verdict that when the hand that shall write it is traceless in the grave it shall live the embodiment of the hope of a free people and a monument to the stability of our institutions. . . .

THE VERDICT AND SENTENCE

The *Jury* retired, and after a short time, returned to the court room. The foreman handed the following written verdict to the clerk: "We, the jury, find the defendant *guilty* as charged in the indictment.—A.L. Peart, Foreman."

JUDGE WADE. Is there anything to be said now why sentence should not be imposed upon this defendant?

Mrs. O'Hare. Yes, your Honor: I was taught in high school that law was pure logic. Abstract law may be pure logic but the application of the law of testimony in this case seems to have gone far afield from logic. As your Honor knows, I am a professional woman, following the profession of delivering lectures whereby I hope to induce my hearers to study the philosophy of socialism. In the regular course of my profession and work I delivered during this year lectures all over the United States—in North Carolina when the draft riots were at their height; in Arizona two or three days following the deportations from Bisbee,[2] and on the day when the strike vote was taken, when excitement ran high and passions were having their sway; in San Francisco during the Mooney[3] case, and in Portland, Idaho, and the Northwestern lumber regions during the great I. W. W. [Industrial Workers of the World] excitement; and at all of these lectures conditions were as tense as conditions could be. The men who were in the employ of the United States in the Department of Justice were present at my meetings. These men were trained, highly efficient, and highly paid, detectors of crime and criminals. In all these months, when my lecture was under the scrutiny of this kind of men, there was no suggestion at any time that there was anything in it that was objectionable, treasonable or seditious. It was the custom of my meetings to send complimentary tickets to the district attorney and the marshal and deputy marshal of the district in order that they might hear the lecture.

And then in the course of the trip I landed at Bowman—a little, sordid, wind-blown, sun-blistered, frost-scarred town on the plains of Western Dakota. There was nothing unusual in my visit to Bowman, except the fact that it was unusual to make a town of this size. The reason I did was because there was one man whose loyalty and faithfulness and unselfish service to the cause to which I had given my life wanted me to come, and I felt he had a right to demand my services. I delivered my lecture there just as I had delivered it many, many times

---

2. **Bisbee:** In the Bisbee Deportation of 1917, more than one thousand striking miners and supporters were kidnapped by vigilantes and taken in cattle cars two hundred miles across the desert to New Mexico.
3. **Mooney:** Tom Mooney, West Coast labor leader thought to have been framed in a terror bombing case.

before. There was nothing in the audience that was unusual except the fact that it was a small audience — a solid, substantial, stolid type of farmer crowd. There was not the great enthusiasm that had prevailed at many of my meetings. There was nothing to stir me or arouse me or cause me to make a more impassioned appeal than usual. There was nothing at all in that little sordid, wind-blown town, that commonplace audience, that should have for a moment overbalanced my reason and judgment and common sense and have caused me to have been suddenly smitten with hydrophobia of sedition. But I found there were peculiar conditions existing at Bowman, and they are common to the whole state of North Dakota. In this State in the last year and a half the greatest and most revolutionary social phenomena that has occurred since the foundation of this Government, has taken place. The story is one that is so well known that I need spend little time on it. Here to these wind-blown, frost-scarred plains came men hard of face and feature and muscle who subdued this desert and made it bloom and produce the bread to feed the world; and these men, toiling in their desperate struggle with adverse conditions and with nature, gradually had it forced on their minds that in some way they were not receiving a just return for the labor expended; that after their wheat was raised and garnered in the processes of marketing, men who toiled not and suffered none of the hardships of production were robbing them of the product of their labor. . . .

And your Honor, it seems to me one of those strange grotesque things that can only be the outgrowth of this hysteria that is sweeping over the world today that a judge on the bench and a jury in the box and a prosecuting attorney should attempt to usurp the prerogatives of God Almighty and look down into the heart of a human being and decide what motives slumber there. There is no charge that if my intent or my motive was criminal that that intent or motive ever was put into action — only the charge that in my heart there was an intent, and on that strange charge of an intent so securely buried in a human heart that no result and no effect came from it, I went to trial. . . .

Your Honor, there are 100,000 people in the United States who know me personally. They have listened to my voice, looked in my face and have worked side by side with me in every great reform movement of the last twenty years. My life has been an open book to them. They know down to this time I have given all that I am, all that I have, from my earliest girlhood, my girlhood, my young womanhood, even my motherhood. And, your Honor, no judge on earth and no ten thousand judges or ten thousand juries can ever convince these hundred thousand people who know me and have worked with me, and these millions who have read my writings, that I am a criminal, or that I have ever given anything to my country except my most unselfish devotion and service. You cannot convince the people who know me that I am dangerous to the United States Government. They are willing to admit I am dangerous to some things in the United States, and I thank God that I am. I am dangerous to the invisible government of the United States; to the special privileges of the United States; to the white-slaver and the saloonkeepers, and I thank God that at this hour I am dangerous to the war profiteers of this country who rob the people on the one hand and rob and debase the Government on the other, and then with their pockets and wallets stuffed with the blood-stained profits of war, wrap the sacred folds of the Stars and Stripes about them and shout their blatant hypocrisy to the world. You can convince the people that I am dangerous to these men; but no jury and no judge can convince them that I am a dangerous woman to the best interests of the United States. . . .

JUDGE WADE. It is never a pleasant duty for me to sentence any one to prison, and it certainly is not a pleasant duty to send a woman to prison; in the course of a trial, in all the years I have been on the bench in the State and Federal courts, I have made it a rule to try to find out who I am sending to prison, because we all make mistakes in this world at times. On the spur of the moment and under excitement, sometimes people are misled and commit offenses, and I have a hard time to reconcile my view of things with heavy sentences in those cases. Therefore, when this case was closed, I made up my mind that I would find out before imposing sentence in this case what were the activities of this defendant.

She testified here to her loyalty, and her support of the President, and I was hoping in my heart that somewhere I would find out that after all, she was such a woman as she has here pictured herself today, and that thus a small penalty for this offense might be adequate, because I realize this is a serious business. The Nation is at war. Every sane man and woman knows that there is only one way that this war can be won, and that is by having men and money and spirit. Those three things are necessary—spirit in the men, in the service, and spirit in the men and women behind the men. And it was because of these absolute essentials that Congress enacted the Espionage law, to reach out and take hold of those who are trying to kill the spirit of the American people, in whole or in part; trying to put in their hearts hate toward this Government and towards the officials of this Government conducting the war. And realizing that this was such a grave matter, I investigated it as far as possible to find out really what character of woman this defendant is, and had been, in her work. I heard the evidence in this case. I had nothing to do with the question of whether she was guilty or innocent. The jury settled that question, and in my judgment, settled it right.

I received information from another town in North Dakota, and this information was given in the presence of counsel for the defendant that at Garrison, in her lecture there, she made the statement that mothers who reared sons to go into the army, were no better than animals on a North Dakota farm; that this war was in behalf of the capitalists, and that if we had loaned our money to Germany instead of to the allies, we would be now fighting with Germany instead of with the allies. That she had boys, but that they are not old enough to go to war, but that if they were, they would not go. That the way to stop the war was to strike, and if the laboring men of this nation would strike, the war would soon be ended. Of course that was an *ex parte* matter. I have heard enough of testimony in my life, and I have seen enough of human nature to know that sometimes these things are stretched because of the feeling on one side or another of the question. So I thought I would go back and see what she had been doing. I wired the Postoffice Department at Washington, and I received a telegram which states:

Party is on editorial staff of publication, *Social Revolution*, Saint Louis, Missouri, which has been barred from the mails for gross violations of Espionage Act, and is successor to *Ripsaw*. The party appears to be of the extreme type who have attempted to handicap the Government in every way in the conduct of the present war.

That was only a statement of an opinion. I tried to get copies of the *Social Revolution*, and have not succeeded in getting either the number for June or July. At some period during that time the Postmaster General barred this from the mails. I have the April and May numbers. In April they published from Eugene Debs this statement:

As we have said, the bankers are for bullets—for the fool patriots that enlist at paupers' wages to stop the bullets, while the bankers clip coupons, boost food prices, increase dividends, and pile up millions and billions for themselves. Say, Mr. Workingman, suppose you have sense enough to be as patriotic as the banker, but not a bit more so. When you see the bankers on the firing line with guns in their hands ready to stop bullets as well as start them, then it is time enough for you to be seized with the patriotic itch and have yourself shot into a crazy-quilt for their profit and glory. Don't you take a fit and rush to the front until you see them there. They own the country and if they don't set the example of fighting for it, why should you?

This was in April, before the war was declared. Up to that time I realize that every person in this country had the right to discuss the war, express their opinions against the war, give any reasons they might have against the war. But you will find here in this statement the note which rings out from the statement of the defendant here in court this afternoon and which forms the foundation of the entire gospel of hate which she and her associates are preaching to the American people: That the Nation is helpless, prostrate, down-trodden by a few capitalists, and that the average man has not a chance on earth; that this war is a war of capitalism; that it was brought about by capital and in the interest of capital; that 100, 200, or 300 millionaires and billionaires if you please, in these United States dominate the souls and consciences of the other 99,000,000 American people.

19

Suppressing the "Dreadful Curse of Liquor"
Carrie Nation

Carrie Nation, America's most notorious temperance advocate, was born Carrie Moore in Kentucky in 1846 to a slave-owning family that had been impoverished by emancipation and disrupted by her mother's delusion that she was the Queen of England. In 1867 Nation married Dr. Charles Gloyd and later gave birth to a disabled daughter. The marriage soon fell apart because of Gloyd's severe alcoholism, which Nation believed had caused their daughter's disabilities. After her divorce, Nation worked as a teacher, struggling with poverty and caring for her disabled daughter. In 1877 she married David Nation, an itinerant minister, lawyer, newspaper editor, and failed farmer, who moved them from place to place, finally settling in Medicine Lodge, Kansas, where Carrie became interested in politics and, in 1894, helped organize a chapter of the Women's Christian Temperance Union (WCTU).

The WCTU was a nineteenth-century women's social reform organization that had won several important legislative victories in Kansas during the late 1880s, including raising the age of sexual consent in Kansas from ten to eighteen, banning the sale of tobacco to children under sixteen, and gaining women's suffrage in municipal elections. Nation soon became a recognized leader, preaching the evils of alcohol to schools across Kansas, writing a prohibitionist newspaper column, and organizing antidrinking conventions. However, it wasn't until June 1900 that Nation received what she said was a vision from God that called her to become the famous "smasher" of saloons.

Six feet tall and one hundred seventy-five pounds, she was large by the standards of her time and terrified drinkers in saloons with attacks that combined an element of surprise, her physical stature, and the frightening spike-ended hatchet she wielded that had replaced the rocks that she used in her first "smashings." A committed advocate of women's suffrage, she defended herself in court by arguing that she had been forced into "hatchetations" by having no right to vote on Prohibition. In the last years of her life, she published her own newspaper, The Hatchet, *sold souvenir mini-hatchets from her home at Hatchet Hall, and appeared in vaudeville. She died in 1911, nine years before the national legislation that would ban alcohol and grant women the right to vote. The document that follows describes how she began her ten year campaign as America's most famous prohibitionist, vandal, and social reformer.*

Carry Amelia Nation, *The Use and Need of Carry A. Nation, written by herself* (Topeka: F.M. Steves & Sons, 1905).

Questions to Consider

1. Why do you think that women like Carrie Nation often linked alcohol prohibition with women's suffrage?
2. What effect, positive and/or negative, do you think Carrie Nation's gender had on the success of her campaign?
3. What does Nation believe are the negative effects of alcohol on families, society, public health, and the political system?
4. Prohibition has been judged a failure by most historians. How do you think that Nation would answer historical critics?

At the time these dives were open, contrary to the statutes of our state, the officers were really in league with this lawless element. I was heavily burdened and could see "the wicked walking on every side, and the vilest men exalted." I was ridiculed and my work was called "meddler" "crazy," was pointed at as a fanatic. I spent much time in tears, prayer and fasting. . . .

On the 6th of June, before retiring, as I often did, I threw myself face downward at the foot of my bed and told the Lord to use me any way to suppress the dreadful curse of liquor; that He had ways to do it, that I had done all I knew, that the wicked had conspired to take from us the protection of homes in Kansas; to kill our children and break our hearts. I told Him I wished I had a thousand lives, that I would give Him all of them, and wanted Him to make it known to me, some way. The next morning, before I awoke, I heard these words very distinctly: "Go to Kiowa, and" (as in a vision and here my hands were lifted and cast down suddenly.) "I'll stand by you." I did not hear these words as other words; there was no voice, but they seemed to be spoken in my heart. I sprang from my bed as if electrified, and knew this was directions given me, for I understood that it was God's will for me to go to Kiowa to break, or smash the saloons. I was so glad, that I hardly looked in the face of anyone that day, for fear they would read my thoughts, and do something to prevent me. I told no one of my plans, for I felt that no one would understand, if I should.

I got a box that would fit under my buggy seat, and every time I thought no one would see me, I went out in the yard and picked up some brick-bats, for rocks are scarce around Medicine Lodge, and I wrapped them up in newspapers to pack in the box under my buggy seat. . . .

I was doing my own work at the time God spoke to me; cooking, washing and ironing; was a plain home keeper. I cooked enough for my husband until next day, knowing that I would be gone all night. I told him I expected to stay all night with a friend, Mrs. Springer. I hitched my horse to the buggy, put the box of "smashers" in, and at half past three o'clock in the afternoon, the sixth of June, 1900, I started to Kiowa. Whenever I thought of the consequences of what I was going to do, and what my husband and friends would think, also what my enemies would do, I had a sensation of nervousness, almost like fright, but as soon as I would look up and pray, all that would leave me, and things would look bright. And I might say I prayed almost every step of the way. . . . I got there at 8:30 P.M. and stayed all night with a friend. Early next morning I had my horse put to the buggy and drove to the first place, kept by Mr. Dobson.

I put the smashers on my right arm and went in. He and another man were standing behind the bar. These rocks and bottles being wrapped in paper looked like packages bought from a store. Be wise as devils and harmless as doves. I did not wish my enemies to know what I had.

I said: "Mr. Dobson, I told you last spring, when I held my county convention here, (I was W. C. T. U. president of Barber County,) to close this place, and you didn't do it. Now I have come with another remonstrance. Get out of the way. I don't want to strike you, but I am going to break tip this den of vice."

I began to throw at the mirror and the bottles below the mirror. Mr. Dobson and his companion jumped into a corner, seemed very much terrified. From that I went to another saloon, until I had destroyed three, breaking some of the windows in the front of the building. In the last place, kept by Lewis, there was quite a young man behind the bar. I said to him: "Young man, come from behind that bar, your mother did not raise you for such a place." I threw a brick at the mirror, which was a very heavy one, and it did not break, but the brick fell and broke everything in its way. I began to look around for something that would break it. I was standing by a billiard table on which there was one ball. I said: "Thank God," and picked it up, threw it, and it made a hole in the mirror. . . .

The other dive keepers closed up, stood in front of their places and would not let me come in. By this time, the streets were crowded with people; most of them seemed to look puzzled. There was one boy about fifteen years old who seemed perfectly wild with joy, and he jumped, skipped and yelled with delight. I have since thought of that as being a significant sign. For to smash saloons will save the boy.

I stood in the middle of the street and spoke in this way: "I have destroyed three of your places of business, and if I have broken a statute of Kansas, put me in jail; if I am not a law-breaker your mayor and councilmen are. You must arrest one of us, for if I am not a criminal, they are."

One of the councilmen, who was a butcher, said: "Don't you think we can attend to our business."

"Yes," I said, "You can, but you won't. As Jail Evangelist of Medicine Lodge, I know you have manufactured many criminals and this county is burdened down with taxes to prosecute the results of these dives. Two murders have been committed in the last five years in this county, one in a dive I have just destroyed. You are a butcher of hogs and cattle, but they are butchering men, women and children, positively contrary to the laws of God and man, and the mayor and councilmen are more to blame than the jointist, and now if I have done wrong in any particular, arrest me." When I was through with my speech I got in my buggy and said: "I'll go home."

The marshal held my horse and said: "Not yet; the mayor wishes to see you."

I drove up where he was, and the man who owned one of the dive-buildings I had smashed was standing by Dr. Korn, the mayor, and said: "I want you to pay for the front windows you broke of my building."

I said: "No, you are a partner of the dive-keeper and the statutes hold your building responsible. The man that rents the building for any business is no better than the man who carries on the business, and you are 'particepts criminus' or party to the crime." They ran back and forward to the city attorney several times. At last they came and told me I could go. As I drove through the streets the reins fell out of my hands and I, standing up in my buggy; lifted my hands twice, saying: "Peace on earth, good will to men." This action I know was done through the inspiration of the Holy Spirit. "Peace on earth, good will to men" being the result of the destruction of saloons and the motive for destroying them. . . .

This smashing aroused the people of the county to this outrage and these dive-keepers were arrested, although we did not ask the prosecuting attorney to get out a warrant, or sheriff to make an arrest. Neither did we take the case before any justice of the peace in Kiowa or Medicine Lodge, for they belong to the republican party and would prevent the prosecution. The cases were taken out in the country several miles from Kiowa before Moses E. Wright, a Free Methodist and a justice of the peace of Moore township.

The men were found guilty, and for the first time in the history of Barber County, all dives were closed. . . .

I will here speak of the attitude of some of the W. C. T. U. concerning the smashing. Most of this grand body of grand women endorsed me from the first. A few weeks after the Kiowa raid, I held a convention in Medicine Lodge. I got letters from various W. C. T. U. workers of the state that they would hold my convention for me. I said: "No, I will hold my own convention."

Up to this time, no one had ever offered to hold my convention, and I fully understood, although I did not say anything, that the W. C. T. U. did not want it to go out that they endorsed me in my work at Kiowa. The state president came to my home the first day of the convention. I believe this was done, thinking I would ask her to preside at the meeting, or convention. I was glad to see her and asked her to conduct a parliamentary drill. She came to me privately and asked me to state to the convention that the W. C. T. U. knew nothing about the smashing at Kiowa and was not responsible for this act of mine. I did so, saying the "honor of smashing the saloons at Kiowa would have to be ascribed to myself alone, as the W. C. T. U. did not wish any of it. . . .

The Free Methodists, although few in number, and considered a church of but small influence, have been a great power in reform. They were the abolitionists of negro slavery to a man, and now they are the abolitionists of the liquor curse to a man. They were also my friends in this smashing. Father Wright and Bro. Atwood were at the convention I speak of. Father Wright, who has been an old soldier for the defence of Truth for many years said to me: "Never mind, Sister Nation, when they see the way the cat jumps, you will have plenty of friends." The ministers were also my friends and approved of the smashing. . . .

I never explained to the people that God told me to do this for some months, for I tried to shield myself from the almost universal opinion that I was partially insane. . . .

[Nation was then sued for slander of the prosecuting attorney who she had accused of taking bribes and was found guilty.]

The jury brought in a verdict of guilty; but the damages to the character of this republican county attorney was one dollar, and of course I sent him the dollar, but the cost which was, including all, about two hundred dollars was assessed to me and a judgement put on a piece of property, which I paid off, by the sale of my little hatchets, and lectures. Strange these trials never caused me to become discouraged, rather the reverse. I knew I was right, and God in his own time would come to my help. The more injustice I suffered, the more cause I had to resent the wrongs. I always felt that I was keeping others out of trouble, when I was in. I had resolved that at the first opportunity I would go to Wichita and break up some of the bold outlawed murder mills there. I thought perhaps it was God's will to make me a sacrifice as he did John Brown, and I knew this was a defiance of the national intrigue of both republican and democratic parties, when I destroyed this malicious property, which afforded them a means of enslaving the people, taxing them to gather a revenue they could squander, and giving them political jobs, thus creating a force to manage the interest and take care of the results of a business where the advantage was in the graft it gave to them and the brewers and distillers.

In two weeks from the close of this trial, on the 27th of December, 1900, I went to Wichita, almost seven months after the raid in Kiowa. . . .

I took a valise with me, and in that valise I put a rod of iron, perhaps a foot long, and as large around as my thumb. I also took a cane with me. I found out by smashing in Kiowa that I could use a rock but once, so I took the cane with me. I got down to Wichita about seven o'clock in the evening, that day, and went to the hotel near the Santa Fe depot and left my valise. I went up town to select the place I would begin at first. I went into about fourteen places, where men were drinking at bars, the same as they do in licensed places. The police standing with the others. This outrage of law and decency was in violation of the oaths taken by every city officer, including mayor and councilmen, and they were as much bound to destroy these joints as they would be to arrest a murderer, or break up a den of thieves, but many of these so-called officers encouraged the violation of the law and patronized these places. I have often explained that this was the scheme of politicians and brewers to make prohibition a failure, by encouraging in every way the violation of the constitution. I felt the outrage deeply, and would gladly have given my life to redress the wrongs of the people. As Esther said: "How can I see the desolation of my people? If I perish." As Patrick Henry said: "Give me liberty or give me death."

I finally came to the "Carey Hotel," next to which was called the Carey Annex or Bar. The first thing that struck me was the life-size picture of a naked woman, opposite the mirror. This was an oil painting with a glass over it, and was a very fine painting hired from the artist who painted it, to be put in that place for a vile purpose. I called to the bartender; told him he was insulting his own mother by having her form stripped naked and hung up in a place where it was not even decent for a woman to be in when she had her clothes on. I told him he was a law-breaker and that he should be behind prison bars, instead of saloon bars. He said nothing to me but walked to the back of his saloon. It is very significant that the picture of naked women are in saloons. Women are stripped of everything by them. Her husband is torn from her, she is robbed of her sons, her home, her food and her virtue, and then they strip her clothes off and hang her up bare in these dens of robbery and murder. Well does a saloon make a woman bare of all things! The motive for doing this is to suggest vice, animating the animal in man and degrading the respect he should have for the sex to whom he owes his being, yes, his Savior also.

I decided to go to the Carey for several reasons. It was the most dangerous, being the finest. The low doggery will take the low and keep them low but these so-called respectable ones will take the respectable, make them low, then kick them out. A poor vagabond applied to a bar tender in one of these hells glittering with crystalized tears and fine fixtures. The man behind the bar said, "You get out, you disgrace my place." The poor creature, who had been his mother's greatest treasure, shuffled out toward the door. Another customer came in, a nice looking young man with a good suit, a white collar, and looking as if he had plenty of money. The smiling bar tender mixed a drink and was handing it to him. The poor vagabond from the door called out, "Oh, don't begin on him. Five years ago, I came into your place, looking just like that young man. You have made me what you see me now. Give that drink to me and finish your work. Don't begin on him."

I went back to the hotel and bound the rod and cane together, then wrapped paper around the top of it. I slept but little that night, spending most of the night in prayer. I wore a large cape. I took the cane and walked down the back stairs the next morning, and out in the alley I picked up as many rocks as I could carry under my cape. I walked into the Carey Bar-room, and threw two rocks at the picture; then turned and smashed the mirror that covered almost the entire side of the large room. Some men drinking at the bar ran at breakneck speed; the bartender was wiping a glass and he seemed transfixed to the spot and never moved. I took the cane and broke up the sideboard, which had on it all kinds of intoxicating drinks. Then I ran out across the street to destroy another one. I was arrested at 8:30 A.M., my rocks and cane taken from me, and I was taken to the police headquarters, where I was treated very nicely by the Chief of Police, Mr. Cubbin, who seemed to be amused at what I had done. This man was not very popular with the administration, and was soon put out. I was kept in the office until 6:30 P.M. Gov. Stanley was in town at that time, and I telephoned to several places for him. I saw that he was dodging me, so I called a messenger boy and sent a note to Gov. Stanley, telling him that I was unlawfully restrained of my liberty; that I wished him to call and see me, or try to relieve me in some way. The messenger told me, when he came back, that he caught him at his home, that he read the message over three times, then said: "I have nothing to say," and went in, and closed the door. This is the man who taught Sunday School in Wichita for twenty years, where they were letting these murder shops run in violation of the law. Strange that this man should pull wool over the eyes of the voters of Kansas. I never did have any confidence in him. . . .

Kansas has learned some dear lessons, and she will be wise indeed when she learns that only Prohibitionists will enforce prohibition laws. That republicans and democrats are traitors, and no one belonging to these parties should ever hold office, especially in Kansas.

Urban Industrial America

"The photographers of the American city during the nineteenth and early twentieth centuries," writes a historian of the photography of American urbanization, "were explorers in a cultural frontier.... They advertised and celebrated change—most fundamentally the transformation of America from a rural and agrarian nation to an urban and industrial one." By the early twentieth century New York City housed over four million people, Chicago over two million, and Philadelphia over one and a half million, making them among the largest cities in the world at that time. Urban life was strange and uncomfortable: vast crowds with languages and manners that were foreign to many Americans; furious construction; monumental traffic jams; dense jungles of overhead wires; and the dilemmas of slums, disease, crime, vice, and corruption. At the same time, the city swelled with promise and opportunity: it was a place to escape age-old restrictions; gain new experience; achieve wealth; secure education; discover new entertainments, like amusement parks, dance halls, concerts, and nickelodeons; or simply observe people in venues like the Bowery or Coney Island, where they seemed unusual or glamorous enough to be worth watching.

Photographers helped explore this new territory. Some celebrated the vitality of the urban scene, while others allied with journalists, urban planners, and social workers to bring the problems of the poor and the successes of reform movements to public gaze. Armed with important technological improvements—such as the more convenient dry plate photographic chemistry (which soon gave rise to the popular Kodak camera), crude forms of flash photography, and the halftone process that allowed the direct printing of photographs in books, newspapers, and magazines—these photographers documented their fascination with the changes overtaking the older American scene.

Each spread in this portfolio highlights the work of a different photographer from this classic age of reform and urban photography: Alvin Langdon Coburn, one of the first of his generation to depict the city and industry as subjects worthy of an artist; Jacob A. Riis, who wedded photography to social reform, calculatingly introducing scenes and themes new to the history of American photography; and Lewis Wickes Hine, who raised social reform photography to a high art.

Figure 1. Alvin Langdon Coburn, "Workers, New York," from Alvin Langdon Coburn, *New York*, 1910.

Alvin Langdon Coburn (1882–1936; Figures 1–3) was part of a group of early-twentieth-century photographers who wished to establish photography as a high art. Working in a style of softened focus that emulated aspects of the Impressionist movement, which was then dominating the other visual arts, Coburn turned his camera away from traditional subjects to the new vistas of the urban landscape. In what ways are Figures 1, 2, and 3 a critique of the modern urban life that was emerging at the time? In what ways are they a celebration? What visual elements do all three images share and how do these shared elements set a tone? How do the three images differ? How do you think Coburn's view of the evolving American city may have been different from

Above: **Figure 2.**
Alvin Langdon
Coburn, "Pillars of
Smoke," Pittsburgh,
1910.

Right: **Figure 3.**
Alvin Langdon
Coburn, "Skyscrap-
ers, Manhattan,"
from Alvin Langdon
Coburn, *New York*,
1910.

Left: **Figure 4.** Jacob A. Riis, "An Ancient Police Station Lodger with the Plank on Which She Slept at the Eldridge Street Station," c. 1898.

Below left: **Figure 5.** Jacob A. Riis, "Shoemaker in Ludlow Street Cellar," c. 1890.

Right: **Figure 6.** Jacob A. Riis, "Baxter Street Court (22 Baxter Street)," c. 1890.

Joseph Finnerty's or William Steinway's (Documents 8 and 9) in Part Two? How do you think the workers from the Triangle Shirtwaist Company (Document 14) would have felt about Coburn's representation of modern cities?

Unlike Coburn, who wanted to make art with his camera, journalist Jacob A. Riis (1849–1914; Figues 4–6) chose to use photography as a tool to provide powerfully convincing visual evidence to document the reality of urban slums. His images gave an emotional dimension to the statistics and facts that he brought before his audiences in lectures, articles, and books about social problems and the need for reform. Most Americans did not understand the impoverished, overcrowded, disease-ridden world of the slums. How did Riis's stark photographs

Above: **Figure 7.** Lewis Wickes Hine, "Doffer Girl in New England Mill, 1909," from *Lewis W. Hine's Workbooks for the National Child Labor Committee.*

Above right: **Figure 8.** Lewis Wickes Hine, "Young Women in Mill," c. 1910, from *Lewis W. Hine's Workbooks for the National Child Labor Committee.*

Below right: **Figure 9.** Lewis Wickes Hine, "Young Woman outside Mill," c. 1910, from *Lewis W. Hine's Workbooks for the National Child Labor Committee.*

support his view that these slum dwellers were not, as many middle-class and upper-class people supposed, victims of their own personal shortcomings?

Riis sometimes staged his photographs for greater effect. In what ways can you imagine this makes them a less accurate account of people's lives and in what ways do you think it might make them more accurate? In fact, Riis's campaign led to improvements in sanitation and the demolition of some of the more notorious tenements that he targeted. How do you think Riis's use of more static images than those of Langdon reflects their respective visions of urban life?

Between 1908 and 1917 Lewis Wickes Hine (1874–1940; Figures 7–9) traveled more than 50,000 miles as the staff photographer for the National Child Labor Committee to assemble "photographic proof" of the extent of child labor in the United States. All three of these prints are in his *Workbooks for the National Child Labor Committee,* which contain page after page of photographs like these, each with its own negative number so that concerned individuals and

groups could purchase copies of the images to use in articles, exhibitions, or posters that argued against the evils of child labor.

What similarities do you see among Figures 7, 8, and 9 and contemporary images circulated on the Internet by groups fighting child labor around the world today? In what ways are these photographs different?

FOR CRITICAL THINKING

1. What do you think the smoke in Figures 1, 2, and 3 symbolizes for the photographer, Alvin Langdon Coburn? What point is he making in choosing the subjects he does?
2. Hine, like Riis carefully posed his subjects. How do the various poses and subjects create a different feeling in viewers and how does this reflect similar and different approaches to promoting reform?
3. What details can you find to distinguish the different young mill women in Figure 8? (*Hint*: Look at their hands.) How does the young mill woman in Figure 9 relate to her place of employment?
4. In what ways do you think these three photographers shared a vision of cities and industry? In what ways do you think they differed? Which images do you think have the most impact today? Why?
5. Compare and contrast the way you imagine the subjects of Figures 4–9 would have felt looking at photos of themselves many years later.

PART FOUR

A New Society

Between the Wars

Worl War I and its social, political, and technological effects helped to transform the economic organization of America and move it into the "consumer" age. A rapidly expanding advertising industry encouraged Americans to embrace new consumer goods, a trend explored in the advertisements featured on pages 187–88. They responded with alacrity, purchasing cars, radios, and other items for their homes. Many developed doubts about whether the political and cultural values that had worked for a previous generation would work as well for them. These doubts fueled creativity in literature, the arts, and social movements, but also triggered defensive reassertions of nineteenth-century values. These social tensions were displayed in many arenas. The Scopes trial pitted William Jennings Bryan, the hero of rural America, against the renowned defense lawyer Clarence Darrow and other champions of modernism like the critic H. L. Mencken and underscored the chasm in terms of their religious and social values that separated fundamentalists and modernists. The Harlem Renaissance, which brought poet Langston Hughes to New York City, revealed new possibilities in race relations exhilarating to some Americans but frightening to many others. And Margaret Sanger's crusade for birth control challenged traditional attitudes in the sensitive areas of family planning and sexuality.

The assumption that modern American life meant unending growth, expansion, and prosperity came into question during the Great Depression of the 1930s. Although citizens everywhere encountered the same overwhelming set of events, the degree to which people were affected by the Depression varied. Some ruminated over fortunes lost on the stock market; others joined radical organizations; still others, like Morey Skaret, took to the road, drifting from place to place. And the labor movement evolved a new weapon, the sit-down strike, which created powerful industrywide unions that formed a national political base for labor that raised wages and involved millions of workers and community supporters like Genora Dollinger.

20

In Defense of the Bible

William Jennings Bryan and Clarence Darrow

In July 1925 John T. Scopes was tried for teaching the theory of evolution in the Dayton, Tennessee, high school. The first trial in American history to be broadcast nationally over radio, it was "monkey business" to some and "the trial of the century" to others.

The Tennessee legislature in March 1925 had passed the Butler Act, making it a crime to teach in any state-supported school (including universities) "any theory that denies the story of the Divine Creation of man as taught in the Bible, and to teach instead that man has descended from a lower order of animals." A few Daytonians decided to test the law and persuaded Scopes, a young local high school biology teacher, to become the defendant.

Larger forces, however, were at work. The Protestant churches were sharply dividing between fundamentalists who believed in the literal truth of the Bible and liberals who accepted the findings of science. The split corresponded to a division between urban and rural values, a division that was also sharply reflected in national, and especially Democratic Party, politics. The South was a stronghold of fundamentalism, and laws like the Butler Act had much support throughout the region.

A famous orator led each legal team. William Jennings Bryan (1860–1925), long identified with the values of the countryside, had been the Democratic Party candidate for president in 1896, 1900, and 1908 and had served as Woodrow Wilson's first secretary of state. Clarence Darrow (1857–1938) was a nationally famous trial lawyer and lecturer on evolution and various reforms. When the presiding judge, John T. Raulston, banned the use of expert witnesses on the theory of evolution, Darrow called Bryan himself to the stand as an authority on the Bible. Bryan agreed and the judge permitted the testimony to proceed—but without the jury, which the judge had ruled was not to decide matters of the truth of either evolution or the Bible but only whether Scopes had taught evolution to his high school class. Yet Darrow made it seem as if Bryan, fundamentalism, and perhaps even the Bible were on trial and revealed Bryan's spotty knowledge of scientific matters. The following day the judge changed his mind, expunged all of Bryan's testimony, and sent the case to the jury for the inevitable finding of Scopes's admitted guilt.

Sheldon Norman Grebstein, *Monkey Trial: The State of Tennessee vs. John Thomas Scopes* (Boston: Houghton Mifflin, 1960).

QUESTIONS TO CONSIDER

1. Why do you think William Jennings Bryan agreed to testify?
2. How could Bryan have made his arguments stronger? What values was he defending?
3. What do you think of Darrow's performance? Was he, as some have said, putting the Bible on trial? Was Darrow's devotion to science in any way deserving of challenge?

EXAMINATION OF W. J. BRYAN BY CLARENCE DARROW, COUNSEL FOR THE DEFENSE

The Court: The question is whether or not Mr. Scopes taught man descended from the lower order of animals.

Q: You have given considerable study to the Bible, haven't you, Mr. Bryan?

A: Yes, sir, I have tried to.

Q: Well, we all know you have; we are not going to dispute that at all. But you have written and published articles almost weekly, and sometimes have made interpretations of various things.

A: I would not say interpretations, Mr. Darrow, but comments on the lesson.

Q: If you comment to any extent, these comments have been interpretations?

A: I presume that any discussion might be to some extent interpretations, but they have not been primarily intended as interpretations.

Q: Then you have made a general study of it?

A: Yes, I have; I have studied the Bible for about fifty years, or some time more than that, but, of course, I have studied it more as I have become older than when I was but a boy.

Q: Do you claim that everything in the Bible should be literally interpreted?

A: I believe everything in the Bible should be accepted as it is given there; some of the Bible is given illustratively. For instance: "Ye are the salt of the earth." I would not insist that man was actually salt, or that he had flesh of salt, but it is used in the sense of salt as saving God's people.

Q: You believe the story of the flood to be a literal interpretation?

A: Yes, sir.

Q: When was that flood?

A: I would not attempt to fix the date. The date is fixed, as suggested this morning.

Q: About 4004 B.C.?

A: That has been the estimate of a man that is accepted today. I would not say it is accurate.

Q: That estimate is printed in the Bible?

A: Everybody knows, at least, I think most of the people know, that was the estimate given.

Q: But what do you think that the Bible, itself, says? Don't you know how it was arrived at?

A: I never made a calculation.

Q: What do you think?

A: I do not think about things I don't think about.

Q: Do you think about things you do think about?

A: Well, sometimes.

The Bailiff: Let us have order.

Mr. Darrow: Mr. Bryan, you have read these dates over and over again?

A: Not very accurately; I turn back sometimes to see what the time was.

Q: You want to say now you have no idea how these dates were computed?

A: No, I don't say, but I have told you what my idea was. I say I don't know how accurate it was.

Q: You say from the generation of man—

Gen. Stewart: I am objecting to his cross-examining his own witness.

Mr. Darrow: He is a hostile witness.

The Court: I am going to let Mr. Bryan control—

The Witness: I want him to have all the latitude he wants, for I am going to have some latitude when he gets through.

Mr. Darrow: You can have latitude and longitude.

The Court: Order.

Gen. Stewart: The witness is entitled to be examined as to the legal evidence of it. We were supposed to go into the argument today, and we have nearly lost the day, your Honor.

Mr. McKenzie: I object to it.

Gen. Stewart: Your Honor, he is perfectly able to take care of this, but we are attaining no evidence. This is not competent evidence.

The Witness: These gentlemen have not had much chance—they did not come here to try this case. They came here to try revealed religion. I am here to defend it, and they can ask me any question they please.

The Court: All right.

Mr. Darrow: Great applause from the bleachers.

The Witness: From those whom you call "yokels."

Mr. Darrow: I have never called them yokels.

The Witness: That is the ignorance of Tennessee, the bigotry.

Mr. Darrow: You mean who are applauding you?

The Witness: Those are the people whom you insult.

Mr. Darrow: You insult every man of science and learning in the world because he does not believe in your fool religion.

The Court: I will not stand for that.

Mr. Darrow: For what he is doing?

The Court: I am talking to both of you.

Gen. Stewart: This has gone beyond the pale of a lawsuit, your Honor. I have a public duty to perform under my oath, and I ask the Court to stop it. Mr. Darrow is making an effort to insult the gentleman on the witness stand and I ask that it be stopped, for it has gone beyond the pale of a lawsuit.

The Court: To stop it now would not be just to Mr. Bryan. He wants to ask the other gentleman questions along the same line.

Gen. Stewart: It will all be incompetent.

The Witness: The jury is not here.

The Court: I do not want to be strictly technical.

Mr. Darrow: Then your Honor rules, and I accept.

Gen. Stewart: The jury is not here.

Mr. Darrow: How long ago was the flood, Mr. Bryan?

A: Let me see Ussher's calculation[1] about it?

Mr. Darrow: Surely.

A: I think this does not give it.

Q: It gives an account of Noah. Where is the one in evidence? I am quite certain it is there.

The Witness: Oh, I would put the estimate where it is, because I have no reason to vary it. But I would have to look at it to give you the exact date.

Q: I would, too. Do you remember what book the account is in?

A: Genesis.

Mr. Hays: Is that the one in evidence?

Mr. Neal: That will have it; that is the King James Version.

Mr. Darrow: The one in evidence has it.

The Witness: It is given here, as 2,348 years B.C.

Q: Well, 2,348 years B.C. You believe that all the living things that were not contained in the ark were destroyed.

A: I think the fish may have lived.

Q: Outside of the fish?

A: I cannot say.

Q: You cannot say?

A: No, I accept that just as it is; I have no proof to the contrary.

Q: I am asking you whether you believe?

A: I do.

Q: That all living things outside of the fish were destroyed?

A: What I say about the fish is merely a matter of humor.

Q: I understand.

The Witness: Due to the fact a man wrote up here the other day to ask whether all the fish were destroyed, and the gentleman who received the letter told him the fish may have lived.

Q: I am referring to the fish, too.

A: I accept that as the Bible gives it and I have never found any reason for denying, disputing, or rejecting it.

Q: Let us make it definite, 2,348 years?

A: I didn't say that. That is the time given there [*indicating the Bible*] but I don't pretend to say that is exact.

Q: You never figured it out, these generations, yourself?

---

1. **Ussher's calculation:** A seventeenth-century Irish bishop, James Ussher, whose book, *The Annals of the Old Testament*, had calculated the age of the Earth to be about 4,000 years.

A: No, sir; not myself.

Q: But the Bible you have offered in evidence says 2,340 something, so that 4,200 years ago there was not a living thing on the earth, excepting the people on the ark and the animals on the ark and the fishes?

A: There have been living things before that.

Q: I mean at that time.

A: After that.

Q: Don't you know there are any number of civilizations that are traced back to more than 5,000 years?

A: I know we have people who trace things back according to the number of ciphers they have. But I am not satisfied they are accurate.

Q: You are not satisfied there is any civilization that can be traced back 5,000 years?

A: I would not want to say there is because I have no evidence of it that is satisfactory.

Q: Would you say there is not?

A: Well, so far as I know, but when the scientists differ from 24,000,000 to 306,000,000 in their opinion as to how long ago life came here, I want them to be nearer, to come nearer together, before they demand of me to give up my belief in the Bible.

Q: Do you say that you do not believe that there were any civilizations on this earth that reach back beyond 5,000 years?

A: I am not satisfied by any evidence that I have seen.

Q: I didn't ask you what you are satisfied with. I asked you if you believe it?

The Witness: Will you let me answer it?

The Court: Go right on.

The Witness: I am satisfied by no evidence that I have found that would justify me in accepting the opinions of these men against what I believe to be the inspired Word of God.

Q: And you believe every nation, every organization of men, every animal, in the world outside of the fishes—

The Witness: The fish, I want you to understand, is merely a matter of humor.

Q: You believe that all the various human races on the earth have come into being in the last 4,000 years or 4,200 years, whatever it is?

A: No, it would be more than that.

[Here Bryan and Darrow engaged in some calculations as to when man was created, according to the chronology Bryan was defending.]

Q: That makes 4,262 years. If it is not correct, we can correct it.

A: According to the Bible there was a civilization before that, destroyed by the flood.

Q: Let me make this definite. You believe that every civilization on the earth and every living thing, except possibly the fishes, that came out of the ark were wiped out by the flood?

A: At that time.

Q: At that time. And then whatever human beings, including all the tribes, that inhabited the world, and have inhabited the world, and who run their pedigree straight back, and all the animals, have come onto the earth since the flood?

A: Yes.

Q: Within 4,200 years. Do you know a scientific man on the face of the earth that believes any such thing?

A: I cannot say, but I know some scientific men who dispute entirely the antiquity of man as testified to by other scientific men.

Q: Oh, that does not answer the question. Do you know of a single scientific man on the face of the earth that believes any such thing as you stated, about the antiquity of man?

A: I don't think I have ever asked one the direct question.

Q: Quite important, isn't it?

A: Well, I don't know as it is.

Q: It might not be?

A: If I had nothing else to do except speculate on what our remote ancestors were and what our remote descendants have been, but I have been more interested in Christians going on right now to make it much more important than speculation on either the past or the future.

Q: You have never had any interest in the age of the various races and people and civilization and animals that exist upon the earth today, is that right?

A: I have never felt a great deal of interest in the effort that has been made to dispute the Bible by the speculations of men, or the investigations of men.

Q: Are you the only human being on earth who knows what the Bible means?

Gen. Stewart: I object.

The Court: Sustained.

Mr. Darrow: You do know that there are thousands of people who profess to be Christians who believe the earth is much more ancient and that the human race is much more ancient?

A: I think there may be.

Q: And you never have investigated to find out how long man has been on the earth?

A: I have never found it necessary—

Q: For any reason, whatever it is?

A: To examine every speculation; but if I had done it I never would have done anything else.

Q: I ask for a direct answer.

A: I do not expect to find out all those things, and I do not expect to find out about races.

Q: I didn't ask you that. Now, I ask you if you know if it was interesting enough or important enough for you to try to find out about how old these ancient civilizations were?

A: No; I have not made a study of it.

Q: Don't you know that the ancient civilizations of China are 6,000 or 7,000 years old, at the very least?

A: No; but they would not run back beyond the creation, according to the Bible, 6,000 years.

Q: You don't know how old they are, is that right?

A: I don't know how old they are, but probably you do. [*Laughter in the courtyard.*] I think you would give preference to anybody who opposed the Bible, and I give the preference to the Bible.

Q: I see. Well, you are welcome to your opinion. Have you any idea how old the Egyptian civilization is?

A: No.

Q: Do you know of any record in the world, outside of the story of the Bible, which conforms to any statement that it is 4,200 years ago or thereabouts that all life was wiped off the face of the earth?

A: I think they have found records.

Q: Do you know of any?

A: Records reciting the flood, but I am not an authority on the subject.

Q: Now, Mr. Bryan, will you say if you know of any record, or have ever heard of any records, that describe that a flood existed 4,200 years ago, or about that time, which wiped all life off the earth?

A: The recollection of what I have read on that subject is not distinct enough to say whether the records attempted to fix a time, but I have seen in the discoveries of archaeologists where they have found records that described the flood.

Q: Mr. Bryan, don't you know that there are many old religions that describe the flood?

A: No, I don't know.

Q: You know there are others besides the Jewish?

A: I don't know whether these are the record of any other religion or refer to this flood.

Q: Don't you ever examine religion so far to know that?

A: Outside of the Bible?

Q: Yes.

A: No; I have not examined to know that, generally.

Q: You have never examined any other religions?

A: Yes, sir.

Q: Have you ever read anything about the origins of religions?

A: Not a great deal.

Q: You have never examined any other religion?

A: Yes, sir.

Q: And you don't know whether any other religion ever gave a similar account of the destruction of the earth by the flood?

A: The Christian religion has satisfied me, and I have never felt it necessary to look up some competing religions.

Q: Do you consider that every religion on earth competes with the Christian religion?

A: I think everybody who does not believe in the Christian religion believes so —

Q: I am asking what you think?

A: I do not regard them as competitive because I do not think they have the same sources as we have.

Q: You are wrong in saying "competitive"?

A: I would not say competitive, but the religious unbelievers.

Q: Unbelievers of what?

A: In the Christian religion.

Q: What about the religion of Buddha?

A: I can tell you something about that, if you want to know.

Q: What about the religion of Confucius or Buddha?

A: Well, I can tell you something about that, if you would like to know.

Q: Did you ever investigate them?

A: Somewhat.

Q: Do you regard them as competitive?

A: No, I think they are very inferior. Would you like for me to tell you what I know about it?

Q: No.

A: Well, I shall insist on giving it to you.

Q: You won't talk about free silver,[2] will you?

A: Not at all. . . .

---

2. **free silver:** Backing the U.S. dollar with silver in addition to gold, a position Bryan advocated during his 1896 presidential campaign against William McKinley.

21

An Odd Eulogy for William Jennings Bryan

H. L. Mencken

Henry Louis Mencken (1880–1956) was one the most controversial figures of the 1920s. The acid pen of this journalist and author championed science, modern litera-ture, and urban sophistication while attacking religion and democracy in general and fundamentalism and political reform in particular. Beloved of college students who sought to shed the previous generation's Victorian values and described in 1926 as "the most powerful personal influence on this whole generation of educated people," Mencken was also roundly hated by representatives of older, rural values and of fundamentalism, the people who rallied behind William Jennings Bryan. "If a buzzard had laid an egg

---

American Mercury, October 1925, 158–60.

in a dunghill," wrote a minister in the Gospel Call, *"and the sun had hatched a thing like Mencken, the buzzard would have been justly ashamed of its offspring."*

It was Mencken who persuaded Clarence Darrow to enter the Scopes trial. "Nobody gives a damn about that yap schoolteacher," Mencken asserted. "The thing to do is make a fool out of Bryan." Darrow, who had earlier tangled with Bryan in newspaper debates over evolution, was pleased to oblige. Mencken supported the cause—and scandalized the locals—by reporting on the case from Dayton. Unfortunately, the responsibilities of editing his magazine, the American Mercury, *brought him back to Baltimore the weekend before Darrow's famous questioning of Bryan. But Mencken recovered from this missed opportunity a few days later when Bryan died in his sleep at Dayton. Mencken's perspective on the case is presented in this savage obituary. In private conversation, he was even more direct in assessing Bryan's death: "Well, we killed the son-of-a-bitch."*

QUESTIONS TO CONSIDER

1. How would you describe Mencken's view of Bryan? Can you arrive at an adjective to characterize it?
2. How did Mencken's literary style reinforce his views of society? Why, for example, does he refer to country wives as "unyieldingly multiparous," to religion as "purely ghostly concerns," and to conversation in small towns as "simian gabble"?
3. How serious do you think Mencken was about the danger of fundamentalism?
4. What strengths and weaknesses do you see in Mencken's way of fighting fundamentalism? Can you imagine better ways of convincing people?

I

Has it been marked by historians that the late William Jennings Bryan's last secular act on this earth was to catch flies? A curious detail, and not without its sardonic overtones. He was the most sedulous flycatcher in American history, and by long odds the most successful. His quarry, of course, was not *Musca domestica* but *Homo neandertalensis.* For forty years he tracked it with snare and blunderbuss, up and down the backways of the Republic. Wherever the flambeaux of Chautauqua[1] smoked and guttered, and the bilge of Idealism ran in the veins, and Baptist pastors dammed the brooks with the saved, and men gathered who were weary and heavy laden, and their wives who were unyieldingly multiparous and full of Peruna[2]—there the indefatigable Jennings set up his traps and spread his bait. He knew every forlorn country town in the South and West, and he could crowd the most remote of them to suffocation by simply winding his horn. The city proletariat, transiently flustered by him in 1896, quickly penetrated his buncombe and would have no more of him; the gallery jeered him at

---

1. **Chautauqua:** An adult education movement popular in the late nineteenth and early twentieth centuries.
2. **Peruna:** An infamous alcohol-based patent medicine.

every Democratic National Convention for twenty-five years. But out where the grass grows high, and the horned cattle dream away the lazy days, and men still fear the powers and principalities of the air—out there between the corn-rows he held his old puissance to the end. There was no need of beaters to drive in his game. The news that he was coming was enough. For miles the flivver dust would choke the roads. And when he rose at the end of the day to discharge his Message there would be such breathless attention, such a rapt and enchanted ecstasy, such a sweet rustle of amens as the world had not known since Johanan fell to Herod's headsman.

There was something peculiarly fitting in the fact that his last days were spent in a one-horse Tennessee village, and that death found him there. The man felt at home in such scenes. He liked people who sweated freely, and were not debauched by the refinements of the toilet. Making his progress up and down the Main Street of little Dayton, surrounded by gaping primates from the upland valleys of the Cumberland Range, his coat laid aside, his bare arms and hairy chest shining damply, his bald head sprinkled with dust—so accoutred and on display he was obviously happy. He liked getting up early in the morning, to the tune of cocks crowing on the dunghill. He liked the heavy, greasy victuals of the farmhouse kitchen. He liked country lawyers, country pastors, all country people. I believe that this liking was sincere—perhaps the only sincere thing in the man. His nose showed no uneasiness when a hillman in faded overalls and hickory shirt accosted him on the street, and besought him for light upon some mystery of Holy Writ. The simian gabble of a country town was not gabble to him, but wisdom of an occult and superior sort. In the presence of city folks he was palpably uneasy. Their clothes, I suspect, annoyed him, and he was suspicious of their too delicate manners. He knew all the while that they were laughing at him—if not at his baroque theology, then at least at his alpaca pantaloons. But the yokels never laughed at him. To them he was not the huntsman but the prophet, and toward the end, as he gradually forsook mundane politics for purely ghostly concerns, they began to elevate him in their hierarchy. When he died he was the peer of Abraham. Another curious detail: his old enemy, Wilson, aspiring to the same white and shining robe, came down with a thump. But Bryan made the grade. His place in the Tennessee hagiocracy is secure. If the village barber saved any of his hair, then it is curing gallstones down there today.

II

But what label will he bear in more urbane regions? One, I fear, of a far less flattering kind. Bryan lived too long, and descended too deeply into the mud, to be taken seriously hereafter by fully literate men, even of the kind who write school-books. There was a scattering of sweet words in his funeral notices, but it was no more than a response to conventional sentimentality. The best verdict the most romantic editorial writer could dredge up, save in the eloquent South, was to the general effect that his imbecilities were excused by his earnestness— that under his clowning, as under that of the juggler of Notre Dame, there was the zeal of a steadfast soul. But this was apology, not praise; precisely the same thing might be said of Mary Baker G. Eddy, the late Czar Nicholas, or Czolgosz. The truth is that even Bryan's sincerity will probably yield to what is called, in other fields, definitive criticism. Was he sincere when he opposed imperialism in the Philippines, or when he fed it with deserving Democrats in Santo Domingo? Was he sincere when he tried to shove the Prohibitionists under the table, or when he seized their banner and began to lead them with loud whoops? Was he sincere when he bellowed against war, or when he dreamed of himself as a tin-soldier in uniform, with a grave reserved among the generals? Was he sincere when he denounced the late John W. Davis[3] or when he swallowed Davis? Was he sincere when he fawned over Champ Clark[4] or when he betrayed Clark? Was he sincere when he pleaded for tolerance in New York, or when he bawled for the fagot and the stake in Tennessee?

This talk of sincerity, I confess, fatigues me. If the fellow was sincere, then so was P. T. Barnum. The word is disgraced and degraded by such uses. He was, in fact, a charlatan, a mountebank, a zany without shame or dignity. What animated him from end to end of his grotesque career was simply ambition — the ambition of a common man to get his hand upon the collar of his superiors, or, failing that, to get his thumb into their eyes. He was born with a roaring voice, and it had the trick of inflaming half-wits. His whole career was devoted to raising these half-wits against their betters, that he himself might shine. His last battle will be grossly misunderstood if it is thought of as a mere exercise in fanaticism — that is, if Bryan the Fundamentalist Pope is mistaken for one of the bucolic Fundamentalists. There was much more in it than that, as everyone knows who saw him on the field. What moved him, at bottom, was simply hatred of the city men who had laughed at him so long, and brought him at last to so tatterdemalion an estate. He lusted for revenge upon them. He yearned to lead the anthropoid rabble against them, to set *Homo neandertalensis* upon them, to punish them for the execution they had done upon him by attacking the very vitals of their civilization. He went far beyond the bounds of any merely religious frenzy, however inordinate. When he began denouncing the notion that man is a mammal even some of the hinds at Dayton were agape. And when, brought upon Darrow's cruel hook, he writhed and tossed in a very fury of malignancy, bawling against the baldest elements of sense and decency like a man frantic — when he came to that tragic climax there were snickers among the hinds as well as hosannas.

Upon that hook, in truth, Bryan committed suicide, as a legend as well as in the body. He staggered from the rustic court ready to die, and he staggered from it ready to be forgotten, save as a character in a third-rate farce, witless and in execrable taste. The chances are that history will put the peak of democracy in his time; it has been on the downward curve among us since the campaign of 1896. He will be remembered, perhaps, as its supreme impostor, the *reductio ad absurdum* of its pretension. Bryan came very near being President of the United States.

---

3. **John W. Davis:** Democratic Party presidential nominee, 1924.
4. **Champ Clark** (James Beauchamp Clark): Democratic Party Speaker of the House, 1911–1919.

In 1896, it is possible, he was actually elected. He lived long enough to make patriots thank the inscrutable gods for Harding, even for Coolidge. Dullness has got into the White House, and the smell of cabbage boiling, but there is at least nothing to compare to the intolerable buffoonery that went on in Tennessee. The President of the United States doesn't believe that the earth is square, and that witches should be put to death, and that Jonah swallowed the whale. The Golden Text is not painted weekly on the White House wall, and there is no need to keep ambassadors waiting while Pastor Simpson, of Smithsville, prays for rain in the Blue Room. We have escaped something—by a narrow margin, but still safely.

III

That is, so far. The Fundamentalists continue at the wake, and sense gets a sort of reprieve. The legislature of Georgia, so the news comes, has shelved the anti-evolution bill, and turns its back upon the legislature of Tennessee. Elsewhere minorities prepare for battle—here and there with some assurance of success. But it is too early, it seems to me, to send the firemen home; the fire is still burning on many a far-flung hill, and it may begin to roar again at any moment. The evil that men do lives after them. Bryan, in his malice, started something that it will not be easy to stop. In ten thousand country towns his old heelers, the evangelical pastors, are propagating his gospel, and everywhere the yokels are ready for it. When he disappeared from the big cities, the big cities made the capital error of assuming that he was done for. If they heard of him at all, it was only as a crimp for real-estate speculators—the heroic foe of the unearned increment hauling it in with both hands. He seemed preposterous, and hence harmless. But all the while he was busy among his old lieges, preparing for a *jacquerie* that should floor all his enemies at one blow. He did the job competently. He had vast skill at such enterprises. Heave an egg out of a Pullman window, and you will hit a Fundamentalist almost anywhere in the United States today. They swarm in the country towns, inflamed by their pastors, and with a saint, now, to venerate. They are thick in the mean streets behind the gasworks. They are everywhere that learning is too heavy a burden for mortal minds, even the vague, pathetic learning on tap in little red schoolhouses. They march with the Klan, with the Christian Endeavor Society, with the Junior Order of United American Mechanics, with the Epworth League[5] with all the rococo bands that poor and unhappy folk organize to bring some light of purpose into their lives. They have had a thrill, and they are ready for more.

Such is Bryan's legacy to his country. He couldn't be President, but he could at least help magnificently in the solemn business of shutting off the presidency from every intelligent and self-respecting man. The storm, perhaps, won't last long, as time goes in history. It may help, indeed, to break up the democratic delusion, now already showing weakness, and so hasten its own end. But while it lasts it will blow off some roofs and flood some sanctuaries.

---

5. **Epworth League:** National Methodist Episcopal youth organization.

For Critical Thinking

1. Bryan, in agreeing to testify at the Scopes trial, had reserved the right similarly to question Darrow. What questions might Bryan have asked? Construct a set of questions and answers between the two men, with Darrow in the witness box and Bryan doing the questioning.

2. Was the Scopes trial really "the trial of the century"? Which issues of the trial are still matters of debate today? In what ways does discussion of these issues today resemble or differ from arguments at the Scopes trial?

3. Imagine yourself a supporter of Bryan and of his rejection of scientific evidence for evolution. Write an editorial objecting to H. L. Mencken's obituary of William Jennings Bryan.

4. Who do you think was more convincing, Bryan or Darrow, to undecided people and why?

5. In what ways do you think the conflict between Bryan and Darrow might have appeared different seen in the courtroom or heard over the radio, as opposed to reading accounts or transcripts of the trial?

22

The Harlem Renaissance

Langston Hughes

"I went up the steps and out into the bright September sunlight," reports the poet Langston Hughes (1902–1967) in his autobiography. "Harlem! I stood there, dropped my bags, took a deep breath, and felt happy again." What was there, in this Upper East Side Manhattan subway stop of 1921, to excite a young black Midwesterner?

By the standards of most white Americans of the time, little enough. While not yet the congested slum it would become during the Great Depression, Harlem was poor. Among the 73,000 Harlemites in 1920 and close to 200,000 a decade later, there was little in the way of a prosperous middle class. In wealth, residences, stability, and order, Harlem fell in some ways behind black sections of several Southern cities. Nor was it the largest concentration of blacks in the North: the greatest migration was to Chicago.

What gave excitement to Harlem was its reputation as a "race capital"—a center of social and cultural independence. For Harlem residents, being a visible part of the great metropolis, tough and streetwise rather than deferential and under the surveillance of suspicious white neighbors and hostile Southern police, was liberating. The main black civil rights organizations and journals were anchored in Harlem. Black American troops had been honored with a parade in New York City for their services during World War I. And the speakeasies and jazz cabarets as well as the rent parties that turned shabby apartments into informal nightclubs blared with the new exciting sound that would soon make both whites and blacks talk about "the Jazz Age."

In 1921, Harlem was in the first stages of an artistic and literary flowering richer than anything African Americans had yet achieved. In the next several years popular musicians like Duke Ellington and Bessie Smith, writers like Langston Hughes (whose memories of this period are excerpted here), artists, and intellectuals would together create a distinctive cultural energy charged with the rhythms and themes of the African American experience.

The Harlem Renaissance and the jazz explosion soon attracted white patronage. Harlem nightclubs and cabarets began to cater to white patrons also, and Harlem jazz migrated to Broadway in shows like Shuffle Along.

Whites provided audiences for black entertainers and patronage for some African American artists and writers. Langston Hughes himself enjoyed the support of a wealthy patroness until his work turned political, and then the relationship ended. The questions raised by these relationships continue to be at issue in American life. How separate from

Langston Hughes, *The Big Sea* (New York: Hill and Wang, 1963), 223–28, 235–40, 243–47.

or integrated with white society should black culture be? Is there a separate black aes-
thetic? Is it appropriate or corrupting to address white audiences and accept white pa-
tronage? Does success in the arts and entertainment draw energy from the less glamorous
struggle for civil rights, political power, and economic opportunity? Participants in the
Harlem Renaissance struggled with all these questions, and the debate continues today.

QUESTIONS TO CONSIDER

1. What was Langston Hughes's attitude toward the era "when the Negro was in vogue"? What did he like about it, and what did he dislike?
2. What, according to Hughes, was it like to be a writer during the Harlem Renaissance?
3. What was the role of A'Lelia Walker in the Harlem Renaissance? Why does Hughes devote so many paragraphs to her activities? Why does her funeral seem important to him?
4. In what ways is the contemporary relationship between African American entertainment and cultural production and "the mainstream" similar to the Harlem Renaissance? In what ways is it different?

EXCERPT FROM
"WHEN THE NEGRO WAS IN VOGUE"

The 1920's were the years of Manhattan's black Renaissance. It began with *Shuffle Along, Running Wild,* and the Charleston. Perhaps some people would say even with *The Emperor Jones,* Charles Gilpin, and the tom-toms at the Provincetown. But certainly it was the musical revue, *Shuffle Along,* that gave a scintillating send-off to that Negro vogue in Manhattan, which reached its peak just before the crash of 1929, the crash that sent Negroes, white folks, and all rolling down the hill toward the Works Progress Administration.

Shuffle Along was a honey of a show. Swift, bright, funny, rollicking, and gay, with a dozen danceable, singable tunes. Besides, look who were in it: The now famous choir director, Hall Johnson, and the composer, William Grant Still, were part of the orchestra. Eubie Blake and Noble Sissle wrote the music and played and acted in the show. Miller and Lyles were the comics. Florence Mills skyrocketed to fame in the second act. Trixie Smith sang "He May Be Your Man But He Comes to See Me Sometimes." And Caterina Jarboro, now a European prima donna, and the internationally celebrated Josephine Baker were merely in the chorus. Everybody was in the audience—including me. People came back to see it innumerable times. It was always packed.

To see *Shuffle Along* was the main reason I wanted to go to Columbia. When I saw it, I was thrilled and delighted. From then on I was in the gallery of the Cort Theatre every time I got a chance. That year, too, I saw Katharine Cornell in *A Bill of Divorcement,* Margaret Wycherly in *The Verge,* Maugham's *The Circle* with Mrs. Leslie Carter, and the Theatre Guild production of Kaiser's *From Morn Till Midnight.* But I remember *Shuffle Along* best of all. It gave just the proper push—a pre-Charleston kick—to that Negro vogue of the '20's, that spread to books, African sculpture, music, and dancing.

Put down the 1920's for the rise of Roland Hayes,[1] who packed Carnegie Hall, the rise of Paul Robeson in New York and London, of Florence Mills over two continents, of Rose McClendon in Broadway parts that never measured up to her, the booming voice of Bessie Smith and the low moan of Clara on thousands of records, and the rise of that grand comedienne of song, Ethel Waters, singing: "Charlie's elected now! He's in right for sure!" Put down the 1920's for Louis Armstrong and Gladys Bentley and Josephine Baker.

White people began to come to Harlem in droves. For several years they packed the expensive Cotton Club on Lenox Avenue. But I was never there, because the Cotton Club was a Jim Crow club for gangsters and monied whites. They were not cordial to Negro patronage, unless you were a celebrity like Bojangles. So Harlem Negroes did not like the Cotton Club and never appreciated its Jim Crow policy in the very heart of their dark community. Nor did ordinary Negroes like the growing influx of whites toward Harlem after sundown, flooding the little cabarets and bars where formerly only colored people laughed and sang, and where now the strangers were given the best ringside tables to sit and stare at the Negro customers—like amusing animals in a zoo.

The Negroes said: "We can't go downtown and sit and stare at you in your clubs. You won't even let us in your clubs." But they didn't say it out loud—for Negroes are practically never rude to white people. So thousands of whites came to Harlem night after night, thinking the Negroes loved to have them there, and firmly believing that all Harlemites left their houses at sundown to sing and dance in cabarets, because most of the whites saw nothing but the cabarets, not the houses.

Some of the owners of Harlem clubs, delighted at the flood of white patronage, made the grievous error of barring their own race, after the manner of the famous Cotton Club. But most of these quickly lost business and folded up, because they failed to realize that a large part of the Harlem attraction for downtown New Yorkers lay in simply watching the colored customers amuse themselves. And the smaller clubs, of course, had no big floor shows or a name band like the Cotton Club, where Duke Ellington usually held forth, so, without black patronage, they were not amusing at all.

Some of the small clubs, however, had people like Gladys Bentley, who was something worth discovering in those days, before she got famous, acquired an accompanist, specially written material, and conscious vulgarity. But for two or three amazing years, Miss Bentley sat, and played a big piano all night long, literally all night, without stopping—singing songs like "The St. James Infirmary," from ten in the evening until dawn, with scarcely a break between the notes, sliding from one song to another, with a powerful and continuous underbeat of jungle rhythm. Miss Bentley was an amazing exhibition of musical energy—a large, dark, masculine lady, whose feet pounded the floor while her fingers pounded the keyboard—a perfect piece of African sculpture, animated by her own rhythm.

---

1. **Roland Hayes:** Probably the first internationally famous African American male classical singer.

But when the place where she played became too well known, she began to sing with an accompanist, became a star, moved to a larger place, then downtown, and is now in Hollywood. The old magic of the woman and the piano and the night and the rhythm being one is gone. But everything goes, one way or another. The '20's are gone and lots of fine things in Harlem night life have disappeared like snow in the sun—since it became utterly commercial, planned for the downtown tourist trade, and therefore dull.

The lindy-hoppers at the Savoy even began to practise acrobatic routines, and to do absurd things for the entertainment of the whites, that probably never would have entered their heads to attempt merely for their own effortless amusement. Some of the lindy-hoppers had cards printed with their names on them and became dance professors teaching the tourists. Then Harlem nights became show nights for the Nordics.

Some critics say that that is what happened to certain Negro writers, too— that they ceased to write to amuse themselves and began to write to amuse and entertain white people, and in so doing distorted and over-colored their material, and left out a great many things they thought would offend their American brothers of a lighter complexion. Maybe—since Negroes have writer-racketeers, as has any other race. But I have known almost all of them, and most of the good ones have tried to be honest, write honestly, and express their world as they saw it.

All of us know that the gay and sparkling life of the so-called Negro Renaissance of the '20's was not so gay and sparkling beneath the surface as it looked. Carl Van Vechten, in the character of Byron in *Nigger Heaven*, captured some of the bitterness and frustration of literary Harlem that Wallace Thurman later so effectively poured into his *Infants of the Spring*—the only novel by a Negro about that fantastic period when Harlem was in vogue.

It was a period when, at almost every Harlem upper-crust dance or party, one would be introduced to various distinguished white celebrities there as guests. It was a period when almost any Harlem Negro of any social importance at all would be likely to say casually: "As I was remarking the other day to Heywood—," meaning Heywood Broun.[2] Or: "As I said to George—," referring to George Gershwin. It was a period when local and visiting royalty were not at all uncommon in Harlem. And when the parties of A'Lelia Walker, the Negro heiress, were filled with guests whose names would turn any Nordic social climber green with envy. It was a period when Harold Jackman, a handsome young Harlem school teacher of modest means, calmly announced one day that he was sailing for the Riviera for a fortnight, to attend Princess Murat's yachting party. It was a period when Charleston preachers opened up shouting churches as sideshows for white tourists. It was a period when at least one charming colored chorus girl, amber enough to pass for a Latin American, was living in a pent house, with all her bills paid by a gentleman whose name was banker's magic on Wall Street. It was a period when every season there was at

---

2. **Heywood Broun:** A New York City left-wing journalist who later ran for Congress as a Socialist.

least one hit play on Broadway acted by a Negro cast. And when books by Negro authors were being published with much greater frequency and much more publicity than ever before or since in history. It was a period when white writers wrote about Negroes more successfully (commercially speaking) than Negroes did about themselves. It was the period (God help us!) when Ethel Barrymore[3] appeared in blackface in *Scarlet Sister Mary!* It was the period when the Negro was in vogue.

I was there. I had a swell time while it lasted. But I thought it wouldn't last long. (I remember the vogue for things Russian, the season the Chauve-Souris[4] first came to town.) For how could a large and enthusiastic number of people be crazy about Negroes forever? But some Harlemites thought the millennium had come. They thought the race problem had at last been solved through Art plus Gladys Bentley. They were sure the New Negro would lead a new life from then on in green pastures of tolerance created by Countee Cullen, Ethel Waters, Claude McKay, Duke Ellington, Bojangles, and Alain Locke.[5]

I don't know what made any Negroes think that—except that they were mostly intellectuals doing the thinking. The ordinary Negroes hadn't heard of the Negro Renaissance. And if they had, it hadn't raised their wages any. As for all those white folks in the speakeasies and night clubs of Harlem—well, maybe a colored man could find *some* place to have a drink that the tourists hadn't yet discovered.

EXCERPT FROM "HARLEM LITERATI"

During the summer of 1926, Wallace Thurman, Zora Neale Hurston, Aaron Douglas, John P. Davis, Bruce Nugent, Gwendolyn Bennett, and I decided to publish "a Negro quarterly of the arts" to be called *Fire*—the idea being that it would burn up a lot of the old, dead conventional Negro-white ideas of the past, *épater le bourgeois*[6] into a realization of the existence of the younger Negro writers and artists, and provide us with an outlet for publication not available in the limited pages of the small Negro magazines then existing, the *Crisis, Opportunity*, and the *Messenger*—the first two being house organs of inter-racial organizations, and the latter being God knows what.

Sweltering summer evenings we met to plan *Fire*. Each of the seven of us agreed to give fifty dollars to finance the first issue. Thurman was to edit it, John P. Davis to handle the business end, and Bruce Nugent to take charge of distribution. The rest of us were to serve as an editorial board to collect material, contribute our own work, and act in any useful way that we could. For artists and writers, we got along fine and there were no quarrels. But October

---

3. **Ethel Barrymore:** Probably the most famous stage actress of the 1920s.
4. **Chauve-Souris:** A popular after-theater Russian dance performance troupe.
5. All important figures in the Harlem Renaissance. Countee Cullen was a poet; Ethel Waters, a singer; Claude McKay, another prominent poet; Duke Ellington, a musician and band leader; Bojangles, a popular performer; and Alain Locke, a prominent philosopher and educator.
6. *épater le bourgeois*: "Shock the middle class" (Fr.).

came before we were ready to go to press. I had to return to Lincoln, John Davis to Law School at Harvard, Zora Hurston to her studies at Barnard. . . .

Only three of the seven had contributed their fifty dollars, but the others faithfully promised to send theirs out of tuition checks, wages, or begging. Thurman went on with the work of preparing the magazine. He got a printer. He planned the layout. It had to be on good paper, he said, worthy of the drawings of Aaron Douglas. It had to have beautiful type, worthy of the first Negro art quarterly. It had to be what we seven young Negroes dreamed our magazine would be—so in the end it cost almost a thousand dollars, and nobody could pay the bills.

I don't know how Thurman persuaded the printer to let us have all the copies to distribute, but he did. I think Alain Locke, among others, signed notes guaranteeing payments. But since Thurman was the only one of the seven of us with a regular job, for the next three or four years his checks were constantly being attached and his income seized to pay for *Fire*. And whenever I sold a poem, mine went there, too—to *Fire*.

None of the older Negro intellectuals would have anything to do with *Fire*. Dr. Du Bois[7] in the *Crisis* roasted it. The Negro press called it all sorts of bad names, largely because of a green and purple story by Bruce Nugent, in the Oscar Wilde tradition, which we had included. Rean Graves, the critic for the *Baltimore Afro-American*, began his review by saying: "I have just tossed the first issue of *Fire* into the fire." Commenting upon various of our contributors, he said: "Aaron Douglas who, in spite of himself and the meaningless grotesqueness of his creations, has gained a reputation as an artist, is permitted to spoil three perfectly good pages and a cover with his pen and ink hudge pudge. Countee Cullen has written a beautiful poem in his 'From a Dark Tower,' but tries his best to obscure the thought in superfluous sentences. Langston Hughes displays his usual ability to say nothing in many words."

So *Fire* had plenty of cold water thrown on it by the colored critics. The white critics (except for an excellent editorial in the *Bookman* for November, 1926) scarcely noticed it at all. We had no way of getting it distributed to bookstands or news stands. Bruce Nugent took it around New York on foot and some of the Greenwich Village bookshops put it on display, and sold it for us. But then Bruce, who had no job, would collect the money and, on account of salary, eat it up before he got back to Harlem.

Finally, irony of ironies, several hundred copies of *Fire* were stored in the basement of an apartment where an actual fire occurred and the bulk of the whole issue was burned up. Even after that Thurman had to go on paying the printer.

Now *Fire* is a collector's item, and very difficult to get, being mostly ashes.

That taught me a lesson about little magazines. But since white folks had them, we Negroes thought we could have one, too. But we didn't have the money. . . .

---

7. **Dr. Du Bois:** W. E. B. Du Bois (1868–1963), American educator, sociologist, and a founder of the National Association for the Advancement of Colored People.

About the future of Negro literature Thurman was very pessimistic. He thought the Negro vogue had made us all too conscious of ourselves, had flattered and spoiled us, and had provided too many easy opportunities for some of us to drink gin and more gin, on which he thought we would always be drunk. With his bitter sense of humor, he called the Harlem literati, the "niggerati."

Of this "niggerati," Zora Neale Hurston was certainly the most amusing. Only to reach a wider audience, need she ever write books — because she is a perfect book of entertainment in herself. In her youth she was always getting scholarships and things from wealthy white people, some of whom simply paid her just to sit around and represent the Negro race for them, she did it in such a racy fashion. She was full of side-splitting anecdotes, humorous tales, and tragi-comic stories, remembered out of her life in the South as a daughter of a travelling minister of God. She could make you laugh one minute and cry the next. To many of her white friends, no doubt, she was a perfect "darkie," in the nice meaning they give the term — that is a naïve, childlike, sweet, humorous, and highly colored Negro.

But Miss Hurston was clever, too — a student who didn't let college give her a broad *a* and who had great scorn for all pretensions, academic or otherwise. That is why she was such a fine folk-lore collector, able to go among the people and never act as if she had been to school at all. . . .

When Miss Hurston graduated from Barnard she took an apartment in West 66th Street near the park, in that row of Negro houses there. She moved in with no furniture at all and no money, but in a few days friends had given her everything, from decorative silver birds, perched atop the linen cabinet, down to a footstool. And on Saturday night, to christen the place, she had a *hand*-chicken dinner, since she had forgotten to say she needed forks.

She seemed to know almost everybody in New York. She had been a secretary to Fannie Hurst,[8] and had met dozens of celebrities whose friendships she retained. Yet she was always having terrific ups-and-downs about money. She tells this story on herself, about needing a nickel to go downtown one day and wondering where on earth she would get it. As she approached the subway, she was stopped by a blind beggar holding out his cup.

"Please help the blind! Help the blind! A nickel for the blind!"

"I need money worse than you today," said Miss Hurston, taking five cents out of his cup. "Lend me this! Next time, I'll give it back." And she went on downtown.

Harlem was like a great magnet for the Negro intellectual, pulling him from everywhere. Or perhaps the magnet was New York — but once in New York, he had to live in Harlem, for rooms were hardly to be found elsewhere unless one could pass for white or Mexican or Eurasian and perhaps live in the Village — which always seemed to me a very arty locale, in spite of the many real artists and writers who lived there. Only a few of the New Negroes lived in the Village, Harlem being their real stamping ground.

---

8. **Fannie Hurst:** A famous Jewish American novelist and former apartment mate of Hurston's. Her novel *Imitation of Life* was adopted into a 1934 movie that may have been Hollywood's first serious attempt to address the issue of race relations.

EXCERPT FROM "PARTIES"

In those days of the late 1920's, there were a great many parties, in Harlem and out, to which various members of the New Negro group were invited. These parties, when given by important Harlemites (or Carl Van Vechten) were reported in full in the society pages of the Harlem press, but best in the sparkling Harlemese of Geraldyn Dismond who wrote for the *Interstate Tattler*. On one of Taylor Gordon's fiestas she reports as follows:

> What a crowd! All classes and colors met face to face, ultra aristocrats, Bourgeois, Communists, Park Avenuers galore, bookers, publishers, Broadway celebs, and Harlemites giving each other the once over. The social revolution was on. And yes, Lady Nancy Cunard was there all in black (she would) with 12 of her grand bracelets. . . . And was the entertainment on the up and up! Into swell dance music was injected African drums that played havoc with blood pressure. Jimmy Daniels sang his gigolo hits. Gus Simons, the Harlem crooner, made the River Stay Away From His Door and Taylor himself brought out everything from "Hot Dog" to "Bravo" when he made high C.

A'Lelia Walker was the then great Harlem party giver, although Mrs. Bernia Austin fell but little behind. And at the Seventh Avenue apartment of Jessie Fauset, literary soirées with much poetry and but little to drink were the order of the day. The same was true of Lillian Alexander's, where the older intellectuals gathered.

A'Lelia Walker, however, big-hearted, night-dark, hair-straightening heiress, made no pretense at being intellectual or exclusive. At her "at homes" Negro poets and Negro number bankers mingled with downtown poets and seat-on-the-stock-exchange racketeers. Countee Cullen would be there and Witter Bynner, Muriel Draper and Nora Holt, Andy Razaf and Taylor Gordon. And a good time was had by all.

A'Lelia Walker had an apartment that held perhaps a hundred people. She would usually issue several hundred invitations to each party. Unless you went early there was no possible way of getting in. Her parties were as crowded as the New York subway at the rush hour—entrance, lobby, steps, hallway, and apartment a milling crush of guests, with everybody seeming to enjoy the crowding. Once, some royal personage arrived, a Scandinavian prince, I believe, but his equerry saw no way of getting him through the crowded entrance hall and into the party, so word was sent in to A'Lelia Walker that His Highness, the Prince, was waiting without. A'Lelia sent word back that she saw no way of getting His Highness in, either, nor could she herself get out through the crowd to greet him. But she offered to send refreshments downstairs to the Prince's car.

A'Lelia Walker was a gorgeous dark Amazon, in a silver turban. She had a town house in New York (also an apartment where she preferred to live) and a country mansion at Irvington-on-the-Hudson, with pipe organ programs each morning to awaken her guests gently. Her mother made a great fortune from the Madame Walker Hair Straightening Process, which had worked wonders on unruly Negro hair in the early nineteen hundreds—and which continues to work wonders today. The daughter used much of that money for fun. A'Lelia Walker was the joy-goddess of Harlem's 1920's. . . .

When A'Lelia Walker died in 1931, she had a grand funeral. It was by invitation only. But, just as for her parties, a great many more invitations had been issued than the small but exclusive Seventh Avenue funeral parlor could provide for. Hours before the funeral, the street in front of the undertaker's chapel was crowded. The doors were not opened until the cortège arrived—and the cortège was late. When it came, there were almost enough family mourners, attendants, and honorary pallbearers in the procession to fill the room; as well as the representatives of the various Walker beauty parlors throughout the country. And there were still hundreds of friends outside, waving their white, engraved invitations aloft in the vain hope of entering.

Once the last honorary pallbearers had marched in, there was a great crush at the doors. . . .

Soft music played and it was very solemn. When we were seated and the chapel became dead silent, De Lawd[9] said: "The Four Bon Bons will now sing."

A night club quartette that had often performed at A'Lelia's parties arose and sang for her. They sang Noel Coward's "I'll See You Again," and they swung it slightly, as she might have liked it. It was a grand funeral and very much like a party. Mrs. Mary McLeod Bethune[10] spoke in that great deep voice of hers, as only she can speak. She recalled the poor mother of A'Lelia Walker in old clothes, who had labored to bring the gift of beauty to Negro womanhood, and had taught them the care of their skin and their hair, and had built up a great business and a great fortune to the pride and glory of the Negro race—and then had given it all to her daughter, A'Lelia.

Then a poem of mine was read by Edward Perry, "To A'Lelia." And after that the girls from the various Walker beauty shops throughout America brought their flowers and laid them on the bier.

That was really the end of the gay times of the New Negro era in Harlem, the period that had begun to reach its end when the crash came in 1929 and the white people had much less money to spend on themselves, and practically none to spend on Negroes, for the depression brought everybody down a peg or two. And the Negroes had but few pegs to fall.

9. **De Lawd:** Hughes's description of the presiding minister, who looked like the character of God in Marc Connelly's play *Green Pastures*, which had an all-black cast.
10. **Mary McLeod Bethune** (1875–1955): African American educator, civil rights leader, and adviser to FDR.

23

My Fight for Birth Control
Margaret Sanger

Margaret Sanger (1879–1966) was not the first champion of the right to use contraception, but she was an important organizer of the twentieth-century movement to make "birth control"—an expression she coined in 1914—legal and widely available. Her account of the life and death of Sadie Sacks, presented here as written in her autobiography, was discussed in countless speeches throughout her career. While the incident did not initiate her concern for birth control access or for the plight of poor women, it did fix her decision to focus her work on this issue, as she did for the rest of her life.

In 1873 Congress had passed the Comstock Act, which imposed fines and imprisonment for providing information to another person "for the prevention of conception or procuring of abortion." The state of New York had a similar statute. So virtually all Sanger's activities to further her cause were against the law. Opening a birth control clinic in 1916 was an act of civil disobedience—much like the acts practiced by the civil rights movement half a century later. Sanger, by violating the law, forced changes in it.

While contraception was to remain illegal in some states into the 1960s, this determined reformer brought about a major change. When she began her crusade, middle-class women had informal access to birth control information and devices, but poor women generally did not. By 1921 when she formed the American Birth Control League—which in 1942 would become Planned Parenthood—courts had already begun to allow doctors to disseminate birth control information and devices to married women, and prosecutions under the Comstock Act virtually ceased.

QUESTIONS TO CONSIDER

1. Is it, as Margaret Sanger wrote at the beginning of this selection, "futile and useless to relieve . . . misery" if you do not get to its root?
2. When she had her revelation after Mrs. Sacks's death, she wrote, "I could now see clearly the various social strata of our life; all its mass problems seemed to be centered around uncontrolled breeding." Do you agree with this? What are the merits and the dangers of such an argument?
3. What made Brooklyn a good venue for opening her birth control clinic, in Sanger's view?

Margaret Sanger, *My Fight for Birth Control* (New York: Farrar-Rinehart, 1931), 46–56, 152–60.

[1912]

Early in the year 1912 I came to a sudden realization that my work as a nurse and my activities in social service were entirely palliative and consequently futile and useless to relieve the misery I saw all about me. . . .

Were it possible for me to depict the revolting conditions existing in the homes of some of the women I attended in that one year, one would find it hard to believe. There was at that time, and doubtless is still today, a substratum of men and women whose lives are absolutely untouched by social agencies.

The way they live is almost beyond belief. They hate and fear any prying into their homes or into their lives. They resent being talked to. The women slink in and out of their homes on their way to market like rats from their holes. The men beat their wives sometimes black and blue, but no one interferes. The children are cuffed, kicked and chased about, but woe to the child who dares to tell tales out of the home! Crime or drink is often the source of this secret aloofness, usually there is something to hide, a skeleton in the closet somewhere. The men are sullen, unskilled workers, picking up odd jobs now and then, unemployed usually, sauntering in and out of the house at all hours of the day and night.

The women keep apart from other women in the neighborhood. Often they are suspected of picking a pocket or "lifting" an article when occasion arises. Pregnancy is an almost chronic condition amongst them. I knew one woman who had given birth to eight children with no professional care whatever. The last one was born in the kitchen, witnessed by a son of ten years who, under his mother's direction, cleaned the bed, wrapped the placenta and soiled articles in paper, and threw them out of the window into the court below. . . .

In this atmosphere abortions and birth become the main theme of conversation. On Saturday nights I have seen groups of fifty to one hundred women going into questionable offices well known in the community for cheap abortions. I asked several women what took place there, and they all gave the same reply: a quick examination, a probe inserted into the uterus and turned a few times to disturb the fertilized ovum, and then the woman was sent home. Usually the flow began the next day and often continued four or five weeks. Sometimes an ambulance carried the victim to the hospital for a curetage, and if she returned home at all she was looked upon as a lucky woman.

This state of things became a nightmare with me. There seemed no sense to it all, no reason for such waste of mother life, no right to exhaust women's vitality and to throw them on the scrap-heap before the age of thirty-five.

Everywhere I looked, misery and fear stalked—men fearful of losing their jobs, women fearful that even worse conditions might come upon them. The menace of another pregnancy hung like a sword over the head of every poor woman I came in contact with that year. The question which met me was always the same: What can I do to keep from it? or, What can I do to get out of this? Sometimes they talked among themselves bitterly.

"It's the rich that know the tricks," they'd say, "while we have all the kids." Then, if the women were Roman Catholics, they talked about "Yankee tricks," and asked me if I knew what the Protestants did to keep their families down. When I said that I didn't believe that the rich knew much more than they did I was laughed at and suspected of holding back information for money. They would nudge each other and say something about paying me before I left the case if I would reveal the "secret." . . .

Finally the thing began to shape itself, to become accumulative during the three weeks I spent in the home of a desperately sick woman living on Grand Street, a lower section of New York's East Side.

Mrs. Sacks was only twenty-eight years old; her husband, an unskilled worker, thirty-two. Three children, aged five, three and one, were none too strong nor sturdy, and it took all the earnings of the father and the ingenuity of the mother to keep them clean, provide them with air and proper food, and give them a chance to grow into decent manhood and womanhood.

Both parents were devoted to these children and to each other. The woman had become pregnant and had taken various drugs and purgatives, as advised by her neighbors. Then, in desperation, she had used some instrument lent to her by a friend. She was found prostrate on the floor amidst the crying children when her husband returned from work. Neighbors advised against the ambulance, and a friendly doctor was called. The husband would not hear of her going to a hospital, and as a little money had been saved in the bank a nurse was called and the battle for that precious life began.

It was in the middle of July. The three-room apartment was turned into a hospital for the dying patient. Never had I worked so fast, never so concentratedly as I did to keep alive that little mother. Neighbor women came and went during the day doing the odds and ends necessary for our comfort. The children were sent to friends and relatives and the doctor and I settled ourselves to outdo the force and power of an outraged nature.

Never had I known such conditions could exist. July's sultry days and nights were melted into a torpid inferno. Day after day, night after night, I slept only in brief snatches, ever too anxious about the condition of that feeble heart bravely carrying on, to stay long from the bedside of the patient. . . .

At the end of two weeks recovery was in sight, and at the end of three weeks I was preparing to leave the fragile patient to take up the ordinary duties of her life, including those of wifehood and motherhood. Everyone was congratulating her on her recovery. All the kindness of sympathetic and understanding neighbors poured in upon her in the shape of convalescent dishes, soups, custards, and drinks. Still she appeared to be despondent and worried. She seemed to sit apart in her thoughts as if she had no part in these congratulatory messages and endearing welcomes. I thought at first that she still retained some of her unconscious memories and dwelt upon them in her silences.

But as the hour for my departure came nearer, her anxiety increased, and finally with trembling voice she said: "Another baby will finish me, I suppose."

"It's too early to talk about that," I said, and resolved that I would turn the question over to the doctor for his advice. When he came I said: "Mrs. Sacks is worried about having another baby."

"She well might be," replied the doctor, and then he stood before her and said: "Any more such capers, young woman, and there will be no need to call me."

"Yes, yes—I know, Doctor," said the patient with trembling voice, "but," and she hesitated as if it took all of her courage to say it, "*what* can I do to prevent getting that way again?"

"Oh ho!" laughed the doctor good naturedly. "You want your cake while you eat it too, do you? Well, it can't be done." Then, familiarly slapping her on the back and picking up his hat and bag to depart, he said: "I'll tell you the only sure thing to do. Tell Jake to sleep on the roof!"

With those words he closed the door and went down the stairs, leaving us both petrified and stunned.

Tears sprang to my eyes, and a lump came in my throat as I looked at that face before me. It was stamped with sheer horror. I thought for a moment she might have gone insane, but she conquered her feelings, whatever they may have been, and turning to me in desperation said: "He can't understand, can he? —he's a man after all—but you do, don't you? You're a woman and you'll tell me the secret and I'll never tell it to a soul."

She clasped her hands as if in prayer, she leaned over and looked straight into my eyes and beseechingly implored me to tell her something—something *I really did not know*. It was like being on a rack and tortured for a crime one had not committed. To plead guilty would stop the agony; otherwise the rack kept turning.

I had to turn away from that imploring face. I could not answer her then. I quieted her as best I could. She saw that I was moved by the tears in my eyes. I promised that I would come back in a few days and tell her what she wanted to know. The few simple means of limiting the family like *coitus interruptus* or the condom were laughed at by the neighboring women when told these were the means used by men in the well-to-do families. That was not believed, and I knew such an answer would be swept aside as useless were I to tell her this at such a time.

A little later when she slept I left the house, and made up my mind that I'd keep away from those cases in the future. I felt helpless to do anything at all. I seemed chained hand and foot, and longed for an earthquake or a volcano to shake the world out of its lethargy into facing these monstrous atrocities.

The intelligent reasoning of the young mother—how to *prevent* getting that way again—how sensible, how just she had been—yes, I promised myself I'd go back and have a long talk with her and tell her more, and perhaps she would not laugh but would believe that those methods were all that were really known.

But time flew past, and weeks rolled into months. That wistful, appealing face haunted me day and night. I could not banish from my mind memories of that trembling voice begging so humbly for knowledge she had a right to have. I was about to retire one night three months later when the telephone rang and an agitated man's voice begged me to come at once to help his wife who was sick again. It was the husband of Mrs. Sacks, and I intuitively knew before I left the telephone that it was almost useless to go.

I dreaded to face that woman. I was tempted to send someone else in my place. I longed for an accident on the subway, or on the street—anything to prevent my going into that home. But on I went just the same. I arrived a few minutes after the doctor, the same one who had given her such noble advice. The woman was dying. She was unconscious. She died within ten minutes after my arrival. It was the same result, the same story told a thousand times before— death from abortion. She had become pregnant, had used drugs, had then consulted a five-dollar professional abortionist, and death followed.

After I left that desolate house I walked and walked and walked; for hours and hours I kept on, bag in hand, thinking, regretting, dreading to stop; fearful of my conscience, dreading to face my own accusing soul. At three in the morning I arrived home still clutching a heavy load the weight of which I was quite unconscious.

I entered the house quietly, as was my custom, and looked out of the window down upon the dimly lighted, sleeping city. . . .

. . . For hours I stood, motionless and tense, expecting something to happen. I watched the lights go out, I saw the darkness gradually give way to the first shimmer of dawn, and then a colorful sky heralded the rise of the sun. I knew a new day had come for me and a new world as well.

It was like an illumination. I could now see clearly the various social strata of our life; all its mass problems seemed to be centered around uncontrolled breeding. There was only one thing to be done: call out, start the alarm, set the heather on fire! Awaken the womanhood of America to free the motherhood of the world! I released from my almost paralyzed hand the nursing bag which unconsciously I had clutched, threw it across the room, tore the uniform from my body, flung it into a corner, and renounced all palliative work forever.

I would never go back again to nurse women's ailing bodies while their miseries were as vast as the stars. I was now finished with superficial cures, with doctors and nurses and social workers who were brought face to face with this overwhelming truth of women's needs and yet turned to pass on the other side. They must be made to see these facts. I resolved that women should have knowledge of contraception. They have every right to know about their own bodies. I would strike out—I would scream from the housetops. I would tell the world what was going on in the lives of these poor women. I *would* be heard. No matter what it should cost. *I would be heard.*

[1916]

The selection of a place for the first birth control clinic was of the greatest importance. No one could actually tell how it would be received in any neighborhood. I thought of all the possible difficulties: The indifference of women's organizations, the ignorance of the workers themselves, the resentment of social agencies, the opposition of the medical profession. Then there was the law—the law of New York State.

Section 1142 was definite. It stated that *no one* could give information to prevent conception to *anyone* for any reason. There was, however, Section

1145, which distinctly stated that physicians *(only)* could give advice to prevent conception for the cure or prevention of disease. I inquired about the section, and was told by two attorneys and several physicians that this clause was an exception to 1142 referring only to venereal disease. But anyway, as I was not a physician, it could not protect me. Dared I risk it?

I began to think of the doctors I knew. Several who had previously promised now refused. I wrote, telephoned, asked friends to ask other friends to help me find a woman doctor to help me demonstrate the need of a birth control clinic in New York. None could be found. No one wanted to go to jail. No one cared to test out the law. Perhaps it would have to be done without a doctor. But it had to be done; that I knew.

Fania Mindell, an enthusiastic young worker in the cause, had come on from Chicago to help me. Together we tramped the streets on that dreary day in early October, through a driving rainstorm, to find the best location at the cheapest terms possible. . . .

Finally at 46 Amboy Street, in the Brownsville section of Brooklyn, we found a friendly landlord with a good place vacant at fifty dollars a month rental; and Brownsville was settled on. It was one of the most thickly populated sections. It had a large population of working-class Jews, always interested in health measures, always tolerant of new ideas, willing to listen and to accept advice whenever the health of mother or children was involved. I knew that here there would at least be no breaking of windows, no hurling of insults into our teeth; but I was scarcely prepared for the popular support, the sympathy and friendly help given us in that neighborhood from that day to this.

With a small bundle of handbills and a large amount of zeal, we fared forth each morning in a house-to-house canvass of the district in which the clinic was located. Every family in that great district received a "dodger" printed in English, Yiddish and Italian. . . .

It was on October 16, 1916, that the three of us—Fania Mindell, Ethel Byrne and myself—opened the doors of the first birth control clinic in America. I believed then and do today, that the opening of those doors to the mothers of Brownsville was an event of social significance in the lives of American womanhood.

News of our work spread like wildfire. Within a few days there was not a darkened tenement, hovel or flat but was brightened by the knowledge that motherhood could be voluntary; that children need not be born into the world unless they are wanted and have a place provided for them. For the first time, women talked openly of this terror of unwanted pregnancy which had haunted their lives since time immemorial. The newspapers, in glaring headlines, used the words "birth control," and carried the message that somewhere in Brooklyn there was a place where contraceptive information could be obtained by all overburdened mothers who wanted it.

Ethel Byrne, who is my sister and a trained nurse, assisted me in advising, explaining, and demonstrating to the women how to prevent conception. As all of our 488 records were confiscated by the detectives who later arrested us for violation of the New York State law, it is difficult to tell exactly how many more women came in those few days to seek advice; but we estimate that it was far more than five hundred. As in any new enterprise, false reports were maliciously spread about the clinic; weird stories without the slightest foundation of truth. We talked plain talk and gave plain facts to the women who came there. We kept a record of every applicant. All were mothers; most of them had large families.

It was whispered about that the police were to raid the place for abortions. We had no fear of that accusation. We were trying to spare mothers the necessity of that ordeal by giving them proper contraceptive information. It was well that so many of the women in the neighborhood knew the truth of our doings. Hundreds of them who had witnessed the facts came to the courtroom afterward, eager to testify in our behalf.

One day a woman by the name of Margaret Whitehurst came to us. She said that she was the mother of two children and that she had not money to support more. Her story was a pitiful one—all lies, of course, but the government acts that way. She asked for our literature and preventives, and received both. Then she triumphantly went to the District Attorney's office and secured a warrant for the arrest of my sister, Mrs. Ethel Byrne, our interpreter, Miss Fania Mindell, and myself.

I refused to close down the clinic, hoping that a court decision would allow us to continue such necessary work. I was to be disappointed. Pressure was brought upon the landlord, and we were dispossessed by the law as a "public nuisance." In Holland the clinics were called "public utilities."

When the policewoman entered the clinic with her squad of plain clothes men and announced the arrest of Miss Mindell and myself (Mrs. Byrne was not present at the time and her arrest followed later), the room was crowded to suffocation with women waiting in the outer room. The police began bullying these mothers, asking them questions, writing down their names in order to subpoena them to testify against us at the trial. These women, always afraid of trouble which the very presence of a policeman signifies, screamed and cried aloud. The children on their laps screamed, too. It was like a panic for a few minutes until I walked into the room where they were stampeding and begged them to be quiet and not to get excited. I assured them that nothing could happen to them, that I was under arrest but they would be allowed to return home in a few minutes. That quieted them. The men were blocking the door to prevent anyone from leaving, but I finally persuaded them to allow these women to return to their homes, unmolested though terribly frightened by it all.

Crowds began to gather outside. A long line of women with baby carriages and children had been waiting to get into the clinic. Now the streets were filled, and police had to see that traffic was not blocked. The patrol wagon came rattling through the streets to our door, and at length Miss Mindell and I took our seats within and were taken to the police station.

On the Road during the Great Depression
Morey Skaret

The Great Depression of the 1930s was devastating to many American families. As people lost their jobs and depleted their savings, millions of families were forced to abandon their homes, some living on the street or, if they were lucky, doubling and tripling up with relatives and friends. While such compromises made sense economically, they often led to tensions and explosive outbreaks among families used to having their own space. Domestic violence and depression were all too common, and many families were unable to survive the stress, causing males who had been breadwinners to take to the road. Some were thrown out by women unable to cope with their inability to secure work. Others stole away in the middle of the night, the shame of not taking care of their families too much to bear. Perhaps they believed they were doing their families a favor by reducing the number of mouths to feed while increasing their prospects for finding work.

So many men took to the road during this period that a subculture developed around this lifestyle that came to be called hobo. *A hobo was a homeless man living on the cheap, illegally hopping freight trains, sleeping where he could, all the while looking for work. Hobos shared a supposed camaraderie of nights beneath the stars and the romance of the road, evolving their own vocabulary and ethical codes, which they used to distinguish themselves from more traditional tramps who also "rambled," but without an interest in employment.*

The classic depiction of the hobo is of a shabbily dressed man carrying all his belongings tied into a cloth at the end of a stick with a sign asking for money, work, or food. Hobos were featured in movies, comics, books, songs, and radio dramas. Despite serious housing shortages after World War II, the robust postwar economy and record lows in unemployment largely put an end to the hobo lifestyle. However, a new generation of postwar artists and writers, who had grown up in a more comfortable and predictable economic environment, would celebrate it in songs, poetry, and fiction.

The following account is by Morest L. "Morey" Skaret, born in Norway in 1913, but who moved to Seattle with his family at the age of ten. After completing a fifth year of high school, thanks to a special program offered by the Seattle school district in response to record unemployment levels, Skaret took to the road. He eventually became a police officer and wrote his autobiography, from which this account is taken.

Morest L. "Morey" Skaret, June 15, 2001, courtesy HistoryLink.org.

1. During the Great Depression high schoolers like Skaret tried to stay in school after graduation; in fact, the City University of New York, which was free at the time, had its greatest expansion in students ever. Why do you think so many people saw school as a response to economic crisis?
2. Although there were women, like "Boxcar" Bertha, who lived the hobo life during the Depression, it was almost entirely men who took to the road. Why do you think this was the case?
3. What were some of the dangers and hardships that Morey and Charlie faced?
4. How do representations of hobos compare with the way homeless people are regarded today?

ON THE BUM

By the time I got to high school, the whole town was well into the Great Depression. It was tough times. I got my diploma but I couldn't afford to go to university so I took advantage of the extra year of high school that the district offered. After that, I did what a lot of young men from large families did then to relieve the load on the home place: I went on the bum. Charlie Shellfisher, my good friend all through school, and I went together. Although Native American not Norwegian, his family was similar to mine — hard-working and hard-pressed. We left Seattle in the spring and returned before winter.

Charlie and I usually rode freight trains. When a gondola car was empty of grain or coal, we could get shelter from the wind inside. A boxcar was even better because it would also keep us dry. If we couldn't get inside a freight car, we rode the rods under it. Two thick rods about five feet apart span between the front and rear wheels of a freight car to give it strength. To "ride the rods," you would lie on a plank wired across those two rods. You could usually count on finding a plank and some wire in the rail yard. The wire is essential because, if your plank falls off when the train's going 40 miles an hour or so, you're dead. Charlie and I always tried to put our planks together so we could get some warmth from each other.

If no freight train was coming, we would catch a passenger train and "ride the blinds." Similar to our articulated buses now, the accordion-like folds of a train's blinds are what enabled it to "bend" around curves. The blinds of one passenger car would butt up to the blinds of the car in front of it to make an articulated compartment. At the time, trains were powered by coal. Where the coal car met the first passenger car, you had just a single, open blind. Charlie and I would jump in there and cuddle in the corner away from the wind. The railroads didn't like you riding their passenger trains and we would do it only as a last resort. If you didn't get off before the train reached the yard, the bulls [railway security officers] would come after you with those big sticks they had.

One day Charlie and I scrambled out from under a car to face a yard bull in Cheyenne, Wyoming. "How much money do you have, boys?" he demanded.

"We don't have any," I responded.

"Well, this town has an ordinance that says, if you don't have at least 35 cents, you're a vagrant and under arrest," he said. "Come on."

We figured out later that, when someone in town needed workers, the yard bull would provide them! We happened along when the town needed to move its library from one side of the street to the other. For four days, Charlie and I carried books. We spent three nights in jail, where our meals arrived in a bucket! When we were finished, the sheriff drove us in an old Dodge panel truck out to the edge of town.

"That's the way to Laramie," he said, pointing down a gray ribbon of highway. "Don't you ever come back to Cheyenne."

"No sir, we won't!" I said. We thumbed our way to the next town and sought out the hobo jungle near the railroad tracks where we could find out when to catch a train going north.

To sustain ourselves, Charlie and I would first ask for work in exchange for a meal, then if we couldn't get work, we would ask for a meal. Because most of the places we asked were on the regular routes that bums traveled, feeding them got to be too much for many of those dear, kind people.

We were in one jungle when Charlie got sick and was shaking with cold. I found a long cardboard box, the kind that a hot-water tank might have come in, and put it under a bridge out of the rain. Charlie crawled inside and I stuffed newspapers all around him for warmth. I went into the town and asked the baker for work in order to get my sick friend something to eat. He said he was asked all the time and usually said no but he had garbage cans out back that needed cleaning and I could have that job.

Never clean a baker's garbage cans! The stuff on the sides was as hard as concrete. I pretty much had to chisel them clean! When I got finished, the baker's wife saw that I had worked hard and she put a full piece of beef steak inside each of two sandwiches. When I got back to Charlie with this food, an old Negro man had come in with a few other hobos and started a fire. They took a square five-gallon tin can and cut one end out to feed in the wood and a hole in the other end to get the draft going and it made a darn good stove. The old man got the beef steak all heated and cut up for Charlie. He began to feel better and soon we were back on our way to Seattle.

One story from that time I know to be true but I'm not sure who did it. It could have been Charlie; I know it wasn't me because such a deception wasn't in my nature.

We were hungry one day when we came across a little boy playing near an irrigation ditch. Charlie thought a minute and then all of a sudden he grabbed the kid by the neck of his shirt and dunked him under the water. Charlie carried the dripping kid to the mother and said, "Your little boy fell in the irrigation ditch!"

"Oh my goodness," she said. "I'm so glad you were there! Johnny, I told you not to go near that irrigation ditch. Now you thank the nice man." Well, of course, the kid's eyes got big and he backed away and started to cry. He didn't want to have anything to do with Charlie! We got a good meal out of it but it was a dirty trick.

On the bum, you're always moving. At first you're searching, anxious to get to the next town or farming area because that may be where you find a job. After you realize that nothing's out there, you're hurrying home. We got as far as Cheyenne before we decided we'd better turn around.

Oldtimers had warned us against riding through a long tunnel—that we could suffocate from the fumes. We took a chance, though, and made it through one long tunnel north of Everett and another just before Union Station in Seattle. As we came out of the second tunnel, we hung on the side of the car and paced with one foot to tell if the train had slowed enough for us to jump. When I jumped, I landed right in the cinders. Charlie was more nimble and made it fine.

We brushed ourselves off and walked down to Skid Road with just 10 cents between us. We got a bowl of soup and dry bread for 5 cents each at the Klondike Café, then walked home. Mother was glad to see me. I had turned 20 on the bum.

25

Taking a Stand:
The Sit-Down Strikes of the 1930s
Genora Dollinger

While the New Deal's reform efforts began to wane after a flurry of legislation in 1935 known as the second hundred days, organized labor's drive in 1936 and 1937 toward national organization levied a powerful tool that both gave the New Deal an institutional base and solidified opposition to it. Labor's new weapon was the sit-down strike.

Early in 1936, the Firestone Rubber Company of Akron, Ohio, fired several unionists for organizing against a proposed wage cut. In defense of their sacked union brothers, workers remained after their work shifts to occupy the factory. Within just two days Firestone gave in. When a similar situation occurred across town at Goodyear, the police deputized 150 strikebreakers to help clear the factory. There they were met by thousands of angry workers from all over Akron. Goodyear, too, surrendered, and the new strategy spread across the nation. Over five hundred sit-downs occurred between 1936 and 1937, achieving more success for unionization in a year than labor had accomplished in decades.

Why did the sit-down strike work? Businessmen were fearful of having equipment dashed along with their hopes of industrial recovery. And the new strategy prevented management from hiring nonunion "scab" workers to replace strikers. Both federal and state governments no longer expected public support for the use of force that had once been their response to labor militancy. So industry after industry yielded to the workers' new aggressiveness. In 1936, before the sit-downs began, scarcely four million workers had belonged to unions. By the end of 1937 the figure was over seven million. The nation entered World War II with over eleven million workers organized.

The most famous sit-down strike occurred in December 1936 at General Motors' Fisher Body Plant in Flint, Michigan, in response to the firing of two union members. The following account is by Genora Dollinger, as told to an oral history interviewer from the United Auto Workers in 1995. Dollinger was twenty-three at the time and realized early in the strike that police would find it difficult to physically attack women. She organized the Women's Auxiliary of the United Auto Workers (UAW) and the Women's Emergency Brigade, providing food and key physical defense for the striking workers.

Questions to Consider

1. What are the advantages for workers of a sit-down strike over a conventional picket? What are the disadvantages to workers of this strategy?
2. How does the sit-down strike depend on different types of external support?
3. Why was the sit-down strike so effective in the 1930s? Do you think it would be as effective today? Why or why not?

Conditions in Flint before the strike were very, very depressing for working people. We had a large influx of workers come into the city from the deep South. They came north to find jobs, because there was no work back home. They came with their furniture strapped on old jalopies and they'd move into the cheapest housing that they could find. Usually these were just little one or two-room structures with no inside plumbing and no inside heating arrangements. They just had kerosene heaters to heat their wash water, their bath water, and their homes. You could smell kerosene all over their clothing. They were very poor. . . .

Before the strike, the women didn't have the opportunity to participate in any activities. The small neighborhood churches were the only places they had to go to. They knew some of their neighbors and they would go to some of these little churches, but that's all. The men frequented the beer gardens and talked to other men about shop problems or whatever. They got to be shop buddies.

When you worked in the factory in those days, no one cared what your name was. You became "Whitey" if you happened to be blonde. Or you might be "Blacky" if you had black hair. If you asked, "Well, who is he?" you'd get, "I don't know, he works in department so-and-so, Plant 4, on the line half way down." It was just "Blacky" or "Shorty" or some nickname. They were wage slaves with a complete loss of identity and rights inside the plant.

At first, when these workers were approached to join the union, they were afraid they might lose this job that was so very valuable to them. At that time, men working in the auto plants were getting around forty-five cents an hour. The younger girls that worked in the A.C. Sparkplug division of General Motors, were being paid twelve-and-a-half cents an hour to make minor car instruments. That was the only plant that employed women.

I'll tell you about the conditions of these young women. After the strike, a Senate investigating committee found that in one department of A.C. alone, the girls had all been forced to go to the county hospital and be treated for venereal disease traced to one foreman. Those were the conditions that young women had to accept in order to support their families. Sometimes they earned just enough to provide food for the family and they couldn't lose their jobs because nobody else in the family had a job.

Flint was a General Motors town—lock, stock and barrel! If you drove past one of the huge GM plants in Flint, you could see workers sitting on the front lawns along the side of the plant just waiting for a foreman to come to the door and call them in. And maybe they'd work them for an hour or maybe for a day, and that was it. But workers were so desperate that they would come and sit every day on that lawn in the hopes of being called in and possibly getting a permanent job. That's how poor these General Motors workers really were, at least the ones in hopes of getting a job at GM. . . .

Conditions were terrible inside the plants, which were notorious for their speed-up systems. They had men with stop watches timing the workers to see if they could squeeze one or two more operations in. You saw Charlie Chaplin in the movie, *Modern Times*? Well, this is exactly what happened. They did everything but tie a broom to their tail. It was so oppressive that there were several cases of men just cracking up completely and taking a wrench and striking their foreman. When that happened, the worker was sentenced to what was then called an insane asylum in Pontiac, Michigan.

The speed-up was the biggest issue. The men just couldn't take it. They would come home at night, and they couldn't hold their forks in their swollen fingers. They would just lie down on the floor. Many of them wound up in beer gardens to try to forget their problems and their aches and pains. . . .

They used to say, "Once you pass the gates of General Motors, forget about the United States Constitution." Workers had no rights when they entered that plant. If a foreman didn't like the way you parted your hair—or whatever he didn't like about you—you may have looked at him the wrong way, or said something that rubbed him the wrong way—he could fire you. No recourse, no nothing. And practically all foremen expected workers to bring them turkeys on Thanksgiving and gifts for Christmas and repair their motor cars and even paint their houses. The workers were kept intimidated because if they didn't comply with what the foreman told them to do, they would lose their jobs and their families would starve. You can see what a feeling of slavery and domination workers felt inside the GM plants.

Not only that, but when workers started talking about organizing, management hired lip-readers to watch the men talk to each other, even when they were right close to each other, so they could tell if they were talking union. One of our friends who was a member of the Socialist Party wore the first UAW button into the Chevrolet plant. He was fired immediately. He didn't even get to his job. They spotted the button and that was it. If you went into a beer garden or other place like that and began to talk about unions, very often you didn't get home without getting an awful beating by GM-hired thugs.

That was the condition inside the plants. Combined with the bad conditions on the outside: poor living conditions, lack of proper food, lack of proper medical attention and everything else, the auto workers came to the conclusion that there was no way they could ever escape any of this injustice without joining a union. But they didn't all decide at one time. . . .

The first sit-down was on December 30 in the small Fisher Body Plant 2 over a particularly big grievance that had occurred. The workers were at the point where they had just had enough, and under a militant leadership, they sat down. When the UAW leaders in the big Fisher Body Plant 1 heard about the sit-down in Fisher 2, they sat down, also. That took real guts, and it took political leadership. The leaders of the political parties knew what they had to do because they'd studied labor history and the ruthlessness of the corporations.

Picket lines were established and also a big kitchen in the south end of Flint, across from the large Fisher 1 plant. Every day, gallons and gallons of food were prepared, and anybody who was on the picket lines would get a ticket with notification that they had served on the line so they'd be able to get a good hot meal.

The strike kitchen was primarily organized by the Communist Party women. They brought a restaurant man from Detroit to help organize this huge kitchen. They were the ones who made all of those good meals.

We also had what we called scavengers, groups of people who would go to the local farmers and ask for donations of food for the strikers. Many people in these small towns surrounding Flint were factory workers who would also raise potatoes, cabbages, tomatoes, corn or whatever. So great quantities of food were sent down to be made into dishes for the strikers. People were very generous. . . .

After the first sit-down started, I went down to see what I could do to help. I was either on the picket lines or up at the Pengelly Building all the time, but some of the strike leaders didn't know who I was and didn't know that I had been teaching classes in unionism and so on. So they said, "Go to the kitchen. We need a lot of help out there." They didn't know what else to tell a woman to do. I said, "You've got a lot of little, skinny men around here who can't stand to be out on the cold picket lines for very long. They can peel potatoes as well as women can." I turned down the idea of kitchen duty.

Instead, I organized a children's picket line. I got Bristol board and paints, and I was painting signs for this children's picket line. One of my socialist comrades came up and said, "Hey, Genora, what are you doing here?" I said, "I'm doing your job." Since he was a professional sign painter, I turned the sign-painting project over to him and that was the beginning of the sign-painting department.

We could only do the children's picket line once because it was too dangerous, but we got an awful lot of favorable publicity from it, much of it international. The picture of my two-year-old son, Jarvis, holding a picket sign saying, "My daddy strikes for us little tykes," went all over the nation, and people sent me articles from French newspapers and from Germany and from other European countries. I thought it was remarkable that the news traveled so far.

26

Advertising in the Interwar Years
ScotTissue and Brer Rabbit
Molasses Advertisements

Since Volney Palmer opened the first advertising agency in 1841 in Philadelphia, Americans have had a love-hate relationship with advertising. Advertisements are attacked for appealing to our fears and anxieties, imposing arbitrary and impossible-to-attain standards of beauty, fitness, personal hygiene, and affluence, and promoting stereotypical attributes of gender, race, and class. Yet they also help us define our identities by influencing our decisions about the music we listen to, the clothing we buy, the cars we drive, and the places we vacation. There is rarely a day when we do not hear a sales pitch, watch an ad, or read a corporate logo; museums, parks, schools, and many sports and entertainment venues carry the names of corporate sponsors.

Much of the contemporary dominance of advertising originated in the 1920s, when mass production of consumer goods and the growing affluence of the post–World War I era led to national distribution networks and increased competition among rapidly growing corporations like Coca-Cola, Palmolive, and Ford. During this golden age of advertising, companies across the country began to compete for the best artists, writers, and musicians, whom they lured with the promise of regular paychecks and mass recognition for their work. Advertisements in newspapers and magazines, on billboards, and on the radio flooded into every nook and cranny of the built environment.

Hated around the world for its sometimes compelling beauty, unapologetic crassness, and power to influence the subconscious, advertising remains both the best and the worst of U.S. popular culture. These two ads, one from 1926 and the other from 1934, are examples of the ways in which advertising has long exploited desires and insecurities.

The techniques of advertising could be used to market any product: even toilet paper could become a status symbol. By the 1920s toilet paper had become widespread in urban America and there were suddenly many competitors producing new products like sanitary napkins, known at first as "cellu-naps," tissues and other "hygiene"-related products but they were still difficult to advertise nationally given the social sensibilities of the time. This ad for ScotTissue presents two women having tea together. What elements of the image and text combine to make the case for ScotTissue as the choice of "discriminating women" in "well-conducted homes"? What is the "it" that "women sense . . . immediately"? How is the product described in the ad's text and how would the words used have helped sell it? What is "intuitive daintiness"? Note that while this ad features words and large, detailed illustrations, the product itself is clearly but discretely placed. Why?

In contrast to the sophisticated women taking tea in the ScotTissue ad, the Brer Rabbit Molasses ad features a cozier scene of a young husband enjoying his wife's home-made gingerbread. The woman lets the reader know that her husband likes the ginger-bread so much because it reminds him of the "plantation molasses he used to have when he was a boy . . . thanks to Brer Rabbit." The ad also features Brer Rabbit dressed up in the clothing worn by servants and seemingly in a hurry to deliver a platter of ginger-bread. What is Alice's problem and what strategies does she devise to overcome it? What instincts and appetites of her husband does she appeal to? How is the contemporary packaging, marketing, and branding of Brer Rabbit Molasses (see http://www.bgfoods .com/brand_brerrabbit.asp) different from what it was in the 1930s? Why do you think that the company made the specific changes in the product that it did?

Questions to Consider

1. How does each product claim to bring happiness to its consumers? How does each ad shape the public image of the product it is selling?
2. Why do you think that companies selling consumer products often tar-geted women first? What particular female concerns (or anxieties) did ads such as these two play on?
3. The ScotTissue ad dates from 1926; the Brer Rabbit Molasses ad from 1934. How do the style and content between the two ads differ? What historical changes during the eight-year interim might account for these differences? (*Hint:* Note the Roosevelt administration National Recov-ery Act (NRA) seal in the lower right-hand corner.)
4. Compare these advertisements with contemporary ones for products in magazines or on the Internet. How has advertising changed? How has it remained the same?

Women sense it immediately ∾ ∾

—that atmosphere of elegance and refinement—those necessary little appointments, noticed but not discussed, which contribute so much to the comfort and well-being of guests and family.

ScotTissue has made a place for itself in well-conducted homes. It is the choice of discriminating women everywhere, because of its hygienic purity and safety.

A highly-absorbent, snow-white, soothing tissue, marvelously soft as fine old linen. Kind to the most sensitive skin. Peculiarly adapted to the needs of women of intuitive daintiness. Ask your doctor.

No conversation. Just say "ScotTissue" to your storekeeper and receive a big, economical, dustproof roll.

SCOTT PAPER COMPANY, Chester, Pa.

Another Thirsty Fibre Product
3 rolls 25c

Soft as old Linen
ScotTissue
The absorbent soft white Toilet paper

Scott Paper Company
Chester, Pa., U.S.A.

15 cents a roll

Our Offer

If your dealer cannot supply you, send us 15 cents with your dealer's name and we will send you a full size roll of ScotTissue, prepaid.

© S. P. Co.

ScotTissue advertisement, *Saturday Evening Post*, September 11, 1926.

Her Saturday Night
Gingerbread
brought him back to her

Brer Rabbit Molasses advertisement, *Ladies Home Journal,* January 1934.

PART FIVE

"The American Century"

War, Affluence, and Uncertainty

World War II affected virtually every part of American life. Problems of economic depression vanished with the growth of productivity in war industries and—to the surprise of most economists—did not return after peace was declared. The federal government expanded during the war and never returned to its prewar size. Family life changed dramatically: fathers were absent, mothers were working, families moved to crowded centers of war industry, consumer goods were rationed or unavailable, and divorce rates soared. Science was transformed both by its scale of activities and by its subjection to military security regulations. Loyalties and antipathies shifted in extraordinary ways: the communist Soviet Union became one of the United States' most important allies and bore the brunt of the war's casualties, while German and Italian Americans became suspect, and many Japanese Americans were locked in internment camps.

The readings in Part Five sample the drama of World War II. J. Robert Oppenheimer, who directed scientific work at Los Alamos, recounts the controversy surrounding the creation of the atomic bomb. Paul Tibbets, pilot of the *Enola Gay*, recounts the dropping of the bomb on Hiroshima, and George Weller describes the aftereffects of the bomb on Nagasaki. Fanny Christina Hill was one of the many women dubbed "Rosie the Riveter" in the newspapers who found new opportunities in the war industries. Ben Yorita and Philip Hayasaka describe the internment camps where they and their families were forced to endure much of the war. Several American soldiers remember how they suffered at the hands of the Japanese during the Bataan death march.

Victory in the war planted seeds of hope and fear. Uncertainties about the future of the United States were accompanied by ideological quarrels with the Soviet Union. The anxious transition to a peacetime economy and then back to the quasi-war footing of the cold war provoked the Red Scare, the fear of communist espionage that Oscar-winner Ring Lardner Jr. struggled with during the 1950s.

Cold war propaganda heightened this fear, but as Americans embarked on what proved to be an era of unprecedented prosperity, social commentators became more concerned about the nation growing soft and complacent, even conformist, like the perfectly planned uniform suburbs of Levittown and their many imitators. There were, of course, many Americans, particularly women and minorities, who were left out of the postwar economic boom. Fanny Christina Hill, for instance, found that after the war it was difficult for her to make a living wage. For her and many others, it was a period of struggle, envy, and disappointment.

POINTS OF VIEW

Building and Using an Atomic Bomb (1942–1945)

27

To Build an Atomic Bomb

J. Robert Oppenheimer

The 1920s were a golden age in theoretical physics. Brilliant and dedicated physicists like J. Robert Oppenheimer (1904–1967) ignored society and politics, living in a separate world of new theories and discoveries in relativity and quantum theory that transformed classic Newtonian physics. Then in the early 1930s, with the rise of Hitler, Mussolini, and Stalin, politics began noticeably to intrude even on sciences as remote as theoretical physics. And, less noticeably, scientific theories and discoveries began ever so slowly to intrude on politics. James Chadwick's discovery of the neutron in 1932 and Albert Einstein's emigration from Germany to the United States in 1933 seemed far less important than the rise of Adolf Hitler or the election of Franklin D. Roosevelt. Yet by 1938, when scientists in Germany at last figured out that neutrons could "split" certain atoms and release great quantities of energy, the fate of people and nations suddenly hung in the balance.

Scientists in Great Britain and the United States could only speculate on what progress Hitler's scientists might have been making in harnessing nuclear fission. In June 1942, American and British scientists developed plans for a uranium-based atomic bomb. Full-scale efforts to construct such a bomb, code-named the "Manhattan

---

Jonathan F. Fanton, R. Hae Williams, and Michael B. Stoff, eds., *The Manhattan Project: A Documentary Introduction to the Atomic Age* (New York: McGraw-Hill, 1991), 29–32; Alice Kimball Smith and Charles Weiher, eds., *Robert Oppenheimer: Letters and Recollections* (Cambridge, Mass.: Harvard University Press, 1980), 315–20, 324–25.

Project," thus began in the shadow of Germany's possible head start. (Only later was Germany's lack of progress discovered.)

The Manhattan Project was overseen by the Army Corps of Engineers. Under the direction of General Leslie R. Groves, massive facilities in Los Alamos, New Mexico; Oak Ridge, Tennessee; and Hanford, Washington, were built, involving about 125,000 work-ers and costing $2 billion. Los Alamos—a site chosen by Oppenheimer—was the scien-tific capital of the project and was kept relatively independent of the military despite its strict security.

"My two great loves," the scientist J. Robert Oppenheimer, chosen to lead the proj-ect, often told friends, "are physics and New Mexico. It's a pity they can't be combined." Two decades later his wish came true when the nation's need for secrecy and his own longtime affection for the area made it the appropriate site of a great adventure for many physicists and their families.

At Los Alamos, scientists who were accustomed to open communications lived under the rule of secrecy and military security. They could not tell relatives where they were going or what they were doing; even their spouses might not have known what the labo-ratory's mission was. Often they did not know what other units in the laboratory were working on, and few knew what the ultimate objective of the project was. Oppenheimer recruited scientists worldwide and directed their work on the tightest of deadlines to-ward their ultimate goal: beating the Germans to the bomb. Their success, and the ironies of that success, are the subjects of Oppenheimer's autobiographical sketch and his November 1945 speech.

QUESTIONS TO CONSIDER

1. What changed J. Robert Oppenheimer from an unworldly scientist to a man who could direct a large and important enterprise?
2. What responsibilities did he see for scientists after the war?
3. After he opposed the development of the hydrogen bomb, Oppen-heimer lost his security clearance to engage in or advise government re-search on nuclear weapons. What foreshadowings of his doubts about nuclear weapons do you see in Oppenheimer's speech?

AUTOBIOGRAPHICAL SKETCH (1954)

I was born in New York in 1904. My father had come to this country at the age of 17 from Germany. He was a successful businessman and quite active in com-munity affairs. My mother was born in Baltimore and before her marriage was an artist and teacher of art. I attended Ethical Culture School and Harvard Col-lege, which I entered in 1922. I completed the work for my degree in the spring of 1925. I then left Harvard to study at Cambridge University and in Goettin-gen, where in the spring of 1927 I took my doctor's degree. . . . I had learned a great deal in my student days about the new physics; I wanted to pursue this myself, to explain it and to foster its cultivation. I had had many invitations to university positions, 1 or 2 in Europe, and perhaps 10 in the United States. I ac-cepted concurrent appointments as assistant professor at the California Institute of Technology in Pasadena and at the University of California in Berkeley. For the coming 12 years, I was to devote my time to these 2 faculties.

Starting with a single graduate student in my first year in Berkeley, we gradually began to build up what was to become the largest school in the country of graduate and postdoctoral study in theoretical physics, so that as time went on, we came to have between a dozen and 20 people learning and adding to quantum theory, nuclear physics, relativity and other modern physics.

My friends, both in Pasadena and in Berkeley, were mostly faculty people, scientists, classicists, and artists. I studied and read Sanskrit with Arthur Rider. I read very widely, mostly classics, novels, plays, and poetry; and I read something of other parts of science. I was not interested in and did not read about economics or politics. I was almost wholly divorced from the contemporary scene in this country. I never read a newspaper or a current magazine like *Time* or *Harper's*; I had no radio, no telephone; I learned of the stock-market crash in the fall of 1929 only long after the event; the first time I ever voted was in the presidential election of 1936. To many of my friends, my indifference to contemporary affairs seemed bizarre, and they often chided me with being too much of a highbrow. I was interested in man and his experience; I was deeply interested in my science; but I had no understanding of the relations of man to his society.

Beginning in late 1936, my interests began to change. These changes did not alter my earlier friendships, my relations to my students, or my devotion to physics; but they added something new. I can discern in retrospect more than one reason for these changes. I had had a continuing, smoldering fury about the treatment of Jews in Germany. I had relatives there, and was later to help in extricating them and bringing them to this country. I saw what the depression was doing to my students. Often they could get no jobs, or jobs which were wholly inadequate. And through them, I began to understand how deeply political and economic events could affect men's lives. I began to feel the need to participate more fully in the life of the community. But I had no framework of political conviction or experience to give me perspective in these matters. . . .

Ever since the discovery of nuclear fission, the possibility of powerful explosives based on it had been very much in my mind, as it had in that of many other physicists. We had some understanding of what this might do for us in the war, and how much it might change the course of history. In the autumn of 1941, a special committee was set up by the National Academy of Sciences under the chairmanship of Arthur Compton to review the prospects and feasibility of the different uses of atomic energy for military purposes. I attended a meeting of this committee; this was my first official connection with the atomic-energy program.

After the academy meeting, I spent some time in preliminary calculations about the consumption and performance of atomic bombs, and became increasingly excited at the prospects. At the same time I still had a quite heavy burden of academic work with courses and graduate students. I also began to consult, more or less regularly, with the staff of the Radiation Laboratory in Berkeley on their program for the electromagnetic separation of uranium isotopes. I was never a member or employee of the laboratory; but I attended many of its staff and policy meetings. With the help of two of my graduate students, I developed an invention which was embodied in the production plants at Oak Ridge. I attended the conference in Chicago at which the Metallurgical Laboratory (to produce plutonium) was established and its initial program projected.

In the spring of 1942, Compton called me to Chicago to discuss the state of work on the bomb itself. During this meeting Compton asked me to take the responsibility for this work, which at that time consisted of numerous scattered experimental projects. Although I had no administrative experience and was not an experimental physicist, I felt sufficiently informed and challenged by the problem to be glad to accept. At this time I became an employee of the Metal-lurgical Laboratory.

After this conference I called together a theoretical study group in Berke-ley, in which Hans Bethe, Emil Konopinski, Robert Serber, Edward Teller, John H. Van Vleck, and I participated. We had an adventurous time. We spent much of the summer of 1942 in Berkeley in a joint study that for the first time really came to grips with the physical problems of atomic bombs, atomic explo-sions, and the possibility of using fission explosions to initiate thermonuclear reactions. I called this possibility to the attention of Dr. Vannevar Bush during the late summer; the technical views on this subject were to develop and change from then until the present day.

After these studies there was little doubt that a potentially world-shattering undertaking lay ahead. We began to see the great explosion at Alamogordo[1] and the greater explosions at Eniwetok[2] with a surer foreknowledge. We also began to see how rough, difficult, challenging, and unpredictable this job might turn out to be. . . .

In later summer, after a review of the experimental work, I became con-vinced, as did others, that a major change was called for in the work on the bomb itself. We needed a central laboratory devoted wholly to this purpose, where people could talk freely with each other, where theoretical ideas and ex-perimental findings could affect each other, where the waste and frustration and error of the many compartmentalized experimental studies could be eliminated, where we could begin to come to grips with chemical, metallurgical, engineer-ing, and ordnance problems that had so far received no consideration. We therefore sought to establish this laboratory for a direct attack on all the problems inherent in the most rapid possible development and production of atomic bombs.

In the autumn of 1942 General Leslie R. Groves assumed charge of the Manhattan Engineer District. I discussed with him the need for an atomic bomb laboratory. . . .

In early 1943, I received a letter signed by General Groves and Dr. James B. Conant, appointing me director of the laboratory, and outlining their conception

1. **Alamogordo:** New Mexico site of first detonation of an atomic device.
2. **Eniwetok:** Pacific island used as an atomic test site.

of how it was to be organized and administered. The necessary construction and assembling of the needed facilities were begun. All of us worked in close collaboration with the engineers of the Manhattan District.

The site of Los Alamos was selected in part at least because it enabled those responsible to balance the obvious need for security with the equally important need of free communication among those engaged in the work. Security, it was hoped, would be achieved by removing the laboratory to a remote area, fenced and patrolled, where communication with the outside was extremely limited. Telephone calls were monitored, mail was censored, and personnel who left the area—something permitted only for the clearest of causes—knew that their movements might be under surveillance. On the other hand, for those within the community, fullest exposition and discussion among those competent to use the information was encouraged. . . .

The program of recruitment was massive. Even though we then underestimated the ultimate size of the laboratory, which was to have almost 4,000 members by the spring of 1945, and even though we did not at that time see clearly some of the difficulties which were to bedevil and threaten the enterprise, we knew that it was a big, complex and diverse job. Even the initial plan of the laboratory called for a start with more than 100 highly qualified and trained scientists, to say nothing of the technicians, staff, and mechanics who would be required for their support, and of the equipment that we would have to beg and borrow since there would be no time to build it from scratch. We had to recruit at a time when the country was fully engaged in war and almost every competent scientist was already involved in the military effort.

The primary burden of this fell on me. To recruit staff I traveled all over the country talking with people who had been working on one or another aspect of the atomic-energy enterprise, and people in radar work, for example, and underwater sound, telling them about the job, the place that we were going to, and enlisting their enthusiasm.

In order to bring responsible scientists to Los Alamos, I had to rely on their sense of the interest, urgency, and feasibility of the Los Alamos mission. I had to tell them enough of what the job was, and give strong enough assurance that it might be successfully accomplished in time to affect the outcome of the war, to make it clear that they were justified in their leaving other work to come to this job.

The prospect of coming to Los Alamos aroused great misgivings. It was to be a military post; men were asked to sign up more or less for the duration; restrictions on travel and on the freedom of families to move about to be severe; and no one could be sure of the extent to which the necessary technical freedom of action could actually be maintained by the laboratory. The notion of disappearing into the New Mexico desert for an indeterminate period and under quasi-military auspices disturbed a good many scientists, and the families of many more. But there was another side to it. Almost everyone realized that this was a great undertaking. Almost everyone knew that if it were completed successfully and rapidly enough, it might determine the outcome of the war. Almost everyone knew that it was an unparalleled opportunity to bring to bear the basic knowledge and art of science for the benefit of his country. Almost everyone knew that this job, if it were achieved, would be a part of history. This sense of excitement, of devotion and of patriotism in the end prevailed. Most of those with whom I talked came to Los Alamos. Once they came, confidence in the enterprise grew as men learned more of the technical status of the work; and though the laboratory was to double and redouble its size many times before the end, once it had started it was on the road to success.

We had information in those days of German activity in the field of nuclear fission. We were aware of what it might mean if they beat us to the draw in the development of atomic bombs. The consensus of all our opinions, and every directive that I had, stressed the extreme urgency of our work, as well as the need for guarding all knowledge of it from our enemies. . . .

The story of Los Alamos is long and complex. Part of it is public history. For me it was a time so filled with work, with the need for decision and action and consultation, that there was room for little else. I lived with my family in the community which was Los Alamos. It was a remarkable community, inspired by a high sense of mission, of duty and of destiny, coherent, dedicated, and remarkably selfless. There was plenty in the life of Los Alamos to cause irritation; the security restrictions, many of my own devising, the inadequacies and inevitable fumblings of a military post unlike any that had ever existed before, shortages, inequities and in the laboratory itself the shifting emphasis on different aspects of the technical work as the program moved forward; but I have never known a group more understanding and more devoted to a common purpose, more willing to lay aside personal convenience and prestige, more understanding of the role that they were playing in their country's history. Time and again we had in the technical work almost paralyzing crises. Time and again the laboratory drew itself together and faced the new problems and got on with the work. We worked by night and by day; and in the end the many jobs were done. . . .

SPEECH TO THE ASSOCIATION
OF LOS ALAMOS SCIENTISTS

Los Alamos, November 2, 1945

I am grateful to the Executive Committee for this chance to talk to you. I should like to talk tonight—if some of you have long memories perhaps you will regard it as justified—as a fellow scientist, and at least as a fellow worrier about the fix we are in. I do not have anything very radical to say, or anything that will strike most of you with a great flash of enlightenment. I don't have anything to say that will be of an immense encouragement. In some ways I would have liked to talk to you at an earlier date—but I couldn't talk to you as a Director. I could not talk, and will not tonight talk, too much about the practical political problems which are involved. . . . I don't think that's important. I think there are issues which are quite simple and quite deep, and which involve us as a group of scientists—involve us more, perhaps than any other group in the world. I think that it can only help to look a little at what our situation is—at what has happened to us—and that this must give us some honesty, some insight, which will be a source of strength in what may be the not-too-easy days ahead.

The real impact of the creation of the atomic bomb and atomic weapons—to understand that one has to look further back, look, I think, to the times when physical science was growing in the days of the renaissance, and when the threat that science offered was felt so deeply throughout the Christian world. The analogy is, of course, not perfect. You may even wish to think of the days in the last century when the theories of evolution seemed a threat to the values by which men lived. The analogy is not perfect because there is nothing in atomic weapons—there is certainly nothing that we have done here or in the physics or chemistry that immediately preceded our work here—in which any revolutionary ideas were involved. I don't think that the conceptions of nuclear fission have strained any man's attempts to understand them, and I don't feel that any of us have really learned in a deep sense very much from following this up. It is in a quite different way. It is not an idea—it is a development and a reality—but it has in common with the early days of physical science the fact that the very existence of science is threatened, and its value is threatened. This is the point that I would like to speak a little about.

I think that it hardly needs to be said why the impact is so strong. There are three reasons: one is the extraordinary speed with which things which were right on the frontier of science were translated into terms where they affected many living people, and potentially all people. Another is the fact, quite accidental in many ways, and connected with the speed, that scientists themselves played such a large part, not merely in providing the foundation for atomic weapons, but in actually making them. In this we are certainly closer to it than any other group. The third is that the thing we made—partly because of the technical nature of the problem, partly because we worked hard, partly because we had good breaks—really arrived in the world with such a shattering reality and suddenness that there was no opportunity for the edges to be worn off.

But when you come right down to it the reason that we did this job is because it was an organic necessity. If you are a scientist you cannot stop such a thing. If you are a scientist you believe that it is good to find out how the world works; that it is good to find out what the realities are; that it is good to turn over to mankind at large the greatest possible power to control the world and to deal with it according to its rights and its values.

There are many people who try to wiggle out of this. They say the real importance of atomic energy does not lie in the weapons that have been made; the real importance lies in all the great benefits which atomic energy, which the various radiations, will bring to mankind. There may be some truth in this. I am sure that there is truth in it, because there has never in the past been a new field opened up where the real fruits of it have not been invisible at the beginning. I have a very high confidence that the fruits—the so-called peacetime applications—of atomic energy will have in them all that we think, and more. There are others who try to escape the immediacy of this situation by saying that, after all, war has always been very terrible; after all, weapons have always gotten worse and worse; that this is just another weapon and it doesn't create a great change; that they are not so bad; bombings have been bad in this war and this is not a change in that—it just adds a little to the effectiveness of bombing; that some sort of protection will be found. I think that these efforts to diffuse and weaken the nature of the crisis make it only more dangerous. I think it is for us to accept it as a very grave crisis, to realize that these atomic weapons which we have started to make are very terrible, that they involve a change, that they are not just a slight modification: to accept this, and to accept with it the necessity for those transformations in the world which will make it possible to integrate these developments into human life.

. . . It is a new field, in which the position of vested interests in various parts of the world is very much less serious than in others. It is serious in this country, and that is one of our problems. It is a new field, in which the role of science has been so great that it is to my mind hardly thinkable that the international traditions of science, and the fraternity of scientists, should not play a constructive part. It is a new field, in which just the novelty and the special characteristics of the technical operations should enable one to establish a community of interest which might almost be regarded as a pilot plant for a new type of international collaboration. I speak of it as a pilot plant because it is quite clear that the control of atomic weapons cannot be in itself the unique end of such operation. The only unique end can be a world that is united, and a world in which war will not occur. But those things don't happen overnight, and in this field it would seem that one could get started, and get started without meeting those insuperable obstacles which history has so often placed in the way of any effort of cooperation. Now, this is not an easy thing, and the point I want to make, the one point I want to hammer home, is what an enormous change in spirit is involved. There are things which we hold very dear, and I think rightly hold very dear; I would say that the word democracy perhaps stood for some of them as well as any other word. There are many parts of the world in which there is no democracy. There are other things which we hold dear, and which we rightly should. And when I speak of a new spirit in international affairs I mean that even to these deepest of things which we cherish, and for which Americans have been willing to die—and certainly most of us would be willing to die—even in these deepest things, we realize that there is something more profound than that; namely, the common bond with other men everywhere. It is only if you do that that this makes sense; because if you approach the problem and say, "We know what is right and we would like to use the atomic bomb to persuade you to agree with us," then you are in a very weak position and you will not succeed, because under those conditions you will not succeed in delegating responsibility for the survival of men. It is a purely unilateral statement; you will find yourselves attempting by force of arms to prevent a disaster.

I don't have very much more to say. There are a few things which scientists perhaps should remember, that I don't think I need to remind us of; but I will, anyway. One is that they are very often called upon to give technical information in one way or another, and I think one cannot be too careful to be honest. And it is very difficult, not because one tells lies, but because so often questions are put in a form which makes it very hard to give an answer which is not misleading. I think we will be in a very weak position unless we maintain at its highest the scrupulousness which is traditional for us in sticking to the truth, and in distinguishing between what we know to be true from what we hope may be true.

The second thing I think it right to speak of is this: it is everywhere felt that the fraternity between us and scientists in other countries may be one of the most helpful things for the future; yet it is apparent that even in this country not all of us who are scientists are in agreement. There is no harm in that; such disagreement is healthy. But we must not lose the sense of fraternity because of it; we must not lose our fundamental confidence in our fellow scientists.

I think that we have no hope at all if we yield in our belief in the value of science, in the good that it can be to the world to know about reality, about nature, to attain a gradually greater and greater control of nature, to learn, to teach, to understand. I think that if we lose our faith in this we stop being scientists, we sell out our heritage, we lose what we have most of value for this time of crisis.

But there is another thing: we are not only scientists; we are men, too. We cannot forget our dependence on our fellow men. I mean not only our material dependence, without which no science would be possible, and without which we could not work; I mean also our deep moral dependence, in that the value of science must lie in the world of men, that all our roots lie there. These are the strongest bonds in the world, stronger than those even that bind us to one another, these are the deepest bonds — that bind us to our fellow men.

28

To Use an Atomic Bomb

Paul Tibbets and George Weller

The decision to drop the atomic bombs on the cities of Hiroshima and Nagasaki on August 6 and 9, 1945, was not an easy one. Nazi Germany surrendered on May 8, 1945, and had been carved up into occupation zones by the increasingly rivalrous British, French, U.S., and Soviet armies. Alone, Japan was hopelessly overmatched and facing inevitable defeat. The June capture of Okinawa, considered by most Japanese to be part of their nation, provided the United States and its allies with an important strategic base close to the main Japanese island. All that remained was to decide the terms under which Japan would cease fighting.

Paul Tibbets, interview by Studs Terkel, *The Guardian*, August 6, 2002; Paul Weller, published with the permission of Anthony Weller, Gloucester, Massachusetts, through Dunow & Carlson Literary Agency, New York via Tuttle-Mori Agency, Inc., Tokyo.

The leaders of the United States had determined that they needed nothing short of unconditional surrender, but many Japanese generals found such terms unacceptable. While the leaders of Japan searched for a formula that would allow them to cease fighting, the Allies prepared for an invasion of the main Japanese island. Adding to the complexity was the fact that Roosevelt and Stalin had agreed at the February Yalta Conference that the Soviet Union would declare war in the Pacific and invade Japan within three months of Germany's capitulation. Casualties on both sides were expected to be enormous, since it was assumed that the Japanese would fight to the death.

These were the challenges faced by President Harry Truman and his advisers in deciding whether to use the new and incredibly powerful secret weapon that J. Robert Oppenheimer discusses in Document 28. On August 6, 1945, the United States dropped an atomic bomb on the Japanese city of Hiroshima. Three days later, the United States dropped another bomb, this one on the city of Nagasaki. That was enough. Emperor Hirohito broadcast to the Japanese people his acceptance of surrender. Under some minor terms, which included allowing the Japanese to keep their emperor as a purely symbolic figure, Japan came under American occupation.

Hiroshima and Nagasaki brought just what the U.S. government wanted. Its troops were spared the enormous bloodshed sure to accompany an invasion. But the question of the morality of the bombings has haunted the world ever since. Did the United States and its allies have to demand total surrender, when a few concessions, such as allowing Japanese war crimes to be tried in Japanese courts, might have avoided both invasion and the horror of the two atomic bombs? Were there fewer civilian casualties from the two bombs than the millions who might have died had the U.S. military invaded Japan, as defenders of Truman's decision have argued? Was the desire to avoid the type of power sharing between the United States and the Soviet Union that had occurred in Europe after the Nazi surrender part of Truman's calculation? Finally, what is the future of a world where such devices may be built and used by one nation, forcing others to develop similar technologies?

In the first excerpt, a pilot of the Enola Gay, *Paul Tibbets, talks with journalist Studs Terkel in 2002 about dropping the bomb over Hiroshima. In the second excerpt, Pulitzer Prize–winning journalist George Weller, the first American reporter to enter Nagasaki after the dropping of the second atomic bomb, describes the devastation. The head of the U.S. occupation forces in Japan, General MacArthur, suppressed the series of stories about what Weller had witnessed, and they were released to the public for the first time in June 2005, just three years after Weller's death at the age of ninety-five.*

Questions to Consider

1. How would you characterize Paul Tibbets's feelings about his role in dropping the atomic bomb? Explain any reservations that he might have had about his role along with his justifications for his actions.

2. What do you learn from George Weller of the deaths and illnesses that came as a result of the bombing of Nagasaki?

3. Why do you think MacArthur decided to censor Weller's stories? In your view, might Weller's point of view have played a part in the decision to keep his writings from the public?

PAUL TIBBETS

An Interview with the Pilot of the Enola Gay

Studs Terkel: You got the go-ahead on August 5.

Paul Tibbets: Yeah. We were in Tinian[1] at the time we got the OK. They had sent this Norwegian to the weather station out on Guam[2] and I had a copy of his report. We said that, based on his forecast, the sixth day of August would be the best day that we could get over Honshu.[3] So we did everything that had to be done to get the crews ready to go: airplane loaded, crews briefed, all of the things checked that you have to check before you can fly over enemy territory.

General Groves had a brigadier-general who was connected back to Washington, D.C., by a special teletype machine. He stayed close to that thing all the time, notifying people back there, all by code, that we were preparing these airplanes to go any time after midnight on the sixth. And that's the way it worked out. We were ready to go at about four o'clock in the afternoon on the fifth and we got word from the president that we were free to go: "Use 'em as you wish." They give you a time you're supposed to drop your bomb on target and that was 9:15 in the morning, but that was Tinian time, one hour later than Japanese time. I told Dutch, "You figure it out what time we have to start after midnight to be over the target at 9 A.M."

Studs Terkel: That'd be Sunday morning.

Paul Tibbets: Well, we got going down the runway at right about 2:15 A.M. and we took off, we met our rendezvous guys, we made our flight up to what we call the initial point, that would be a geographic position that you could not mistake. Well, of course we had the best one in the world with the rivers and bridges and that big shrine. There was no mistaking what it was.

Studs Terkel: So you had to have the right navigator to get it on the button.

Paul Tibbets: The airplane has a bombsight connected to the autopilot and the bombardier puts figures in there for where he wants to be when he drops the weapon, and that's transmitted to the airplane. We always took into account what would happen if we had a failure and the bomb bay doors didn't open: we had a manual release put in each airplane so it was right down by the bombardier and he could pull on that. And the guys in the airplanes that followed us to drop the instruments needed to know when it was going to go. We were told not to use the radio, but, hell, I had to. I told them I would say, "One minute out," "Thirty seconds out," "Twenty seconds" and "Ten" and then I'd count, "Nine, eight, seven, six, five, four seconds," which would give them a time to drop their cargo. They knew what was going on because they knew where we were. And that's exactly the way it worked, it was absolutely perfect.

After we got the airplanes in formation I crawled into the tunnel and went back to tell the men. I said, "You know what we're doing today?" They said,

---

1. **Tinian:** The U.S. island base in the Pacific.
2. **Guam:** The United States' westernmost territory.
3. **Honshu:** The island on which Hiroshima stands.

"Well, yeah, we're going on a bombing mission." I said, "Yeah, we're going on a bombing mission, but it's a little bit special." My tailgunner, Bob Caron, was pretty alert. He said, "Colonel, we wouldn't be playing with atoms today, would we?" I said, "Bob, you've got it just exactly right." So I went back up in the front end and I told the navigator, bombardier, flight engineer, in turn. I said, "OK, this is an atom bomb we're dropping." They listened intently but I didn't see any change in their faces or anything else. Those guys were no idiots. We'd been fiddling round with the most peculiar-shaped things we'd ever seen.

So we're coming down. We get to that point where I say "one second" and by the time I'd got that second out of my mouth the airplane had lurched, because 10,000 lbs had come out of the front. I'm in this turn now, tight as I can get it, that helps me hold my altitude and helps me hold my airspeed and everything else all the way round. When I level out, the nose is a little bit high and as I look up there the whole sky is lit up in the prettiest blues and pinks I've ever seen in my life. It was just great.

I tell people I tasted it. "Well," they say, "what do you mean?" When I was a child, if you had a cavity in your tooth the dentist put some mixture of some cotton or whatever it was and lead into your teeth and pounded them in with a hammer. I learned that if I had a spoon of ice-cream and touched one of those teeth I got this electrolysis and I got the taste of lead out of it. And I knew right away what it was.

OK, we're all going. We had been briefed to stay off the radios: "Don't say a damn word, what we do is we make this turn, we're going to get out of here as fast as we can." I want to get out over the sea of Japan because I know they can't find me over there. With that done we're home free. Then Tom Ferebee has to fill out his bombardier's report and Dutch, the navigator, has to fill out a log. Tom is working on his log and says, "Dutch, what time were we over the target?" And Dutch says, "Nine-fifteen plus 15 seconds." Ferebee says: "What lousy navigating. Fifteen seconds off!"

Studs Terkel: Did you hear an explosion?

Paul Tibbets: Oh yeah. The shockwave was coming up at us after we turned. And the tailgunner said, "Here it comes." About the time he said that, we got this kick in the ass. I had accelerometers installed in all airplanes to record the magnitude of the bomb. It hit us with two and a half G.[4] Next day, when we got figures from the scientists on what they had learned from all the things, they said, "When that bomb exploded, your airplane was 10 and half miles away from it."

Studs Terkel: Did you see that mushroom cloud?

Paul Tibbets: You see all kinds of mushroom clouds, but they were made with different types of bombs. The Hiroshima bomb did not make a mushroom. It was what I call a stringer. It just came up. It was black as hell, and it had light and colours and white in it and grey colour in it and the top was like a folded-up Christmas tree.

---

4. **G:** G-force; 1 G is equal to the force of Earth's gravity.

Studs Terkel: Do you have any idea what happened down below?

Paul Tibbets: Pandemonium! I think it's best stated by one of the historians, who said: "In one micro-second, the city of Hiroshima didn't exist."

Studs Terkel: You came back, and you visited President Truman.

Paul Tibbets: We're talking 1948 now. I'm back in the Pentagon and I get notice from the chief of staff, Carl Spaatz, the first chief of staff of the air force. When we got to General Spaatz's office, General Doolittle was there, and a colonel named Dave Shillen. Spaatz said, "Gentlemen, I just got word from the president he wants us to go over to his office immediately." On the way over, Doolittle and Spaatz were doing some talking; I wasn't saying very much. When we got out of the car we were escorted right quick to the Oval Office. There was a black man there who always took care of Truman's needs and he said, "General Spaatz, will you please be facing the desk?" And now, facing the desk, Spaatz is on the right, Doolittle and Shillen. Of course, militarily speaking, that's the correct order: because Spaatz is senior, Doolittle has to sit to his left.

Then I was taken by this man and put in the chair that was right beside the president's desk, beside his left hand. Anyway, we got a cup of coffee and we got most of it consumed when Truman walked in and everybody stood on their feet. He said, "Sit down, please," and he had a big smile on his face and he said, "General Spaatz, I want to congratulate you on being first chief of the air force," because it was no longer the air corps. Spaatz said, "Thank you, sir, it's a great honour and I appreciate it." And he said to Doolittle: "That was a magnif-icent thing you pulled flying off of that carrier," and Doolittle said, "All in a day's work, Mr. President." And he looked at Dave Shillen and said, "Colonel Shillen, I want to congratulate you on having the foresight to recognize the po-tential in aerial refueling. We're gonna need it bad some day." And he said thank you very much.

Then he looked at me for 10 seconds and he didn't say anything. And when he finally did, he said, "What do you think?" I said, "Mr. President, I think I did what I was told." He slapped his hand on the table and said: "You're damn right you did, and I'm the guy who sent you. If anybody gives you a hard time about it, refer them to me."

Studs Terkel: Anybody ever give you a hard time?

Paul Tibbets: Nobody gave me a hard time.

Studs Terkel: Do you ever have any second thoughts about the bomb?

Paul Tibbets: Second thoughts? No. Studs, look. Number one, I got into the air corps to defend the United States to the best of my ability. That's what I be-lieve in and that's what I work for. Number two, I'd had so much experience with airplanes . . . I'd had jobs where there was no particular direction about how you do it and then of course I put this thing together with my own thoughts on how it should be because when I got the directive I was to be self-supporting at all times.

On the way to the target I was thinking: I can't think of any mistakes I've made. Maybe I did make a mistake: maybe I was too damned assured. At 29 years of age I was so shot in the ass with confidence I didn't think there was anything I couldn't do. Of course, that applied to airplanes and people. So, no, I had no problem with it. I knew we did the right thing because when I knew we'd be doing that I thought, yes, we're going to kill a lot of people, but by God we're going to save a lot of lives. We won't have to invade [Japan].

GEORGE WELLER

The First American Report on the Bombing of Nagasaki

NAGASAKI, Sept. 8 — The following conclusions were made by the writer — as the first visitor to inspect the ruins — after an exhaustive, though still incomplete study of this wasteland of war.

Nagasaki is an island roughly resembling Manhattan in size and shape, running north and south in direction with ocean inlets on both sides. What would be the New Jersey and Manhattan sides of the Hudson river are lined with huge war plants owned by the Mitsubishi and Kawasaki families. . . .

It is about two miles from the scene of the bomb's 1,500 feet high explosion where the harbor has narrowed to the 250 feet wide Urakame River that the atomic bomb's force begins to be discernible.

The area is north of downtown Nagasaki, whose buildings suffered some freakish destruction, but are generally still sound.

The railroad station, destroyed except for the platforms is already operating. Normally it is sort of a gate to the destroyed part of the Urakame valley. . . . For two miles stretches a line of congested steel and some concrete factories with the residential district "across the tracks." The atomic bomb landed between and totally destroyed both with half [illegible] living persons in them. The known dead number 20,000[;] police tell me they estimate about 4,000 remain to be found.[5]

The reason the deaths were so high — the wounded being about twice as many according to Japanese official figures — was twofold:

1. Mitsubishi air raid shelters were totally inadequate and the civilian shelters remote and limited.
2. That the Japanese air warning system was a total failure.

I inspected half a dozen crude short tunnels in the rock wall valley which the Mitsubishi Co., considered shelters. I also picked my way through the tangled iron girders and curling roofs of the main factories to see concrete shelters four inches thick but totally inadequate in number. Only a grey concrete building topped by a siren, where the clerical staff had worked had reasonable cellar shelters, but nothing resembling the previous had been made.

A general alert had been sounded at seven in the morning, four hours before two B-29's appeared, but it was ignored by the workmen and most of the population. The police insist that the air raid warning was sounded two minutes before the bomb fell, but most people say they heard none. . . .

---

5. The actual number of deaths was approximately 75,000, with many thousands more to die in the years to follow due to radiation poisoning.

All around the Mitsubishi plant are ruins which one would gladly have spared. The writer spent nearly an hour in 15 deserted buildings in the Nagasaki Medical Institute hospital. . . . Nothing but rats live in the debris choked halls. On the opposite side of the valley and the Urakame river is a three story concrete American mission college called Chin Jei, nearly totally destroyed.

Japanese authorities point out that the home area flattened by American bombs was traditionally the place of Catholic and Christian Japanese.

But sparing these and sparing the allied prison camp, which the Japanese placed next to an armor plate factory would have meant sparing Mitsubishi's ship parts plant with 1,016 employees who were mostly Allied. It would have spared a Mounting factory connecting with 1,750 employees. It would have spared three steel foundries on both sides of the Urakame, using ordinarily 3,400 workers but that day 2,500. And besides sparing many sub-contracting plants now flattened it would have meant leaving untouched the Mitsubishi torpedo and ammunition plant employing 7,500 which was nearest where the bomb [detonated].

All these latter plants today are hammered flat. But no saboteur creeping among the war plants of death could have placed the atomic bomb by hand more scrupulously given Japan's inertia about common defense.

NAGASAKI, Saturday, Sept. 8 — In swaybacked or flattened skeletons of the Mitsubishi arms plants is revealed what the atomic bomb can do to steel and stone, but what the riven atom can do against human flesh and bone lies hidden in two hospitals of downtown Nagasaki. Look at the pushed-in facade of the American consulate, three miles from the blast's center, or the face of the Catholic cathedral, one mile in the other direction, torn down like gingerbread, and you can tell that the liberated atom spares nothing in the way. . . .

Showing them to you, as the first American outsider to reach Nagasaki since the surrender, your propaganda-conscious official guide looks meaningfully in your face and wants to know: "What do you think?" What this question means is: do you intend saying that America did something inhuman in loosing this weapon against Japan? That is what we want you to write about.

Several children, some burned and others unburned but with patches of hair falling out, are sitting with their mothers. Yesterday Japanese photographers took many pictures with them. About one in five is heavily bandaged, but none are showing signs of pain.

Some adults are in pain as they lie on mats. They moan softly. One woman caring for her husband, shows eyes dim with tears. It is a piteous scene and your official guide studies your face covertly to see if you are moved.

Visiting many litters, talking lengthily with two general physicians and one X-ray specialist, gains you a large amount of information and opinion on the victims. . . .

Most of the patients who were gravely burned have now passed away and those on hand are rapidly curing. Those not curing are people whose unhappy lot provides the mystery aura around the atomic bomb's effects. They are victims of what Lt. Jakob Vink, Dutch medical officer and now allied commandant of prison camp 14 at the mouth of Nagasaki Harbor, calls "disease." Vink himself was in the allied prison kitchen abutting the Mitsubishi armor plate department when the ceiling fell in but he escaped this mysterious "disease X" which some allied prisoners and many Japanese civilians got.

Vink points out a woman on a yellow mat in the hospital, who according to hospital doctors Hikodero Koga and Uraji Hayashida have just been brought in. She fled the atomic area but returned to live. She was well for three weeks except a small burn on her heel. Now she lies moaning with a blackish mouth stiff as though with lockjaw and unable to utter clear words. Her exposed legs and arms are speckled with tiny red spots in patches.

Near her lies a 15-year-old fattish girl who has the same blotchy red pinpoints and nose clotted with blood. A little farther on is a widow lying down with four children, from one to about 8, around her. The two smallest children have lost some hair. Though none of these people has either a burn or a broken limb, they are presumed victims of the atomic bomb.

Dr. Uraji Hayashida shakes his head somberly and says that he believes there must be something to the American radio report about the ground around the Mitsubishi plant being poisoned. But his next statement knocks out the props from under this theory because it develops that the widow's family has been absent from the wrecked area ever since the blast yet shows symptoms common with those who returned.

According to Japanese doctors, patients with these late developing symptoms are dying now a month after the bomb's fall, at the rate of about 10 daily. The three doctors calmly stated that the disease has them nonplussed and that they are giving no treatment whatever but rest. . . .

NAGASAKI, Sept. 9—The atomic bomb's peculiar "disease," uncured because it is untreated and untreated because it is not diagnosed, is still snatching away lives here.

Men, women, and children with no outward marks of injury are dying daily in hospitals, some after having walked around three or four weeks thinking they have escaped.

The doctors here have every modern medication, but candidly confessed in talking to the writer—the first Allied observer to Nagasaki since the surrender—that the answer to the malady is beyond them. Their patients, though their skin is whole, are all passing away under their eyes.

Kyushu's leading X-ray specialist, who arrived today from the island's chief city Fukuoka, elderly Dr. Yosisada Nakashima, told the writer that he is convinced that these people are simply suffering from the atomic bomb's beta Gamma, or the neutron ray is taking effect.

"All the symptoms are similar," said the Japanese doctor. "You have a reduction in white corpuscles, constriction in the throat, vomiting, diarrhea and small hemorrhages just below the skin. All of these things happen when an overdose of Roentgen rays is given. Bombed children's hair falls out. That is natural because these rays are used often to make hair fall artificially and sometimes takes several days before the hair becomes loose.". . .

At emergency hospital No. 2, commanding officer young Lt. Col. Yoshitaka Sasaki, with three rows of campaign ribbons on his breast, stated that 200 patients died of 343 admitted and that he expects about 50 more deaths.

Most severe ordinary burns resulted in the patients' deaths within a week after the bomb fell. But this hospital began taking patients only from one to two weeks afterward. It is therefore almost exclusively "disease" cases and the deaths are mostly therefrom.

Nakashima divides the deaths outside simple burns and fractures into two classes on the basis of symptoms observed in the post mortem autopsies. The first class accounts for roughly 60 percent of the deaths, the second for 40 percent. Among exterior symptoms in the first class are falling hair from the head, armpits, and pubic zones, spotty local skin hemorrhages looking like measles all over the body, lip sores, diarrhea but without blood discharge, swelling in the throat . . . and a descent in numbers of red and white corpuscles. Red corpuscles fall from a normal 5,000,000 to one-half, or one-third while the whites almost disappear, dropping from 7,000 or 8,000 to 300 to 500. Fever rises to 104 and stays there without fluctuating. . . .

Nakashima considers that it is possible that the atomic bomb's rare rays may cause deaths in the first class, as with delayed X-ray burns. But the second class [deaths] has him totally baffled. These patients begin with slight burns which make normal progress for two weeks. They differ from simple burns, however, in that the patient has a high fever. Unfevered patients with as much as one-third of the skin area burned have been known to recover. But where fever is present after two weeks, healing of burns suddenly halts and they get worse. They come to resemble septic ulcers. Yet patients are not in great pain, which distinguishes them from ordinary X-ray burn victims.

Up to five days from the turn to the worse, they die. Their bloodstream has not thinned as in the first class and their organs after death are found in a normal condition of health. But they are dead—dead of the atomic bomb—and nobody knows why.

Twenty-five Americans are due to arrive Sept. 11 to study the Nagasaki bombsite. The Japanese hope that they will bring a solution to Disease X.

FOR CRITICAL THINKING

1. Compare and contrast Oppenheimer's views of the atomic bomb with Tibbets's and Weller's views. What stance, if any, does each of these men take toward the bomb, and how is this reflected in their writing? Note in particular any differences or similarities in their reaction to the power of the atomic bomb.

2. Joseph Rothblat, a Polish scientist recruited to work at Los Alamos, insisted on leaving the project at the end of 1944 when it became apparent that there was no danger of any other nation's building a nuclear weapon before the United States. Based on your reading of these

selections, what do you think of his decision? Should other scientists have followed his lead? Why or why not?

3. At Hiroshima and Nagasaki in August 1945, and at the World Trade Center on September 11, 2001, civilians were specifically targeted for the sake of larger objectives: in the one case, military victory; in the other, a terrorist act in the name of Islam. In modern warfare, distinguishing between fighting an enemy military and attacking an enemy population may be impossible. If this is the case, how does one distinguish between just and unjust kinds of warfare? Do you believe that in future wars such distinctions will be available?

29

Rosie the Riveter

Fanny Christina Hill

World War II brought with it a massive need for a larger labor force. Millions of men were under arms, and the United States, billing itself the "Arsenal of Democracy" for the Allied forces, strove for giant increases in the production of planes, ships, trucks, tanks, armaments, food, clothing, and all the other supplies that fuel a war. In 1940, 11.5 million women were employed outside the home, principally single women, widows, and wives from poor families. African American women like Fanny Christina Hill expected to work in whatever jobs were available to them—most commonly domestic service.

On Columbus Day 1942, President Franklin D. Roosevelt called for a new attitude in the workplace: "In some communities employers dislike to hire women. In others they are reluctant to hire Negroes. We can no longer afford to indulge such prejudices." Soon women like Hill shifted from "women's jobs" to defense work, prompting others who previously had not worked to adopt these new roles as well.

War production peaked in 1944. By the middle of that year, pressure grew to persuade women to return to their homes even before the war reached its conclusion. Defense plant newspapers replaced features on women production workers with "cheesecake" contests. Tales of neglected children became a theme of popular journalism. Yet seventy-five percent of women surveyed in 1944 and 1945 expressed the desire to continue working after the war. A cultural battle had begun that would outlast wartime.

QUESTIONS TO CONSIDER

1. How was Fanny Christina Hill's life affected by her work during the war?
2. Why did she continue working after the war? Was she influenced by the pressure to cease working?
3. What examples of prejudice affecting her life do you find? How did she deal with them?

I went to a little small town—Tyler, Texas. . . . And the only thing I could do there for a living was domestic work and it didn't pay very much. So I definitely didn't like it.

Sherna Berger Gluck, *Rosie the Riveter Revisited* (Boston: Twayne, 1987), 28–33, 35–38, 40–45, 48–49.

But I left Tyler. I was saying, "I don't like it here because you can't make any money." I discovered I didn't have any trade. I had nothing I could do other than just that, and that wasn't what I wanted. So I decided I'd better get out of this town. I didn't like Dallas because that was too rough. Then someone told me, "Well, why don't you try California?" So then I got Los Angeles in my mind. I was twenty and I saved my money till I was twenty-one. In August 1940, I came here.

When I first came, when my aunt met me down at the station, I had less then ten dollars. I went on to her house and stayed. In less than ten days I had found a job living on the place doing domestic work. I stayed there from some time in August until Christmas. I was making thirty-five dollars a month. That was so much better than what I was making at home, which was twelve dollars a month. I saved my money and I bought everybody a Christmas present and sent it. Oh, I was the happiest thing in the world! . . .

I liked to go on outings a lot. So when I first came to California, when I'd have my day off, I'd go to the parks and to the beach and museum. Just go sight-seeing; walking and look in the windows. Sometimes my aunt would go along with me or I'd find another girlfriend. But then I had a sister here pretty soon.

Los Angeles was a large city but I adjusted to it real well. It didn't take me long to find a way about it. I knew how to get around, and I knew how to stay out of danger and not take too many chances. I read the *Eagle* and I still get the *Sentinel*[1] once in a while. I have to get it to keep up with what the black people are doing. I used to read those papers when I was a child back home. That's what give me a big idea. I used to read a little paper called the *Kansas City Call*, and they had a *Pittsburgh Courier* that all the Negroes read. . .

[She returns to Texas to get married.] I stayed there for about nine months until he went into the service. Then I came to Los Angeles. I told my sister, "Well, I better get me a good job around here working in a hotel or motel or something. I want to get me a good job so when the war is over, I'll have it." And she said, "No, you just come on out and go in the war plants and work and maybe you'll make enough money where you won't have to work in the hotels or motels.". . .

I don't remember what day of the week it was, but I guess I must have started out pretty early that morning. When I went there, the man didn't hire me. They had a school down here on Figueroa and he told me to go to the school. I went down and it was almost four o'clock and they told me they'd hire me. You had to fill out a form. They didn't bother too much about your experience because they knew you didn't have any experience in aircraft. Then they give you some kind of little test where you put the pegs in the right hole.

There were other people in there, kinda mixed. I assume it was more women than men. Most of the men was gone, and they weren't hiring too many men unless they had a good excuse. Most of the women was in my bracket, five

---

1. the *Eagle* and . . . the *Sentinel:* Newspapers that covered news events in the African American community.

or six years younger or older. I was twenty-four. There was a black girl that hired in with me. I went to work the next day, sixty cents an hour.

I think I stayed at the school for about four weeks. They only taught you shooting and bucking rivets and how to drill the holes and to file. You had to use a hammer for certain things. After a couple of whiles, you worked on the real thing. But you were supervised so you didn't make a mess.

When we went into the plant, it wasn't too much different than down at the school. It was the same amount of noise; it was the same routine. One difference was there was just so many more people, and when you went in the door you had a badge to show and they looked at your lunch. I had gotten accustomed to a lot of people and I knew if it was a lot of people, it always meant something was going on. I got carried away: "As long as there's a lot of people here, I'll be making money." That was all I could ever see.

I was a good student, if I do say so myself. But I have found out through life, sometimes even if you're good, you just don't get the breaks if the color's not right. I could see where they made a difference in placing you in certain jobs. They had fifteen or twenty departments, but all the Negroes went to Department 17 because there was nothing but shooting and bucking rivets. You stood on one side of the panel and your partner stood on this side, and he would shoot the rivets with a gun and you'd buck them with the bar. That was about the size of it. I just didn't like it. I didn't think I could stay there with all this shooting and a'bucking and a'jumping and a'bumping. I stayed in it about two or three weeks and then I just decided I did *not* like that. I went and told my foreman and he didn't do anything about it, so I decided I'd leave.

While I was standing out on the railroad track, I ran into somebody else out there fussing also. I went over to the union and they told me what to do. I went back inside and they sent me to another department where you did bench work and I liked that much better. You had a little small jig that you would work on and you just drilled out holes. Sometimes you would rout them or you would scribe them and then you'd cut them with a cutters.

I must have stayed there nearly a year, and then they put me over in another department, "Plastics." It was the tail section of the B-Bomber, the Billy Mitchell Bomber. I put a little part in the gun-sight. You had a little ratchet set and you would screw it in there. Then I cleaned the top of the glass off and put a piece of paper over it to seal it off to go to the next section. I worked over there until the end of the war. Well, not quite the end, because I got pregnant, and while I was off having the baby the war was over. . .

Some weeks I brought home twenty-six dollars, some weeks sixteen dollars. Then it gradually went up to thirty dollars, then it went up a little bit more and a little bit more. And I learned somewhere along the line that in order to make a good move you gotta make some money. You don't make the same amount everyday. You have some days good, sometimes bad. Whatever you make you're supposed to save some. I was also getting that fifty dollars a month from my husband and that was just saved right away. I was planning on buying a home and a car. And I was going to go back to school. My husband came back, but I never was laid off, so I just never found it necessary to look for another job or to go to school for another job.

I was still living over on Compton Avenue with my sister in this small little back house when my husband got home. Then, when Beverly was born, my sister moved in the front house and we stayed in the back house. When he came back, he looked for a job in the cleaning and pressing place, which was just plentiful. All the people had left these cleaning and pressing jobs and every other job; they was going to the defense plant to work because they was paying good. But in the meantime he was getting the same thing the people out there was getting, $1.25 an hour. That's why he didn't bother to go out to North American [Aircraft Company]. But what we both weren't thinking about was that they did have better benefits because they did have an insurance plan and a union to back you up. Later he did come to work there, in 1951 or 1952.

I worked up until the end of March and then I took off. Beverly was born the twenty-first of June. I'd planned to come back somewhere in the last of August. I went to verify the fact that I did come back, so that did go on my record that I didn't just quit. But they laid off a lot of people, most of them, because the war was over.

It didn't bother me much—not thinking about it jobwise. I was just glad that the war was over. I didn't feel bad because my husband had a job and he also was eligible to go to school with his GI bill. So I really didn't have too many plans—which I wish I had had. I would have tore out page one and fixed it differently; put my version of page one in there.

I went and got me a job doing day work. That means you go to a person's house and clean up for one day out of the week and then you go to the next one and clean up. I did that a couple of times and I discovered I didn't like that so hot. Then I got me a job downtown working in a little factory where you do weaving—burned clothes and stuff like that. I learned to do that real good. It didn't pay too much but it paid enough to get me going, seventy-five cents or about like that.

When North American called me back, was I a happy soul! I dropped that job and went back. That was a dollar an hour. So, from sixty cents an hour, when I first hired in there, up to one dollar. That wasn't traveling fast, but it was better than anything else because you had hours to work by and you had benefits and you come home at night with your family. So it was a good deal.

It made me live better. I really did. We always say that Lincoln took the bale off of the Negroes. I think there is a statue up there in Washington, D.C., where he's lifting something off the Negro. Well, my sister always said— that's why you can't interview her because she's so radical—"Hitler was the one that got us out of the white folks' kitchen." . . .

[She recalls the discrimination faced by black workers at North American Aircraft.] But they had to fight. They fought hand, tooth, and nail to get in there. And the first five or six Negroes who went in there, they were well educated, but they started them off as janitors. After they once got their foot in the door and was there for three months—you work for three months before they say you're hired—then they had to start fighting all over again to get off of that broom and get something decent. And some of them did.

But they'd always give that Negro man the worst part of everything. See, the jobs have already been tested and tried out before they ever get into the department, and they know what's good about them and what's bad about them. They always managed to give the worst one to the Negro. The only reason why the women fared better was they just couldn't quite give the woman as tough a job that they gave the men. But sometimes they did. . .

There were some departments, they didn't even allow a black person to walk through there let alone work in there. Some of the white people did not want to work with the Negro. They had arguments right there. Sometimes they would get fired and walk on out the door, but it was one more white person gone. I think even to this very day in certain places they still don't want to work with the Negro. I don't know what their story is, but if they would try then they might not knock it.

But they did everything they could to keep you separated. They just did not like for a Negro and a white person to get together and talk. Now I am a person that you can talk to and you will warm up to me much better than you can a lot of people. A white person seems to know that they could talk to me at ease. And when anyone would start—just plain, common talk, everyday talk—they didn't like it. . .

And they'd keep you from advancing. They always manage to give the Negroes the worst end of the deal. I happened to fall into that when they get ready to transfer you from one department to the next. That was the only thing that I ever ran into that I had to holler to the union about. And once I filed a complaint downtown with the Equal Opportunity.

The way they was doing this particular thing—they always have a lean spot where they're trying to lay off or go through there and see if they can curl out a bunch of people, get rid of the ones with the most seniority, I suppose. They had a good little system going. All the colored girls had more seniority in production than the whites because the average white woman did not come back after the war. They thought like I thought: that I have a husband now and I don't have to work and this was just only for the war and blah, blah, blah. But they didn't realize they was going to need the money. The average Negro was glad to come back because it meant more money than they was making before. So we always had more seniority in production than the white woman.

All the colored women in production, they was just one step behind the other. I had three months more than one, the next one had three months more than me, and that's the way it went. So they had a way of putting us all in [the] Blueprint [department]. We all had twenty years by the time you got in Blueprint and stayed a little while. Here come another one. He'd bump you out and then you went out the door, because they couldn't find nothing else for you to do—so they said. They just kept doing it and I could see myself: "Well, hell, I'm going to be the next one to go out the door!"

So I found some reason to file a grievance.[2] I tried to get several other girls: "Let's get together and go downtown and file a grievance." I only got two girls to go with me. That made three of us. I think we came out on top, because we all kept our jobs and then they stopped sending them to Blueprint, bumping each other like that. So, yeah, we've had to fight to stay there...

When I bought my house in '49 or '48, I went a little further on the other side of Slauson, and I drove up and down the street a couple of times. I saw one colored woman there. I went in and asked her about the neighborhood. She said there was only one there, but there was another one across the street. So I was the third one moved in there. I said, "Well, we's breaking into the neighborhood."

I don't know how long we was there, but one evening, just about dusk, here comes this woman banging on my door. I had never seen her before. She says, "I got a house over here for sale, you can tell your friends that they can buy it if they want to." I thought to myself, "What in the hell is that woman thinking about?" She was mad because she discovered I was there. Further down, oh, about two streets down, somebody burned a cross on a lawn.

Then, one Sunday evening, I don't know what happened, but they saw a snake in the yard next door to us. Some white people were staying there and the yard was so junky, I tell you. Here come the snake. We must have been living there a good little while, because Beverly was old enough to bring the gun. Everybody was looking and they had a stick or something. I don't know how, but that child came strutting out there with the gun to shoot the snake. My husband shot the snake and from that point on, everybody respected us—'cause they knew he had a gun and could use it.

I was talking to a white person about the situation and he said, "Next time you get ready to move in a white neighborhood, I'll tell you what you do. The first thing you do when you pull up there in the truck, you jump out with your guns. You hold them up high in the air." He says, "If you don't have any, borrow some or rent 'em, but be sure that they see you got a gun. Be sure one of them is a shotgun and you go in there with it first. They going to be peeping out the window, don't you worry about it. They going to see you. But if they see those guns going in first, they won't ever bother you."

I did like he said, moved in here with some guns, and nobody come and bothered me. Nobody said one word to me.

Working at North American was good. I did make more money and I did meet quite a few people that I am still friends with. I learned quite a bit. Some of the things, I wouldn't want to go back over. If I had the wisdom to know the difference which one to change and which one not to, I would. I would have fought harder at North American for better things for myself.

I don't have too many regrets. But if I had it to do over again, if I had to tamper with page one, I would sure get a better education. I would never have stopped going to school. I took several little classes every so often—cosmetol-

---

2. **grievance:** A discrimination complaint filed with the Equal Opportunities Employment Commission.

ogy, photography, herbs. For a little while, I did study nursing. I would have finished some of them. I would have went deeper into it.

We always talking about women's lib and working. Well, we all know that the Negro woman was the first woman that left home to go to work. She's been working ever since because she had to work beside her husband in slavery— against her will. So she has always worked. She knows how to get out there and work. She has really pioneered the field. Then after we've gotten out here and proved that it can be done, then the white woman decided: "Hey, I don't want to stay home and do nothing." She zeroed in on the best jobs. So we're still on the tail-end, but we still back there fighting.

30

Memories of the Internment Camp
Ben Yorita and Philip Hayasaka

During World War II, the United States was more careful about protecting the civil lib-
erties of its citizens than it had been after its entrance into World War I. There was, how-
ever, one glaring exception: the internment of 110,000 Japanese Americans in camps
euphemistically called "relocation centers." (A similar attempt to relocate Italian and
German Americans from areas along the West Coast was quickly recognized as imprac-
tical and soon abandoned.) The military director of the internment program declared that
the "Japanese race is an enemy race and while many second and third generation Japa-
nese born on United States soil, possessed of United States Citizenship, have become Amer-
icanized, the racial strains are undiluted. . . . It, therefore, follows that along the vital
Pacific coast over 112,000 potential enemies, of Japanese extraction, are at large today."
These people, seventy thousand of them native-born citizens of the United States, were
forced to evacuate their homes within forty-eight hours (losing about $500 million in
property along with their jobs) and made to live for long periods of time in tar-papered
barracks behind barbed wire.

The Supreme Court of the United States, in two major decisions, supported the
constitutionality of internment. Justice Robert Jackson warned in a dissenting opinion
that the case established a precedent that "lays about like a loaded weapon." In 1988,
Congress, in recognition of the wrong that the government inflicted, appropriated com-
pensation for internees.

This reading, from interviews and commentary conducted by Archie Satterfield in
the 1970s, is about the experiences of two Japanese Americans who suffered through
this period of injustice.

QUESTIONS TO CONSIDER

1. What were the main fears aroused among Japanese Americans by the
   internment?
2. What did Japanese Americans lose by the internment?
3. What were the likely psychological effects on Japanese Americans of
   the internment?
4. Compare the treatment of Japanese Americans in the United States
   with that of Jews in Germany. What was similar? What was different?

Archie Satterfield, *The Home Front: An Oral History of the War Years in America, 1941–1945* (New
York: Playboy Press, 1981), 330–38.

BEN YORITA

"Students weren't as aware of national politics then as they are now, and Japanese–Americans were actually apolitical then. Our parents couldn't vote, so we simply weren't interested in politics because there was nothing we could do about it if we were.

"There were two reasons we were living in the ghettos: Birds of a feather flock together, and we had all the traditional aspects of Japanese life—Japanese restaurants, baths, and so forth; and discrimination forced us together. The dominant society prevented us from going elsewhere.

"Right after Pearl Harbor we had no idea what was going to happen, but toward the end of December we started hearing rumors and talk of the evacuation started. We could tell from what we read in the newspapers and the propaganda they were printing—guys like Henry McLemore,[1] who said he hated all Japs and that we should be rounded up, gave us the idea of how strong feelings were against us. So we were expecting something and the evacuation was no great surprise.

"I can't really say what my parents thought about everything because we didn't communicate that well. I never asked them what they thought. We communicated on other things, but not political matters.

"Once the evacuation was decided, we were told we had about a month to get rid of our property or do whatever we wanted to with it. That was a rough time for my brother, who was running a printshop my parents owned. We were still in debt on it and we didn't know what to do with all the equipment. The machines were old but still workable, and we had English type and Japanese type. Japanese characters had to be set by hand and were very hard to replace. Finally, the whole works was sold, and since nobody would buy the Japanese type, we had to sell it as junk lead at 50¢ a pound. We sold the equipment through newspaper classified ads: 'Evacuating: Household goods for sale.' Second-hand dealers and everybody else came in and bought our refrigerator, the piano, and I had a whole bunch of books I sold for $5, which was one of my personal losses. We had to sell our car, and the whole thing was very sad. By the way, it was the first time we had ever had a refrigerator and it had to be sold after only a few months.

"We could take only what we could carry, and most of us were carrying two suitcases or duffel bags. The rest of our stuff that we couldn't sell was stored in the Buddhist church my mother belonged to. When we came back, thieves had broken in and stolen almost everything of value from the church.

"I had a savings account that was left intact, but people who had their money in the Japanese bank in Seattle had their assets frozen from Pearl Harbor until the late 1960s, when the funds were finally released. They received no interest.

---

1. **Henry McLemore:** Syndicated columnist for the Hearst newspapers who strongly supported mass evacuation of Japanese Americans from the West Coast to the interior.

"They took all of us down to the Puyallup fairgrounds, Camp Harmony,[2] and everything had been thrown together in haste. They had converted some of the display and exhibit areas into rooms and had put up some barracks on the parking lot. The walls in the barracks were about eight feet high with open space above and with big knotholes in the boards of the partitions. Our family was large, so we had two rooms.

"They had also built barbed-wire fences around the camp with a tower on each corner with military personnel and machine guns, rifles, and searchlights. It was terrifying because we didn't know what was going to happen to us. We didn't know where we were going and we were just doing what we were told. No questions asked. If you get an order, you go ahead and do it.

"There was no fraternization, no contact with the military or any Caucasian except when we were processed into the camp. But the treatment in Camp Harmony was fairly loose in the sense that we were free to roam around in the camp. But it was like buffalo in cages or behind barbed wire.

"There was no privacy whatsoever in the latrines and showers, and it was humiliating for the women because they were much more modest then than today. It wasn't so bad for the men because they were accustomed to open latrines and showers.

"We had no duties in the sense that we were required to work, but you can't expect a camp to manage itself. They had jobs open in the kitchen and stock room, and eventually they opened a school where I helped teach a little. I wasn't a qualified teacher, and I got about $13 a month. We weren't given an allowance while we were in Camp Harmony waiting for the camp at Minidoka[3] to be finished, so it was pretty tight for some families.

"From Camp Harmony on, the family structure was broken down. Children ran everywhere they wanted to in the camp, and parents lost their authority. We could eat in any mess hall we wanted, and kids began ignoring their parents and wandering wherever they pleased.

"Eventually they boarded us on army trucks and took us to trains to be transported to the camps inland. We had been in Camp Harmony from May until September. There was a shortage of transportation at the time and they brought out these old, rusty cars with gaslight fixtures. As soon as we got aboard we pulled the shades down so people couldn't stare at us. The cars were all coaches and we had to sit all the way to camp, which was difficult for some of the older people and the invalids. We made makeshift beds out of the seats for them, and did the best we could.

"When we got to Twin Falls,[4] we were loaded onto trucks again, and we looked around and all we could see was that vast desert with nothing but sagebrush. When the trucks started rolling, it was dusty, and the camp itself wasn't completed yet. The barracks had been built and the kitchen facilities were there, but the laundry room, showers, and latrines were not finished. They had

2. **Camp Harmony:** Temporary assembly center in Puyallup, Washington.
3. **Minidoka:** Relocation center in Idaho.
4. **Twin Falls:** Transfer city in Idaho.

taken a bulldozer in the good old American style and leveled the terrain and then built the camp. When the wind blew, it was dusty and we had to wear face masks to go to the dining hall. When winter came and it rained, the dust turned into gumbo mud. Until the latrines were finished, we had to use outhouses.

"The administrators were civilians and they tried to organize us into a chain of command to make the camp function. Each block of barracks was told to appoint a representative, who were called block managers. Of course we called them the Blockheads.

"When winter came, it was very cold and I began withdrawing my savings to buy clothes because we had none that was suitable for that climate. Montgomery Ward and Sears Roebuck[5] did a landslide business from the camps because we ordered our shoes and warm clothing from them. The people who didn't have savings suffered quite a bit until the camp distributed navy pea coats. Then everybody in camp was wearing outsize pea coats because we were such small people. Other than army blankets, I don't remember any other clothing issues.

"The barracks were just single-wall construction and the only insulation was tar paper nailed on the outside, and they never were improved. The larger rooms had potbellied stoves, and we all slept on army cots. Only the people over sixty years old were able to get metal cots, which had a bit more spring to them than the army cots, which were just stationary hammocks.

"These camps were technically relocation centers and there was no effort to hold us in them, but they didn't try actively to relocate us until much later. On my own initiative I tried to get out as soon as I could, and started writing letters to friends around the country. I found a friend in Salt Lake City who agreed to sponsor me for room and board, and he got his boss to agree to hire me. I got out in May 1943, which was earlier than most. In fact, I was one of the first to leave Minidoka.

"Of course I had to get clearance from Washington, D.C., and they investigated my background. I had to pay my own way from Twin Falls to Salt Lake City, but after I left, the government had a program of per diem for people leaving.

"I got on the bus with my suitcase, all by myself, my first time in the outside world, and paid my fare and began looking for a seat, then this old guy said: 'Hey, Tokyo, sit next to me.'

"I thought, Oh, my God, Tokyo! I sat next to him and he was a friendly old guy who meant well."

Yorita's friend worked in a parking garage across the street from the Mormon tabernacle, and the garage owner let them live in the office, where the two young men cooked their own meals. One nearby grocery-store owner wouldn't let them buy from him, and a barber in the neighborhood hated them on sight. Yorita parked a car once that had a rifle and pair of binoculars in the back seat, and he and his friend took the binoculars out and were looking

---

5. **Montgomery Ward and Sears Roebuck:** Two mail-order catalog companies.

through them when the barber looked out and saw them studying the Mormon tabernacle. He called the FBI, and two agents were soon in the garage talking to the young men.

Yorita wasn't satisfied with his job in Salt Lake City, and soon left for Cincinnati, then Chicago, which he enjoyed because most Chicago people didn't care what nationality he was. He and a brother were able to find good jobs and a good place to live, and they brought their parents out of the Idaho camp to spend the rest of the war in Chicago.

PHILIP HAYASAKA

Philip Hayasaka was a teen-ager when Pearl Harbor was attacked. Unlike most Japanese-Americans, his parents had been able to find a home in a predominantly Caucasian neighborhood because his father was a wholesale produce dealer and most of his business was conducted with Caucasians. Consequently, when the family was interned, Hayasaka was a stranger to most of the other families.

Still, he and his family understood well the rationale of the Little Tokyos along the West Coast.

"If you could become invisible, you could get along. We were forced into a situation of causing no trouble, of being quiet, not complaining. It was not a matter of our stoic tradition. I've never bought that. We did what we had to do to survive.

"There was a lot of hysteria at the time, a lot of confusion, and the not knowing what was going to happen created such a fear that we became super-cautious. We would hear that the FBI was going into different houses and searching, and we would wonder when they were coming to our house. We just knew that they were going to come and knock on the door and that we wouldn't know what to do when they came.

"A lot of people were burning things that didn't need to be burned, but they were afraid suspicion would be attached to those things. All those wonderful old calligraphies were destroyed, priceless things, because they thought someone in authority would believe they represented allegiance to Japan. One time I was with my mother in the house, just the two of us, and there was a knock on the door. My mother had those rosary-type beads that the Buddhists use for prayer, and she put them in my pocket and sent me outside to play and stay out until whoever was at the door left. She was afraid it was the FBI and they would take them away from us. It sounds silly now, but that kind of fear was pervasive then. It was tragic.

"When this happened, my dad's business went to hell. Suddenly all his accounts payable were due immediately, but all the accounts receivable weren't. People knew the guy wasn't going to be around much longer, so they didn't pay him. I knew at one time how much he lost that way—we had to turn in a claim after the war—but I've forgotten now. But it was a considerable amount. Those claims, by the way, didn't give justice to the victims; it only legitimized the government. We got about a nickel on the dollar.

"It was kind of interesting how different people reacted when they came to Camp Harmony to see friends, and how we reacted in return. Friends from Seattle would come down to see me, and we had to talk through the barbed-wire fences. [Note: Nobody was permitted to stand closer than three feet to the fence, which meant conversations were held at least six feet from each other, with guards standing and watching.] There was one instance when I saw a close friend from high school just outside the fence, and he had come down to see me. He hadn't seen me inside, so I hid rather than going out to see him. The whole evacuation did funny things to your mind.

"All the leaders of the community were taken away, and my dad was interned before we were and taken to the interrogation camp in Missoula. It was one of the greatest shocks of my life when the FBI came and picked him up. Here was a guy who had followed all the rules, respected authority, and was a leader in the company. And all of the sudden he was behind bars for no reason. He stayed there several months before they let him join us at Minidoka."

When the war ended and the camps were closed, about the only people left in them were young children and the elderly. All who could leave for jobs did so, and the experience had a scattering effect on the Japanese-American communities across the Pacific Coast. Several families settled on the East Coast and in the Midwest, and when those with no other place to go, or who didn't want to migrate away from the Coast, returned to their hometowns, they usually found their former ghettos taken over by other minority groups. Consequently, whether they wanted to or not, they were forced to find housing wherever it was available. It was difficult returning to the cities, however. Everybody dreaded it, and some of the elderly people with no place to go of their own were virtually evacuated from the camps. They had become accustomed to the life there and were afraid to leave.

Some Caucasians, such as Floyd Schmoe and the Reverend Emory Andrews, worked with the returning outcasts to help them resettle as smoothly as possible. A few farms had been saved for the owners, but four years of weeds and brush had accumulated. Schmoe was back teaching at the University of Washington by that time, and he organized groups of his students to go out on weekends and after school to help clear the land for crops again. Some people returning found their former neighbors had turned against them in their absence, and grocery-store owners who had become Jap-haters during the war would not sell them food.

The farmers who did get their crops growing again were often so discriminated against that they could not sell their produce, or get it delivered into the marketplace. Schmoe was able to solve this problem for one farmer by talking a neighbor, a Filipino, into taking the Japanese-American's produce and selling it as his own. Hayasaka's father was able to get back into the wholesale produce business by becoming partners with a young Japanese-American veteran of the famed 442d Regiment, the most highly decorated group in the war. The veteran put up a sign over the office saying the business was operated by a veteran, which made it difficult for buyers to avoid it.

BEN YORITA

"The older people never recovered from the camps. The father was the traditional breadwinner and in total command of the family. But after going into the camps, fathers were no longer the breadwinners; the young sons and daughters were. Most of them couldn't even communicate in English, so all the burdens fell on the second generation. And most of us were just kids, nineteen or twenty. Consequently there was a big turnover of responsibility and authority, and the parents were suddenly totally dependent on their children. When we returned to the cities after the war, it was the second generation again that had to make the decisions and do all the negotiating with landlords, attorneys, and the like."

31

The Bataan Death March

Blair Robinett et al.

*In the months immediately after the December 7, 1941, attack on Pearl Harbor—as
Japanese Americans were being herded into internment camps—the Axis powers were on
the march. Hitler's armies threatened Moscow and the Suez Canal, while his submarine
navy was sinking British and American ships far more rapidly than they could be replaced:
nearly 750,000 tons a month. In the Pacific, Japan captured the key British naval base of
Singapore as well as Burma, most of the East Indies, and the Philippines, where General
Douglas MacArthur directed troops in a gallant but futile defense.*

*When the Philippine stronghold of Bataan fell on April 9, 1942, after a three-month
siege, Japanese soldiers forced their prisoners—about seventy thousand Americans and Filipinos—to evacuate quickly and without adequate food or water. Thousands died on this
infamous Bataan death march amid tortures and horrors that the following selections only
begin to describe.*

*The death march joined the sneak attack on Pearl Harbor as a focus for many
Americans' hatred of all things Japanese. Most Americans believed that the cruelty was
deliberate and planned. In reality, as the historian John Toland has written, "There
had been no plan at all. About half of the prisoners rode in trucks . . . and suffered
little. Some who walked saw almost no brutalities and were fed, if not well, at least
occasionally. Yet others a mile behind were starved, beaten and killed by brutal guards."
Perhaps seven to ten thousand men died on the march, about 2,330 of them Americans.
The Japanese generals, in Toland's view, had seriously underestimated how many
soldiers had surrendered as well as how sick and near starvation the prisoners already
were. Their responsibility for the general misery as well as the gratuitous violence
inflicted on the prisoners stemmed not from some deliberate plan but from indifference to suffering, the habitual brutality of the Japanese Army (officers routinely beat
enlisted men), and the Japanese officers' lack of control over their own soldiers.*

QUESTIONS TO CONSIDER

1. What evidence can you find in the readings to corroborate or disprove
   John Toland's view of how the death march occurred?
2. How would you try to explain the way the guards acted?
3. How did the prisoners whose accounts you will read survive the march?

Donald Knox, *Death March: The Survivors of Bataan* (New York: Harcourt Brace Jovanovich, 1981),
122–39.

PFC. BLAIR ROBINETT

Company C, 803d Engineers

My group came up the road from Mariveles another half mile or so when a Jap soldier stepped out, came across, and took my canteen out of its cover. He took a drink, filled his canteen out of mine, poured the rest of my water on the ground, and dropped the canteen at my feet. I thought he was going to walk back to the line of Jap troops standing across the road, so I bent over to pick up my canteen. But he turned around and hit me on the head with his rifle butt. Put a crease in the top of my head that I still have. I fell face down on the cobblestones. I crawled back up to my knees, debating whether to pick up the canteen again. I figured the best course of action was to stand up and leave the canteen alone. Soon as the Jap troops moved off, I squatted down and picked it up. A little later a Jap soldier came over to one of the lieutenants out of our company, and when he found out his canteen was empty he beat the lieutenant to his knees with the canteen. Just kept slapping him back and forth across the face.

We moved down the ridge a ways when we saw this GI. He was sick. I figured he had come out of the hospital that was in tents out under the trees. He was wobbling along, uneasy on his feet. There were Japanese infantry and tanks coming down the road alongside us. One of these Jap soldiers, I don't know whether he was on our side or if he deliberately came across the road, but he grabbed this sick guy by the arm and guided him to the middle of the road. Then he just flipped him out across the road. The guy hit the cobblestone about five feet in front of a tank and the tank pulled on across him. Well, it killed him quick. There must have been ten tanks in that column, and every one of them came up there right across the body. When the last tank left there was no way you could tell there'd ever been a man there. But his uniform was embedded in the cobblestone. The man disappeared, but his uniform had been pressed until it had become part of the ground.

Now we knew, if there had been any doubts before, we were in for a bad time.

CPL. HUBERT GATER

200th Coast Artillery

Suddenly the hill rocked under us. There was a roar to the left, to the right, and then several back to our rear. The Japs had moved their field guns into position around us on Cabcaben Field.

"Why the dirty bastards!" the man next to me said. "They're using us as a shield to fire on Corregidor." It was true. We should have realized then what to expect as their prisoners.

A flight of Jap bombers were flying over Corregidor. Our officers cautioned us not to watch them because if our anti-aircraft fire hit any of them we would cheer in spite of ourself. Our chief worry was, would Corregidor return fire on the guns that surrounded us?

Corregidor didn't, but a gunboat out in the Bay did. I don't know the size of the shells; they were some smaller than our 3-inch. The first shell was to our right. Apparently, a dud. It skidded through the grass and set it on fire. Some of the men flattened out; others stood up ready to run to cover. Our officers motioned us down. There were a lot of Japs around us now.

The second shell burst to the rear and center of us. At the time I thought it had hit some of our men. A Jap soldier got part of his chin tore off. He was a terrible looking sight running around, evidently half out of his mind. From chin to waist he was covered with blood.

A young Jap officer who had been silently watching us motioned with his hand for us to take cover. About 300 of us ran across Cabcaben Field to get behind a hill. The rest ran the other way, up the road.

SGT. RALPH LEVENBERG

17th Pursuit Squadron

Eventually they started to systematically put us in groups of about 100 or so and marched us off. There were one, two, sometimes four guards, you never knew.

I was fortunate in two respects. First, I had a new pair of shoes, and second, I had some chlorine pills. The shoes I had kept with me ever since we left the barracks outside Manila, and the chlorine I had just managed to pick up. I don't know why, maybe because of my upbringing, I was taught to be protective of my physical being. I was therefore able from time to time, when we stopped near a creek which had dead bodies and horses floating in it, to get some water and purify it with the chlorine.

One of the tricks the Japs played on us—thought it was funny, too—was when they would be riding on the back of a truck, they would have these long black snake whips, and they'd whip that thing out and get some poor bastard by the neck or torso and drag him behind their truck. 'Course if one of our guys was quick enough he didn't get dragged too far. But, if the Japs got a sick guy. . . .

CAPT. MARK WOHLFELD

27th Bombardment Group

We were all mixed up—privates, officers, Scout officers, 31st Infantry, 192d Tank Battalion, 200th New Mexico Coast Artillery—just a jumbled mass of humanity.

My group stopped at a small bridge up above Cabcaben to let some Jap horse artillery through. They were in a real hurry to get these guns in place and start on Corregidor. Right behind the artillery there arrived a great big 1942 Cadillac equipped with a freshly cut wooden camera platform attached to the roof. As soon as they saw us they stopped and the cameraman jumped out and placed his tripod and camera on the platform. He had his big box camera which he looked down into. A white-shirted Japanese interpreter staged us for the cameraman. He told us to line up and put our hands over our heads. We should look depressed and dejected. That wasn't hard. The cameraman took his pictures and started back down the road in his Cadillac towards Corregidor, while we started marching in the other direction. That picture eventually appeared in *Life* magazine.

An hour or so later we halted and fell out near a ditch where there were about five dead Filipinos lying around. They looked like swollen rag dolls. I used a handkerchief knotted at the four corners to keep the sun from my head. I asked the Japanese guard, part talk, part pantomime, "Can I have a helmet? Dead, Filipino. Sun, hot, hot." He finally gave in, but I wondered whether he'd shoot me when I got as far as the ditch: "Fuck it, I'll try it." There was this dead Filipino lying there, and because his face was so puffed up I could only barely manage to get the chin strap off. He was full of maggots and flies. I finally got the helmet off and wiped out the inside with a part of his uniform that wasn't soiled. Then I hung it from my belt so it would dry. Who cared for germs at a time like that? I came back from the ditch and sat next to Major Small. "Boy," he said, "could I stand a Coca-Cola now." I started thinking about my girlfriend then. She worked in Grand Central Station in a real estate office, and I knew she used to go downstairs on her break and get a nice Coke with lots of ice chips in it. I started to take the helmet off my belt and put it on my head, when I noticed the dead Filipino had scratched the name Mary in his helmet liner. The amazing thing was my girlfriend's name was also Mary!

After a column of trucks carrying landing craft passed us, we resumed our march. We fell in behind another group marching out. We'd gone a little farther when we pulled off to the side of the road again to let some trucks roll by. Some of our young guys started asking the Japs whether they could have a drink of water. I looked to my right and saw a buffalo wallow about fifty yards off the road. It looked like green scum. The guards started to laugh and said. "O.K., O.K." So all these kids, eighteen or nineteen year old enlisted men, run for the water and began drowning each other trying to get a drink. The Japs thought it was hilarious. I noticed at the end of the scum some others drinking through handkerchiefs, thinking that would filter the bacteria out. Finally, a Japanese officer came along and began shouting at the men in the water. There must have been fifty of them, and they scattered and ran back for the road. That wasn't the end of it. This officer found some Jap soldiers who had been watching us and ordered them to pull out of the line any Americans who had water stains on their uniforms. When we marched out, after a short while we heard shooting behind us.

That night when we stopped, most of us had had no water all day. Our tongues were thick with dust. We had come into this abandoned barrio and were now sitting in a field. My small group was made up of some senior officers, even a few full colonels. I noticed one, Col. Edmund Lillie, who had been my reserve unit instructor back in the States ten years before. I went up to him, but of course he didn't remember me. We started to talk and began wondering how we could get some water. There was an artesian well near us that had water dribbling out of it, but we were afraid that we'd be shot if we went to get any. Desperate as we were, Colonel Lillie asked a guard whether we could go and get water. The Jap agreed. Most of these officers did not have canteens, but I spotted an old pail, and since I was only a captain, I went over to get it. Inside the pail, stuck to the bottom, was some dried manure. "Maybe I can rinse it out," I said. Lillie told me, "Don't waste the water rinsing it, just fill it up." When I got to the well, one of the Jap guards kept urging me to hurry up. As soon as I got as much as I could, without running the risk of being bayoneted, I came back to the group. There wasn't much water in the pail, but it was something. Lillie told us we could each have only one full mouthful before we passed the pail to the next man. In those days an officer's word meant something, so that's just what we did. Each of us took one full gulp. That way there was enough for everyone.

CAPT. LOYD MILLS

Company C, 57th Infantry, Philippine Scouts

The nights were the worst times for me. We walked all day, from early morning until dusk. Then we were put into barbed-wire enclosures in which the conditions were nearly indescribable. Filth and defecation all over the place. The smell was terrible. These same enclosures had been used every night, and when my group got to them, they were covered by the filth of five or six nights.

I had dysentery pretty bad, but I didn't worry about it because there wasn't anything you could do about it. You didn't stop on "the March" because you were dead if you did. They didn't mess around with you. You didn't have time to pull out and go over and squat. You would just release wherever you were. Generally right on yourself, or somebody else if they happened to be in your way. There was nothing else to do. Without food it was water more than anything. It just went through me . . . bang.

I was in a daze. One thing I knew was that I had to keep going. I was young, so I had that advantage over some of the older men. I helped along the way. If someone near you started stumbling and looked like he was going to fall, you would try to literally pick him up and keep him going. You always talked to them. Tried to make them understand that if they fell they were gone. 'Course, there was nothing you could do about the people who fell in the back.

STAFF SGT. HAROLD FEINER

17th Ordnance Company, Provisional Tank Group

I don't know if the guards were Korean or Taiwanese. I was so miserable on that Death March that I couldn't tell you what they were. I know one thing about them, though—they were mean, sadistic, brutal. And yet, on "the March" I was befriended.

I had been hit at Cabcaben and had a piece of Corregidor shrapnel in my leg. It was the size of a piece of pencil lead and was laying along my shinbone. I had wrapped an old white towel around it and had managed to walk about fifteen miles, but I was getting weaker and more feverish the further I went. I was in bad shape. Guys had to help me. They would kind of hold onto me. If you fell, you were dead. They bayoneted you right away. No bullshit! If you fell, bingo, you were dead.

We finally stopped for the night near a small stream and I laid down. About an hour later this guy comes crawling along. He looked like an Italian, swarthy, kind of muscular. "Hey, fellows, any of you guys need any help?" he was whispering. "I'm a doctor." Didn't give us his name. When he got to me, he stopped and I told him about my leg. Just then a young guard saw us and came over. The first thing they did was hit you with their rifle butts. He spoke atrocious English and he yelled for us to separate. The doctor kept talking, and asked him would it be all right if he took the shrapnel out of my leg. "Wait, wait, wait," and he ran out into the road to see if anyone was coming. Then he came back and said, "Hurry, hurry." I remember the doctor saying, "Soldier, this is going to hurt. If you can take it, I'll get it out." He never had to worry about me hurting. As soon as he touched it, bam, I passed out. He took it out and wrapped a hand towel around my shin. When he left he said, "Yeah, well, I hope to God you make it. God bless you." He disappeared and I never got to know his name.

The Jap guard came up to me during the night and gave me a cup of sweetened chocolate, tasted like milk. I hadn't had any food and no water for days. I didn't speak one single word of Japanese then, but he could speak a little English, but with a really horrible accent. "Someday me go Hollywood, me going to be movie star." That's the way he talked. He made me laugh. All through the night he gave me something, because he knew I needed strength. In the morning he was gone. His squad had been replaced by another. The orders were given, "Everybody up, up, up." We got in line and I found I couldn't walk. My leg hurt so much. Some guys held me up and I was carried about 100 feet to the road. There we were told to stop and sit down. Then we were told to get up. We waited about a half an hour before we were permitted to sit down again. Then we were turned around and marched back to where we started. Wait . . . rest . . . wait . . . march . . . turn around . . . go back. We did this the whole day. I never had to walk, and by the time we started out the next day I had enough strength to limp along on my own. I'm not a religious man, but God said keep those men there, we want to save that man. I don't know what it was. I know I wouldn't have made it, if I had to march that day.

Blacklist: Post–World War II Red Scare

Ring Lardner Jr.

Following each of the world wars of the twentieth century, American politics shifted from progressive to conservative and went through a "red scare," a heightened fear of communism. The Truman administration conducted a rigid internal security program to weed out disloyal or potentially subversive federal employees (although it fired many more homosexuals than political activists). And Truman pursued a foreign policy of unparalleled aggressiveness against the Soviet Union. Despite this he was successfully attacked by Republicans as "soft" on communism. Teachers and professors were fired for political reasons, the National Association for the Advancement of Colored People was branded an instrument of international communism, and the 1954 landmark decision in Brown v. Board of Education, *which paved the way for the integration of public schools, was regularly cited across the South as evidence of communist infiltration of the U.S. Supreme Court.*

The Red Scare affected the entertainment industry particularly. Both Hollywood and New York had been centers of political radicalism in the 1930s. Highly organized citizens' groups pressured the entertainment industry to blacklist writers, directors, and actors, among others. This greatly influenced what Americans did and did not see on television or at the movies and left hundreds of industry workers unemployed.

Ring Lardner Jr. was one of many such entertainment industry workers who suffered from the postwar Red Scare. An open member of the Communist Party, Lardner had contributed to writing the movie A Star is Born *and won the 1942 Academy Award for Best Original Screenplay for* Woman of the Year *(starring Katharine Hepburn) at the age of twenty-six. Five years later, he was subpoenaed by the House Un-American Activities Committee (HUAC) and asked the infamous question, "Are you now or have you ever been a member of the Communist Party?" Knowing that answering would provide the legal opening for HUAC to ask many other questions and force him to "name names," he gave the famous response, "I could answer it, but if I did, I would hate myself in the morning." He was subsequently cited for contempt of Congress, blacklisted, and served one year in prison. The government never took away Lardner's passport, as had happened to African American singer, athlete, actor, writer, and lawyer Paul Robeson, enabling Lardner to wait out the 1950s abroad, writing under pseudonyms and through "fronts" (nonblacklisted people paid to pretend to have written scripts). When he finally returned to working under his own name, he won a second Oscar for writing the screenplay for the movie* M*A*S*H. *During the 1970s he*

"Notes on the Blacklist: Lardner," interviewed by Barry Strugatz, *Film Comment*, September/October 1988, 52–69.

wrote twenty-two episodes of the television adaptation of M*A*S*H *and several movies, including* The Greatest, *about Muhammad Ali. This interview with Lardner from 1988 details his experiences in the period leading up to and during his time on the blacklist.*

QUESTIONS TO CONSIDER

1. Do you think that a screenwriter's politics are a public issue or a private matter? Explain your answer.
2. If you have seen any of Ring Lardner's movies or television shows, do you see a connection between his beliefs and his life facing the blacklist and the movie scripts he wrote?
3. Are there current issues today that might be similar to those that arose in the entertainment industry during the 1950s? If yes, how are they similar to and how are they different from the Red Scare of the post–World War II period?

When did you join the Party?
In 1936.
You knew Schulberg[1] in Russia?
I met him first there. He and Maurice Rapf were students there; they were both students at this institute at the University of Moscow. We didn't know each other very well there, but we spoke.
He was very political back then.
Very. As a matter of fact, Budd really recruited me into the Communist Party. We were working together on *A Star Is Born* or had started on that thing for Merian Cooper; I know we were collaborating on something. I had written a letter on Selznick International stationery to *Time* magazine, which they published in connection with something they had said about the Stalin-Trotsky rivalry, and I was correcting a point of fact. Somebody apparently in the Communist unit to which Budd belonged said, "Hey, isn't this the guy you are working with? And if he is writing this kind of pro-Stalinist letter, why haven't you recruited him?"
So Budd went to work on me.
How did he do that?
It wasn't very hard.
The people who were in the Communist Party, were they a social group?
Yes. Over the next couple of years, not only were most of my friends writers but they were mostly Communists. Both tendencies were, I think, unfortunate: It's not good always to be with like-minded people.
Schulberg and his wife were romantic figures in a way, weren't they?
Yes, she was a very glamorous, very beautiful woman, and Budd, who was not at all prepossessing in appearance or speech—he stuttered; it was more pronounced then than it is now—was nevertheless regarded by everyone as an

---

1. **Schulberg:** Budd Schulberg (b. 1914), Hollywood screenwriter and winner of the 1954 Oscar for his screenplay of *On the Waterfront*.

extremely devoted and idealistic fellow as well as a very talented individual. So they were definitely a sort of role model.

What was the general political climate in Hollywood?

People were becoming quite political about the Spanish Civil War, which broke out in the middle of that year, and about what was going on in Germany. The most popular political organization in Hollywood at that time was the Hollywood Anti-Nazi League, which Donald Ogden Stewart was chairman of, but most of the work was done by Herbert Bibberman and Beatrice Buchman, Sidney Buchman's wife.

Also, toward the end of 1936, the Screenwriters Guild, which had been effectively smashed a couple of years before, began to reorganize because of the Wagner Labor Relations Act,[2] and we were working toward a Labor Board election, which took place in the spring of 1937. There was also a strike going on, in '36–'37, of the various crafts, the non-IATSE-AFL[3] crafts—carpenters and painters—supported by the office workers and readers; and the Screen Actors Guild was heading toward its first contract and, as an AFL union, was in a position where they had to decide whether to support the IATSE or this other AFL group. It was a very close battle, and there was a big political fight in SAG. At one point they actually passed a straw vote to support the strikers and respect picket lines, but when it came to an actual vote, they didn't.

What did it mean to be an active member of the Party? What do you think you accomplished by being a member? What do you think the Party accomplished?

What it meant to be an active member was mostly spending a lot of time at meetings of various sorts. . . . I had meetings of the Guild board once a week and usually a committee meeting another evening of the week, and there was a regular Party branch meeting about once a week, and very often a writers' faction—these were writers who were members of the Party, as well as a few who, for various reasons, were not but were very close to the Party. They would meet and would discuss policy in the Guild. With one thing and another, I found I was going to meetings five or six nights a week. And Sylvia, who joined some months after we were married, was going to a good many of those, too. And there were other types of meetings as well.

We did play a part, I think, in most everything that was going on in the Hollywood scene. Organizations such as the Motion Picture Committee to Aid Spanish Democracy, the Hollywood Anti-Nazi League, and the League of American Writers would not really have functioned anywhere near to the extent that they did without the very active participation of Communists in their forefront; nor, I think, would the unions that were being formed or reformed at that time—the guilds of actors, writers, and directors, etc., and the emerging

---

2. **Wagner Labor Relations Act:** Officially known as the National Labor Relations Act, this bill, enacted in 1935, established the rights of workers to join trade unions without fear of management reprisal.

3. **IATSE:** International Alliance of Theatrical Stage Engineers; labor union representing technicians, artisans, and craftspersons in the entertainment industry; **AFL:** American Federation of Labor, known since 1955 as the AFL-CIO; the largest federation of labor unions in the United States.

office workers union, etc.—have gotten as strong as fast as they did without the extra work that the Communists put into organizing and recruiting people for them.

The nature of the work we did changed twice during that period. Once in the fall of 1939, with the outbreak of the war in Europe and the Nazi-Soviet Pact, the Russian war against Finland, etc., when there was a very sharp division for a while between Communists and liberals—most of the latter being supporters of the British and French in the war and most of us remaining pretty skeptical about what the Allies were up to in the war. And then, of course, when Hitler invaded the Soviet Union, and when Pearl Harbor was attacked, there was another big shift, and with much more unity on the liberal and left side of things.

Why were you skeptical of the Allies in the beginning?

The basic skepticism was what I still think is a well-founded fear: That the people who were in charge of those governments—Neville Chamberlain in England and Deladier in France—were likely to, if they got a chance, make some kind of a deal with Hitler to turn the war against the Soviet Union, which was a very popular idea in British and French circles.

What did you think of the non-aggression pact?

We thought it was just that: a non-aggression pact. And we justified it on the ground that Stalin and the Soviet Union generally had kept advocating collective security in Czechoslovakia and Poland, etc.; that they had finally despaired of ever getting an agreement to oppose fascism collectively and, in self-defense, because they feared German aggression backed by the Western powers, they had signed the pact to give them time.

But gradually it emerged that there was more to it than that: There was the active splitting up of Poland; there were certain economic exchanges going on that were distasteful. But still, as we saw it—as I saw it, anyway, and I think most of my comrades did, too—this was understandable and could be justified.

How did you see your politics as they related to your writing?

It was pretty difficult to find much relationship between them, except to the extent that when I was able—after *Woman of the Year*—to make some selection in what I was doing, I tried to get assignments that had some potential for progressive content.

We had what was called a clinic within the Communist Party, where writers used to meet and discuss each other's problems with scripts and sometimes with other kinds of writing: books, etc. That was, I think, helpful to many individuals in just working out certain technical story problems and things in conjunction with their colleagues. But I can't say that it had much of a broad effect on the content of what was done in the movies.

Did the studios or the Party try to influence the political content of scripts?

When they finally came before the House Un-American Activities Committee in 1947, the heads of the studios maintained that there was never any real question about the content of pictures because they retained control of content. And largely this was true; they did. What things a few writers might have been able to sell them on or slip into a script were of minor consequence.

Basically it was the studio heads who had charge of the content of the films, and there was nothing we could do about it. . . .

When the war ended, did you detect a change in the political atmosphere—the beginning of the Cold War, etc.?

Yes, quite rapidly. I think it probably came quicker in Hollywood than in most other places because during the last six months of the war, most of the same group that had been involved in that strike back in the late Thirties under the leadership of a man named Herbert Sorrell started a strike against the studios. And it was the position of the Communist Party during the war that there should be no strikes and no support for strikes until the war was over. So we did not actively help. There was some money raised, because we were basically sympathetic with what was going on, but we thought they had called the strike prematurely.

And when the war ended in the summer of 1945, the strike was still going on, and that condition persisted for six months after that. As I recall, it was a long, drawn-out, and quite violent struggle, with a lot of violence taking place on picket lines. Many of us marched on those picket lines in '45 and '46. That strike divided Hollywood very much into a sort of liberal-left camp that supported the strike in varying degrees and the conservative element in the Screen Actors Guild, which, by the time it was over, I think included a new president, Ronald Reagan.

At the same time there was an organization called the Hollywood Independent Citizens Committee of the Arts, Sciences & Professions, or HICCASP. The New York office was called NICCASP; in Hollywood it was HICCASP. The members were very enthusiastic supporters of Roosevelt during his fourth election campaign, and many supported what Henry Wallace stood for subsequently. But there did arise a split between those who were more inclined toward Harry Truman's policies and those of us who thought Henry Wallace was the man who should run in 1948. . . .

On the national scene, we knew that there were big industrial conflicts going on. The United Electrical Workers Union and other unions that had a somewhat left orientation were trying to carry on strikes, and they were being opposed by the hierarchy in the AFL. I guess the AFL and the CIO were still separate at that time. This was the time when the so-called Truman Doctrine in regard to Greece and Turkey was promulgated, and when Winston Churchill made his Iron Curtain speech in Fulton, Missouri, with President Truman seated alongside him. This was the time when we all seemed to be going in the wrong direction.

When were you served with a subpoena? Do you remember that moment?

It was in September, I think, of 1947. I remember it particularly because we had just bought a new house. I had been divorced and remarried to Frances, my present wife, who was the widow of my brother David, who was killed in the Spanish Civil War. We were married in 1946, and in the summer of 1947 we bought a house in Santa Monica with a tennis court—generally quite a nice place—and we were in escrow with it when subpoenas arrived. We had been aware of the possibility of this threat. . . .

Dalton Trumbo[4] and I had a couple of times discussed what we would do if it came up. We decided that it was not a good idea to deny membership in the Communist Party, although some of our colleagues had done that before the California State Un-American Activities Committee. We just felt that there were too many stool pigeons and various other ways to find out, and you could get yourself in a much worse situation for perjury; it would be very hard to organize any sympathy around that. On the other hand, we thought it would be a bad idea to answer "Yes" to the question because the studios would probably use it against us and also because it made it less feasible to refuse to answer further questions about other people.

You anticipated that they would proceed along those lines?

Yes. We therefore felt the most sensible policy was just not to answer questions and to challenge the right of the committee to ask any questions at all. The two of us had agreed that was the position we thought best to take.

It was only after it became known that there were 19 of us who had received subpoenas, known as "unfriendly" witnesses—as opposed to people who had received subpoenas who we believed were going to be cooperative witnesses—that we got together at meetings in Hollywood, all 19 of us, with the exception of Bertolt Brecht, who was then in a considerably different position. He was an enemy alien all during the war; the rest of us were citizens.

We met with some lawyers, and Trumbo and I brought up this idea of not answering any questions. There were problems with that position. There were several people who wanted to say yes, they were Communists; they felt it was time to raise the face of the Party. But we raised the point—and the lawyers agreed with us—that it would then be very difficult to take a position against naming practically everybody they knew.

We discussed the Fifth Amendment, and there was some dispute as to whether that would really work. The Smith Act,[5] under which the Communist Party leaders were later convicted, had not been invoked against them at that time; it wasn't until the next year that they were arrested. So we would be saying: "It's a crime to be a Communist and therefore I plead "self-incrimination." But beyond that, we thought that that position would not do anything to challenge the right of the committee to function.

In other words, it was a freedom of speech issue?

Yes. We were saying: "Under the First Amendment there is freedom of speech and freedom of the press—and that includes the movie business. Therefore Congress cannot legislate in this field—and Congress has no right to investigate where it cannot legislate."

What about the issue of political affiliation? Did that come under the First Amendment also?

---

4. **Dalton Trumbo:** Novelist and screenwriter who was blacklisted as a Communist after testifying before the House Un-American Activities Committee.
5. **Smith Act:** During the 1940s and 1950s, hundreds of communists were prosecuted under this act, which made it a criminal offense to be a member of any group that advised the overthrow of the U.S. government.

Yes; that it was our business what political party we belonged to or believed in. And Alvah Bessie[6] at that time pointed out to the committee that Dwight Eisenhower was then refusing to say whether he was a Democrat or a Republican—and we should have the same rights as he did.

So gradually the policy of not answering questions and of challenging the committee was agreed upon: More or less, we all agreed that we were going to do that, although we didn't want to seem to be doing it by agreement. Our lawyers additionally advised us that it was a good idea to say we were answering the question, but in our own way, while never actually answering it.

And we went along with this last tactic, which actually turned out to be a bad idea and just made us seem to be more evasive than we were, and it didn't accomplish anything in the end.

Could you describe what it was like testifying? What was going through your head?

I was somewhat frightened, I guess, of the idea of appearing before this committee. . . .

I had no great confidence in my ability to be articulate before this committee or to make any great points at such a hearing. The experience of my colleagues who had preceded me—the way they were jumped on and shut up—made me less confident.

I just couldn't see any real good coming out of it and determined that I would try to make a couple of points about why I wasn't answering these questions; that that was about the maximum good you could accomplish—namely, to get in a phrase or two.

And that's what I tried to do.

Jumping ahead to after your sentence. What was your prison experience like? Were you scared?

Yes, that was really a considerable unknown, both as to what it would actually be like in prison and what it would be like with our particular offense. I faced that with a good deal of uncertainty and pessimism because I didn't think it was going to go well.

It turned out, on the whole, not to be nearly as bad as I anticipated. . . .

Lester Cole[7] and I were both sent to Danbury, where my mother, who was only about 13 miles away, was able to visit once a week.

Were you put in the same cell?

No. In Danbury every new inmate went through an orientation course, which involved living in a segregated part of the prison in a kind of dormitory and spending a few days learning about prison life and discipline and so on. Then we were released into the general population and assigned jobs according to whether we were classified as maximum security or moderate security or light security. Those who were light security were allowed to have jobs working outside the prison walls. . . .

---

6. **Alvah Bessie:** Writer blacklisted during the 1950s anti-Communist witch hunts.
7. **Lester Cole:** Screenwriter who cofounded the writers guild of America and was blacklisted as a Communist.

When did you first realize you were blacklisted?

We returned from the hearings in Washington not sure of what was going to happen. We thought we had a pretty good chance to win the case based on the court decisions so far, and we thought if we won the case, the studios would not take any action, would not get enough support to take any blacklisting action.

However, there was a meeting called the very next month in New York: The heads of companies in New York met and passed a resolution that ten of us would not work—and anyone else who took the same position couldn't work—until we had been cleared by the committee, and that they would not knowingly hire a Communist or anyone who refused to answer questions of a congressional committee. So that was then put into effect in varying degrees. Only five of the ten of us were actually working at studios then.

Where were you?

I was under contract at 20th Century-Fox. I was in kind of a special situation because after I came back from the hearing, Otto Preminger asked if I would work on an adaptation of a book he had bought, and we started working on it. So they were giving me a new assignment after the hearing.

This later became an issue in a civil case when a jury decided that they had waived their right to fire me by giving me a new assignment. But a judge threw that out, and at a second trial we settled out of court for a relatively minor amount of money. Anyway, Darryl Zanuck made a public statement that he wasn't going to fire anybody unless he was specifically urged to do so by his board of directors. But the 20th Century-Fox board got together and obliged him. I was the only person at the studio. . . .

How did they let you know?

I was in Otto's office—we were talking about the story—when a message came that Zanuck wanted to see me. And Otto said, "Not both of us?" [laughter], and the message was, "No, just Lardner."

And then when I went to Zanuck's office, I was shunted off and did not get to Zanuck himself but to his assistant, Lou Schreiber, who told me that my contract was terminated and I was supposed to leave the premises.

I told this to Otto. He was very distressed but couldn't think of anything to do about it.

When you learned that people like Schulberg were cooperating with the blacklisters, were you hurt, disappointed, or did you see it coming?

There was some surprise and some disappointment. . . .

But then during the rest of that year, 1951, there were more hearings in Washington, and later in the fall, in Los Angeles, a number of people had testified. Some of them I was quite surprised by. But, in particular, I knew that Budd had had nothing to do with the Party since 1940–41, and I had once talked to him and he felt very strongly about some Russian writers that he had met when we were both in Moscow in 1934 who had since been purged. But, still, that Budd volunteered, really, to appear before the committee because someone had named him—he wasn't subpoenaed and he wasn't working in Hollywood at the time, and there was no particular reason why he had to clear himself—surprised me.

But others were more understandable. Some of them did it under quite strong pressure and didn't, like Budd, Kazan,[8] and some others, have some other kinds of work that they could do. Some of them were extremely dependent on Hollywood to support themselves.

What was the impact of the blacklist?

Well, the impact was to create intimidation in the motion picture business and in the emerging television business. It affected the content of pictures to some extent, because people avoided subjects they thought were controversial. The studios started making anti-Communist pictures, which the committee more or less specifically asked for, and, although they didn't do very well, there was a tendency to stay away from material that might be controversial. There was, I think, an increased kind of escapism in pictures. Certainly the impact was strongest on the 300 or more who were blacklisted. But it also threatened people who sort of got nervous about being revealed as entertaining dangerous thoughts.

Do you think this was an attack on freedom of speech?

Yes, I think it certainly had a limiting effect on freedom of expression in Hollywood.

8. **Kazan:** Elia Kazan (1909–2003). A prominent director of such critical and box office hits as *On the Waterfront* and *Gentleman's Agreement*. Kazan was one who named names when called to testify before HUAC.

33

Levittown: Making America Suburban
Homeowners' Guide and Images

The majority of Americans currently live in suburban settlements, usually composed of modest single-family homes, with a patch of grass in front and a small, fenced-in yard in back. But this was not always the case. Until the late 1940s the towns just at the edge of major cities were typically privileged enclaves of the elite, and most Americans lived and worked in cities, small towns, or the countryside. Many did not have the money to own a home.

The end of World War II in 1945 brought the return of sixteen million GIs, many of whom expected to start families. There was no place to house them. The decade of economic depression during the 1930s and five years of war in the 1940s had left the country with a severe housing shortage, estimated at five million units or more. Returning soldiers and their families were sometimes compelled to live in barns, abandoned trolley cars, unheated bungalows, and tool sheds.

Abraham Levitt and his two sons helped change all this in 1947, by building Levittown, the first modern mass-produced suburb, on an abandoned Long Island potato farm just outside New York City. Helped by their low-interest "GI loans," returning soldiers and their families (indeed, anyone with a little bit of money) could buy a Levittown home outfitted with a modern stove, refrigerator, washing machine, and oil burner for just a $90 deposit and $58 a month. Levitt took advantage of the housing crisis to transform homebuilding, avoiding union labor, building on poured concrete slabs, in violation of laws requiring basements, and undermining traditional craftsmen by factory cutting building materials in his lumberyard and nail factory in California.

The growing car culture and affluent postwar consumer culture favored Levitt's creation, which was so popular that in 1950 Levitt was featured on the cover of Time *magazine, having constructed over 15,000 homes at the rate of thirty per day. Levitt's vision would literally transform the landscape, determining the pattern of life for generations of Americans.*

The following document is taken from a homeowners' guide Levitt provided for new residents of the Buck's County, Pennsylvania, Levittown. The images are a photograph of a typical Levittown street and the cover of a Levittown brochure. In its twenty-seven sections the guide covers everything from how to use a fireplace to maintenance of door locks. Since many Levittown homeowners were from cities and had never lived in a single-family house before, five pages are devoted to garden-maintenance

---

"Homeowners' Guide: Some Information for Residents of Levittown to Help Them Enjoy Their New Homes," 1, 2–3, 4, 12–13, 16, 20.

tasks, including how often good neighbors should mow the lawn. Though there is nothing in the handbook about it, Levitt and Sons decided early on to restrict their planned community to white people only. The federal government accepted this and, as a result, Levittowns remain disproportionately white to this day.

Questions to Consider

1. In what ways did owning a Levittown home change the way families coming from cities lived?
2. How do you think people who already lived in the area viewed the arrival of Levittown and their new neighbors? How do you imagine their lives changing?
3. Many people have criticized Levittown for homogenizing American housing and creating vast, ugly suburban sprawl. What is your perspective on the pluses and minuses of these new suburbs? How do the images included inform your perspective?
4. What arguments does this guide make to motivate first time homeowners to do things "by the book"?
5. Compare and contrast the photograph of Levittown and the brochure cover. What differences do you notice right away? How do you account for those differences?

Street in Levittown.

Levittown sales brochure, 1957.

TEACHING CITY FOLK TO BE SUBURBANITES

Welcome to Levittown!

You have just purchased what we believe to be the finest house of its size in America. We wish you health and happiness in Levittown for many years to come.

In order that you may enjoy your house, and derive the utmost pleasure from it, we have undertaken to prepare this handbook so that you may better understand our position and your responsibilities. . . .

Electrical

Now let us start at the front door and walk through your new home. The two electrical switches as you enter control the foyer light and the light over the front door in the Country Clubber. In the Jubilee the two switches control the outside light and a receptacle on the front wall of the living room. In your kitchen you will find the oil burner emergency switch, clearly identified by a red plate.

Your circuit breaker is located in the #2 bedroom closet of the Jubilee, and in the garage of the Country Clubber. No fuses are required. Upon any lighting failure check your circuit breaker first. Simply reset the switch by returning it to its normal position. Repeated tripping of the breaker indicates a short circuit.

You will find ample receptacles conveniently located throughout the house. In rooms not provided with a lighting fixture the wall switch controls the nearest receptacle. Do not use any greater than 60 watt bulbs or 75 watt spot type bulbs in your ceiling recessed fixtures. You must supply a 40 watt 48 inch "rapid" starting fluorescent bulb for the bathroom of the Jubilee. In the Country Clubber you must supply four standard light bulbs for each bathroom. You will find that 40 watt bulbs will supply ample illumination.

Your dining room light fixture was designed for a standard 100 watt bulb.

Condensation

Condensation is the formation of water, usually on a very smooth surface. It takes place when warm, moist air comes in contact with a cold surface. Your new home has been tightly constructed and well insulated. Moisture created by your living activities in the house and the operation of your modern home appliances can therefore only be expelled by adequate ventilation. The normal living habits of a family of four people, using shower, washing dishes, cooking, and the use of automatic appliances, create 18 gallons of moisture each weak. Be sure to air out your home for at least a few minutes each day. The use of your exhaust fan and adequate window ventilation are the simple, practical steps that can be taken by you to allow moisture to escape. . . .

The Lawn and Its Upkeep

No single feature of a suburban residential community contributes so much to the charm and beauty of the individual home and locality as well-kept lawns. Stabilization of values, yes, increase in values, will most often be found in those neighborhoods where lawns show as green carpets, and trees and shrubbery join to impart the sense of residential elegance. Where lawns and landscape material are neglected the neighborhood soon assumes a sub-standard or blighted appearance and is naturally shunned by the public. Your investment in your garden is large at the beginning, but will grow larger and larger as the years go by. For while furniture, houses and most material things tend to depreciate with the years, your lawn, trees and shrubs become more valuable both esthetically and monetarily.

We grade your premises, fertilize the soil, then seed and roll the lawn. After that we turn the newly made lawn over to you for your care. The first thing to do is to water for many hours a day. The grass seed will not germinate otherwise; most of the seed will dry up. There is one way and only one way to water a lawn. Use an *OVERHEAD SPRINKLER* on one spot for a short time then shift the sprinkler to another spot. If you use it too long on any one place on a lawn, it will create puddles and will wash out the seed. *DON'T USE THE HOSE WITH NOZZLE ATTACHED; THE SEED WILL BE WASHED AWAY.* Don't step on a soft lawn especially with high heeled shoes; use a board or several of them. Try to keep children from running over the new soil, though we admit that is no easy task.

The Care of Trees, Shrubs, and Evergreens

Now the first thing to do to newly transplanted material is to water it. We have given this advice again and again and to see the neglect of many owners in this respect is extremely disheartening. Many who attempt to water do more harm than good. There is but one way to water a newly transplanted tree, shrub or evergreen. Place the hose (*WITHOUT NOZZLE*) at the root of the plant and give it a good soaking. For a large tree proceed from several positions. The hole or holes made by rushing water should be plugged up when through watering.

Important

Never use a hose to water your lawn. Always use an overhead sprinkler. You cannot grow a lawn if you water it with a hose, especially with a nozzle attached. Don't even keep a nozzle on your premises; it will only do harm!

PART SIX

Contested Boundaries

Moral Dilemmas at Home and Abroad

In the twentieth century an American national culture came to dominate all regions of the country and much of the world. Consumerism ruled national markets, the mass media shaped our most personal aspirations, and active federal and state governments provided services and regulations that were both desired and distrusted. The United States took on the role of global policeman and became an immense military superpower.

The powerful civil rights movement that African Americans had begun in the 1950s intensified in the 1960s, giving rise to unrest and a political idealism among young people reflected in the letters sent home by student civil rights workers in Mississippi during the "Freedom Summer" of 1964 and in the photographs included in the Visual Portfolio (pages 300–306). The middle class was greatly enlarged and became more mobile and vocal, awakening new political movements on both the right and left. Inspired by the dramatic struggle of African Americans to regain many of the rights they had lost when Reconstruction was reversed in 1877, myriad groups like the Young Lords, La Raza, the American Indian Movement (AIM), and the Gay Liberation Front contested old boundaries and tried to fight their way into the mainstream. And as had happened during the antislavery movement in the nineteenth century, women became frustrated at being denied, by their male colleagues, the respect and equality these various groups claimed to fight for. This led to a revival of the women's liberation movement. Across the United States women began to publicly question the political and personal aspects of gender inequality. The consciousness-raising sessions described by Kathie Sarachild were one of the tools used by the women's movement to encourage women to become involved.

Overshadowing all American lives during this period, however, was the Vietnam War—the nation's longest war. The massacre at My Lai in 1968 became a

243

potent symbol of what the war — and, many feared, the nation — had become. By 1979, when Islamic militants seized the American embassy in Iran and held embassy personnel hostage for more than a year, the United States had been defeated on the battlefield by Vietnamese communists, the years of protest were largely over, and a sizable segment of society was calling for the restoration of order and traditional values.

In 1980 former movie actor Ronald Reagan was elected president on a promise to make America strong again. His legacy was at best uneven. He projected strength, but used the military against striking workers at home and tiny nations like Grenada and Nicaragua abroad. He slashed school breakfast programs for children from poor families and oversaw an unprecedented expansion of the prison system, at the same time most Americans found themselves working longer hours for less pay. He funded and supplied the Afghan Islamists who would later become the Taliban. However, when he declared, in his folksy, intimate way, "It's morning in America," it was difficult to disagree with the powerful optimism of this president who had provided amnesty for three million excluded and undocumented immigrants like those whose voices were captured in "Border Crossings."

POINTS OF VIEW

The My Lai Massacre and Its Aftermath (1968–1970)

34

Disbelief and Corroboration

Ronald L. Ridenhour et al.

Throughout the twentieth century, civil wars have led to atrocities, and Vietnam was no exception. Such wars rarely obey the international rules of warfare and often control areas through deliberate terror. When the Vietcong (VC, Vietnamese communists) captured the ancient city of Hué during the Tet Offensive of 1968, they murdered hundreds, perhaps thousands, some of whom were buried alive. The attempt to eradicate guerrillas from among a population, any member of whom might be a friend, an enemy, or simply a poor peasant wanting to be left alone, usually produces episodes of indiscriminate killing of civilians. One U.S. "pacification" effort in a Mekong Delta province in 1969, for example,

Peers Report, vol. 1, 1–7 to 1–11; My Lai File, Army Crimes Records Center, Fort Belvoir, Virginia; Peers Report, vol. 4, 299–300; Peers Report, vol. 4, exhibit M–21, 111.

produced an official body count of eleven thousand Vietcong killed. That only 748 weapons were captured makes it likely that very many of those dead were noncombatants.

The massacre at My Lai on March 16, 1968, was the most notorious atrocity committed by American soldiers in Vietnam, causing many around the world to forget the discipline and restraint of countless other American troops since the beginning of the intervention. Company C (Charlie) of Task Force Barker, part of the American Division, after a particularly forceful briefing in which the men were reminded of previous casualties they had suffered at the hands of the VC, attacked the village of My Lai, known to be a VC stronghold. Finding no enemy forces there, they nevertheless opened fire on the old men, women, and children who remained in the hamlet, killing somewhere between two and four hundred. Rapes preceded several of the killings.

However awful the war in Vietnam and however frequent the atrocities on all sides, the men of Charlie Company and those who heard about My Lai knew that they had done something far out of the ordinary. Neither they nor their superiors wanted to talk about what happened. The standard press release, although written by an eyewitness, made no reference to atrocities. A cover-up had begun that lasted until a year later when Ronald L. Ridenhour (1946–1998), a former infantryman, wrote a letter to Congress, forcing an investigation that made available the documents reproduced here.

QUESTIONS TO CONSIDER

1. Why did Ronald L. Ridenhour write his letter? Does the letter convincingly present the need for an investigation?
2. Are there any indications in the documents that military personnel during the raid objected to what was happening?

LETTER TO CONGRESS FROM RON RIDENHOUR

Mr. Ron Ridenhour
1416 East Thomas Road #104
Phoenix, Arizona

March 29, 1969

Gentlemen:

It was late in April, 1968 that I first heard of "Pinkville"[1] and what allegedly happened there. I received that first report with some skepticism, but in the following months I was to hear similar stories from such a wide variety of people that it became impossible for me to disbelieve that something rather dark and bloody did indeed occur sometime in March, 1968 in a village called "Pinkville" in the Republic of Viet Nam. . . .

In late April, 1968 I was awaiting orders for a transfer from HHC, 11th Brigade to Company "E," 51st Inf. (LRP), when I happened to run into Pfc "Butch" Gruver, whom I had known in Hawaii. Gruver told me he had been assigned to "C" Company 1st of the 20th until April 1st when he transferred to

---

1. **"Pinkville":** Army slang for the vicinity around My Lai.

the unit that I was headed for. During the course of our conversation he told me the first of many reports I was to hear of "Pinkville."

"Charlie" Company 1/20 had been assigned to Task Force Barker in late February, 1968 to help conduct "search and destroy" operations on the Batangan Peninsula, Barker's area of operation. The task force was operating out of L. F. Dottie, located five or six miles north of Quang Nhai city on Viet Namese National Highway 1. Gruver said that Charlie Company had sustained casualties; primarily from mines and booby traps, almost everyday from the first day they arrived on the peninsula. One village area was particularly troublesome and seemed to be infested with booby traps and enemy soldiers. It was located about six miles northeast of Quang Nhai city at approximate coordinates B.S. 728795. It was a notorious area and the men of Task Force Barker had a special name for it: they called it "Pinkville." One morning in the latter part of March, Task Force Barker moved out from its firebase headed for "Pinkville." Its mission: destroy the trouble spot and all of its inhabitants.

When "Butch" told me this I didn't quite believe that what he was telling me was true, but he assured me that it was and went on to describe what had happened. The other two companies that made up the task force cordoned off the village so that "Charlie" Company could move through to destroy the structures and kill the inhabitants. Any villagers who ran from Charlie Company were stopped by the encircling companies. I asked "Butch" several times if all the people were killed. He said that he thought they were, men, women and children. He recalled seeing a small boy, about three or four years old, standing by the trail with a gunshot wound in one arm. The boy was clutching his wounded arm with his other hand, while blood trickled between his fingers. He was staring around himself in shock and disbelief at what he saw. "He just stood there with big eyes staring around like he didn't understand; he didn't believe what was happening. Then the captain's RTO (radio operator) put a burst of 16 (M-16 rifle) fire into him." It was so bad, Gruver said, that one of the men in his squad shot himself in the foot in order to be medivac-ed out of the area so that he would not have to participate in the slaughter. Although he had not seen it, Gruver had been told by people he considered trustworthy that one of the company's officers, 2nd Lieutenant Kally (this spelling may be incorrect) had rounded up several groups of villagers (each group consisting of a minimum of 20 persons of both sexes and all ages). According to the story, Kally then machine-gunned each group. Gruver estimated that the population of the village had been 300 to 400 people and that very few, if any, escaped.

After hearing this account I couldn't quite accept it. Somehow I just couldn't believe that not only had so many young American men participated in such an act of barbarism, but that their officers had ordered it. There were other men in the unit I was soon to be assigned to, "E" Company, 51st Infantry (LRP), who had been in Charlie Company at the time that Gruver alleged the incident at "Pinkville" had occurred. I became determined to ask them about "Pinkville" so that I might compare their accounts with Pfc Gruver's.

When I arrived at "Echo" Company, 51st Infantry (LRP) the first men I looked for were Pfc's Michael Terry, and William Doherty. Both were veterans of "Charlie" Company, 1/20 and "Pinkville." Instead of contradicting "Butch" Gruver's story they corroborated it, adding some tasty tidbits of information of their own. Terry and Doherty had been in the same squad and their platoon was the third platoon of "C" Company to pass through the village. Most of the people they came to were already dead. Those that weren't were sought out and shot. The platoon left nothing alive, neither livestock nor people. Around noon the two soldiers' squad stopped to eat. "Billy and I started to get out our chow," Terry said, "but close to us was a bunch of Vietnamese in a heap, and some of them were moaning. Kally (2nd Lt. Kally) had been through before us and all of them had been shot, but many weren't dead. It was obvious that they weren't going to get any medical attention so Billy and I got up and went over to where they were. I guess we sort of finished them off." Terry went on to say that he and Doherty then returned to where their packs were and ate lunch. He estimated the size of the village to be 200 to 300 people. Doherty thought that the population of "Pinkville" had been 400 people.

If Terry, Doherty and Gruver could be believed, then not only had "Charlie" Company received orders to slaughter all the inhabitants of the village, but those orders had come from the commanding officer of Task Force Barker, or possibly even higher in the chain of command. Pfc Terry stated that when Captain Medina (Charlie Company's commanding officer Captain Ernest Medina) issued the order for the destruction of "Pinkville" he had been hesitant, as if it were something he didn't want to do but had to. Others I spoke to concurred with Terry on this.

It was June before I spoke to anyone who had something of significance to add to what I had already been told of the "Pinkville" incident. It was the end of June, 1968 when I ran into Sargent Larry La Croix at the USO in Chu Lai. La Croix had been in 2nd Lt. Kally's platoon on the day Task Force Barker swept through "Pinkville." What he told me verified the stories of the others, but he also had something new to add. He had been a witness to Kally's gunning down of at least three separate groups of villagers. "It was terrible. They were slaughtering the villagers like so many sheep." Kally's men were dragging people out of bunkers and hootches and putting them together in a group. The people in the group were men, women and children of all ages. As soon as he felt that the group was big enough, Kally ordered an M-60 (machine-gun) set up and the people killed. La Croix said that he bore witness to this procedure at least three times. The three groups were of different sizes, one of about twenty people, one of about thirty people, and one of about forty people. When the first group was put together Kally ordered Pfc Torres to man the machine-gun and open fire on the villagers that had been grouped together. This Torres did, but before everyone in the group was down he ceased fire and refused to fire again. After ordering Torres to recommence firing several times, Lieutenant Kally took over the M-60 and finished shooting the remaining villagers in that first group himself. Sargent La Croix told me that Kally didn't bother to order anyone to take the machine-gun when the other two groups of villagers were formed. He simply manned it himself and shot down all villagers in both groups.

This account of Sargent La Croix's confirmed the rumors that Gruver, Terry and Doherty had previously told me about Lieutenant Kally. It also convinced me that there was a very substantial amount of truth to the stories that all of these men had told. If I needed more convincing, I was to receive it.

It was in the middle of November, 1968 just a few weeks before I was to return to the United States for separation from the army that I talked to Pfc Michael Bernhardt. Bernhardt had served his entire year in Viet Nam in "Charlie" Company 1/20 and he too was about to go home. "Bernie" substantiated the tales told by the other men I had talked to in vivid, bloody detail and added this. "Bernie" had absolutely refused to take part in the massacre of the villagers of "Pinkville" that morning and he thought that it was rather strange that the officers of the company had not made an issue of it. But that evening "Medina (Captain Ernest Medina) came up to me ("Bernie") and told me not to do anything stupid like write my congressman" about what had happened that day. Bernhardt assured Captain Medina that he had no such thing in mind. He had nine months left in Viet Nam and felt that it was dangerous enough just fighting the acknowledged enemy.

Exactly what did, in fact, occur in the village of "Pinkville" in March, 1968 I do not know for *certain*, but I am convinced that it was something very black indeed. I remain irrevocably persuaded that if you and I do truly believe in the principles, of justice and the equality of every man, however humble, before the law, that form the very backbone that this country is founded on, then we must press forward a widespread and public investigation of this matter with all our combined efforts. I think that it was Winston Churchill who once said "A country without a conscience is a country without a soul, and a country without a soul is a country that cannot survive." I feel that I must take some positive action on this matter. I hope that you will launch an investigation immediately and keep me informed of your progress. If you cannot, then I don't know what other course of action to take.

I have considered sending this to newspapers, magazines, and broadcasting companies, but I somehow feel that investigation and action by the Congress of the United States is the appropriate procedure, and as a conscientious citizen I have no desire to further besmirch the image of the American serviceman in the eyes of the world. I feel that this action, while probably it would promote attention, would not bring about the constructive actions that the direct actions of the Congress of the United States would.

Sincerely,
/s/ Ron Ridenhour

TESTIMONY OF ROBERT T'SOUVAS

Q: Have you ever heard of Pinkville?

A: Yes. As far as I remember Pinkville consisted of My Lai (4), My Lai (5), and My Lai (6), and maybe some other Hamlets. The Pinkville area was mostly our area of operation, to my knowledge.

Q: Is there one operation in the Pinkville area that stands out in your mind?

A: Yes. In March 1968 we went on an operation to My Lai (4) which is in the Pinkville area. This area stands out in my mind because there was so many women, children, and men killed.

I do not remember the name of my Platoon Leader or my Platoon Sergeant. After we got out of the helicopters, we organized. As soon as I got out the helicopter threw a smoke bomb and I and my Squad were told to look for the Viet Cong in the vicinity where the helicopter had dropped the smoke bomb. Names are hard to remember and I do not know at this time who the soldiers were that accompanied me. We searched for the Viet Cong, but we could not find them until the helicopter radioed and hovered at a certain spot right over the Viet Cong. Personnel in our Company went to the busy area and found a weapon. I do not know if they found the Viet Cong. I was there with my machine gun. After this my Platoon moved into the Hamlet and we just had to search and destroy mission. I seen people shot that didn't have weapons. I've seen the hootches burn, animals killed—just like saying going to Seoul and start burning hootches and shooting—a massacre wherein innocent people were being killed, hootches being burned, everything destroyed. They had no weapons and we were told that they were VC sympathizers. To come right to the point, we carried out our orders to the very point—Search and Destroy. In my mind, that covered the whole situation.

Q: How many people do you think was shot by C Company in My Lai (4)?

A: This is hard to say—from my personal observation I would say 80 that I have seen myself.

Q: What did the people that you saw shot consist of?

A: Women, men, children and animals.

Q: Did you at anytime receive hostile fire?

A: I was told that we were fired upon, but I myself did not receive direct fire.

Q: Were there still any people living in the Hamlet when you came through?

A: When we got there there was still people alive in the Hamlet and the Company was shooting them, however, when we left the Hamlet there was still some people alive.

Q: Did you see a trail in the village with a pile of dead women and children?

A: I seen dead women, children and men in groups and scattered on the trails and the rice paddies. I seen people running and just innocently being shot.

Q: Did you shoot 2 wounded children laying on the trail outside of My Lai (4)?

A: I opened up on people that were running. I do not remember that I shot at 2 children that were laying down on the trail. However, I do remember I did shoot a girl that was sitting there amongst 5 or more people, sitting there completely torn apart. She was screaming. I felt just as if it was my mother dying. I shot her to get her out of her misery. She was around 15. This happened inside the hamlet. However, I do not remember about the 2 children laying on the trail. I also shot 5 wounded villagers because they did not give them medical aid. They refused to give them medical aid. . . .

Q: Was the combat assault on My Lai (4) different than any of the others you were on?

A: Yes, I never heard anything so stupid as to search and destroy and to kill all those people.

Q: Is there anything else you would like to say?

A: I wanted to talk about this for a long time—and am glad now that it is off my chest—it is wrong. Even before it was investigated, I wanted to write about it to my Senator, but I didn't know how to go about it. This is all that I know about the incident. It is such a long time ago and it is hard to remember the exact sequence of events and I am not too good a map reader and I will not be able to draw a sketch of the Hamlet and show how we went through the Hamlet.

JOURNAL OF THOMAS R. PARTSCH

Mar. 16 Sat.

Got up at 5:30 left at 7:15 we had 9 choppers. 2 lifts first landed had mortar team with us. We started to move slowly through the village shooting everything in sight children men and women and animals. Some was sickening. There legs were shot off and they were still moving it was just hanging there. I think there bodies were made of rubber. I didn't fire a round yet and didn't kill anybody not even a chicken I couldn't. We are [now] suppose to push through 2 more it is about 10 A.M. and we are taken a rest before going in. We also got 2 weapons M1 and a carbine our final destination is the Pinkville suppose to be cement bunkers we killed about 100 people after a while they said not to kill women and children. Stopped for chow about 1 P.M. we didn't do much after that. . . .

Mar. 17 Sun.

Got up at 6:30 foggy out. We didn't go to Pinkville went to My Lai 2, 3, and 4 no one was there we burned as we pushed. We got 4 VC and a nurse. . . .

Mar. 18 Mon.

We got with company and CA out to Dottie [their base] there is a lot of fuss on what happened at the village a Gen was asking questions. There is going to be an investigation on MEDINA. We are not supposed to say anything. I didn't think it was right but we did it at least I can say I didn't kill anybody. I think I wanted to but in another way I didn't.

CAPTAIN BRIAN LIVINGSTON'S LETTER
TO HIS WIFE

Saturday 16 March 68

Dear Betz,

Well its been a long day, saw some nasty sights. I saw the insertion of infantry-men and were they animals. The[y] preped the area first, then a lot of women and kids left the village. Then a gun team from the shark[s], a notorious killer of civilians, used their minny guns, people falling dead on the road. I've never seen so many people dead in one spot. Ninety-five percent were women and kids. We told the grunts on the ground of some injured kids. They helped them al[l-]right. A captain walked up to this little girl, he turned away took five steps, and fired a volly of shots into her. This Negro sergeant started shooting people in the head. Finally our OH23 saw some wounded kids, so we acted like medivacs [mede-vacs]. Another kid whom the grunts were going to "take care of" was next on our list. The OH23 took him to Quang Nai [Ngai] hospital. We had to do this while *we* held machine guns on our own troops—American troops. I'll tell you something it sure makes one wonder why we are here. I can also see why they hate helicopter pilots. If I ever [hear] a shark open his big mouth I'm going to shove my fist into his mouth.

We're trying to get the captain and sergeant afore mentioned reprimanded. I don't know if we will be successful, but we're trying. Enough for that.

Brian

35

Cover-Up and Outcome

General Westmoreland, President Nixon et al.

Between March 1968 when the massacre at My Lai occurred and December 1969 when the New York Times *and* Life *magazine broke the story, the Reverend Martin Luther King Jr. and Robert Kennedy were both assassinated; ghettoes across the country erupted in riots; the Democratic National Convention degenerated into violence; Alabama governor George Wallace conducted his divisive presidential campaign; antiwar demonstrations escalated enormously; and despite a strategy of "disengagement" (that was being renamed "Vietnamization") American casualties were greater in 1969 than in any previous year.*

With so much wrong it became difficult to assign responsibility for the massacre. A thorough and careful investigation, directed by the highly respected General William R. Peers, recommended charges against fourteen officers: two generals, two colonels, two lieutenant colonels, four majors, two captains, and two first lieutenants. In the end only Lieutenant William Calley was found guilty of killing. He was convicted of the deaths of "at least" twenty-two people and sentenced to life in prison. Several higher officers

Peers Report, vol. 4, 245; *Peers Report*, vol. 4, Exhibit M–22, 113; *Peers Report*, vol. 4, 401–5; *Peers Report*, vol. 4, 264–65; *Peers Report*, vol. 3, 261–62; *Peers Report*, vol. 2, bk. 24, 44–50; William C. Westmoreland, *A Soldier Reports* (New York: Doubleday, 1976), 377–78; Richard M. Nixon, *RN: The Memoirs of Richard Nixon* (New York: Grosset, 1978), 449–50.

suffered administrative penalties: demotions, lost decorations, and letters of censure placed in their files for covering up the incident, although according to military law they could have been held responsible for criminal acts of which they should have been aware. The documents you will read present evidence of the cover-up and some of the reasons that it occurred.

Calley's conviction stirred massive controversy. Some regarded him a scapegoat for higher-ranking officers; others argued that amid the confusion over who was a friend and who was an enemy in Vietnam, his acts could not be considered criminal. Jimmy Carter, then governor of Georgia, thought it unfair to single out Calley for punishment. President Richard Nixon reduced his sentence, and in March 1974 he was paroled. When hearing of Calley's parole, General Peers told reporters: "To think that out of all those men, only one, Lieutenant William Calley, was brought to justice. And now, he's practically a hero. It's a tragedy." And in My Lai, Nyugen Bat, a hamlet chief who was not a Vietcong before the massacre, recalled, "After the shooting, all the villagers became Communists."

QUESTIONS TO CONSIDER

1. Why did the Barker report and the Henderson investigation cover up the events at My Lai? What light does the Vietcong document throw on this question?
2. How does the testimony of Herbert L. Carter help you to understand why participants and observers at My Lai did not reveal what had happened?
3. How does General Westmoreland explain the My Lai incident? How persuasive is his explanation?
4. Why did President Nixon reduce Calley's sentence? Was this the right thing to do?

SERGEANT JAY ROBERTS, PRESS RELEASE ON MY LAI, 1968

CHU LAI, Vietnam—For the third time in recent weeks, the American Division's 11th Brigade infantrymen from Task Force Barker raided a Viet Cong stronghold known as "Pinkville" six miles northeast of Quang Ngai, killing 128 enemy in a running battle.

The action occurred in the coastal town of My Lai where, three weeks earlier, another company of the brigade's Task Force Barker fought its way out of a VC ambush, leaving 80 enemy dead.

The action began as units of the task force conducted a combat assault into a known Viet Cong stronghold. "Shark" gunships[1] of the 174th Aviation Company escorted the troops into the area and killed four enemy during the assault. Other choppers from the 123d Aviation Battalion killed two enemy.

---

1. **"Shark" gunships:** Helicopters.

"The combat assault went like clockwork," commented LTC Frank Barker, New Haven, Conn., the task force commander. "We had two entire companies on the ground in less than an hour."

A company led by CPT Ernest Medina, Schofield Barracks, Hawaii, killed 14 VC minutes after landing. They recovered two M1 rifles, a carbine, a short-wave radio and enemy documents.

CAPTAIN BRIAN LIVINGSTON'S
LETTER TO HIS WIFE

19 March 68

Dear Betz,

... You remember I told you about the massacre I witnessed, well I read a follow-up story in the paper. The article said I quote "The American troops were in heavy combat with an unknown number of V. C. Two Americans were killed, seven wounded, and 128 V. C. killed." Thats a bunch of bull. I saw four V. C., that is, those with weapons, and the amazing thing about that, is two of them got away. It made me sick to watch it.

Brian

LIEUTENANT COLONEL FRANK A. BARKER JR.,
"COMBAT ACTION REPORT" ON MY LAI

28 March 1968

8. *Intelligence:* Enemy forces in the area of operation were estimated to be one local force battalion located in the vicinity of My Lai, BS 728795 as shown in Inclosure 1. This information was based upon previous combat operations in this area, visual reconnaissance, and PW and agent reports. During the operation it was estimated that only two local force companies supported by two to three local guerrilla platoons opposed the friendly forces. The area of operation consisted of six hamlets to varying degree of ruin, each separated by rice paddies which were bounded by a series of hedge rows and tree lines. The area was also honeycombed with tunnels and bunkers. . . .

9. *Mission:* To destroy enemy forces and fortifications in a VC base camp and to capture enemy personnel, weapons and supplies.

10. *Concept of Operation:* Task Force Barker conducts a helicopter assault on 160730 Mar 68 on a VC base camp vicinity BS 728795 with Company C, 1st Battalion, 20th Infantry landing to the west and Company B, 4th Battalion, 3d Infantry landing to the southeast of the VC base camp. Company A, 3d Battalion, 1st Infantry moves by foot to blocking positions north of the base camp prior to the helicopter assault. . . .

11. *Execution:* The order was issued on 14 March 1968. Coordination with supporting arms reconnaissance and positioning of forces was conducted

on 15 Mar 68. On 160726 Mar 68 a three minute artillery preparation began on the first landing zone and at 0730 hours the first lift for Co C touched down while helicopter gunships provided suppressive fires. At 0747 hours the last lift of Co C was completed. The initial preparation resulted in 68 VC KIA's[2] in the enemy's combat outpost positions. Co C then immediately attacked to the east receiving enemy small arms fire as they pressed forward. At 0809H a three minute artillery preparation on the second landing zone began and the first lift for Co B touched down at 0815 hours. At 0827 the last lift of Co B was completed and Co B moved to the north and east receiving only light enemy resistance initially. As Co B approached the area of the VC base camp, enemy defensive fires increased. One platoon from Co B flanked the enemy positions and engaged one enemy platoon resulting in 30 enemy KIA. Throughout the day Co B and Co C received sporadic sniper fire and encountered numerous enemy booby traps. . . . At 1715 hours Co C linked-up with Co B and both units went into a perimeter defense for the night in preparation for conducting search and destroy operations the next day. With the establishment of the night defensive position at 161800 March 1968 the operation was terminated.

12. *Results:*

A. Enemy losses:

    (1) Personnel:

        128 KIA
          11 VCS CIA

    (2) Equipment captured:

          1 M-1 rifle
          2 M-1 carbines
        10 Chicom hand grenades
         8 US M-26 hand grenades
      410 rounds small arms ammo
         4 US steel helmets with liners
         5 US canteens with covers
         7 US pistol belts
         9 sets US web equipment
         2 short wave transistor radios
         3 boxes of medical supplies

    (3) Equipment and facilities destroyed:

        16 booby traps
         1 large tunnel complex
      14 small tunnel complexes
         8 bunkers
           numerous sets of web equipment

---

2. **KIA's:** Military acronym for "killed in action."

B. Friendly losses:
   2 US KHA
   11 US WHA[3]

15. *Commander Analysis:* This operation was well planned, well executed and successful. Friendly casualties were light and the enemy suffered heavily. On this operation the civilian population supporting the VC in the area numbered approximately 200. This created a problem in population control and medical care of those civilians caught in fires of the opposing forces. However, the infantry unit on the ground and helicopters were able to assist civilians in leaving the area and in caring for and/or evacuating the wounded.

A VIETCONG LEAFLET ON MY LAI

Since the Americans heavy loss in the spring they have become like wounded animals that are crazy and cruel. They bomb places where many people live, places which are not good choices for bombings, such as the cities within the provinces, especially in Hue, Saigon, and Ben Tre. In Hue the US newspapers reported that 70% of the homes were destroyed and 10,000 people killed or left homeless. The newspapers and radios of Europe also tell of the killing of the South Vietnamese people by the Americans. The English tell of the action where the Americans are bombing the cities of South Vietnam. The Americans will be sentenced first by the Public in Saigon. It is there where the people will lose sentiment for them because they bomb the people and all people will soon be against them. The world public objects to this bombing including the American public and that of its Allies. The American often shuts his eye and closes his ear and continues his crime.

In the operation of 15 March 1968 in Son Tinh District the American enemies went crazy. They used machine guns and every other kind of weapon to kill 500 people who had empty hands, in Tinh Khe (Son My) Village (Son Tinh District, Quang Ngai Province). There were many pregnant women some of which were only a few days from childbirth. The Americans would shoot everybody they saw. They killed people and cows, burned homes. There were some families in which all members were killed.

When the red evil Americans remove their prayer shirts they appear as barbaric men.

When the American wolves remove their sheepskin their sharp meat-eating teeth show. They drink our peoples blood with animal sentimentalities.

Our people must choose one way to beat them until they are dead, and stop wriggling.

---

3. **KHA; WHA:** Military acronyms for "killed by hostile action" and "wounded by hostile action."

COLONEL FRANK HENDERSON,
REPORT OF INVESTIGATION
OF MY LAI INCIDENT

24 April 1968

Commanding General
Americal Division
APO SF 96374

1. (U) An investigation has been conducted of the allegations cited in In-closure 1. The following are the results of this investigation.

2. (C) On the day in question, 16 March 1968, Co C 1st Bn 20th Inf and Co B 4th Bn 3rd Inf as part of Task Force Barker, 11th Inf Bde, conducted a combat air assault in the vicinity of My Lai Hamlet (Son My Village) in east-ern Son Tinh District. This area has long been an enemy strong hold, and Task Force Barker had met heavy enemy opposition in this area on 12 and 23 February 1968. All persons living in this area are considered to be VC or VC sympathizers by the District Chief. Artillery and gunship preparatory fire were placed on the landing zones used by the two companies. Upon landing and during their advance on the enemy positions, the attacking forces were supported by gunships from the 174th Avn Co and Co B, 23rd Avn Bn. By 1500 hours all enemy resistance had ceased and the remaining enemy forces had withdrawn. The results of this operation were 128 VC soldiers KIA. Dur-ing preparatory fires and the ground action by the attacking companies 20 noncombatants caught in the battle area were killed. US Forces suffered 2 KHA and 10 WHA by booby traps and 1 man slightly wounded in the foot by small arms fire. No US soldier was killed by sniper fire as was the alleged reason for killing the civilians. Interviews with LTC Frank A. Barker, TF Commander; Maj Charles C. Calhoun, TF S3; CPT Ernest L. Medina, Co Co C, 1–20 and CPT Earl Michles, Co Co B, 4–3 revealed that at no time were any civilians gathered together and killed by US soldiers. The civilian habitants in the area began withdrawing to the southwest as soon as the oper-ation began and within the first hour and a half all visible civilians had cleared the area of operations.

3. (C) The Son Tinh District Chief does not give the allegations any importance and he pointed out that the two hamlets where the incidents is alleged to have happened are in an area controlled by the VC since 1964. CC Toen, Cmdr 2d Arvn Div reported that the making of such allegations against US Forces is a common technique of the VC propaganda machine. Inclosure 2 is a translation of an actual VC propaganda message targeted at the ARVN soldier and urging him to shoot Americans. This message was given to this headquarters by the CO, 2d ARVN Division o/a 17 April 1968 as matter of information. It makes the same allegations as made by the Son My Village Chief in addition to other claims of atrocities by American soldiers.

4. (C) It is concluded that 20 non-combatants were inadvertently killed when caught in the area of preparatory fires and in the cross fires of the US and

VC forces on 16 March 1968. It is further concluded that no civilians were gathered together and shot by US soldiers. The allegation that US Forces shot and killed 450–500 civilians is obviously a Viet Cong propaganda move to discredit the United States in the eyes of the Vietnamese people in general and the ARVN soldier in particular.

5. (C) It is recommended that a counter-propaganda campaign be waged against the VC in eastern Son Tinh District.

TESTIMONY OF HERBERT L. CARTER

Q: Did you ever hear anything about an investigation into the My Lai incident?

A: Yes.

Q: What did you hear?

A: I heard that they said if anybody asks around or any questions about what happened at My Lai, to tell them that we were fired upon and say that a sniper round had come in or something.

Q: Whom did you hear this from?

A: I was in the hospital at this time at Qui Nhon, and a couple of guys from the company came over. I'm not bragging, but most of the guys in that company liked me. I didn't bother nobody. I did my job and they did their job. We drank together.

Q: They came to see you in the hospital?

A: Yes. A lot of guys came over. You know, when they came back through, they would come over.

Q: Captain MEDINA told us that soon after this operation he got the company together and told them that there was an investigation and it would be better if nobody talked about it while the investigation was underway. Did your friends say anything about this?

A: No. The way they ran it down to me was like somebody was trying to cover something up or something, which I knew they were. They had to cover up something like that.

Q: I think you know that it took a long time for the story of My Lai to get out. What is your opinion as to why this wasn't reported right at the time? You did mention about some of your friends coming and telling you to keep quiet. Do you know anything else?

A: Like a lot of people wondered how come I didn't say something. Now, who would believe me. I go up to you with a story like that and you would call me a nut. You would tell me I am a nut and that there was nothing like this going on. You would think that nothing like this goes on in the United States. Just like I was in a bar a couple of weeks ago, and there was a drunk in there. He was standing there reading a paper and he was asking me if I believed that things like that actually went on, and I said, "I wouldn't know, pal." It was kind of weird. This happened three different times. One time I was sitting up there with a friend of mine, and my partner told me to be quiet about the whole mess.

Some people want to talk that talk all day long, and they just don't know this and that about what they are talking about.

Q: Did you or the other members of the company ever think about these killings as a war crime?

A: Not at that time. No. I didn't want to think about anything at the time.

Q: In your statement to Mr. CASH you spoke of it as murder?

A: Yes.

Q: You looked at it as being murder, but you didn't think about it as being a war crime?

A: That's right. I thought it was just the poor misfortunes of war.

GENERAL WILLIAM C. WESTMORELAND

In the criminal cases, acquittal resulted in all but that of a platoon leader, First Lieutenant William L. Calley Jr. Charged with the murder of more than a hundred civilians, he was convicted on March 29, 1971, of the murder of "at least" twenty-two. He was sentenced to dismissal from the service and confinement at hard labor for life, but the latter was reduced by judicial review to twenty years and further reduced after my retirement by Secretary of the Army Howard Callaway to ten years, an action that President Nixon sustained. The case was subsequently and for a long time under judicial appeal in the federal courts.

Lieutenant Calley was legally judged by a jury whose members all were familiar with the nature of combat in Vietnam and well aware that even the kind of war waged in Vietnam is no license for murder. The vast majority of Americans in Vietnam did their best to protect civilian lives and property, often at their own peril. That some civilians, even many, died by accident or inevitably in the course of essential military operations dictated by the enemy's presence among the people was no justification or rationale for the conscious massacre of defenseless babies, children, mothers, and old men in a kind of diabolical slow-motion nightmare that went on for the better part of a day, with a cold-blooded break for lunch. I said at the time of the revelation: "It could not have happened—but it did."

Although I can in no way condone Lieutenant Calley's acts—or those of any of his colleagues who may have participated but went unpunished—I must have compassion for him. Judging from the events at My Lai, being an officer in the United States Army exceeded Lieutenant Calley's abilities. Had it not been for educational draft deferments, which prevented the Army from drawing upon the intellectual segment of society for its junior officers, Calley probably never would have been an officer. Denied that usual reservoir of talent, the Army had to lower its standards. Although some who became officers under those conditions performed well, others, such as Calley, failed.

An army has a corps of officers to insure leadership: to see that orders are given and carried out and that the men conduct themselves properly. Setting aside the crime involved, Lieutenant Calley's obvious lack of supervision and failure to set a proper example himself were contrary to orders and policy, and the supervision he exercised fell far short.

In reducing standards for officers, both the United States Army and the House Armed Services Committee, which originated the policy of deferments for college students, must bear the blame. It would have been better to have gone short of officers than to have accepted applicants whose credentials left a question as to their potential as leaders.

PRESIDENT RICHARD M. NIXON

On March 29, 1971, just days after the withdrawal of ARVN troops from Laos, First Lieutenant William Calley Jr. was found guilty by an Army court-martial of the premeditated murder of twenty-two South Vietnamese civilians. . . .

It was in March 1968, ten months before I became President, that Calley led his platoon into My Lai, a small hamlet about 100 miles northeast of Saigon. The village had been a Vietcong stronghold, and our forces had suffered many casualties trying to clear it out. Calley had his men round up the villagers and then ordered that they be shot; many were left sprawled lifeless in a drainage ditch.

Calley's crime was inexcusable. But I felt that many of the commentators and congressmen who professed outrage about My Lai were not really as interested in the moral questions raised by the Calley case as they were interested in using it to make political attacks against the Vietnam War. For one thing, they had been noticeably uncritical of North Vietnamese atrocities. In fact, the calculated and continual role that terror, murder, and massacre played in the Vietcong strategy was one of the most underreported aspects of the entire Vietnam War. Much to the discredit of the media and the antiwar activists, this side of the story was only rarely included in descriptions of Vietcong policy and practices.

On March 31 the court-martial sentenced Calley to life in prison at hard labor. Public reaction to this announcement was emotional and sharply divided. More than 5,000 telegrams arrived at the White House, running 100 to 1 in favor of clemency.

John Connally and Jerry Ford recommended in strong terms that I use my powers as Commander in Chief to reduce Calley's prison time. Connally said that justice had been served by the sentence, and that now the reality of maintaining public support for the armed services and for the war had to be given primary consideration. I talked to Carl Albert and other congressional leaders. All of them agreed that emotions in Congress were running high in favor of presidential intervention.

I called Admiral Moorer on April 1 and ordered that, pending Calley's appeal, he should be released from the stockade and confined instead to his quarters on the base. When this was announced to the House of Representatives, there was a spontaneous round of applause on the floor. Reaction was particularly strong and positive in the South. George Wallace, after a visit with Calley, said that I had done the right thing. Governor Jimmy Carter of Georgia said that I had made a wise decision. Two days later I had Ehrlichman[4] announce

---

4. **Ehrlichman:** John Ehrlichman, one of President Nixon's closest advisers.

that I would personally review the Calley case before any final sentence was carried out.

By April 1974, Calley's sentence had been reduced to ten years, with eligibility for parole as early as the end of that year. I reviewed the case as I had said I would but decided not to intervene. Three months after I resigned, the Secretary of the Army decided to parole Calley.

I think most Americans understood that the My Lai massacre was not representative of our people, of the war we were fighting, or of our men who were fighting it; but from the time it first became public the whole tragic episode was used by the media and the antiwar forces to chip away at our efforts to build public support for our Vietnam objectives and policies.

FOR CRITICAL THINKING

1. Why did the My Lai massacre occur? Does the response to it, including both the cover-up and the outcome, suggest why it could occur?
2. What responsibility did higher-ranking officers bear for the massacre? What policies encouraged such an occurrence?
3. Should Calley have been required to serve a larger part of his sentence, or were the actions of President Nixon and other officials the right ones to take?
4. General Westmoreland claimed that "the vast majority of Americans in Vietnam did their best to protect civilian lives and property, often at their own peril," while President Nixon argued strenuously that My Lai "was not representative of our people, of the war we were fighting, or of our men who were fighting it." Judging from these documents and what else you may know about the Vietnam War, do you agree with these statements? Would Ron Ridenhour have agreed with them? What about Captain Brian Livingston? Why or why not?

36

Feminism and Consciousness-Raising

Kathie Sarachild

In November 1967 Shulamith Firestone, Anne Koedt, Carol Hanisch, and Kathie Sarachild, four of the founding mothers of the second-wave feminist movement, met with other women in Koedt's apartment in New York City and soon began the practice of feminist consciousness-raising. The idea was that part of what made women's oppression possible was their isolation from one another and their inability to identify their problems as more than interpersonal difficulties between individuals. Consciousness-raising, or CR, was an attempt to take a systematic view of the feelings and experiences of women and use that view to generalize about the status of women and the things that needed changing.

As these women began meeting regularly, deepening their understanding of the similarity of their oppression and developing a broader analysis of the status of women, they sought to bring the practice to more women. On Thanksgiving Day 1968, the author of this selection, Kathie Sarachild, who is famous for coining the expression "Sisterhood is powerful," presented "A Program for Feminist Consciousness-Raising" at the First National Women's Liberation Conference in Illinois. Soon groups like Redstockings and New York Radical Feminists were organizing neighborhood consciousness-raising groups throughout New York City. Over the next few years the practice spread to communities across the United States. By the time Kathie Sarachild gave the following speech to the feminist flight attendant group Stewardesses for Women's Rights in 1973, CR was a nationwide phenomenon that had grown to encompass politics, therapy, personal development, and community building.

QUESTIONS TO CONSIDER

1. Some feminists have criticized consciousness-raising for limiting the analysis of women's oppression to personal feelings and experiences and thus limiting political impact. What do you see as the pros and cons of this critique?
2. Can you identify other social movements that have employed different or similar means for raising the consciousness of their collective circumstances?
3. How relevant do you think the approach outlined by Kathie Sarachild might be to address contemporary problems for women?

Kathie Sarachild, "Consciousness-Raising: A Radical Weapon," in *Feminist Revolution* (New York: Random House, 1978), 144–50.

CONSCIOUSNESS-RAISING: A RADICAL WEAPON

The Idea

To be able to understand what feminist consciousness-raising is all about, it is important to remember that it began as a program among women who all considered themselves radicals.

Before we go any further, let's examine the word "radical." It is a word that is often used to suggest extremist, but actually it doesn't mean that. The dictionary says radical means root, coming from the Latin word for root. And that is what we meant by calling ourselves radicals. We were interested in getting to the roots of problems in society. You might say we wanted to pull up weeds in the garden by their roots, not just pick off the leaves at the top to make things look good momentarily. Women's Liberation was started by women who considered themselves radicals in this sense.

Our aim in forming a women's liberation group was to start a *mass movement of women* to put an end to the barriers of segregation and discrimination based on sex. We knew radical thinking and radical action would be necessary to do this. We also believed it necessary to form Women's Liberation groups which excluded men from their meetings.

In order to have a radical approach, to get to the root, it seemed logical that we had to study the situation of women, not just take random action. How best to do this came up in the women's liberation group I was in — New York Radical Women, one of the first in the country — shortly after the group had formed. We were planning our first public action and wandered into a discussion about what to do next. One woman in the group, Ann Forer, spoke up: "I think we have a lot more to do just in the area of raising our consciousness," she said. "Raising consciousness?" I wondered what she meant by that. I'd never heard it applied to women before.

"I've only begun thinking about women as an oppressed group," she continued, "and each day, I'm still learning more about it — my consciousness gets higher."

Now I didn't consider that I had just started thinking about the oppression of women. In fact, I thought of myself as having done lots of thinking about it for quite a while, and lots of reading too. But then Ann went on to give an example of something she'd noticed that turned out to be a deeper way of seeing it for me, too.

"I think a lot about being attractive," Ann said. "People don't find the real self of a woman attractive." And then she went on to give some examples. And I just sat there listening to her describe all the false ways women have to act: playing dumb, always being agreeable, always being nice, not to mention what we had to do to our bodies, with the clothes and shoes we wore, the diets we had to go through, going blind not wearing glasses, all because men didn't find our real selves, our human freedom, our basic humanity "attractive." And I realized I still could learn a lot about how to understand and describe the particular oppression of women in ways that could reach other women in the way this had just reached me. The whole group was moved as I was, and we decided on the spot that what we needed—in the words Ann used—was to "raise our consciousness some more."

At the next meeting there was an argument in the group about how to do this. One woman—Peggy Dobbins—said that what she wanted to do was make a very intensive study of all the literature on the question of whether there really were any biological differences between men and women. I found myself angered by that idea.

"I think it would be a waste of time," I said. "For every scientific study we quote, the opposition can find their scientific studies to quote. Besides, the question is what we want to be, what we think we are, not what some authorities in the name of science are arguing over what we are. It is scientifically impossible to tell what the biological differences are between men and women—if there are any besides the obvious physical ones—until all the social and political factors applying to men and women are equal. Everything we have to know, have to prove, we can get from the realities of our own lives. For instance, on the subject of women's intelligence. We know from our own experience that women play dumb for men because, if we're too smart, men won't like us. I know, because I've done it. We've all done it. Therefore, we can simply deduce that women are smarter than men are aware of, and that there are a lot of women around who are a lot smarter than they look and smarter than anybody but themselves and maybe a few of their friends know."

In the end the group decided to raise its consciousness by studying women's lives by topics like childhood, jobs, motherhood, etc. We'd do any outside reading we wanted to and thought was important. But our starting point for discussion, as well as our test of the accuracy of what any of the books said, would be the actual experience we had in these areas. One of the questions, suggested by Ann Forer, we would bring at all times to our studies would be—who and what has an interest in maintaining the oppression in our lives. The kind of actions the groups should engage in, at this point, we decided—acting upon an idea of Carol Hanisch, another woman in the group—would be consciousness-raising actions . . . actions brought to the public for the specific purpose of challenging old ideas and raising new ones, the very same issues of feminism we were studying ourselves. Our role was not to be a "service organization," we decided, nor a large "membership organization." What we were talking about being was, in effect, Carol explained, a "zap" action, political agitation and education group something like what the Student Non-Violent Coordinating Committee (S.N.C.C.) had been. We would be the first to dare to say and do the undareable, what women really felt and wanted. The first job now was to raise awareness and understanding, our own and others'—awareness that would prompt people to organize and to act on a mass scale.

The decision to emphasize our own feelings and experiences as women and to test all generalizations and reading we did by our own experience was actually the scientific method of research. We were in effect repeating the 17th century challenge of science to scholasticism: "study nature, not books," and put all theories to the test of living practice and action. It was also a method of radical organizing tested by other revolutions. We were applying to women and to ourselves as women's liberation organizers the practice a number of us had learned as organizers in the civil rights movement in the South in the early 1960's.

Consciousness-raising—studying the whole gamut of women's lives, starting with the full reality of one's own—would also be a way of keeping the movement radical by preventing it from getting sidetracked into single issue reforms and single issue organizing. It would be a way of carrying theory about women further than it had ever been carried before, as the groundwork for achieving a radical solution for women as yet attained nowhere.

It seemed clear that knowing how our own lives related to the general condition of women would make us better fighters on behalf of women as a whole. We felt that all women would have to see the fight of women as their own, not as something just to help "other women," that they would have to see this truth about their own lives before they would fight in a radical way for anyone. "Go fight your own oppressors," Stokely Carmichael had said to the white civil rights workers when the black power movement began. "You don't get radicalized fighting other people's battles," as Beverly Jones put it in the pioneering essay "Toward a Female Liberation Movement."

The Resistance

There turned out to be tremendous resistance to women's simply studying their situation, especially without men in the room. In the beginning we had set out to do our studying in order to take better action. We hadn't realized that just studying this subject and naming the problem and problems would be a radical action in itself, action so radical as to engender tremendous and persistent opposition from directions that still manage to flabbergast me. The opposition often took the form of misinterpretations and misrepresentations of what we were doing that no amount of explanation on our part seemed able to set straight. The methods and assumptions behind consciousness-raising essentially grew out of both the scientific and radical political traditions, but when we applied them to women's situation, a whole lot of otherwise "scientific" and "radical" people—especially men—just couldn't see this.

Whole areas of women's lives were declared off limits to discussion. The topics we were talking about in our groups were dismissed as "petty" or "not political." Often these were the key areas in terms of how women are oppressed as a particular group—like housework, childcare and sex. Everybody from Republicans to Communists said that they agreed that equal pay for equal work was a valid issue and deserved support. But when women wanted to try to figure out why we weren't *getting* equal pay for equal work anywhere, and wanted to take a look in these areas, then what we were doing wasn't politics, economics or even study at all, but "therapy," something that women had to work out for themselves individually.

When we began analyzing these problems in terms of male chauvinism, we were suddenly the living proof of how backward women are. Although we had taken radical political action and risks many times before, and would act again and again, when we discussed male chauvinism, suddenly we were just women who complained all the time, who stayed in the personal realm and never took any action.

Some people said outright they thought what we were doing was dangerous. When we merely brought up concrete examples in our lives of discrimination against women, or exploitation of women, we were accused of "man-hating" or "sour grapes." These were more efforts to keep the issues and ideas we were discussing out of the realm of subjects of genuine study and debate by defining them as psychological delusions. . . .

Our meetings were called coffee klatches, hen parties or bitch sessions. We responded by saying, "Yes, bitch, sisters, bitch," and by calling coffee klatches a historic form of women's resistance to oppression. The name calling and attacks were for us a constant source of irritation and sometimes of amazement as they often came from other radicals who we thought would welcome this new mass movement of an oppressed group. Worse yet, the lies prevented some women we would have liked to reach from learning about what we were really doing.

The Program

There was no denying, though, that we ourselves were learning a tremendous amount from the discussions and were finding them very exciting. From our consciousness-raising meetings was coming the writing which was formulating basic theory for the women's liberation movement. Shulamith Firestone, who wrote the book *The Dialectic of Sex*, Anne Koedt, who wrote the essay "The Myth of the Vaginal Orgasm," Pat Mainardi, who wrote the essay "The Politics of Housework," Carol Hanisch, who wrote the essay "The Personal Is Political," Kate Millett, who wrote *Sexual Politics*, Cindy Cisler, who led the groundbreaking abortion law repeal fight in New York, Rosalyn Baxandall, Irene Peslikis, Ellen Willis, Robin Morgan and many others participated in these discussions. Most of us had thought we were only beginning to have a radical understanding of women—and of other issues of class, race and revolutionary change.

Our group was growing rapidly. Other women were as fascinated as we about the idea of doing something politically about aspects of our lives as women that we never thought could be dealt with politically, that we thought we would just have to work out as best we could alone. Most of these issues the National Organization for Women (NOW) wouldn't touch. Was it because these subjects were "petty" or really hitting at the heart of things—areas of deepest humiliation for all women? Neither was NOW then organizing consciousness-raising groups. This only happened after 1968, when the new and more radical groups formed, with a mass perspective. Our group's first public action after putting out a journal was an attempt to reach the masses with our ideas on one of those so-called petty topics: the issue of appearance. We protested and picketed the Miss America Contest, throwing high heels, girdles and other objects of female torture into a freedom trash can. It was this action in 1968 which first awakened widespread awareness of the new "Women's Liberation Movement," capturing world interest and giving the movement its very name.

Our study groups were radicalizing our own consciousness and it suddenly became apparent that women could be doing on a mass scale what we were doing in our own group, that the next logical radical action would be to get the word out about what we were doing. . . .

Six Years Later

Since 1967, consciousness-raising has become one of the prime educational, organizing programs of the women's liberation movement. Feminist groups and individual women who at first didn't think they needed it are all doing it. As consciousness-raising became popular, many other groups and individuals have become involved in it and its nature has been changed to suit various purposes. The term consciousness-raising has become widely used in contradictory contexts. A recent *New York Times* article referred to a meeting called by Henry Kissinger to talk to the executives of the major television networks about the content of their programs as a "curious 'consciousness-raising' session with a Secretary of State."

Even in the women's liberation movement there are all kinds of proponents of consciousness-raising, people who are looked at as "experts in the field" and people who are drawing up all kinds of guidelines and rules for its use. In all of this, the original purpose of consciousness-raising, its connection with revolutionary change for women, is all too often getting lost. This is why a look at the origins of consciousness-raising provides such an important perspective.

The purpose of women's liberation was to defeat male supremacy and give women equality. We felt this was such a monumental task. How to approach it? Consciousness-raising seemed to be what was needed.

The male supremacist Establishment and its forces of discrimination against women that consciousness-raising set out to critique have rolled with the punch. Now the opposition to consciousness-raising frequently comes under the guise of support or partial support. The Establishment is trying to change consciousness-raising, weaken, dilute, and take away its strength so it won't cause any more changes.

Going to the sources, the historic roots, to the work that set the program in motion, is one of the ways to fight this process. The wellspring of consciousness-raising's power is the commitment to a radical approach, a radical solution. What actually went on in the original consciousness-raising program which turned out to be so provocative, the thinking behind it, the literature which the original group produced, form the kernel experience from which all other lessons grew. From it we can also discover what may have been wrong in the original thinking that allowed some organizing to go off the track. But any corrections in the original idea must be done to make the weapon of consciousness-raising in the hands of women sharper, not duller.

Checking Out the Original Sources

The people who started consciousness-raising did not see themselves as beginners at politics, including, in many cases, feminism. Yet they intended consciousness-raising as much for themselves as for people who really were beginners. Consciousness-raising was seen as both a method for arriving at the truth and a means for action and organizing. It was a means for the organizers themselves to make an analysis of the situation, and also a means to be used by the people they were organizing and who were in turn organizing more people. Similarly, it wasn't seen as merely a stage in feminist development which would then lead to another phase, an action phase, but as an essential part of the overall feminist strategy.

To get consciousness-raising started we, as organizers, gave it priority in our actions and outreach political work. In that sense we saw it as a first stage—to awaken people, to get people started thinking and acting. But we also saw it as an ongoing and continuing source of theory and ideas for action. We made the assumption, an assumption basic to consciousness-raising, that most women were like ourselves—not different—so that our self-interest in discussing the problems facing women which most concerned us would also interest other women. Daring to speak about our own feelings and experiences would be very powerful. Our own rising feminist consciousness led us to that assumption by revealing that all women faced oppression as women and had a common interest in ending it. . . .

From the beginning of consciousness-raising—as you can see in the first program outlined in 1968—there has been no one method of raising consciousness. What really counts in consciousness-raising are not methods, but results. . . .

. . . There have been a number of formalized "rules" or "guidelines" for consciousness-raising which have been published and distributed to women's groups with an air of authority and as if they represented the original program of consciousness-raising. But new knowledge is the source of consciousness-raising's strength and power. Methods are simply to serve this purpose, to be changed if they aren't working.

Radical Principles Bring Results

For instance, the aim of going around the room in a meeting to hear each woman's testimony, a common—and exciting—practice in consciousness-raising, is to help stay focused on a point, to bring the discussion back to the main subject after exploring a tangent, to get the experience of as many people as possible in the common pool of knowledge. The purpose of hearing from everyone was never to be nice or tolerant or to develop speaking skill or the "ability to listen." It was to get closer to the truth. Knowledge and information would make it possible for people to be "able" to speak. The purpose of hearing people's feelings and experience was not therapy, was not to give someone a chance to get something off her chest . . . that is something for a friendship. It was to hear what she had to say. The importance of listening to a woman's feelings was collectively to analyze the situation of women, not to analyze *her*. The idea was not to change women, was not to make "internal changes" except in the sense of knowing more. It was and is the conditions women face, it's male supremacy, we want to change.

Though usually very provocative, fascinating and informative, "going around the room" can become deadening and not at all informative, even defeating the purpose of consciousness-raising, when it is saddled with rigid rules like "no interruptions," "no tangents," "no generalizations." The idea of consciousness-raising was never to end generalizations. It was to produce truer ones. The idea was to take our own feelings and experience more seriously than any theories which did not satisfactorily clarify them, and to devise new theories which did reflect the actual experience and feelings and necessities of women.

Consciousness-raising, then, is neither an end in itself nor a stage, a means to a different end, but a significant part of a very inclusive commitment to winning and guaranteeing radical changes for women in society. . . .

Nor does consciousness-raising, as some have implied, assume that increased awareness, knowledge, or education alone will eliminate male supremacy. In consciousness-raising, through shared experience, one learns that uncovering the truth, that naming what's really going on, is necessary but insufficient for making changes. With greater understanding, one discovers new necessity for action—and new possibilities for it. Finding the solution to a problem takes place through theory and action both. Each leads to the other but both are necessary or the problem is never really solved. . . .

37

Mississippi Freedom Summer
Student Workers

In the summer of 1964, after nearly a decade of civil rights demonstrations, more than a thousand people, most of them white Northern college students, volunteered to travel to Mississippi to help African Americans register to vote and to teach African American children their own history in "freedom schools." The Mississippi Freedom Summer project was a high point and nearly the end of the integrated, nonviolent civil rights movement of the 1950s and 1960s. Although twelve hundred new African American voters registered in the state, it was a hard summer. Consider this macabre score: at least one African American and two white civil rights workers were killed, not including an uncertain number of African American Mississippians who died mysteriously; more than eighty volunteers were wounded and more than a thousand were arrested; thirty-five African American churches were burned; and thirty homes and other buildings were bombed.

But another score can be calculated. Mississippi Freedom Summer contributed to the success of the Voting Rights Act of 1965, which prohibits discrimination in voting practices because of race or color and quickly secured for millions of Southern blacks the right to vote. And the murders of James Chaney, Michael Schwerner, and Andrew Goodman forced federal authorities to infiltrate and destroy the Ku Klux Klan in Mississippi. These letters home from participants in the project (some supplied without attribution) testify to the intensity of the volunteers' experiences that summer.

Questions to Consider

1. Why did these young men and women travel to Mississippi in 1964?
2. What difficulties did they encounter there, and what were their rewards?
3. Had you been a college student in 1964, would you have gone to Mississippi?
4. Compare the risks faced by the volunteers and those they were helping. What did David Dennis argue in his eulogy for the murdered civil rights workers? Do you think his accusations were fair?

Elizabeth Sutherland, *Letters from Mississippi* (New York: McGraw-Hill, 1965).

Mileston, August 18

Dear folks,

One can't move onto a plantation cold; or canvas a plantation in the same manner as the Negro ghetto in town. It's far too dangerous. Many plantations—homes included—are posted, meaning that no trespassing is permitted, and the owner feels that he has the prerogative to shoot us on sight when we are in the house of one of *his* Negroes.

Before we canvas a plantation, our preparation includes finding out whether the houses are posted, driving through or around the plantation without stopping, meanwhile making a detailed map of the plantation.

We're especially concerned with the number of roads in and out of the plantation. For instance, some houses could be too dangerous to canvas because of their location near the boss man's house and on a dead end road.

In addition to mapping, we attempt to talk to some of the tenants when they are off the plantation, and ask them about conditions. The kids often have contacts, and can get on the plantation unnoticed by the boss man, with the pretense of just visiting friends.

Our canvassing includes not only voter registration, but also extensive reports on conditions—wages, treatment by the boss man, condition of the houses, number of acres of cotton, etc. Much more such work needs to be done. The plantation system is crucial in Delta politics and economics, and the plantation system must be brought to an end if democracy is to be brought to the Delta. . . .

Love,
Joel

July 18

. . . Four of us went to distribute flyers announcing the meeting. I talked to a woman who had been down to register a week before. She was afraid. Her husband had lost his job. Even before we got there a couple of her sons had been man-handled by the police. She was now full of wild rumors about shootings and beatings, etc. I checked out two of them later. They were groundless. This sort of rumorspreading is quite prevalent when people get really scared. . . .

At 6 P.M. we returned to Drew for the meeting, to be held in front of a church (they wouldn't let us meet inside, but hadn't told us not to meet outside). A number of kids collected and stood around in a circle with about 15 of us to sing freedom songs. Across the street perhaps 100 adults stood watching. Since this was the first meeting in town, we passed out mimeoed song sheets. Fred Miller, Negro from Mobile, stepped out to the edge of the street to give somebody a sheet. The cops nabbed him. I was about to follow suit so he wouldn't be alone, but Mac's[1] policy was to ignore the arrest. We sang on

---

1. **Mac:** Charles McLaurin, the project director and member of the Student Nonviolent Coordinating Committee, a civil rights group.

mightily "Ain't going to let no jailing turn me around." A group of girls was sort of leaning against the cars on the periphery of the meeting. Mac went over to encourage them to join us. I gave a couple of song sheets to the girls. A cop rushed across the street and told me to come along. I guess I was sort of aware that my actions would get me arrested, but felt that we had to show these girls that we were not afraid. I was also concerned with what might happen to Fred if he was the only one.

. . . The cop at the station was quite scrupulous about letting me make a phone call. I was then driven to a little concrete structure which looked like a power house. I could hear Fred's courageous, off-key rendition of a freedom song from inside and joined him as we approached. He was very happy to see me. Not long thereafter, four more of our group were driven up to make their calls. . . .

Holly Springs

Dear Mom and Dad:

The atmosphere in class is unbelievable. It is what every teacher dreams about — real, honest enthusiasm and desire to learn anything and everything. The girls come to class of their own free will. They respond to everything that is said. They are excited about learning. They drain me of everything that I have to offer so that I go home at night completely exhausted but very happy. . . .

I start out at 10:30 teaching what we call the Core Curriculum, which is Negro History and the History and Philosophy of the Movement, to about fifteen girls ranging from 15 to 25 years of age. I have one girl who is married with four children, another who is 23 and a graduate from a white college in Tennessee, also very poorly educated. The majority go to a Roman Catholic High School in Holly Springs and have therefore received a fairly decent education by Mississippi standards. They can, for the most part, express themselves on paper but their skills in no way compare to juniors and seniors in northern suburban schools.

In one of my first classes, I gave a talk on Haiti and the slave revolt which took place at the end of the eighteenth century. I told them how the French government (during the French Revolution) abolished slavery all over the French Empire. And then I told them that the English decided to invade the island and take it over for a colony of their own. I watched faces fall all around me. They knew that a small island, run by former slaves, could not defeat England. And then I told them that the people of Haiti succeeded in keeping the English out. I watched a smile spread slowly over a girl's face. And I felt the girls sit up and look at me intently. Then I told them that Napoleon came to power, reinstated slavery, and sent an expedition to reconquer Haiti. Their faces began to fall again. They waited for me to tell them that France defeated the former slaves, hoping against hope that I would say that they didn't. But when I told them that the French generals tricked the Haitian leader Toussaint to come aboard their ship, captured him and sent him back to France to die, they knew that there was no hope. They waited for me to spell out the defeat.

And when I told them that Haiti did succeed in keeping out the European powers and was recognized finally as an independent republic, they just looked at me and smiled. The room stirred with a gladness and a pride that this could have happened. And I felt so happy and so humble that I could have told them this little story and it could have meant so much.

We have also talked about what it means to be a Southern white who wants to stand up but who is alone, rejected by other whites and not fully accepted by the Negroes. We have talked about their feelings about Southern whites. One day three little white girls came to our school and I asked them to understand how the three girls felt by remembering how it feels when they are around a lot of whites. We agreed that we would not stare at the girls but try to make them feel as normal as possible. . . .

Every class is beautiful. The girls respond, respond, respond. And they disagree among themselves. I have no doubt that soon they will be disagreeing with me. At least this is one thing that I am working towards. They are a sharp group. But they are under-educated and starved for knowledge. They know that they have been cheated and they want anything and everything that we can give them.

I have a great deal of faith in these students. They are very mature and very concerned about other people. I really think that they will be able to carry on without us. At least this is my dream. . . .

Love,
Pam

Ruleville

To my brother,

Last night, I was a long time before sleeping, although I was extremely tired. Every shadow, every noise—the bark of a dog, the sound of a car—in my fear and exhaustion was turned into a terrorist's approach. And I believed that I heard the back door open and a Klansman walk in, until he was close by the bed. Almost paralyzed by the fear, silent, I finally shone my flashlight on the spot where I thought he was standing. . . . I tried consciously to overcome this fear. To relax, I began to breathe deep, think the words of a song, pull the sheet up close to my neck . . . still the tension. Then I rethought why I was here, rethought what could be gained in view of what could be lost. All this was in rather personal terms, and then in larger scope of the whole Project. I remembered Bob Moses[2] saying he had felt justified in asking hundreds of students to go to Mississippi because he was not asking anyone to do something that he would not do. . . . I became aware of the uselessness of fear that immobilizes an individual. Then I began to relax.

---

2. **Bob Moses:** Robert P. Moses, a young African American high school teacher from New York who organized a team of SNCC workers to join other civil rights workers in Mississippi that summer.

"We are not afraid. Oh Lord, deep in my heart, I do believe. We Shall Overcome Someday" and then I think I began to truly understand what the words meant. Anyone who comes down here and is not afraid I think must be crazy as well as dangerous to this project where security is quite important. But the type of fear that they mean when they, when we, sing "we are not afraid" is the type that immobilizes. . . . The songs help to dissipate the fear. Some of the words in the songs do not hold real meaning on their own, others become rather monotonous—but when they are sung in unison, or sung silently by oneself, they take on new meaning beyond words or rhythm. . . . There is almost a religious quality about some of these songs, having little to do with the usual concept of a god. It has to do with the miracle that youth has organized to fight hatred and ignorance. It has to do with the holiness of the dignity of man. The god that makes such miracles is the god I do believe in when we sing "God is on our side." I know I am on that god's side. And I do hope he is on ours.

Jon, please be considerate to Mom and Dad. The fear I just expressed, I am sure they feel much more intensely without the relief of being here to know exactly how things are. Please don't go defending me or attacking them if they are critical of the Project. . . .

They said over the phone "Did you know how much it takes to make a child?" and I thought of how much it took to make a Herbert Lee[3] (or many others whose names I do not know). . . . I thought of how much it took to be a Negro in Mississippi twelve months a year for a lifetime. How can such a thing as a life be weighed? . . .

With constant love,
Heather

Tchula, July 16

Yesterday while the Mississippi River was being dragged looking for the three missing civil rights workers, two bodies of Negroes were found———one cut in half and one without a head. Mississippi is the only state where you can drag a river any time and find bodies you were not expecting. Things are really much better for rabbits—there's a closed season on rabbits.

Meridian, August 4

Last night Pete Seeger was giving a concert in Meridian. We sang a lot of freedom songs, and every time a verse like "No more lynchings" was sung, or "before I'd be a slave I'd be buried in my grave," I had the flash of understanding that sometimes comes when you suddenly think about the meaning of a familiar song. . . . I wanted to stand up and shout to them, "Think about what you are singing—people really have died to keep us all from being slaves." Most of the people there still did not know that the bodies had been found. Finally just before

---

3. **Herbert Lee:** Mississippi farmer killed by a local white politician after registering to vote in a Student Nonviolent Coordinating Committee campaign in 1961.

the singing of "We Shall Overcome," Pete Seeger made the announcement. "We must sing 'We Shall Overcome' now," said Seeger. "The three boys would not have wanted us to weep now, but to sing and understand this song." That seems to me the best way to explain the greatness of this project—that death can have this meaning. Dying is not an everpresent possibility in Meridian, the way some reports may suggest. Nor do any of us want to die. Yet in a moment like last night, we can feel that anyone who did die for the Project would wish to be remembered not by tributes or grief but by understanding and continuation of what he was doing. . . .

As we left the church, we heard on the radio the end of President Johnson's speech announcing the air attacks on Vietnam. . . . I could only think "This must not be the beginning of a war. There is still a freedom fight, and we are winning. We must have time to live and help Mississippi to be alive." Half an hour before, I had understood death in a new way. Now I realized that Mississippi, in spite of itself, has given real meaning to life. In Mississippi you never ask, "What is the meaning of life?" or "Is there any point to it all?" but only that we may have enough life to do all that there is to be done. . . .

Meridian, August 5

At the Freedom school and at the community center, many of the kids had known Mickey and almost all knew Jimmy Chaney. Today we asked the kids to describe Mickey and Jimmy because we had never known them.

"Mickey was a big guy. He wore blue jeans all the time." . . . I asked the kids, "What did his eyes look like?" and they told me they were "friendly eyes" "nice eyes" ("nice" is a lovely word in a Mississippi accent). "Mickey was a man who was at home everywhere and with anybody," said the 17-year-old girl I stay with. The littlest kids, the 6, 7, 8 years olds, tell about how he played "Frankenstein" with them or took for drives or talked with them about Freedom. Many of the teen-age boys were delinquents until Mickey went down to the bars and jails and showed them that one person at least would respect them if they began to fight for something important. . . . And the grownups too, trusted him. The lady I stay with tells with pride of how Mickey and Rita came to supper at their house, and police cars circled around the house all during the meal. But Mickey could make them feel glad to take the risk.

People talk less about James Chaney here, but feel more. The kids describe a boy who played with them—whom everyone respected but who never had to join in fights to maintain this respect—a quiet boy but very sharp and very understanding when he did speak. Mostly we know James through his sisters and especially his 12-year-old brother, Ben. Today Ben was in the Freedom School. At lunchtime the kids have a jazz band (piano, washtub bass, cardboard boxes and bongos as drums) and tiny Ben was there leading all even with his broken arm, with so much energy and rhythm that even Senator Eastland[4] would have had to stop and listen if he'd been walking by. . . .

4. **Senator Eastland:** James Eastland, a U.S. senator from Mississippi from 1943 to 1978 and an outspoken supporter of segregation.

Meridian, August 11

. . . In the line I was in, there were about 150 people — white and Negro — walking solemnly, quietly, and without incident for about a mile and a half through white and Negro neighborhoods (segregation is like a checkerboard here). The police held up traffic at the stoplights, and of all the white people watching only one girl heckled. I dislike remembering the service — the photographers with their television cameras were omnipresent, it was really bad. And cameras when people are crying . . . and bright lights. Someone said it was on television later. I suppose it was.

Dave Dennis spoke — it was as if he was realizing his anger and feeling only as he spoke. As if the deepest emotion — the bitterness, then hatred — came as he expressed it, and could not have been planned or forethought. . . .

Laurel, August 11

Dear Folks,

. . . The memorial service began around 7:30 with over 120 people filling the small, wooden-pew lined church. David Dennis of CORE,[5] the Assistant Director for the Mississippi Summer Project, spoke for COFO.[6] He talked to the Negro people of Meridian — it was a speech to move people, to end the lethargy, to make people stand up. It went something like this:

"I am not here to memorialize James Chaney, I am not here to pay tribute — I am too sick and tired. Do YOU hear me, I am S-I-C-K and T-I-R-E-D. I have attended too many memorials, too many funerals. This has got to stop. Mack Parker, Medgar Evers, Herbert Lee, Lewis Allen, Emmett Till, four little girls in Birmingham, a 13-year-old boy in Birmingham, and the list goes on and on. I have attended these funerals and memorials and I am SICK and TIRED. But the trouble is that YOU are NOT sick and tired and for that reason YOU, yes YOU, are to blame. Everyone of your damn souls. And if you are going to let this continue now then you are to blame, yes YOU. Just as much as the monsters of hate who pulled the trigger or brought down the club; just as much to blame as the sheriff and the chief of police, as the governor in Jackson who said that he 'did not have time' for Mrs. Schwerner when she went to see him, and just as much to blame as the President and Attorney General in Washington who wouldn't provide protection for Chaney, Goodman and Schwerner when we told them that protection was necessary in Neshoba County. . . . Yes, I am angry, I AM. And it's high time that you got angry too, angry enough to go up to the courthouse Monday and register — everyone of you. Angry enough to take five and then other people with you. Then and only then can these brutal killings be stopped. Remember it is your sons and your daughters who have been killed all these years and you have done nothing about it, and if you don't do nothing NOW baby, I say God Damn Your Souls.". . .

5. **CORE:** Congress of Racial Equality, a civil rights group.
6. **COFO:** Congress of Federated Organizations, an organization of the civil rights groups operating in Mississippi that summer.

Mileston, August 9

Dear Blake,

. . . Dave finally broke down and couldn't finish and the Chaney family was moaning and much of the audience and I were also crying. It's such an impossible thing to describe but suddenly again, as I'd first realized when I heard the three men were missing when we were still training up at Oxford, [Ohio,] I felt the sacrifice the Negroes have been making for so long. How the Negro people are able to accept all the abuses of the whites—all the insults and injustices which make me ashamed to be white—and then turn around and say they want to love us, is beyond me. There are Negroes who want to kill whites and many Negroes have much bitterness but still the majority seem to have the quality of being able to look for a future in which whites will love the Negroes. Our kids talk very critically of all the whites around here and still they have a dream of freedom in which both races understand and accept each other. There is such an overpowering task ahead of these kids that sometimes I can't do anything but cry for them. I hope they are up to the task, I'm not sure I would be if I were a Mississippi Negro. As a white northerner I can get involved whenever I feel like it and run home whenever I get bored or frustrated or scared. I hate the attitude and position of the Northern whites and despise myself when I think that way. Lately I've been feeling homesick and longing for pleasant old Westport and sailing and swimming and my friends. I don't quite know what to do because I can't ignore my desire to go home and yet I feel I am a much weaker person than I like to think I am because I do have these emotions. I've always tried to avoid situations which aren't so nice, like arguments and dirty houses and now maybe Mississippi. I asked my father if I could stay down here for a whole year and I was almost glad when he said "no" that we couldn't afford it because it would mean supporting me this year in addition to three more years of college. I have a desire to go home and to read a lot and go to Quaker meetings and be by myself so I can think about all this rather than being in the middle of it all the time. But I know if my emotions run like they have in the past, that I can only take that pacific sort of life for a little while and then I get the desire to be active again and get involved with knowing other people. I guess this all sounds crazy and I seem to always think out my problems as I write to you. I am angry because I have a choice as to whether or not to work in the Movement and I am playing upon that choice and leaving here. I wish I could talk with you 'cause I'd like to know if you ever felt this way about anything. I mean have you ever despised yourself for your weak conviction or something. And what is making it worse is that all those damn northerners are thinking of me as a brave hero. . . .

Martha

38

The Young Lords
Pablo Guzmán

The Young Lords Party, founded in 1969, was one of the many left-wing urban youth organizations that developed out of the political turmoil of the late 1960s. Modeled after the Black Panthers, the Young Lords was a loose confederation of Puerto Rican youth groups that skirted the boundary between a civil rights organization, a street gang, and a third-world anticolonial liberation army. They brought together a remarkable mix of Puerto Ricans, from upwardly mobile "college kids" to street toughs, prostitutes, and recent immigrants from the island. The Young Lords, along with the Black Panthers and other minority youth organizations that sprang up around the same time, articulated the political voice of a generation of nonwhite teenagers that had been shaped by growing up on the excluded margins of the greatest economic boom in world history.

Heavily influenced by the Marxist revolutions in Cuba, Vietnam, and China, the Young Lords attempted to weld traditional ethnic community organizations to their politics of revolution through neighborhood study groups, educational meetings, and the kind of confrontational, direct political action that had made the black power movement so frightening to the authorities. Like the Panthers, they often carried guns and used paramilitary tactics borrowed from third-world guerrilla movements to gain attention. Their political banditry included commandeering a hospital van to provide free mobile medical services to their communities. They also provided a free-breakfast program for schoolchildren and produced a weekly radio program and newspapers.

The New York Police Department and the FBI eventually managed to destabilize the group, but for six years the Young Lords captured the imagination of many in urban America, particularly in New York City with its sizable Puerto Rican community. A large number of the group's leaders went on to become successful journalists, television and radio personalities, union organizers, academics, and authors. Pablo Guzmán, the author of this memoir, became a television reporter after his time in the Young Lords.

Pablo Guzmán, *"La Vida Pura:* A Lord of the Barrio," in Andrés Torres and José E. Velázquez, eds., *The Puerto Rican Movement: Voices from the Diaspora* (Philadelphia: Temple University Press, 1998), 155–58, 164–67. Originally appeared in the *Village Voice,* March 21, 1995.

Questions to Consider

1. What were the main objectives of the Young Lords?
2. Why do you think the Young Lords gained support from their community?
3. What does Guzmán reveal about how he now feels about his involvement with the Young Lords?

RAÍCES/ROOTS

We called ourselves the Young Lords Organization. In June 1969, two small groupings from Spanish Harlem and one from the Lower East Side, consisting overwhelmingly of guys between seventeen and twenty-two, decided to merge. I was in the Sociedad de Albizu Campos, named for the leader of the old Nationalist Party of Puerto Rico. Primarily college students, we had begun meeting three months before. I had just returned from a semester of study in Cuernavaca, Mexico, completing the required "in-the-field" half of my freshman year at the State University at the brand-new Old Westbury. I left as Paul Guzman, a nervous only child of a Puerto Rican-Cuban mother and a Puerto Rican father, both of whom were born "here"—stateside. I came back to the states as Pablo Guzmán. The other East Harlem group consisted mostly of high-school dudes who met in an after-school photo workshop run by Hiram Maristany. The Lower East Side group was a mix of college and high-school aged guys who we later found out had already been penetrated by two or three NYPD Red Squad agents.

Immediately after the merger, Mickey, David, and I drove in Mickey's Volkswagen Beetle to Chicago. We didn't know at the time about the Brown Berets or La Raza Unida among the Chicanos and the Mexicans of the West and Southwest. But Mauricio and I had read in that week's *Guardian* about what the Chicago Panthers called a "Rainbow Coalition" they had put together. The Panthers had turned (or were trying to turn) two Chicago gangs, the Young Patriots (poor Whites with Appalachian roots) and the Young Lords (Puerto Ricans and Mexicans), away from 'banging and toward something more constructive. If there was already a Latino group in action, we reasoned, why not throw in together? The Lords' chairman, Cha Cha Jiménez, breezily gave us permission to organize as the New York chapter of the YLO. The affiliation with Chicago was where we got our purple berets—even though they claimed to be moving away from street life, the Lords weren't giving up their colors.

This whole gang thing was fairly jolting. Although to this day people think the New York group was a gang because of that name, we never were, and except for Felipe Luciano (one of the few New Yorkers who had been in a gang himself), we walked lightly around the Chicago boys. Nevertheless, it was a Mexican member of the Chicago Lords, Omar López, who came up with our slogan, *"Tengo Puerto Rico en Mi Corazón"*—"I Have Puerto Rico in My Heart." We loved it, and it soon spread throughout Puerto Rican circles. Only years later did we learn that it contained a slight grammatical error, a testimonial to the bad Spanish most of us "spoke." We were truly examples of Ricans raised in the states.

I wasn't yet nineteen. My folks would have freaked if they'd known what their only child—the altar boy from Our Lady of Pity who was supposed to use his Bronx science diploma and college scholarship to bust out of the ghetto—was really doing on his summer vacation. But it didn't come from nowhere—my parents and my grandparents, after all, had first instilled in me a sense that there was far too long a history of injustice in this society. "Only," as my father would say later at my trial, "your mother and I never thought you would actually try to do something about it. Not on such a scale, anyhow."

By the time of that trial, the Young Lords Party—we split from Chicago in April 1970 because we felt they hadn't overcome being a gang—had been targeted by Hoover's FBI as the Latino version of the Panthers and the Weather Underground. Although we never kept a roster, I tallied our New York membership at the end of 1970, and we had grown to more than a thousand, with storefront offices in *El Barrio*, the Lower East Side, and the South Bronx. We had branches in Newark-Hoboken, Bridgeport, Philadelphia, and Puerto Rico, active supporters in Detroit, Boston, Hawaii, in the military and in the prisons. We published a weekly newspaper, *Pa'lante*. We had organized workers, including medical professionals, in the city's hospitals and had a sizeable following on campuses across the country, where we often spoke. . . .

"WHERE ARE THE DAMN GUNS!"

In early October 1970, two of our members, Bobby Lemus and Julio Roldán, were arrested basically for drinking beer and hanging out with some guys on a stoop one night. This was 1970, remember. The next morning, Julio was found hung in his cell at the "Tombs" (Manhattan House of Detention), the latest in a series of controversial "suicides" in jails and police precincts, often with autopsies returned that did not indicate unassisted death. We had been covering the issue in *Pa'lante*. Julio was a quiet, unassuming little guy of about thirty who joined mainly because he believed in independence. His main contribution was cooking at one of our communal apartments at East Harlem.

Surrounded by five thousand demonstrators, we carried his casket from the González Funeral Home on Madison Avenue and marched to the church on 111th that we had taken over a year before. We took it over again, suddenly, posting armed guards at the entrance and at either side of the casket. The standoff would continue, we said, until conditions in the prisons changed. It was the first time we had ever been connected with weapons. We caught even most of our own organization by surprise. Given the risk involved, and the infiltration we took as a given, we had to. The police, already at war with the "soft" Lindsay administration, were furious, but the mayor did not want a confrontation, and so he negotiated. The cops vented their frustration in other ways.

Very soon after the takeover, the Central Committee received reports from inmates in cells next to Julio indicating that he may have taken his own life. This created a debate that split the leadership. My view was that we should admit to doubts and cut our losses immediately. By this time Felipe was not part of the leadership, and indeed, soon he would be gone altogether. Meanwhile, a hard-liner named Gloria Fontanez, recruited from Gouverneur Hospital in the Lower East Side, had risen rapidly through the ranks. She argued that we should stick with our issue regardless of its actual truth, and the majority went along so as not to undermine the months of work we'd put into the UN march scheduled for October 1970. Because I continued to argue, I was suspended. In five and a half years of hard work, that is the only episode of which I am not proud—that and not doing more to get Gloria tossed out.

The march to the UN came off spectacularly, as it probably would have had we left the church earlier. But when the march was over with, we were still there. Negotiations were ongoing, however, and by God they budged: The Board of Corrections would institute sweeping reforms, and José Torres would get a seat on the board.

So now there was the matter of getting out of the church. Past the ring of cops waiting to bust us for the guns. The deal with the city included an amnesty clause that the city was sure would backfire on us. The cops would be allowed in to make sure there were no guns, and only upon their OK could we walk with no charges against us. Because the police had the place surrounded and had infiltrators inside, they were sure they were going to catch us sneaking guns out. And then, all bets would be off. On the appointed day, the police arrived, and at the front door I had the captain and his escort put up against the wall and frisked. "Sorry, Captain," I said, "but we agreed: no weapons. And that includes you. We don't want to say anybody planted anything, right?" The captain acquiesced, and because this occurred within view of reporters covering the "surrender," the image of the Young Lords telling a police captain to assume the position spread. The PBS (Policemen's Benevolent Association) and indignant editorialists called for his head, on a stake right next to ours.

The cops searched thoroughly and found nothing. To this day, I have had police veterans ask me how we pulled it off. Later that day, I had to break policy and get the story from the Lord in charge, David Pérez. "Never underestimate the power of the people," he said laughing. "The cops stopped everybody they thought looked like a Young Lord a block from the church. 'Where are the damn guns?!' one cop yelled at me. But we've spent the last year and change organizing this whole community, not just a part of it. They've been stopping everyone under thirty-five. We broke the weapons down and hid them under the coats of *las viejitas*, the little old ladies who look like your grandmother. Hey, those little old ladies were down."

GERALDO RIVERA SAVES MY ASS

In April 1970, a seven-month effort by Juan González was to culminate in the takeover of Lincoln Hospital. Juan and his team had organized doctors, nurses, other health-care providers, and patients in Manhattan and the Bronx in revealing exposés of just how poorly the system works for poor folks. From lead poisoning and tuberculosis, we had gone on to report the wave of unnecessary hysterectomies performed on Latin women, organized disgruntled rank-and-file workers within 1199,[1] "liberated" an X-ray truck, promoted preventive medicine, and tried to show the links between the pharmaceutical companies, the AMA establishment, hospitals, and insurance outfits that made up the multibillion-dollar health-care industry. But our immediate plan was to take over Lincoln Hospital in the South Bronx and run it with the help of staff who were fed up with rats in the emergency room, antiquated equipment, meager supplies, and chronic personnel shortages.

Lincoln was a mess. For twenty-five years it awaited demolition, and for twenty-five years the city never funded the construction of its replacement. Getting spics a better hospital was the last thing on their agenda. I was from the South Bronx, and growing up I had heard the stories of a stabbing victim crawling two blocks to the catchment zone where the ambulance would take him to Morrisania (which would eventually be shut down as well). Apocryphal, perhaps, but it reflected Lincoln's street rep.

At dawn, we moved in, sneaking through windows and doors opened by doctors and nurses working with us. From inside, we told the guards they could go on a "lo-o-o-ng" break. A huge Puerto Rican flag was flown from the roof. The city was notified, and acute-care patients were transferred, but all other patients were treated by a reenergized staff. A phalanx of cops in riot gear sealed off the area outside, and the standoff was on. We held a news conference in the hospital auditorium, me in an Afro and white lab coat, and made our case against the city. Deputy Mayor Aurelio sent Sid Davidoff and Barry Gottehrer and their Latino "liaison," Arnie Segarra (who went on to become Dinkins's[2] appointment aide). Negotiations began. By late afternoon, we had won: A new Lincoln would be built. And, of course, the participants would receive amnesty.

The cops were not going for this amnesty bullshit. And they could give a f—— that Lindsay was their boss—he was as hated as Dinkins. So a few blocks from the hospital, I was chased by four detectives in an unmarked car. I thought I had given them the slip, but a dog, a goddamn dog, came nipping after me and slowed me down, and I was collared. Just before they got the cuffs on, I pulled my beret from my back pocket and waved it to the onlookers. "Call the Young Lords!" I vainly cried out. Then my wrists got pinched tight, and my head was slammed on the car roof before I was thrown inside.

They gave me a few more shots, but I knew I was in for a serious beating back at the precinct. As spokesmen, Felipe and I were the biggest targets. On two occasions, cops arrested guys they mistook for me, breaking one's leg and another's arm. In Chicago, I spoke at a rally at the start of the Chicago 7 trial, and as I was finishing, word came that the cops were going to bust me. I managed to escape but learned later that once again the cops grabbed a look-alike and beat the shit out of him. I had been shot at by cops and nearly run over by a squad car in both Chicago and New York. And now my charmed existence had come to an end.

---

1. **1199:** Health Care Workers Union.
2. **Dinkins:** David Dinkins, the first African American mayor of New York City (1989–1993).

At the 40th Precinct, I was put in a "bing," or holding cell. Louie Perez, who had been assigned as my security when he left Lincoln, was already there. This Negro detective put on a show for his White comrades. They had taken Louie's nunchakus, the "karate sticks" many Lords used. "So, this is what you use against cops, huh?" the lackey said. "Well, let's see how it stands up against this"—and he patted one of the three guns he was visibly packing. His boys laughed, and I knew we were goners. "This is America, c——s——." He was leaning in close through the bars. His hand was at the lock. "And you oughta be taught what happens to punks who want to mess it up for the rest of us." He was going for the key. Louie and I braced ourselves.

Suddenly, there was a commotion. Bustling sounds from below. Shouting, growing louder. Gerry Rivera materialized, with what seemed like half the precinct coming up the stairs behind him, Keystone Kops–style. He dodged a cop, leaped over a railing, dodged another, and got to our cell. "You OK?" he asked. I was ready to kiss his feet. "Yeah, yeah," I panted. "You just made it. Behind you, watch out!" He turned just before the first cop could grab him. I'malawyerthesearemyclientsyoutouchanyoneofusI'lltakeallyourbadges." Cops froze in mid air.

From an office, a supervisor emerged looking down at some paper. "Jesus! I just got off the phone with headquarters. Do we have some Young Lord here for the hospital thing, they're getting all kinds of calls from the media—" He finally looked up and took the scene in. "What the f—— is all this?" Gerry waded through fifty or so cops and glibly explained. I had to laugh; he was a piece of work.

Gerry burst into our collective lives soon after we had opened the first office, interrupting a meeting with our lawyers to charge that we had no Latino representation, like, for instance, him, even though one of our attorneys was a Puerto Rican he knew personally. Appalled though we were, we admired his chutzpah. But when he tried to join we drew the line. "This is an adventure for you, bro," he was told. "You're not really into the ideology." Still, he had a lot of heat, and he loved the street battles—and the press conferences. Eventually he took advantage of a scholarship to the Columbia School of Journalism that I had turned down because it would have meant leaving the Lords. We wished him well. Once out of Columbia, he got a gig with WABC-TV and hit the ground running. And that's how the Young Lords Party unleashed Geraldo Rivera on an unsuspecting universe. . . .

By our sixth year, it was over. Partly because of destabilization by arrest and government infiltration but mainly because we were young and prone to mistakes—mistakes of leadership, of vulnerability to betrayal, and of the same movement infighting that we had once so despised. But before we dissolved, the Young Lords Party had left its mark:

- A new Lincoln Hospital was built in the South Bronx after we seized a facility that the city had run out of a condemned building for twenty-five years.

- We forced the city to use the lead-poisoning and tuberculosis detection tests gathering dust in some agency's basement after we liberated them and exposed epidemics in both diseases—which are now making comebacks.
- We pushed the Board of Corrections into reforming prison conditions just before the Attica uprising—which our sixteen-year-old chief of staff, Juan "Fi" Ortíz, witnessed as our representative on the negotiation team.
- We encouraged schools to teach Puerto Rican history. Some, at least, now do.
- We created a climate for the start of bilingual education. Never intended as a parallel track, but as a way of mainstreaming Spanish-dominant kids to English proficiency, it has since been sabotaged by educators who were against it from the beginning.
- We produced the first radio show by a New York-born Latino (myself, over WBAI).
- Ask any Latino professional in Nueva York who advanced in government or the corporate world between, say, 1969 and 1984, and you'll be told they owe part of their opportunity to the sea change in perception that the Young Lords inspired.
- We helped raise the understanding, first among Latinos and then the society at large, that Puerto Ricans possessed a culture on a par with anyone's.

39

An American Hostage in Tehran
Barry Rosen

On November 4, 1979, five hundred Iranian students seized the American embassy in Iran in response to the U.S. government allowing the recently deposed Iranian dictator Shah Reza Pahlevi to enter the United States for medical treatment. It was the beginning of a hostage drama that would last for 444 days, involve fifty-two captive embassy personnel, and bring down a U.S. president, Jimmy Carter. This was not the first time that Americans had been taken hostage for political reasons, but what made the Iran crisis different was that it gave ordinary Americans their first real view of the power and intensity of anti-American sentiment abroad. Though the North Vietnamese had fought ferociously against the American invaders, Vietnamese Communists had generally avoided anti-American rhetoric, hoping to win support for their cause from drafted soldiers and sympathetic Americans. In Iran it was different. Nightly news coverage showed large angry mobs burning the Stars and Stripes and chanting "death to Carter, death to America" in the streets of Tehran, while Islamic militants paraded members of the U.S. Marine embassy guard, bound and blindfolded, in front of television cameras. For over a year Americans watched in horror as an entire country, led by a revolutionary Islamic government, vented rage against the United States for its support of the shah's brutal and repressive regime.

The Iranian students were not just holding Americans captive, as Islamic militants later did in Lebanon. They were occupying American sovereign territory in flagrant violation of international law and custom. President Carter devoted much of his last year in office to freeing the hostages, finally resorting to a disastrous military rescue operation which ended before it began with three helicopters crashing in a sandstorm. After this failure Secretary of State Cyrus Vance resigned, leaving Carter's presidency even more compromised. These failures prepared the way for the victory of the conservative Republican Ronald Reagan in the 1980 election. A short time after the new president took office, he announced that the hostages had been freed.

Barry Rosen, the writer of the following selection, specialized in Persian and Central Asian studies and ran Voice of America's Uzbek service in the 1970s. In November 1978 he became the American embassy press attaché in Tehran and was in the embassy when it was taken over. His knowledge of Iranian culture made him a leader among the hostages and he became well known to both Iranians and Americans during his 444 days of captivity.

Barbara and Barry Rosen, with George Feifer, *The Destined Hour: The Hostage Crisis and One Family's Ordeal* (Garden City, NY: Doubleday, 1982), 128–34, 136–38.

QUESTIONS TO CONSIDER

1. Why, according to Barry Rosen, did the Iranian students hate the United States?
2. What did the students hope to accomplish by taking the embassy?
3. What does Rosen reveal about his opinion of the shah and U.S. policy in Iran in this document?

November 4 dawned a drizzly day that prompted daydreams of Florida with Barbara. It was Sunday, a normal workday in Iran. The embassy staff numbered about eighty now, up from the forty of the early months after the revolution. Many of the additions were on temporary duty; some were assigned to help businessmen who had returned to complete contracts. We did not consider that the beginning of resumption of heavy involvement in the country.

Back in my office from Isfahan, I first checked the press to prepare our report for the morning staff meeting. Most newspapers provided their readers with times and routes of major demonstrations. Apparently nothing anti-American was scheduled for the day. There were just the usual relevant items to summarize for Washington, which on that day were few: no unusually strident charges or complaints against America.

My cable drafted, I took a telephone call from a magazine called *Message of Peace*, based in the holy city of Qom. The journal had a strong anti-Western bias, but the call informed me that I was expected in Qom to discuss the possibility of exchanging Islamic and Christian theological students between Iran and America. Then I pondered how to fulfill a directive from a more exalted ICA [intelligence] officer. He *had* to be exalted—and isolated—in order to have devised this particular project: a blueprint of Iran's current power structure. At my level this seemed like a request to photograph air. Washington naturally wanted outlines and diagrams, but the situation remained so amorphous and fluid that few Iranians themselves had a clear idea of who reported to whom and who was responsible for what. The new order's most characteristic trait still seemed to me that there *was* no power structure. Power was largely up for grabs among the clergy, various revolutionary organs, and street mobs unleashed for specific jobs.

Our ICA offices were now in a small building fifty yards directly inside the Embassy's main gate. Takht-e Jamshid, the street outside the gate, had been renamed Taleghani, in honor of a recently dead progressive ayatollah. At ten o'clock or so, the sidewalks and roadway began to fill up with demonstrators, slowly at first, then with a surge. When their noise grew more clamorous than usual, I got up from my typing and went into my secretary's office for a better view. Several dozen young men and women sporting plastic-covered pictures of the Imam on their chests were visible through the gate. The boys wore old suit jackets over turtleneck sweaters; many of the girls were in black chadors or kerchiefs. Both sexes were in their late teens and early twenties: a collection of types who took their anti-Americanism very seriously.

"God is great!"

"Long live Khomeini!"

Although they seemed no more worked up than earlier protestors, some-thing held me at my secretary's desk, watching the swelling cluster. Suddenly there were not several dozen but several hundred demonstrators. Then twice that or more. No better trained or disciplined than ever, our crew of embassy guards—those we ourselves had hired—were overwhelmed by the new arrivals.

"God is great!"

"Long live Khomeini!"

"Death to America!"

Just as suddenly, a handful of seemingly designated men started climbing over the gates. Their scrambling appeared both preposterous and utterly nat-ural, as if fated. Some had pistols and lead pipes. Another cut the chain with a large bolt cutter. With the gate flung open, a roar of triumph sounded and a rush of demonstrators, more than we'd seen, poured in like a flood of frenzy. The Embassy's defenses had been breached in seconds.

Thick clubs waved in the air, mingling with portraits of Khomeini held high like icons. The rush was now a tidal wave of field jackets, mustaches, sweat, and grimaces of hatred. The roar had become an unholy howl—but for some reason I couldn't yet react seriously. "There goes my great report on the so-called power structure," I smirked to myself. "And there goes Iran. I bet we close the Embassy by tomorrow."

Even though the gate remained wide open, some of the fist-waving men kept demonstrating their valor by climbing over the wall. A hundred bodies were now inside the compound, twitching with menace, lining up in a kind of battle order. A lieutenant of the National Police Force—in whose Academy I had taught—skipped up to embrace the scruffy invaders. The Revolutionary Guards who had taken over as our protectors from Masha'allah had been sta-tioned outside the compound; I could picture them joining the invaders. The game was up. I felt a certain relief at that, mixed with the excitement of observ-ing a historic moment.

When "shock troops" had captured the Embassy nine months before and marched us out of the vault where we had taken refuge, we assumed we were about to be shot in our own blinding tear gas. When they grabbed my beard and ordered me to open safes whose combinations I didn't know, I believed the end was very near. As much as anything else, the invaders' inexperience made me apprehensive. They were so frightened by what they were doing and so amazed by their ease in penetrating the imperialist monsters' outpost that they made themselves doubly dangerous through nervousness. More experienced this time, they also seemed more determined—which, curiously, boded better for our safety than during the previous invasion. I was less worried about get-ting shot thanks to somebody's jumpiness.

The fifty yards that separated us from the main gate seemed to shrink to ten. We were right on top of the action and totally cut off, since the Chancery was several minutes' run away. The first detachment of boys and girls—I re-fused to think of them as men and women—rushed directly for our outer door, which I had naturally locked and barred. I instructed my secretary not to open it for anyone, then ran into my own office to search for classified materials that might not have been locked away in the Chancery with the others. The unsettling sounds of my colleagues being routed from nearby offices penetrated the walls while I was searching. Together with their Iranian employees, they were being driven to the Commercial Library in a nearby wing. The "Death to America" chanting was now so violent that its vibrations almost shook my floor.

As I was rushing through the papers in my last desk drawer, the scrape of the bar being removed from my secretary's door stiffened the hairs on my neck. "Mary, what are you doing?" I screamed. "DON'T OPEN THAT DOOR!" But Mary had children. Her husband was unemployed. Most dangerous for her, she was Armenian: a minority who, like the Jews, had been protected under the Shah and now feared for their safety. Good and loyal as she was, it was too much to ask her to jeopardize everything. By the time I had raced back into the outer room, its door was open.

The exultant victors squeezed in too fast to separate them as individuals. My first impression was of unkemptness. I noticed several girls with clubs among the first dozen. They were in chadors or kerchiefs wrapped heavily around their heads.

"GET OUT!" I shouted in Farsi.

"Either you move out of this room or we're going to drag you out," several voices answered simultaneously.

"This is United States property. Get out of this building immediately!"

This was more than bravado. The presence of that mob in my office made me very angry. To sympathize with the revolution's original aim was one thing, but to believe that revolutionaries had a right to violate diplomatic immunity and custom—to commit this barefaced offense against America—was quite another.

But this was probably too abstract and too patriotic to explain my stubbornness. Most of all I was acting on a childish insistence that *I*, which in this case meant my country, be treated with dignity. And although I was quaking, something in me was confident that I wasn't courting death. Perhaps it was naïve, but I reckoned the revolution, despite its anti-foreign passion, had killed very few foreigners.

Half a dozen intruders began ransacking the office, tearing through my press files and news-agency teletape rolls. Mary hunched in a corner, trembling. (She would be released that evening.) But most of the attention was devoted to me. My resistance seemed both to infuriate and, by enhancing their image of themselves as valiant fighters, to please the intruders.

"Leave this room immediately or you will be hurt," barked one of the leaders while his closest assistants waved clubs in the direction of my head. "This is no joke. You are flouting the will of the Iranian people."

"*You* leave immediately. You have no right to set foot in here, any of you. It is totally illegal."

I was also aware of the element of gamesmanship in my defense of principle. Iranians love to bargain and play brinksmanship, pitting one side against the other. Although the outcome was inevitable, I wanted to see how far I could go with *this* game. They respected a show of strength, which I was determined to carry through.

I gave up when the closest clubs swished inches from my nose. A squad led me to join the others in the Commercial Library. If I had dreamed that this was going to be the first of a dozen substitute cells, I would have been appalled and depressed instead of cocky. . . .

"It's going to be a trade: the Shah for you," said one of the group guarding us in the Commercial Library. That was the first hint that we might be in for something longer than the brief encounter of the Embassy's seizure and its personnel's expulsion. Surely Washington wouldn't, and shouldn't, succumb to terrorism by surrendering the Shah. I felt bitter about the staff meeting of October 22, when we were told about the decision to admit him for medical treatment. But once there, he could not be given up on a plate by a humbled American Government. And if he was not, would we in fact be flying home to a nice holiday with our families the next day?

I was in a group of about fifty captives in the Commercial Library. A handful were Americans. Many of our Iranian staff became panicky and pleaded to call home. Something had snapped in Mary's back; she lay on the floor with my jacket to ease the pain. My attempt to soothe and calm lost out to the wailing of our ordinarily cheerful cleaning woman: "You don't know how brutal they can be. I have children; let me out.". . .

. . . Peering out the window, I saw young men and women spray-painting "Nest of Spies" on the chancery walls, while others denounced the Shah through bullhorns. If the Chancery's steel doors held, as I was certain they would, at least some of our staff were calling for help from the government. However, there were no signs of anyone arriving to restore order. After two heavy hours, the Americans in the library were selected to leave, but not to pack our things or for a ride directly to the airport, as I'd half assumed.

As the other Americans were being blindfolded, I kissed Mary good-bye and shook as many Iranian hands as I could. My own blindfold, a piece of khaki that might have been ripped from the uniform of one of our marines, was an outrage—yet I wanted it, in a way. When one guard asked another, "Is he an American too?" I almost shouted, "Yes I am, and take me with the others!" The blindfold was tight, but I could tell I was being led—alone—to the back end of the compound, toward the Ambassador's residence. The guards debated in whispers. I was pulled one way and then another. Apparently only the break-in itself had been organized.

When the blindfold came off, I was in a bedroom of one of the Embassy's Pakistani kitchen staff. From across the hall I heard one of the military attachés answering his captors in single syllables. My own guards, who would answer no question about who they were and whom they represented, took up the argument about the United States handing over the Shah.

"Whatever *you* say, your government will give in. You're more important to them than the Shah, that blood-sucking dictator, that animal!"

"I might agree with some things you say about the Shah, but our policy is not to surrender to terrorism—which is what you're engaged in."

"Do any of you Americans, even now, have any idea of what the Shah committed?"

"I can't answer for his mistakes or supposed mistakes. Have *you* made any? Are you going to answer for the one you're committing today?"

After our little debate, my guards posted themselves outside the door, and I strained to hear a radio playing in a nearby room. A local news broadcast announced with near glee that our captors called themselves Students Following the Line of the Imam and that support for their brave and righteous action was pouring in from all over the country. The implication that the seizure might be more, or become more, than an impulse of a band of irate zealots was a glum new hint that our confinement might not end in time for dinner. . . .

They were still unsure about who was who among embassy personnel, and still totally disorganized as to which brother or sister was responsible for which duties with respect to us. But they settled on a simple answer to their chaos. After breakfast I was moved again, this time to the large reception room of the Ambassador's residence, which was on the same floor. Blindfolded again, I could not count the Americans there, but coughing, shuffling, and occasional words suggested we numbered fifteen to twenty. I wondered whether the ghosts and goblins from last week's Halloween party were enriching the Iranians' imagination about our sinister activities. That day and the next, we were tied to chairs, our blindfolds remaining on. I got a masterpiece of modern design with a strip of leather for the seat and another supposedly to support the back. It was fairly torturous after the first few hours, but less than my thoughts of what this frenzied treatment might lead to.

A prohibition against talk accompanied the physical bondage. With shouts and threats we were ordered to say nothing except in answer to guards' questions. During the day I was fed a handful of dates while my blindfold remained on. Totally powerless, with ropes cutting into my hands and feet, I did not seriously consider disobeying. Still, it was demoralizing and shaming that we did obey. The only sentence in English I heard throughout the day was, "I'd like to go to the bathroom." I ate supper with the blindfold off in the already filthy kitchen. Contempt for myself was growing together with growing hatred for *them*.

They examined our watches for two-way radios. They checked our heels for hidden . . . what? Their nervousness was not totally misplaced: From their tone and from everything I knew about them, they were, despite their triumphant bluster, amazed by their success and frightened that American retribution for it was already on the way. But from what I knew about them too, they were operating on a knowledge of America that came chiefly from fantasies stimulated by spy thrillers. . . .

Returning from the bathroom on the third day, I asked a young escort if I might see something from the press. Apparently he hadn't heard or understood the leaders' directive against this, for he gave me a copy of *Kayhan*, which bulged with copy about the seizure. The burning of the American flag and the "liberation" of our Iranian secretaries and drivers were featured among the saga of the Iranian people's glorious victory. Most depressing was the total absence of mention—and apparently of perception—that the take-over was a stunning

violation of diplomatic immunity. As with the students themselves, the editorialists I read might never have heard of international law. It meant nothing
whatever to them. It was a Western, not an Iranian concept, a concept invented
to aid the rape of Third World countries. And Iranians were *finished* with everything Western; the seizure itself was proof of that.

What the newspaper did declare, and what the average Iranians surely felt,
was that America had for too long used its laws—and not only laws—to oppress Iran. When I understood that the Embassy's seizure was regarded as no
wrong, certainly not a crime, I felt a sharp stab of longing to leave the country
forever.

40

Border Crossings
Ramón Pérez et al.

Throughout U.S. history, waves of immigration have shaped the nation's life. Only in the period from 1924 to 1965, when federal racial and ethnic quotas for overseas immigration were imposed, did migration become less common, and even in that period, the overseas immigrants were often replaced by Latin Americans, who were not restricted. Since the mid-1960s, the historic U.S. pattern has reasserted itself, with immigrants—particularly from Asia, the Caribbean, and Latin America—again shaping U.S. social, economic, and cultural life.

The new immigrants are at least as varied as the old: Mexicans, Central Americans, Filipinos, Koreans, Indians, Iranians, Jamaicans, Haitians, Taiwanese, Vietnamese, and others fill the stream of legal immigrants. In addition, large numbers of undocumented immigrants from Mexico and elsewhere in Latin America have swelled the populations of Florida, Texas, Arizona, New Mexico, and Southern California and led to Mexican communities throughout the nation. All have different stories, motives, and prospects. Some have been viewed as potential labor, others as potential welfare cases, and still others as entrepreneurs who will fuel a rebirth of economic growth. The government at times has recognized the value of this new wave of immigration by granting amnesties that allow immigrants to gain legal residence if they can prove that they have been living in the United States for a number of years. Most spectacularly, in 1986, President Ronald Reagan signed the Immigration Reform and Control Act, creating an amnesty that legalized over 2.5 million people.

People use a variety of methods to enter the United States illegally. Faced with the many perils of crossing—from extortion at the hands of Mexican police to death in the desert to capture by la Migra (the U.S. Border Patrol) or the citizen militias that have recently formed to watch desert paths—many of these immigrants turn for help to professional border crossers known as coyotes to coordinate their journey. The ways of the coyotes are questionable and the safety of their clients is not always assured. As you read the accounts by these smugglers, consider whether or not such individuals are making money not just illegally but also immorally. Even with experienced help from coyotes, however, the passage from one country to the next is an uncertain and often dangerous enterprise. Below are three accounts that illustrate the reasons for entering this country

Ramón "Tianguis" Pérez, *Diary of an Undocumented Immigrant*, trans. Dick J. Reavis (Houston: Arte Publico Press, 1991), 12–14, 31–47; Marilyn P. Davis, *Mexican Voices, American Dreams: An Oral History of Mexican Immigration to the United States* (New York: Holt, 1990), 35–37, 109–12, 113–16, 134–37, 131–33.

illegally, the ways in which undocumented immigrants come into the United States, and the challenges they face in doing so.

QUESTIONS TO CONSIDER

1. What goals do these immigrants have? How do these goals compare with those of people born in the United States? How do they compare with those of immigrants from Europe earlier in the century?
2. Compare the accounts of the border crossings written by the immigrants with that written by the coyote. How do these accounts differ? How are they similar?
3. What arguments can you think of for and against allowing these illegal immigrants to become citizens of the United States?
4. What reasons do you think Ronald Reagan may have had for granting an amnesty to so many people?

RAMÓN PÉREZ

Reasons for Going

In 1979, Ramón Pérez left his village in southern Mexico to make the first of a series of journeys to the United States. In 1991, after returning to Mexico to stay, he published an account of his experiences in Diary of an Undocumented Immigrant.

It didn't take a lot of thinking for me to decide to make this trip. It was a matter of following the tradition of my village. One could even say that we're a village of wetbacks. A lot of people, nearly the majority, have gone, come back, and returned to the country to the north; almost all of them have held in their fingers the famous green bills that have jokingly been called "green cards"—immigrant cards—for generations. For several decades, Macuiltianguis—that's the name of my village—has been an emigrant village, and our people have spread out like roots of a tree under the earth, looking for sustenance. My people have had to emigrate to survive. First, they went to Oasaca City, then to Mexico City, and for the past thirty years up to the present, the compass has always pointed towards the United States. . . .

I, too, joined the immigrant stream. For a year I worked in Mexico City as a night watchman in a parking garage. I earned the minimum wage and could barely pay living expenses. A lot of the time I had to resort to severe diets and other limitations, just to pay rent on the apartment where I lived, so that one day I wouldn't come home and find that the owner had put my belongings outside.

After that year, I quit as night watchman and came back home to work at my father's side in the little carpentry shop that supplies the village with simple items of furniture. During the years when I worked at carpentry, I noticed that going to the U.S. was a routine of village people. People went so often that it was like they were visiting a nearby city. I'd seen them leave and come home as changed people. The trips erased for a while the lines that the sun, the wind and the dust put in a peasant's skin. People came home with good haircuts, good clothes, and most of all, they brought dollars in their pockets. In the *cantinas* they paid for beers without worrying much about the tab. When the alcohol rose to their heads, they'd begin saying words in English. It was natural for me to want to try my luck at earning dollars, and maybe earn enough to improve the machinery in our little carpentry shop.

Crossing

In a few minutes, we again hear Shell reading the list, this time for those who are going to Houston. I'm named along with the others. First, the car carrying nine men leaves, and then the station wagon, with sixteen more, just as before. About half an hour later, the station wagon in which I'm riding stops in front of a house. We're told to run inside. I hear the faint rumble of running water. We're on the bank of the Rio Grande. . . .

We wait for about an hour until a fat man arrives. He's shirtless and one of his arms bears a tattoo of an Indian maid. He says that we should be alert to a signal from the River.

Five minutes later, we hear a long and shrill whistle and the same fat man appears from behind a bush, extending five fingers as a signal that five of us should come. Ten minutes later he leans out of the bush again and makes the same signal. This goes on until only four of us are left in the hideaway shack. At the signal we run towards the River. When we get to where the fat man is, he tells us to remove our shoes.

"The river is swollen!" one of us says when we've gotten nearer to its bank. "Two nights ago we crossed it by walking, but that's not possible now. Last night's rain made it swell."

The River *is* swollen and its swift current makes a sound like that of a coming storm. The water is dirty and thick and stained gray, like the color of the dirt on the riverbank. Pieces of wood and branches float on its surface.

A man who's standing waist-high in water near the riverbank tells us to climb into the inflatable raft he's holding with a rope. We squat aboard, one after another. Then the fat man swims into the water and with his free hand pulls the raft into the current.

"Don't move, you *cabrones*!"[1] the fat man says when one of us tries to make himself comfortable.

The fat man is touching bottom when we begin, but the center of the river must be deep, because then he swims a while, and touches bottom, walking again, as we near the opposite bank. Despite his efforts, in crossing we've drifted a good ways downstream. When we get to the American bank, we put our shoes on and reunite with the others who are hiding in a high cane break. A little later, a young, thin man tells us in a low voice that we should follow him, walking in a crouched position. For fifteen minutes we climb up and down little hills. Sometimes he tells us to wait while he advances to reconnoiter, and sometimes

---

1. *cabrones*: Bastards (Sp.).

we run, as he tells us to, until we come to a place where houses begin. A dark man with short, curly hair is waiting for us.

LUPE MARCÍAS

When this interview with Lupe Marcías was conducted in the 1980s, she lived in a five-room apartment in Lynwood, California, with fourteen other people, all members of her husband's family from the same pueblo back in Mexico. Her husband had come to Los Angeles ahead of her but wanted Lupe to come join him. In the spring, she agreed.

Then a *señora* named Rosa, she's a relative, said, "Come on, let's go! I have a friend who is a *coyote*. She has passed a lot of people. Come on, don't be afraid." I was so nervous. *Aye, Dios mio!*[2] I couldn't have imagined all this.

Finally the *coyote* came. She gave me identification and said, "Look, this identification is yours. You are going to pass through the border, but you can't be at all nervous. No shaking! No dancing! You have to pass as if it were nothing. Just in case they ask you, you will tell them you are going for an errand in San Ysidro." Aye, no!

"Listen, you have two daughters. One's name is Monica, she is thirteen, and your other daughter is six."

I said, "Do you think I am going to remember this?"

"Yes. Now tell me, what is your name?" I was supposed to tell her in English. Well, I forgot. She said, "No, no, don't be nervous."

Aye Dios, I said, "This isn't going to be possible."

"Come on, let's see. What is your name? How many children do you have?" I had to learn this in English. *Dios mio,* I was perspiring with fear. "Listen," she said, "you are going to be carrying a bag because you have an errand. You and your husband work in San Ysidro."

Well, I learned everything and just as soon as I did she said, "Okay, you're ready, let's go." We went right to the line, you know where the people walk across. It was a long line with every sort of person carrying all kinds of things. Many were *gringos* carrying bags and bags of souvenirs and things they had bought in Mexico. There were a lot of Mexicans too. Well the *señora* told me, "You get in line here and I will go ahead. In the case that you pass, I will be waiting and give you a sign. Then follow me, but a little behind." I wasn't going to talk to her or even look like I knew her.

The line was very slow. After awhile, I could see they were checking everyone. Oh, no! There was a very fat woman—like this—with her *pistolas.*[3] *Aye madre mia!*[4] And she was sending back so many people. I went asking the benediction of the little saints. Aye, please don't let her turn out the lights! Well, I just kept in the line and as I came up to where they were checking people there was some kind of disagreement or something. A man was in front of them with his

---

2. *Aye, Dios mio!* Oh, my god! (Sp.)
3. *pistolas:* Pistols (Sp.)
4. *Aye madre mia!* Oh my mother! (Sp.; used as an exclamation)

bag open and they had everything out, they were speaking pure English, all of them, and well the fat woman was talking to the man next to her and would you believe, she didn't ask me anything. She just glanced at my card and went back to talking with the other *migra* and off I went. Aye little *Dios*, I passed, I passed!

I went to the store across the street. There were four others who had just passed too, and the woman who was going to bring me up. She just said, "Are you the girl I'm supposed to pick up? Well come on." She had to pick up her daughters at school and she had errands, but wherever she went she took me. She even bought me a hamburger, and I came to know San Diego.

Well, there we were at her house. I helped her wash dishes and just waited. I didn't even think about why we were waiting until a young man arrived and said, "Good, you're here. Now you passed once, but you have to pass again."

I screamed, "Aye, no! Don't tell me I have to pass again!" No, what could I do? Just let God do what he wants. The young man's name was Alexander. He could speak pure English. They told me he would leave me in a car near the airport while he went to buy the tickets. Well, we didn't wait. He drove to the airport right then and he parked the car. I could hear planes but I couldn't actually see any except in the air. Well, he told me that we had to be careful because the *migra* is always around there. *Dios mio*, I was very nervous alone in the car. It was a beautiful car. Well, just a little time passed and he came back. From then on everything happened very quickly.

He left his car and we went in. They told me in English to pass my purse onto this machine. Well I didn't understand what they were saying, but I saw the lady in front of me do it, so I put mine on too. When I saw my purse come out at the other end, I grabbed it. We ran to the plane because they were waiting for us. This Alexander went with me and we were the last ones on.

My husband met us at the airport. This Alexander had to return that same afternoon because he had left his car at the airport in San Diego. He was a North American from San Diego. He pronounced everything perfect.

That was it. I believe my husband paid $500 and the plane fare was included, but now that I was here, I didn't care how much he had to pay. He was the one who wanted me to come, and when he would call on the telephone he would say, "What I want is for you to pass, without problems. I don't want you to pass over the mountains." Later a cousin of my husband's and his wife came. They arrived so dirty because they had to cross in the mountains. It was very difficult for them. No, it's so much fear. You have to take the risk and suffer to get to this side. No, I never imagined how it could be. For me, believe me it was luck. I thanked God that I was able to pass at the line.

"EL MÉXICO"

Confessions of los Coyotes

The coyote who calls himself El México lived in a converted garage in the hills around Tijuana with his wife and six-year-old daughter when he was interviewed. He had built his business since he was a young boy, and now almost every night found him conveying immigrants from Tijuana to San Ysidro just across the U.S. border.

I first started bringing people across when I was about twelve or thirteen. At that time I lived on the other side, in San Ysidro with a woman who is like a mother to me. My parents are in Mexico City and they sent me to live with her when I was young so I could go to school. Our house was right on the border, across from the schoolyard there, and I knew the area with my eyes closed. That's where we played when we were kids. So when I would see people crossing and know that they needed help or they would get caught, I would bring them across. I never charged anything. I guess people got to know me, other guides, and they would ask me to signal for them. That's more or less how it was.

People want to cross with us because they know we are secure and we're serious. They know we are not like those who look for people off the street, or are looking for people to take their money, or those that take people across so they'll have money to drink. We are fathers, we have families to maintain, and our interest is to cross people. When we take someone across and a friend asks them if they know someone, they recommend us. They say, "Oh yes, I know someone secure and responsible."

With those in the street it's no more than an adventure to see if they can make it, and often they're caught or they leave the people with nothing to eat for two or three days. Oh, and there are those who take the people to one side of the fields and leave them when the Immigration isn't around. They tell their clients a vehicle will be by to pick them up, but it never comes.

It's like any other business, if you are a mechanic or an engineer, it takes time to build your clientele. When people see you do good work they will look for you. I am very familiar with the terrain and the techniques. It's like a game of chess. Each one of us takes one or two, and then we reunite, or if it's tranquil we can all go together. Some nights we will have up to twelve people to cross.

Oh, we've been caught. I would say one or two times every six months or maybe four times a year. Each time we give a different name. They want to know your name, where you were born, your father and mother, how old you are, how you entered, and where you entered. You give whatever answer. They put it in a computer, but you answer differently each time.[5] . . .

This is how it is. Tonight we will have these two men to take across and there will be three of us. They will pay $50 each, so we'll make about thirty dollars. That's not much, is it? It's what anyone would make in a day, well, not here in Mexico, but on the other side, even more. A professional or skilled person will make about $50 a day, and this is what someone who is unskilled would make, the minimum. There are times when there are more people and we make more money, but then you have to save some of it for when there is no work. This month we had two weeks with no work. The bad months are from September through Christmas. Then it picks up again. In January we have all the people who went to Mexico for the fiestas, then in the spring farm workers come over, in the summer we have students, and at the end of the summer we have parents

---

5. This account describes procedures from long before the September 11 attacks in 2001.

crossing to take their kids back to school. The people from several little pueblos in Michoacán and Jalisco come to us; the whole pueblo knows us. But we also get people from El Salvador, Guatemala, and Peru.

It's $50 to cross to San Ysidro and $300 to go to Los Angeles. But to go to Los Angeles, you first have to arrive at a house. There is a *señora*, she doesn't like to do this, but she has a son who has an infirmity where he can't walk. The *señora* helps us, taking care of the people. The people she takes in are better off than others, because she does care for them. When we get there, she makes them breakfast, lets them bathe and wash their clothes, for the little bit of money she gets.

Then we have to pay an American with a car. He gets a little more, about one hundred dollars per person. Then arriving in Los Angeles, we have another person we pay to take the people to their houses. Sometimes, when we want to, we go to Los Angeles too, but usually we don't. The person who takes them collects the money when they arrive in Los Angeles. He pays the person who takes them to their houses, and when he returns that night, he pays the *señora* and us. When someone brings us a client we pay them $5 for making the connection. The person who drives has to get paid well because he has to drive a nice car. If it was one of the little old cars we drive, no, they'd stop us for sure.

Those who make good money are the ones who sell drugs. They make money coming and going. Besides all this, the little that one makes, and then the Mexican police want $100 if they catch you with one or two! We play the game on this side to avoid the police, because when you're caught you have to pay $100 or $200 just so they will leave you alone. And think of it, there are the municipal police, the state police, the *federales*, the governors, and beyond that, those that pass for police. And they all have an interest. What can you do? You have no choice. Sometimes you have to pay them.

Protest Movements of the 1960s and 1970s

The sixties is a pocket-sized term for an era that might be dated from the be-ginnings of the civil rights movement in the mid-1950s until the 1970s, when the United States withdrew from Vietnam. It was a time of enormous cultural and social energy and change. Nothing quite like the combination of campus activism, feminism, black and minority rebellion, war protests, and challenges to American society had ever occurred before. While such protest movements were common across the planet during the 1960s, most famously in Paris in 1968, much of the agitation in communities and on university campuses around the United States drew on American traditions of freedom, justice, and the strenuous remaking of the nation, both politically and culturally. The photographs here capture some of the protest movements of the 1960s and 1970s.

In race relations, barriers collapsed that only a few years earlier had looked like permanent fixtures of American life. In 1957, Dwight D. Eisenhower sent troops to Little Rock, Arkansas, to back up a court order for the integration of the city's public schools. The decision was not of his choosing—the defiance by a federal judge acting under the court of the state of Arkansas forced it on him—but it initiated a process of federal military and police intervention in protection of constitutional rights for black Southerners that had been absent since the end of Reconstruction. But especially in the aftermath of the Supreme Court's condemnation of segregation in the 1954 decision *Brown v. Board of Education of Topeka*, black communities in the South had acted on their own to topple white supremacy, most notably in the boycott of segregated busing in Montgomery, Alabama, led by Martin Luther King Jr. in 1956.

Large-scale and sweeping demonstrations for civil rights only intensified during the 1960s. Heeding Martin Luther King's request for nonviolent protest, sit-ins were staged across the segregated South at lunch counters, in schools, on public transportation, and in other public places long denied to African Ameri-cans. Figure 1 shows sit-in protesters Professor John R. Salter, Joan Trunpauer, and Annie Moody at a lunch counter in Jackson, Mississippi, in the spring of 1963. Figure 2 shows another scene of civil rights protest, African Americans picketing outside a store on April 19, 1960. The people in Figures 1 and 2 are engaging in an alternative to fighting: the ability to maintain composure under

Figure 1. Sit-in protesters at Jackson, Mississippi, lunch counter, May 28, 1963.

Figure 2. African American demonstrator mocked in New Bern, North Carolina, April 19, 1960.

attack. What is happening to them? What might you imagine to be their emotions and thoughts as they undergo their ordeals and what sustained their courage? How would you explain the fury of the mobs that tried to resist the integration of blacks in America?

Such public conflicts acted as a catalyst to move President John F. Kennedy in a more activist direction against the Southern segregationists. That much of the civil rights movement came at the initiative of black Southerners is in itself enough to make the period distinctive, for black Americans had, since Reconstruction, been largely perceived as passive, marginal members of the American public. The quick engagement and major presence of white Northerners in the black struggle, most notably in risking their lives in Mississippi during the Freedom Summer of 1964, represented the swift entrance of at least a portion of the white citizenry into the rebellions of the times (see Document 37).

College campuses during the 1960s stirred with an excitement that had been absent since a flurry of campus political activism during the Great Depression. In one of the decade's first student protests, California university students staged a demonstration in San Francisco against the presence of the House Un-American Activities Committee. Although the demonstration was peaceful, San Francisco police drove the students away with fire hoses. In the spring of 1964, the Berkeley Free Speech Movement (FSM) got its start when students organized to protest the University of California Regents' decision to deny students use of a small campus-owned area that had long been employed to recruit civil rights supporters. Figure 3 shows Mario Savio, the most prominent leader of the FSM. The son of socially conscious Roman Catholic parents, Savio had spent the summer of 1963 working with black civil rights workers in Mississippi and was greatly angered by the university's decision. The Berkeley demonstrations that followed drew support from even conservative students, a sign of the growing strength of student movements during this period. The targets of U.S. campus protests ranged widely, from calls for curricular changes to attacks on university-based military research, this latter issue protested most extensively in the uprising at Columbia University in 1968. What the university rebellions shared was a decision on the part of students that study and politics, books and street culture must come together for social change, be the change local and restricted to campus or larger in scope and part of the world beyond the classroom.

The demand among Americans of both races for full equality for blacks sparked movements by other groups for the elimination of legal and cultural forms of discrimination. Feminism, a movement that encouraged women to examine such issues as reproductive rights, equal pay, and the nature of marriage, has had an enduring effect on politics, the family, and the workplace. Feminism was a latecomer to the 1960s' protest movements; as late as the Vietnam antiwar protests, women were expected to make sandwiches and wait on the male leaders of the movement. But in 1968, a small group of women calling themselves New York Radical Women staged a protest against the Atlantic City Miss America contest. This event, shown in Figure 4, caught the attention of the national press and helped to spark a large-scale movement for equality and women's rights. Why do you think the women in this photo targeted the Miss

Figure 3. Mario Savio speaking to demonstrators occupying Sproul Hall at the University of California, Berkeley, 1964.

America contest? Why do you think their protest drew so much attention? Do you think that the issues they were addressing with their protest are still of concern to women?

Several civil rights laws passed in the mid-1960s were a daring use of federal power. Most prominent were a 1964 act that ended discrimination in public places and opened up jobs in businesses that had excluded blacks and a 1965 statute that allowed federal registrars to enroll black voters previously excluded from voting. Another example of the federal government's bold use of constitu-

Figure 4. New York Radical Women protesting the Miss America contest in 1968.

tional resources was the exercise of congressional authority over interstate commerce to compel forms of economic equality.

During the late 1960s, the civil rights movement—at its outset an effort to eliminate racial divisions—acquired a black militant wing that advocated separation from whites. Malcolm X, one of the most complex and enduring figures to emerge from the decade of protest, was the famous leader of the black separatist group the Nation of Islam (NOI). In 1964, however, he turned away from separatism after a pilgrimage to Mecca, founding a political organization dedicated to a world revolution that was not based solely on race. This ultimately led to his assassination shortly afterward by members of the Nation of Islam, who believed that he had betrayed their cause. Despite his short life and uncertain political legacy, he had a remarkable influence on both white and black radical politics of the 1960s.

Practitioners of nonviolence, such as the followers and allies of Martin Luther King Jr., used peaceful civil disobedience to protest racism and, later, the Vietnam War; their method of protest attempted to foster the broadest possible involvement of all concerned citizens. By later in the decade, however, civil rights nonviolence advocates were competing with groups such as the Black Panthers, the Young Lords (see Document 38), the Congress of Racial Equality, and other groups that advocated more militant means of protest. The Black Panther Party was the most famous and notorious of these organizations for its insistence on using the right to publicly bear arms as a statement that they were not opposed to violence in defense of their rights (see Figure 5) and its argument for progressive blacks and whites organizing separately.

Though they called themselves a political party, the Black Panthers never developed any unifying national program or set of policies, making it difficult to generalize about them. In Chicago, they were a force for reform against the reactionary police who broke in and shot leaders of their movement. In New Haven, they had both successes and excesses. In Oakland, where Panthers created programs that provided free sickle-cell anemia testing, the nation's most controversial chapter included prominent leaders, such as Huey Newton,

Figure 5. Armed members of the Black Panthers, 1969.

who were accused of wife beating, drug dealing, pimping, and assassinating local police. The Black Panthers considered it among their projects to give armed protection against police brutality to black neighborhoods. They also opened free-breakfast programs for impoverished black children, but these were mostly indoctrination programs against the police. Radical groups like the Black Panthers often endangered the gains that King's movement had made in the early 1960s as they presented a specter of violent separatism to the general public. How do you explain the intensification of black anger at a time of apparent improvement in civil rights? How would you account for a movement that grew out of the struggle against racism but then adopted forms of black segregation in its political organizing?

As the 1960s and the Vietnam War wore on, clashes that once took place only between left- and right-leaning political believers began to occur within the liberal ranks. Right-wingers had regularly attacked liberals for their softness toward communism and their efforts to gain a more active role for the federal government. But liberals began to face anger from fellow left-wingers for their support of housing programs for the poor (which were likened to the fortified hamlets into which the South Vietnamese regime and its U.S. allies gathered Vietnamese villagers as a way of pacifying them), for their efforts to sustain

an unjust war against the Vietnamese people, and for their use of federal economic programs to control and repress poor Americans at home. These criticisms were launched despite the obvious repressiveness of North Vietnamese communism and the many strikingly humane liberal programs such as the Peace Corps. At the end of the 1960s a strong antiwar movement was born among ordinary civilians, soldiers, and ex-soldiers. Figure 6 shows a Vietnam veteran protesting the war with his fellow active-duty servicemen at a military base. Why do you think that so many soldiers and ex-soldiers opposed the war? How do you think antiwar activity among soldiers affected army life?

Native Americans were also inspired to militant political ac-

Figure 6. Vietnam veteran protesting the war, May 1970.

tion during the late 1960s, founding the American Indian Movement (AIM) in 1968. Like the New York Radical Women, AIM came to national prominence by protesting, in a highly visible and public way, a hallowed American tradition that its members believed oppressed them: Thanksgiving. On Thanksgiving Day 1970 (the 350th anniversary of the *Mayflower* landing), they seized the ship *Mayflower II*. This, combined with their connections to an occupation of Alcatraz Island the previous year, drew them national attention and led to a reemergence of Native American political protest, after the long hiatus that had followed the disastrous defeats of the late nineteenth century. However, this type of movement was new to Native American politics; it was not so much regionally, locally, or tribally based, but rather national in its scope. It argued that a history of oppression and conflict with the larger settler society had galvanized a distinct Native American experience. They sought to unite "Indians of all tribes." AIM's most famous moment came in 1973 with the occupation of the Pine Ridge Reservation in South Dakota (called the Wounded Knee Incident) in protest against police brutality. It lasted seventy-one days and led to the deaths of two people. Figure 7 shows Native American activists at Pine Ridge Reservation during the standoff with federal authorities. What is the significance of hanging an American flag upside down? Can you imagine any of these other protest movements, many of which held similar occupations of public spaces, hanging a flag upside down? Why? Why not?

Advocates for gay rights were also calling for change during this period. Figure 8 shows the Mattachine Society picket line in front of the White House in 1965, protesting government employment discrimination against gays. Founded in 1950 in Los Angeles, the Mattachine Society was one of the United States'

Figure 7. Standoff at the Pine Ridge Reservation, 1973.

earliest gay rights organizations. This was in the early days of the McCarthy witch hunts, when the epithets "commie," "pinko," and "queer" were often linked. Though homosexuals were still an underground subculture, with little public or political face, they were quietly developing vibrant communities in major cities such as San Francisco, New York, Boston, Chicago, Denver, Washington, D.C., and Philadelphia, rapidly following Los Angeles and setting up their own Mattachine chapters in each. San Francisco, in particular, came to be a center of gay culture in the 1950s, as thousands of World War II veterans who had discovered a gay identity in the army chose to remain there, rather than return to the small towns and regional cities where they had grown up. By the time this photo was taken, in the mid-1960s, the Mattachine Society was the principal public organization fighting for gay rights in the United States. It was also in decline, as young, politically active homosexuals were often drawn to other, more glamorous and "mainstream" movements, like African American civil rights and the fledgling antiwar movement. In 1969, after the Stonewall riots in New York City, where gays fought back against police persecution, it opened a new chapter of the gay rights movement—one that made the older and more closeted homosexuals of the Mattachine Society seem stodgy. Young gays were drawn to seemingly more militant and confrontational organizations

Figure 8.
Mattachine Society picket line in front of the White House, 1965. Photo by Kay Tobin Lahusen.

like the Gay Liberation Front. How have these protesters marketed their cause differently from those shown in the other photos? Why do you think they chose this type of presentation? How do you imagine the protesters in the other pictures might respond to the Mattachine Society's protest? How might the presence of a black policeman be explained? How do you imagine that young homosexuals might have felt looking at these protesters in the 1960s?

FOR CRITICAL THINKING

1. Consider the signs carried by those picketing for the different movements. What do the messages ask of their audiences?
2. Photographs can be spontaneous snapshots taken by amateurs on the fly, carefully framed images by professionals that reflect a political or social agenda, or anything in between. Review these images again carefully and consider their relative value in garnering support for the various movements they depict. Do any seem particularly effective or affecting to you? Why?
3. In a novel twist, Mario Savio (Figure 3) was not permitted to speak from a University of California stage of a Greek amphitheater that was dedicated to the Athenian credo of free speech. What do you consider the state of free speech to be on today's college campuses? How might protesters like Savio have influenced the rights that you enjoy today as students?
4. Protest movements typically struggle to convince people and pressure politicians. Compare and contrast the different strategies that these pictures show for accomplishing these two tasks. Who was effective? How? In what ways?

PART SEVEN

Between History and Tomorrow

After the Cold War

When the Berlin Wall came down in 1989, most historians agreed that it was the end of one era and the beginning of another. Some commentators called it globalization, others postmodernity, and the U.S. president, George H. W. Bush, described it as a "new world order." American political scientist Francis Fukuyama attempted a more precise definition in his 1989 article "The End of History?" in which he argued that humankind's evolution through monarchy, fascism, communism, and other political ideologies was finally over, and that Western liberal democracy would be "the final form of human government." He went on to argue that "economic calculation, the endless solving of technical problems, environmental concerns, and the satisfaction of sophisticated consumer demands" would replace the conflicts over big ideas of the past.

For a time it seemed that Fukuyama was right. The Soviet Union peacefully dissolved, Palestinians and Israeli Jews signed a peace accord at Oslo, Irish Catholics and Protestants agreed to settle their differences, and South Africa achieved black majority rule. There was still, as Fukuyama had predicted, ethnic conflict, civil war, and a few isolated dictatorships but none of the ideological battles that had characterized the cold war. Los Angeles and several other cities erupted into violence and anarchy for a few days following a verdict of "not guilty" in the trial of LAPD officers caught on videotape beating African American motorist Rodney King. However, these conflicts might have seemed like Fukuyama's "technical problems" to be solved. In 1991, an international coalition of more than twenty countries, many of which had been enemies only a few years earlier, joined forces to liberate Kuwait from Iraqi occupation, as multinational peacekeeping forces fanned out across the globe.

Americans still fought over social issues like abortion, religion in the schools, immigration, and the death penalty. Bias attacks like the one that killed gay college student Matthew Shepard also continued, but the widespread support for his family, as well as young, charismatic president Bill Clinton's public appearance

309

with Shepard's mother to announce new hate crime laws, suggested a growing consensus over tolerance, liberalism, and civil rights. The economy boomed as trillions of dollars flowed into the stock market from around the world. The information superhighway created a "new economy," producing overnight "dot-com" millionaires; software billionaires; and millions of CEOs, MBAs, and workplace "day-traders." This was also the period of "emerging markets" when globalization and free trade policies ended protectionist tariffs and forced the sale of state sector industries, drawing new capital to modernize aging, inefficient production facilities and forcing the layoff of redundant workers. As new wealth was created, skyscrapers and modern metropolises grew in distant places like Kuala Lumpur and Jakarta while many American inner cities "gentrified."

However, most of the world's population had missed the boom, experiencing it instead as displacement, poverty, and blocked ambition. Many took the traditional path out of misery, leaving home and family to migrate to a wealthier region. As described in Part Six, Mexico lost millions of people as the 1994 devaluation of the peso greatly increased the migration stream, bringing landless peasants, laid-off workers, and suddenly impoverished professionals to the United States. As this decade of excesses ended, ominous changes loomed on the horizon. In 1999 antiglobalization protesters fought the "Battle of Seattle," during a World Trade Organization meeting. They demanded the return to a time when the economy was more local and global warming did not threaten the planet. In 2000 irregularities in the Florida electoral commission tarnished a presidential contest between Al Gore and George W. Bush. Soon afterward, the new economy came crashing down, bringing with it not just dot-com millionaires, but many ordinary people who had invested their hard-earned savings in tech stocks whose value then plummeted. Finally, on September 11, 2001, a series of coordinated suicide attacks by nineteen fundamentalist Muslims in hijacked jetliners killed almost three thousand people and destroyed one of the great symbols of America, the twin towers of the World Trade Center in New York City.

Americans were suddenly forced back into a world of difficult ethical, political, and historical choices that divided people at home and made the nation unpopular abroad. Newly elected president George W. Bush declared a "war on terror" involving a significant abrogation of civil liberties, "renditions," assassinations, and most notoriously, the open-ended detention without trial of suspected enemies of America at the U.S. military base in Guantánamo Bay, Cuba. As war in Iraq followed war in Afghanistan and the expansion of U.S. military operations in the Muslim world, Samuel Huntington's 1993 article "Clash of Civilizations," which described a future of endless cultural, religious, and ethnic conflict seemed to many a better description of the times than Fukuyama's fuzzy optimism.

However, many ordinary Muslims, like James Yee, Shams Alwujude, and Moazzam Begg, who found themselves trapped between Islamic fundamentalists and the war on terror, fought against having to choose between their religion and their nation. Many ordinary Americans, like Erik Saar, an army officer who served at Guantánamo, also came to recognize the problems of forcing such narrow choices, leading to a 2008 electoral campaign that became something of a referendum on Bush and his war on terror. One candidate, Democrat Hillary Rodham Clinton, eliminated during the primaries, had offered a return to the heady Clinton years and the prospect of shattering the glass ceiling that still kept women from many positions of power; another, aging senator and Vietnam War veteran John McCain, represented the hopes of conservatives; and a third, Barack Obama, the first African American to win both a presidential nomination and the White House, promised "change we can believe in" and a new politics far different from the secrecy and unilateralism that characterized the Bush administration. The American people took a chance on "change," ushering in what many hoped would be a new chapter in American history, at home and abroad.

POINTS OF VIEW

Security versus Freedom after September 11, 2001

41

Securing the Nation and Fighting a War on Terror
Gordon Cucullu and John Ashcroft

When the United States first opened the U.S. military detention center at Guantánamo Bay in Cuba to hold suspected terrorists, some Americans and allies as well as enemies around the world were concerned that these prisoners, deemed too criminal to be treated as prisoners of war but not criminal enough to be given a fair trial, were being denied basic human rights. As these open-ended detentions, without trial or external monitoring, continued, concern grew at home and abroad that the United States was becoming a less democratic country where "justice for all" was no longer guaranteed.

The world was watching and criticism of the United States only grew, as the Bush administration kept some eight hundred people in legal limbo. Foreign governments and international rights advocates criticized Gitmo (as the prison at Guantánamo Bay came to be called), while American courts, which seemed to have no power over Gitmo, made numerous judgments against what was happening. Members of Congress, senators, and ordinary people expressed everything from concern to downright shock at what appeared to be gross violations of international norms of justice and legal due process.

Even the U.S. military was embarrassed by Gitmo. Retired officers gave press conferences at which they spoke against the detention center, and the military judge in America's first Guantánamo Bay trial—against Osama bin Laden's driver—wished

Lt. Col. Gordon Cucullu, *Front Page Magazine.com*, June 27, 2005, and June 28, 2005, accessed from http://frontpagemag.com, October 5, 2008.

the defendant "Godspeed" at his sentencing. An army translator published a book of life stories of detainees, who, she claimed, were "innocent men who'd been swept up by mistake" or captured and turned over by bounty hunters in return for money offered by the United States for Al Qaeda militants. According to this translator and many others who worked inside Gitmo, many of the prisoners had no idea why they were there. By the beginning of 2008 Australian David Hicks was the only individual who had been found guilty of any charges, and even his guilt was in doubt because he had accepted a plea bargain in order to be able to return to Australia.

While most accounts by retired army officers and soldiers who served at Gitmo have been harshly critical, a significant number of official visitors have inspected the camp and argued that it is a reasonable response to an undeclared war. Often comparing it favorably with high-security domestic prisons designed for American citizens, these accounts have challenged what they see as a soft and overly liberal orthodoxy opposing the war on terror. The following account of a visit to Gitmo is by Gordon Cucullu, an author and retired lieutenant colonel from the U.S. Special Forces Green Berets, whose service in Vietnam enabled him to work as a political military adviser to the State Department and has allowed him privileged access to Gitmo. The second account is testimony before Congress in 2008 by John Ashcroft, the U.S. attorney general at the time of the September 11, 2001, attacks. Ashcroft reminds us that he and his colleagues were facing a new situation and a nation that wanted guarantees of security for its citizens, at home and abroad.

QUESTIONS TO CONSIDER

1. What are Ashcroft's key arguments in defense of the people who set up Guantánamo Bay Detention Camp?
2. Every policy decision is likely to be a mix of practical problem solving and political posturing. What do you think were the practical issues of collective security that drove the decision to open Guantánamo and what were the political ones?
3. What elements in Ashcroft's testimony suggest that he believes that Guantánamo was the right decision and what elements, if any, suggest that he believes the camp was a mistake?
4. Which of Cucullu's observations seem most reliable and which seem least reliable, and why?

June 27–28, 2005

GORDON CUCULLU

What I Saw at Gitmo

Last week, I was privileged to be part of a Department of Defense trip to the Joint Task Force—Guantánamo Bay, Cuba. I got to see the operations of this "controversial" facility up-close—something particularly important after Sen. Richard Durbin's comparison of its guard to Nazi stormtroopers and calls of leftists to shut the center down. Our group went to GITMO to check out tales that the military was being too tough on these terrorist detainees. We left convinced that America is being extraordinarily lenient — far too lenient.

After speaking with soldiers, sailors, and civilians who collectively staff GITMO, I left convinced that abuse definitely exists at the detention facilities, and it typically fails to receive the press attention it deserves: it's the relentless, merciless attacks on American servicemen and women by these terrorist thugs. Many of the orange jumpsuit-clad detainees fight their captors at every opportunity, openly bragging of their desire to kill Americans. One has promised that, if released, he would find MPs in their homes through the internet, break into their houses at night, and "cut the throats of them and their families like sheep." . . .

We dined with the soldiers, toured several of the individual holding camps, observed interrogations, and inspected cells. We were impressed by the universally high quality of the cadre and the facilities. While it may not be exactly "Club GITMO," as Rush Limbaugh uses to tweak the hard-Left critics who haven't a clue about reality here, GITMO is a far cry from the harshness experienced even by maximum security prisoners in the U.S.

Meals for detainees are ample: we lunched on what several thought was an accumulated single day's ration for detainees. "No," the contract food service manager said with a laugh, "what you're looking at there is today's lunch. A single meal. They get three a day like that." The vegetables, pita bread, and other well-prepared food filled two of the large Styrofoam take-home containers we see in restaurants. Several prisoners have special meal orders like "no tomatoes" or "no peanut products" depending on taste or allergies. "One prisoner," General Hood said, "throws back his food tray if it contains things he has specifically said he doesn't want." How is he punished for this outrageous behavior? His tray is numbered, the food he requested is put on it, and the corrected "order" is delivered to his cell.

The detainees are similarly catered to medically. Almost every one arrived at GITMO with some sort of battlefield trauma. After all, the majority were captured in combat. Today they are healthy, immunized, and well cared for. At a visit to the modern hospital facility — dedicated solely to the detainees and comparable to a well-equipped and staffed small-town hospital with operating, dental, routine facilities — the doctor in charge confirmed that the caloric count for the detainees was so high that while "most detainees arrived undernourished," medics now watch for issues stemming from high cholesterol and being overweight. Each of approximately 520 terrorists currently held in confinement averages about four medical visits monthly, something one would expect from only a dedicated American hypochondriac. Welcome to the rigors of detention under American supervision.

Of the estimated 70,000 battlefield captures that were made in Afghanistan, only a tiny percentage, something on the order of 800-plus, were eventually evacuated to GITMO. These were the worst of the worst. More than 200 have been released back to their home country — if the U.S. is assured that the detainees would not be tortured by local authorities upon return. These men were freed because they were deemed by ongoing official military review processes to no longer pose a threat, or to possess no useful intelligence. And this process has proven too generous at times: more than 10 released GITMO detainees have been killed or recaptured fighting Americans or have been identified as resuming terrorist activities. Still, the process is up and running for review of cases, and if a Washington DC circuit court approves a government appeal, the system for military tribunals will get started. All mechanisms are in place and ready to go as soon as DoD[1] gets a green light. . . .

We've all heard wild tales about the interrogation techniques employed at Guantanamo Bay. Allegedly, these include sleep deprivation, drugs, overheated cells, seductive women, and even Christina Aguilera music (true torture). In addition to enjoying the kind of first-class meal these would-be terrorists enjoy everyday during my trip to Guantanamo Bay last week, I also learned part of their 2,600-calorie daily diet comes in the form of donuts—donuts the terrorists enjoy while being interrogated by sensitive, nurturing, modestly-clad female interrogators.

On my trip last week to Gitmo, I was personally able to observe Joint Task Force specialists conducting interrogations. The detainee wore an orange jump suit—the mark of detainees who refuse to do what guards direct them to do—and was described by JTF officers as "extremely noncompliant." I was surprised to see one detainee, described as "a high level al-Qaeda organizational and financial expert," relaxed during his interrogation session, happily munching from a box of donuts which had been provided by his interrogator. The 30-something woman had an interpreter present during the interrogation, because, although the interrogator speaks Arabic, she says she is more comfortable having "another set of ears" present at each session.

. . . [M]any of the most dangerous inmates regularly attack the guards, pelting them with feces, urine, semen, and spittle, not to mention the constant threats they make against the guards' families. Even this terrorist, casually munching on donut after donut, says he would happily kill every American he could get his hands on: military or civilian; man, woman or child. The woman in charge of behavioral analysis at Gitmo—a dedicated Ph.D. who has two years of experience with these people and has just extended her stay—added, "This man is proud of what he did, the people he killed, the targets he attacked, the plans he made, and the money he raised for al-Qaeda. He met with Osama bin Laden frequently. He tells us these things as a proud jihadist fighter."

I asked why he had not tried to lay a hand on his interrogator, who is much physically weaker than he is. "He knows the drill," replied JTF Commander BG Jay Hood. "He is restrained by leg cuffs and can't reach the interrogators. If he tried—and some have—then he would be denied privileges." Like Krispy Kremes. He eagerly eats the donuts that the interrogator provides at each session, General Hood added, "so that he can throw his food tray at the guards who deliver it to his cell." He attacks guards and his punishment is to be supplied with breakfast pastries: sounds like torture to me.

---

1. **DoD:** Department of Defense.

After learning of the treats given to detainee terrorists, we were surprised to find the modus operandi of the female interrogators was much different than the media and the Left had led us to believe: The women act as caring nurturers, gently lulling the captives into disclosing vital information. "Why did Gitmo employ a female interrogator in the first place?" we asked. We were told that these thugs were especially sensitive about having Western women around them. "We are very effective with some of the detainees," another female interrogator told me. She looks to be in her forties, slight build, light hair. "I dress modestly when I work with the detainees," she said. "Long sleeves and an ankle-length skirt. I act as a mother or perhaps a sister to these men. In their culture those role models are acceptable. Indeed, it provides a comfort level for them to discuss their activities with a motherly/sisterly figure. We don't coerce; we don't pressure. We just talk. And listen very carefully."

"Most importantly," she continued, "we are breaking stereotypes. These men expected to find something quite different. Many are very well educated, in America and Europe, and have much exposure to Western culture. But their ideology has implanted a harsh, critical stereotype of what Western women are like. When we act differently—more in keeping with women's behavior in their family circles—then we connect with their culture and they open up to us."

Gitmo interrogators focus on "building rapport" with the detainees, getting to know them, gaining their trust. They "break down stereotypes" and engage in dialogue. General Hood affirms that "the techniques work." Not all conversation with the detainees is about military or terrorist actions. They chat, talk about family, background, world affairs. One woman bakes cookies for her sessions.

What, after all these years of confinement, do the Gitmo interrogators elicit from these people? One would expect that any important information they possess has long been overtaken by events or grown stale, that these people had been milked of all actionable intelligence months ago and were simply hanging around waiting for ultimate disposition by military tribunal. . . .

They are, instead, critical informants in the War on Terror.

JTF interrogators disclosed that they are continuing to develop a large amount of important intelligence from these detainees, even years after capture, and the information gained is growing daily. Integrating this intelligence with Homeland Security agencies and with military reports from battlefields in Afghanistan and Iraq is helping penetrate the detainee cover stories and break down defenses. One detainee provided personal information on a current Afghan tribal leader that helped Afghanistan forces control a turbulent region. Other detainees gave up operational attack plans that they formulated that had not yet been implemented. Police authorities in Europe and America follow up these leads and continue to break up hidden terrorist sleeper cells.

Another man was silent for almost three years. He successfully maintained a false identity until a captured terrorist half a world away picked him from a photo and gave his name. Once he was confronted with the truth he began to talk. From him we are learning about al-Qaeda's web of financial sources, how funds are moved, and how money laundering takes place. His information enables specialists to dry up money sources that had been, up-to-that-moment, aiding their terrorist jihad.

There are many reasons to hold these very dangerous terrorists, including the wealth of vital information that we continue to elicit. To make this happen, they need to be confined in a special facility secluded from everyone else where they can be controlled effectively and interrogated properly. Guantanamo Bay fits the requirements in ways no other facility would. This base is keeping highly dangerous terrorists from killing more innocent Americans. It is not a gulag or torture camp. . . .

. . . [W]e owe these gallant service men and women a deep debt of gratitude for carrying out this vital but viciously slandered mission, all the while bearing up with great professionalism.

These are the professionals who bear the brunt of the overheated and irresponsible charges of the Left—but if the Left manages to get the government to shut Gitmo down, they won't be its only victims.

JOHN ASHCROFT

Hearing before the House Judiciary Committee
From the DOJ to Guantánamo Bay: Administration Lawyers
and Administration Interrogation Rules

Mr. Chairman, thank you for the opportunity to testify about "United States policies regarding interrogation of persons in the custody of the nation's intelligence services and armed forces." This Committee's prior hearings on this topic have focused principally on three legal opinions authored by the Office of Legal Counsel in August 2002, March 2003, and December 2004. I served as Attorney General when each of these memos was written. Before delving into the specifics of those memos, I would like to make a few preliminary points.

First, during the weeks and months following September 11—and particularly in the summer of 2002, as the first anniversary of that tragic day approached—the Nation greeted each new day with justified awareness that al Qaeda was determined to strike us again. The daily report of national security threats prepared for the President by the intelligence agencies served as a chilling reminder of the danger we faced, and every morning brought new and pressing challenges. As I stated to the 9/11 Commission: "My day beg[an] with a review of the threats to Americans and to American interests that were received in the previous twenty-four hours. If ever there were proof of the existence of evil in the world, it is in the pages of these reports."

After seven years without an attack, it is perhaps easy to forget just how perilous that time was; easy to forget the daily headlines of foiled plots and new threats; easy to forget the color-coded threat levels and the nervous apprehension that hung in the air; easy to forget how strange it seemed to take our shoes off in airport security lines. But at the time—the summer of 2002—reminders of the peril we faced were all about us. During that summer both Zacarias Moussaoui, a confessed co-conspirator in 9/11, and John Walker Lindh, the

American turned Taliban fighter, were being prosecuted by the Justice Department. It was also during that summer that the Department announced the disruption of Jose Padilla's plot to explode a dirty bomb, and the indictment of five leaders of the Islamic terrorist organization Abu Sayyaf. And in August of 2002 the first payments from the September 11 Victim Compensation Fund went out to the families of some of our murdered countrymen.

In short, we in the Justice Department were confronted with daily reminders that the lives of countless Americans depended on the effectiveness of our efforts to prevent another terrorist attack and that even the slightest mistake could result in tragedy. After 9/11, the Administration's overriding goal, which I fully embraced, was to do everything within its power and within the limits of the law—I repeat, within its power *and* within the limits of the law—to keep this country and the American people safe from terrorist attacks. If we had missed some piece of intelligence, or had failed to pursue vigorously every lead—if we had returned to a pre-9/11 way of doing business, with counterproductive firewalls and outdated laws and procedures—I might still be testifying here today, but the topic might be far different. As this Congress and the nation now turn to reevaluate that work with the altered perception of seven years of safety, we would all do well to remember the danger we faced (and still face) and the potentially catastrophic consequences of error.

Second, the process we will discuss here today—the examination of difficult legal questions by OLC, and OLC's reassessment of its opinions when warranted by new concerns, conditions, or information—is a distinct virtue, and reflects this Administration's commitment to the rule of law. There is no room in the Justice Department for an assumption that its work is perfect, nor for an attitude of resistance to reconsideration. The Administration's continual—indeed, almost obsessive—quest for legal guidance and specific authorization for measures necessitated by the War on Terror is evidence of a government striving to keep within the limits of law, not one seeking to ignore or evade those limits. I make no claim that the Department's analyses of the difficult legal questions that arose during my tenure as Attorney General—questions often at the edges of our law—were always flawless, nor that our conclusions were always free from doubt. No Administration can lay claim to such a feat; nor can the oft-divided Supreme Court, which reverses itself, from time to time, on issues of the greatest national importance. I can and do claim, however, that as Attorney General I sought to ensure that the legal advice provided by the Department adhered to the highest professional standards of quality and integrity. . . .

42

What Price Security? The View from Inside Gitmo
Erik Saar et al.

In her 2008 book, My Guantánamo Diary: The Detainees and the Stories They Told Me, *Mahvish Rukhsana Khan, one of the translators at the Guantánamo detention camp, writes that "I came to believe that many, perhaps even most" of the detainees were "innocent men who'd been swept up by mistake." She observes that the American military dropped leaflets across Afghanistan promising up to $25,000, or nearly one hundred times the annual per capita income, to anyone who would turn in members of the Taliban or al Qaeda and that this led bounty hunters to wild errors in a place where hardly anyone in the military spoke any of the national languages. She writes that many of the men she worked with had no idea where Guantánamo was or why they were there. While clearly some prisoners at Gitmo were indeed connected to organizations that were hostile to American security, the question that most people were asking by the time her book came out was whether it was necessary to make so many mistakes to stop genuine terrorists and whether the price of security had been set too high by the Bush administration. For many of the individuals who came in contact with Gitmo, the answer became no.*

Sergeant Erik Saar describes how he went from a gung-ho soldier who wanted to be assigned to Gitmo to an individual deeply disillusioned with the army for the injustices and incompetence that he witnessed at Guantánamo. Moazzam Begg, a British national who was captured in Afghanistan while on a mission to help his fellow Afghanis, tells in an interview and in his published account a harrowing tale of false imprisonment and abuse at the hands of the U.S. military. Finally, James Yee, a career officer and West Point graduate, who acted as army chaplain for Muslims at Gitmo, tells how he attempted to do the job the army set for him and was eventually punished, persecuted, and unjustly imprisoned for his belief in the Constitution and his loyalty to the U.S. Army.

QUESTIONS TO CONSIDER

1. What aspects of these three accounts do you think are the most and least reliable and why?
2. How might these three individuals provide different arguments against John Ashcroft's defense of Gitmo? How might their arguments be similar?
3. Saar and Begg both believe that the war on terror may be producing more terrorists. How do you think Ashcroft would respond to this charge?

Amy Goodman, Interview, May 4, 2005, from http://democracynow.org.

ERIK SAAR

Witness to Interrogations

[Erik Saar]: I volunteered to go to Guantánamo Bay because I believed in the mission, to be honest with you, ma'am. I went there enthusiastically to serve my country and hopefully to use my Arabic skills to contribute to the war on terrorism and to help. I believed I was going to sit face-to-face with those who perpetrated and were responsible for the events of September 11 and those who were—or those who were planning future attacks against the United States.

Amy Goodman: And is that what happened when you went to Guantánamo?

Erik Saar: Well, I went there with one expectation. What I found shortly after I arrived, and then I actually went through a process of realizing that my expectations really clashed with the reality of Guantánamo Bay. And it's not exactly what I found. There were a number of things that troubled me, that ended up leading me to the conclusion that Guantánamo Bay, to me, represents a mistake and a failed strategy in this war.

Amy Goodman: You translated for the interrogators at Guantánamo?

Erik Saar: I did. In the second half of my six-month assignment, I did serve as a translator in a number of interrogations.

Amy Goodman: You describe one scene of a female interrogator. Can you talk about what happened that day and start from the beginning?

Erik Saar: I walked in with her. The prisoner had already been there waiting for a good period of time before we arrived. He was shackled to the floor and forced to hunch over. We were asking him—telling him to be cooperative. She was explaining—saying that, you know, this is going to be unpleasant for you. After a break, we then returned to the interrogation booth, and that was when she started taking off her outer blouse, where she was wearing a tight t-shirt underneath, and she was touching herself and trying to arouse the detainee. . . .

She was saying, you know, it doesn't have to be this way. We could sit across a table and talk like adults, but I could tell—and then she went on to say—I could tell that you're aroused by me. How do you think Allah feels by you being attracted to an American infidel?

We took a break and then we went back. That was when she went and found a red marker to wipe red ink on her hands. We returned to the interrogation, where she told him that she was menstruating and walked around and began to put her hands in her pants and walked around the detainee and then wiped the red ink on the side of his face and told him that it was menstrual blood. . . .

He lunged from the chair and actually he came out of one of the ankle shackles that was on, and the M.P.'s had to come in, the guards had to come in and put him back in the shackles. And all of this, I'd like to say, was with someone that personally based on the intelligence I had access to was someone who was an individual that, to be honest with you, I hope never sees the light of day, and—but of course, goes through some process of justice, in order to be—to face a just punishment, but at the same time, what convinced me and what was so troubling was that, first of all, this was ineffective; secondly, even if it was effective, it was apparent to me that what we were doing there was not in keeping with the values we stand for as a country.

Amy Goodman: Was he responding to you at all?

[Erik Saar]: . . . I actually felt—it was one of the frustrations of dealing with certain interrogations, because as a linguist, you're to take on the role of the interrogator who was with you. So, there was a conflict there in that I wasn't necessarily agreeing with what was taking place, but you had a mission at the same time.

Amy Goodman: And so, when she took the red ink and smeared it on him, did she say to him, this is menstrual blood?

Erik Saar: Yes, she said this is menstrual blood. And then she also said, you know, have fun attempting to pray in your cell tonight when your water is going to be turned off. So they would turn off the water in his cell so he couldn't become ritually clean.

Amy Goodman: And his response?

Erik Saar: His response was really non-verbal. The only thing I can make out that he said was some profanity, but other than that, he really was just despondent, and I guess that's the best way to put it. . . .

Amy Goodman: And as a result of the interrogation, did he reveal anything?

Erik Saar: To my knowledge, Amy, I don't know that he ever did. . . .

Amy Goodman: What about these hundreds of prisoners at Guantánamo? How many of them would you say are what the U.S. government calls terrorists?

Erik Saar: Well, it's difficult for me to say, because that definition seems so ambiguous, but I'll say this, that I was under the impression when I went there that I was going to be sitting face-to-face with hardened terrorists, meaning what our government had said is the worst of the worst. And I took that to mean those individuals that had extensive training from al Qaeda. Additionally, I thought that they were going to be men who had planned attacks against the United States, who were responsible for the events of September 11, or who were planning future attacks against the United States. But what I found to be the case was that—and then I was also told that they were all enemy combatants, supposedly, this new term, that were picked up on the battlefield with weapons; they had taken up arms against Americans. But we knew, to be—I shortly found out after arriving there that that necessarily was not the case with a number of individuals. And we knew that there was a chunk of men there who we really had no idea how they came to us, or we did know that they were turned over by foreign governments or by the Northern Alliance. So, we had no way to ascertain whether or not they had, in fact, ever taken up arms against them, or really even know how to corroborate their story. . . .

One of the things I learned when I joined the intelligence team was that when a V.I.P. visit would take place, meaning it could be a general or could be an executive from the senior government service, one of the intelligence agencies, maybe, or even a congressional delegation, there was a concerted effort to explain to the interrogators that they were to find a detainee who had previously been cooperative and put him in the interrogation booth at the time when the V.I.P. would be visiting and sitting in the observation room. Essentially, they were to find someone who had been cooperative, who they were able to sit across a table with and have a regular dialogue, and someone who would also — had in the past provided adequate intelligence, and then they were to replay that interrogation for the visiting V.I.P.s. And essentially, as an intelligence professional, this was insulting. And I don't think I was alone in feeling this way, to be honest with you, because in the intelligence community your whole existence is in order to provide policymakers with the right information to make the right decisions. So, that's really the existence of the intelligence community, to simply provide the right information. And this concept of creating this fictitious world so Gitmo [looked] like one thing to those visiting, when in reality it was something far different, completely undermined everything that we, as professionals, were trying to do in intelligence. . . .

. . . You know, honestly, ma'am, I didn't know if I thought that the V.I.P.s when they came to visit really believed they were seeing an actual interrogation. I almost find that hard to believe, because if they wanted to see something that might be typical, at least from the military's perspective, regarding what was going on in the interrogation booth, they might have been better off coming unannounced and asking to see an interrogation at 2:00 in the morning. . . .

You know, a lot of the soldiers there shared some of my frustrations, but I don't want to say or act as though they all came to the conclusions exactly in the same way that I did or had the same conclusions. But at the same time I think if you talk to individuals who had been there, you will find someone who has frustrations with some elements of the camp. I mean, it was — the way in which the camp was run, the gray lines that no one knew what was clearly defined as right and wrong, frustrated a number of individuals, and many people even were troubled by the fact that the files on a number of the individuals being held were extremely thin. We knew very little, excuse me, about why they were there. And that bothered some people in thinking that as Americans, we enjoy one way of life, and we say that our system of justice is something that we want to promote around the world, and our democratic values are something that we stand up for, but at the same time we're defying those very same values in Guantánamo Bay. . . .

Amy Goodman: Erik Saar, [were] the words Geneva Conventions ever used at Guantanamo?

Erik Saar: One time, ma'am, I can say, when we were talked to regarding the Geneva Conventions, and there was a meeting that I describe where our leaders of the intelligence group explained to us that the Geneva Convention does not apply at Guantánamo Bay. And they gave us reasons as to why they rationalized that it did not, and that now the detainees, we should understand — of course, we knew this beforehand, but this was in a meeting where they were explaining to us the reasons why — we should understand that these individuals were enemy combatants and to be treated as detainees. And one of the frustrations regarding that is someone who interacted with and had friends who were interrogators, is that the essence of their training, ma'am, when they go through school, is that you were taught a couple of things about the Geneva Convention. First of all, all your training is under the umbrella of the Geneva Convention, and you are told that you never violate the Geneva Conventions as an interrogator, because—for two reasons: Number one, it's illegal; and number two, they're taught that it's ineffective. And if you need to use tactics outside of the scope of the Geneva Conventions, you are going to get bad intelligence anyway. But somehow, no one quite understood how it was determined that now those rules don't need to apply. Plus there's limited, if no training, for how these new rules should be implemented in the interrogation booth, and what is the rationale for why previously, I was taught as an interrogator or one of my colleagues was taught, that these techniques wouldn't work, but now we're saying that maybe they will?

Amy Goodman: Erik Saar, do you think that the abuse was creating terrorists?

Erik Saar: I think, Amy, that what I witnessed at Guantánamo Bay was, on a practical level, counterproductive in the war on terrorism. Because, in fact, as we go throughout the Arab and Muslim world and say that we're going to promote values of democracy and justice and human dignity, but at the same time defy those very same values in Guantanamo Bay, I do think in the long run, it could produce more terrorists.

MOAZZAM BEGG

From Kandahar to Bagram to Guantánamo

Moazzam Begg: I was the world's number one terrorist. I was hog-tied, shackled, kicked and punched. Black hole no end in sight. I cracked up fell in a corner weeping. I can't believe, I, it's incomprehensible for me to think how they would come to the conclusion that I am a threat to Britain. Britain is my home, it's my, it's where I was born, it's where I was raised, I went to school, my friends, my family, everybody is here, my wife and my children are here, they were all born and raised here. I'm as British as I, as, as anybody else.

Q: So you decided to go in 2001 with the family.

Moazzam Begg: That's correct, yes.

Q: To a Taliban administered Afghanistan.

Moazzam Begg: Yes that's correct. . . .

Q: But you are moving from Birmingham where your wife can move freely, where your children can be educated, your girl children can be educated, to a country where, at that point, under Taliban rule, your wife would have to be beneath a burka and your girl children—

Moazzam Begg: I think though in hindsight, when I look back at Afghanistan, there were rules that were austere but they really weren't as bad as, as people have made them out to be—and my evidence for that of course is if you'd speak to some of the other people, who were not of a Muslim background that lived there, and I think they might give you similar story. What I would say, yes, the Taliban rules, I think they were austere, they were strict, to their own detriment, but as far as my wife and my children were concerned it was, they were free to go wherever they wanted. . . .

Channel 4 News, http://www.channel4.com/news/2005/02/week_4/images/24_beggtranscript.doc.

. . . I went to a country where people were a lot more impoverished, I tried to help people that were a little worse off than myself in whatever little way that I could, and perhaps stay away for a year, two years or so, with my family rather than be away from them, and then come back when, when we felt the time was right. . . .

I remember some, somebody coming knocking to the doors. . . . He said America has been attacked. . . .

. . . [A] friend of mine, I'd phoned him and he told me that there could be imminent attacks on Afghanistan, that they're blaming al-Qaeda that's based in around Kandahar for being responsible. . . .

Well we evacuated from Kabul, myself and my family. I really didn't want to give up all the projects that we'd begun, we put a lot of hard work, time, effort and money into all of this.

Q: You are in your house in Islamabad with your wife and your children. Tell us then what happens, this is three months after you have fled from Afghanistan and, and you are all asleep?

Moazzam Begg: I was awake actually, I was, I was sitting in, I think I was playing a game on my computer, I was just about to go to sleep. There was a knock, about 12 o'clock at night, I answered the door, it was sort of strange to get a, receive a visitor at that time, but I answered the door anyway and I was faced with several gun-toting, I don't know who they were, I still maintain to this day that they were thugs and they were not part of the intelligence service and I'll tell you why in a minute. But a gun was put to my head and I was pushed forward into my front room, made to kneel, a black hood was put on my head, my hands were tied behind my back and my legs were shackled and I was physically carried into a vehicle, the back of a vehicle, I think it was a 4x4, and driven off. Never got a chance to say goodbye or a word to my wife or my children. And then everything was to change forever. . . .

They lifted my hood in the vehicle and I saw these two Americans and I remember one, clearly, he said to me, he said, he was wearing an Afghan cap, and he said that, he produced a pair of handcuffs, and he said that do you know why I have got these, gotten these handcuffs from? I said no. He said I was given these handcuffs by one of the wives of the victims of 9/11 to go and catch, capture the perpetrators. I said well wouldn't she think that your are an idiot for having caught the wrong person, and he said nothing.

Next Begg was taken to Bagram airbase—holding center for terror.

Moazzam Begg: They used to take us into freezing ice-cold showers from which people actually dropped from the sheer cold and were taken to hospital for hypothermia. I had witnessed old people, who were older than 80 years old, brought into detention. I had witnessed people have their hearing aids removed from them because it was an electrical device that might possibly cause some security problem. I had witnessed children in detention, 11, 12 year olds. I had witnessed people who had been wounded and brought over and held. So it was very, it was very, very difficult to bear and up until June of 2002, which is almost five months after I had been taken in, I still had no word from my family.

And I remember during one of the interrogations, which was probably one of the hardest ever, in the room next door they had the sound of a woman screaming and at that time I believed it was my wife. . . .

A particularly harsh interrogation took place in May, in which I faced two members of the FBI, one CIA, one major, and one other unknown chap, and I believe it's those, amongst them that date, particularly the FBI and the CIA, which had ordered my punishment or harsh treatment, which included me being hog-tied, left in a room with a bag put over my head, even though I suffered from asthma . . . after which they threatened to have me sent to Egypt, to be tortured, to face electric shocks, to have my fingers broken, to be sexually abused, and, and the like. . . .

I witnessed two people get beaten so badly that I believe it caused their deaths. And one of those deaths was later investigated and those investigators turned up to Guantánamo Bay and asked me if I would be willing to point out the perpetrators of that, those beatings, of what I witnessed and so they subsequently brought over pictures of all the units at the time—asked if I would be willing to stand as a witness. And how ironic it is that after two and a half years in detention, which is when they turned up, that the only crime that I can witness to is one that has been committed by American soldiers. . . .

[Next, Begg was sent to Guantánamo Bay. Three days after arriving he was compelled to sign a false confession by two U.S. intelligence officers.]

Moazzam Begg: They said you can't go any further, you could be sitting here for years, you could face a summary trial, which could mean execution by the electric chair, a lethal injection or gas chamber and all of that, the British government has washed its hands of you, you have no access to any legal courts, to any normal proceedings, so this is your only option to proceed with this. And I thought to myself, I couldn't believe that this was happening and yet, again I asked for a lawyer, again I asked for British consular representation and again it was all denied. And finally I relented, and I put my name, I signed and initialed this document that they had put together and I thought to myself, okay, at least if I get a chance to appear in court that's when I can say this is all rubbish. . . .

I think the interrogation effectively had ended about a few months after I had been there and then I thought that some process might begin but it just became a black hole of incarceration with no end in sight. The worse thing was being cut off from news of current affairs, of what's taken place, even about my own affairs, and the sporadic, intermittent mail, postal service that they'd established, was months on end I would not get any reply. I wouldn't know if my letters had gotten through, and eventually when they did, this is an example of the type of censorship that was so ridiculous. This is a letter from my daughter, who was at the time seven years old. They've blocked out all but maybe six or seven lines. I asked her a few weeks ago, when I had arrived, I said do you remember what you wrote over here? She said yes I did. She said I wrote here: one, two, three, four, five, once I caught a fish alive, six, seven, eight, nine, ten, then I let it go again. When the general appeared, General Hood, I presented this to him, this is an example of several types of letters, and I said what is it possibly that you could be afraid of from a seven year old girl that you would do something like this, that she wrote so lovingly to her father, and he could give me no reply. He put his head down in shame.

[Begg later went on to write a book about his experiences, *Enemy Combatant: A British Muslim's Journey to Guantánamo and Back*. In the excerpt that follows, he describes his new surroundings in Guantánamo Bay.]

Extract from Enemy Combatant

The next time I remember anything was in a daze in Guantánamo. The first sensations I felt were intense heat and humidity. I realized I was out of the plane and the shackles I had on were different. There was a chain going from the waist to the ankles, which restricted my movement even more than before. That was my introduction to the "three-piece suit," which I soon knew only too well. I was still half dazed and vaguely felt there were a lot of MPs around. In and out of a vehicle, in and out of more orange clothes, I was barely conscious. The guards on both sides held me up for a few steps, and I noticed the ground under my feet was very different from anything I'd seen in Afghanistan. There were small light-brown sun-baked rocks, it seemed a lot drier, hotter . . . and I could smell the sea. It was distinctly different to the smell of the sea in Britain. But I could definitely smell the sea.

I was in Camp Echo—or Eskimo, as they called it at that time—although I didn't know it just then. I was taken into a room where they took off my hood, goggles, earmuffs, and facemask. The guards took me to a cell in the corner of the room, asked me to step up and in, and locked the door. Then they asked me to stand up with my back to the door so they could take the shackles off, through the beanhole, an opening in the cell door covered with a metal flap controlled from the outside. They undid the legs first, and then the padlock at the back of the waist, then I had to turn round and hand them over the rest of the chain that had gone from the wrist to the ankles. Then they undid the wrists, and I was free in my little cell. My cell, my new home, measured about eight foot by six foot. It had a toilet in there, an Arab-style toilet, all metal, on the ground.

I didn't know what I was expecting, but it was not this. I looked around in utter bewilderment, almost unbelief. Nothing had changed, in fact things were worse. From Kandahar to Bagram, from Bagram to Guantánamo: each time I thought things were going to get better, but they actually got worse. What could be more bleak, or grimmer, than being in a cage like this? I could not even see out of it clearly as it was covered with a pale green steel mesh, doubled with one part of the mesh set vertically, and the other horizontally, so they crisscrossed one another. I could barely see through it, it was a strain on the eyes. I felt I was really back to square one.

Moazzam Begg, *Enemy Combatant: A British Muslim's Journey to Guantánamo and Back* (New York: Free Press, 2006).

It is considered a sin in Islam to despair, but in Bagram, during the worst days of May 2002, I had been unable to hold despair at bay. Here in Guantánamo, in this steel cage with its mesh sides, steel roof and floor, steel bed, steel toilet, all inside a white, new-looking brightly lit room, I felt despair returning as I took in my surroundings for the first time.

All I had in the cell was a sheet and a roll of toilet paper, not even my glasses. I asked for something that I could use as a prayer mat, and they brought a thin camping mat, which became my mattress for the next two years. . . .

JAMES YEE

Faith and Patriotism under Fire

. . . I was coming home in September of 2003 for what I thought would be a short two-week break. I landed in Jacksonville Naval Air Station, the first stop where U.S. service members come back into the country after being in Guantánamo. The customs officials, they stopped and they searched my bags. It was interesting, because when they directed me to get my bags, I went to the pile of luggage where all of the luggage had been unloaded from the plane, but lo and behold, beside this pile of luggage, were my two bags already set aside, and I was wondering how that happened? Nevertheless, it was very convenient. I was able to grab those two bags and give them to the customs officials. Disturbingly, I would actually learn that it was the FBI—the FBI—who had contacted the customs officials, even as early as the day before my arrival and again the morning of my arrival, requesting them specifically to single me out, identify me before I even get off the plane, and have my bags searched. And that's what happened.

So we no longer have a routine customs search, but instead we have now a search being conducted by an extension of a law enforcement agency, the FBI, without probable cause, a violation, of course, of my Fourth Amendment right to be free from an illegal search and seizure. Didn't matter too much to me, because it's not like I had anything. But then, it would matter, because these customs officials would say, "Oh, we got some suspicious documents in his backpack," and then these suspicious documents were immediately, within seconds, handed over to several federal and military intelligence officers, who, by the way, just happened to be standing by. No, it wasn't a coincidence. It was a sting operation, and then these intelligence officers would say, not only were these documents suspicious, but they are classified documents, and then they would be able to get an arrest warrant, and then I was thrown in jail for which it ultimately would be for 76 days in isolation.

I was arrested in secret, held incommunicado. I never showed up at the airport in Seattle like I was supposed to have, where my wife and daughter were waiting. They didn't know what happened to me. My parents in New Jersey

Radio transcript from DemocracyNow.org, www.democracynow.org/2006/5/22/ex_guantanamo_chaplain_james_yee_on.

had no idea what had happened. I essentially disappeared from society, from the face of the earth. But my family would learn of what happened to me ten days later, when government leaks to the media were then reported, first by the *Washington Times*, that I was now arrested and charged with these heinous crimes of spying, espionage, aiding the enemy, and mutiny and sedition, which is like trying to overthrow the government. All of these capital crimes, and, yes, I was threatened with the death penalty days after my arrest by a military prosecutor.

But now, I was sitting in a super-maximum security prison down in Charleston, South Carolina. Interestingly enough, the prison in which they sent me to is the very same prison in which they hold the U.S. citizen enemy combatants. Foreign enemy combatants, we know, are held down in Guantánamo and these other secret C.I.A. black sites that we've heard about. Enemy combatants declared by our U.S. president that are U.S. citizens are held in Charleston, South Carolina at the Consolidated Naval Brig, and that's where they sent me, and I believe it was a U.S. Southern Command public affairs representative—I believe it was on Amy's[1] show—who said this was only a coincidence that they sent me to this very same prison. But I know it wasn't a coincidence, because of the way in which they transported me there.

I was taken from Jacksonville, shackled like prisoners are shackled down in Guantánamo, at the wrist and at the waist and at the ankles in what we call in the military a three-piece suit, not a three-piece suit like you buy at the mall, made by Armani, a three-piece suit of chains. This is how I was shackled and then thrown in the back of a truck next to an armed guard, two other armed guards in the front. And down on the way, on this trip to Charleston, the guard pulls out of this bag these goggles—they're blackened out, opaque—puts them on my eyes so now I can't see a thing. He takes out these heavy industrial type ear muffs, the likes that you might see a construction worker wearing when he's jack hammering in the middle of the street, puts them on my ears, and now I can't hear a thing. We call this tactic "sensory deprivation." Sensory deprivation, it's something that I recently read that the American Psychiatric Association has included in a draft of their definition of torture.

Sensory deprivation. I was subjected to sensory deprivation, but I knew about this tactic, because that's, of course, how I saw prisoners being treated and subjected to when they are in-processed into Guantánamo when they are flown in from Afghanistan under this very same tactic of sensory deprivation; its purpose, which is meant to instill fear and intimidation. You, yourselves, maybe have seen the pictures with the prisoners wearing the hoods on their head. Well, I feared also that a hood would be then thrown on my head, but fortunately for me, that practice of hooding had just been stopped months before my arrest. I also feared of being kicked and beaten violently, especially after hearing some of the prisoners when I spoke with them down in Guantánamo, how they were kicked and beaten during their transport down to Guantánamo.

1. Amy Goodman, radio host of Democracynow.org.

One prisoner, as I've written about, even said, "Chaplain, if you look in my medical records, you'll see that I've even been treated by Army medics for being kicked and beaten so violently when I was brought here." I feared that I was going to be subjected to this same type treatment. So when they threw me in a cell down in Charleston, South Carolina, in solitary confinement, in isolation, I was at least relieved that I was still alive. But what was life like in that prison cell for me for those seventy-six days down in Charleston?

One of the most ironic parts of this situation is that down in Guantánamo, as the Muslim chaplain, I was able to protect certain religious rights for the alleged, suspected, Taliban and al-Qaeda prisoners down in Guantánamo. I was able to ensure that the call to prayer was made five times a day over a loudspeaker. I was able to ensure that in every cell, an arrow was painted, directing them towards Mecca so they can properly make their prayers. I was able to ensure that every meal that is served to Muslim prisoners in Guantánamo is what we call "halal," meaning "the meat." The meals are prepared according to Islamic guidelines, a concept similar to kosher. I was able to ensure that meal schedules were adjusted during the holy month of Ramadan to accommodate for the holy fasting of that month, but when I, a U.S. citizen, was taken into U.S. military custody and thrown into a maximum security prison, I was denied my religious rights.

Yes, the prison chaplain came to see me, and he knew that I was a Muslim chaplain and, of course, by this time, it's high profile, as it has hit the news. The chaplain asked me if I needed anything, and I said, "Yes, could you get me the five prayer times so that I can make my Muslim prayers during their correct time?" And I even gave him a website, www.islamicfinder.org. Type in the zip code and you can get the prayer times for Charleston, South Carolina. He said, "Sorry, I can't give it to you. The security section won't allow me to give you that type of information."

I said, "Well, how about just a quick confirmation to the northeasterly direction, so that I can at least pray in the right direction, northeast from North America?" Mecca is to the northeast from North America. He said, "Sorry. I can't give you that either. The security section won't allow me to give you even that information." And I interpreted that to mean that if he gave me the northeasterly direction, then I, of course, being a military soldier, would be able to determine which way was north, south, east and west, and that information would help me if I was able to escape from this super-maximum security prison, because then I would know which way to run.

The point is, I was denied my religious rights as a U.S. citizen in military custody, the very same rights that I was able to uphold for prisoners down in Guantánamo. With that, I have to say that after 76 days I was suddenly released. I was never charged officially with those heinous crimes. I was charged with some lesser offenses of mishandling classified documents, which the military tried to prosecute me on. . . .

I didn't receive an apology. Yes, I am an eternal optimist, and I hope one day that I will receive an official apology, and I believe that by speaking out, speaking the truth, and making people aware of what's going on in Guantánamo and letting others know what happened to me, as a U.S. citizen held in this so-called war on terrorism, that one day all of this will lead to a well-deserved apology. Thank you.

FOR CRITICAL THINKING

1. In what ways does point of view affect the way Gitmo is viewed?
2. Why do you think the U.S. government kept Gitmo open, despite the criticisms from so many people who had contact with it?
3. How do you think the U.S. Army might have done things differently to avoid creating such criticisms?

43

Los Angeles Burning, April 1992:
Riots in the Wake of the Rodney King Verdict

On the afternoon of April 29, 1992, Los Angeles exploded in its worst urban violence since the Watts riots of 1965. Like the urban riots of the 1920s, 1940s, and 1960s, it began with one incident, a largely white suburban jury acquitting four white police officers accused of beating African American motorist Rodney King. Like earlier urban riots, it also spread to cities across the United States. However, this incident, which had occurred more than a year earlier, had been captured on videotape by a bystander. Television news audiences around the world had spent the year watching ninety seconds of grainy footage of the four police officers beating King over and over on a street in Los Angeles, as other officers stood and watched. By the time the jury delivered the verdict few people who knew anything about Los Angeles were surprised at the violent reaction.

However, it was not the new technology that put policing onto television that convinced so many that Los Angeles might again burn and take other cities with it. Instead it was the twelve-year buildup of tension and conflict over economic and social changes in African American urban communities across the nation. The riots came at the end of the "Reagan Revolution," which had involved a direct assault on civil rights institutions and economic changes in how the government managed "inner cities"—the contemporary term for center city areas with large non-white, urban working class populations. Between 1981 and 1988, Reagan sponsored massive cuts to the public services and federal housing programs that underwrote much of inner city family life, reduced and retrenched the urban civil service jobs that had become heavily Latino and African American after the civil rights era, and waged a "war on drugs" that swelled urban police forces and gave officers new impunity to arrest and imprison.

Things became even more tense when Reagan's vice president, George H. W. Bush, took the helm. He began his presidential campaign by using the image of Willie Horton, a black felon who had raped a white woman while on a weekend furlough from prison, to attack his opponent, Massachusetts governor Michael Dukakis. Many African Americans were shocked by the racism they felt underlay the Willie Horton ads. Once in office, Bush ramped up the war on drugs, militarized the "inner cities," and raised imprisonment rates for African American men faster than at any time in U.S. history. Social commentators around the world were describing American inner cities as tinder boxes, and by the afternoon of the Rodney King verdict the question that most people in Los Angeles were asking was not if there would be riots, but when, for how long, and with what response from the government.

While the riots clearly had a racial dimension, they spread across neighborhoods and involved many ethnic groups among both rioters and those trying to keep the peace. As an example of this, the most famous incident during the rioting was captured on video-

tape by a news helicopter, allowing the entire nation to watch in horror as Reginald Denny, a white motorist, was dragged from his truck at a traffic light and beaten by a group of black men. What fewer Americans remember is that Denny was then hero-ically saved by another group of black men.

After nearly a week of violence, arson, looting, and vandalism, Los Angeles had fifty-three dead and over two thousand injuries, ten thousand arrested, one thousand destroyed buildings, seven thousand fires, three thousand devastated businesses, and $1 billion in property damage. Although Bush was up for reelection, his response to the riots was to send in the military and remain in Washington for the entire week allowing Demo-cratic Party candidate Bill Clinton to upstage him by visiting the still smoldering ruins of South Central Los Angeles. Though Republicans accused Clinton of exploiting the city's misery for his own electoral gain, many Angelinos, especially African Americans, were reassured and comforted by a candidate who met them face to face in their worst hour and wanted to talk with the "inner cities," rather than militarize them. Many people in the rest of the country asked, "Where was George Bush when Los Angeles was burning?"

QUESTIONS TO CONSIDER

1. How do you think the introduction of portable home video cameras and digital photography has changed the relationship between police and the communities they regulate?

2. How do you think photographs like these might have influenced the debate about whether the government should have committed the same resources to rebuild as is typically provided for a hurricane or other nat-ural disaster?

3. The photo on page 332 (top) shows some of the more than ten thousand people arrested for looting. What impact do you think the wide dissem-ination of such televised images had on the ability of local communities to counter the violence?

Above: Looting suspects handcuffed in the wake of the Los Angeles riots.

Left: Aerial view of smoke-covered Los Angeles, April 30, 1992.

Opposite: Cleaning up South Central Los Angeles, May 1992.

44

Daughter of America
Shams Alwujude

The hyphen that both connects and separates categories of American identity such as Italian-American, Jewish-American, African-American, Korean-American, and so on is often described as a fulcrum that immigrants and their children must use to balance the two cultures that make up their identity. Since September 11, 2001, when nineteen Arab men hijacked airplanes and created the worst terror attack in American history, the hyphen that holds together the word **Arab**-American *has often threatened to break under the strain of the cultural and political baggage loaded on its two sides.*

On the day of the attack, a speech by Osama Bin Laden, believed to be the mastermind behind the attack, aired on international television. In it, he declared that "America will not live in peace" and called on Muslims across the planet to unite against America. In response, many Americans began to fear their Arab-descended neighbors. Soon after the speech, people with "a Middle Eastern appearance" were attacked, a Molotov cocktail was thrown into an Arab-American school, and the FBI detained over one thousand people of Arab descent, sometimes for reasons as flimsy as having the same last name as one of the hijackers.

Arab-American families, some of whom had been in the United States for generations, suddenly found their loyalty to their country questioned, as the FBI asked police departments across the country to interview thousands of "Middle Eastern men." Some local officials, such as police chief Andrew Kirkland of Portland, Oregon, defied the FBI, claiming that such ethnic profiling violated the civil rights of the people he was paid to serve; most complied.

On the Sunday after September 11, President George W. Bush publicly declared "a crusade" against terrorism, raising the memory of the European holy wars of the eleventh through thirteenth centuries, when knights and soldiers from across Europe invaded Arab lands to drive them from Christian holy sites. These wars, recently depicted by the movie **Kingdom of Heaven** *(2005), remain a bitter part of national histories in much of the Muslim world, where schoolchildren learn gory details about the mass slaughter of Muslims and the European practice of using the severed heads of Arab prisoners as battle projectiles in their catapults. The story typically ends with an honorable warrior-king Saleh al Din finally bringing peace to the region by driving the Europeans into the sea.*

Nabeel Abraham and Andrew Shryock, eds., *Arab Detroit: From Margin to Mainstream* (Detroit: Wayne University Press, 2000), 382–90.

Bush's speech immediately inflamed the anger of ordinary people across the Muslim world, made allies groan with discomfort as anti-American rhetoric intensified, and briefly presented Osama Bin Laden, who was widely disliked in the Middle East, as a modern-day Saleh al Din. Many Arab-Americans in places like California, Michigan, and New York wondered how they could sustain the balance between being Arab and American in such an inflammatory climate. Some turned inward and found sanctuary in their Muslim faith and Arab traditions, while others with remaining ties to the Middle East left the United States in fear of persecution. Still, many consciously turned their attention to strengthening the hyphen that links their two sides the way Americans always have, by entering public life and fighting for both parts of their identity.

Since they first began to arrive in significant numbers in the 1880s, Arab-Americans have been barely noticed as an ethnicity, often integrating smoothly into American life. This was particularly the case for Christian Arabs, who constitute the majority of the roughly 3.5 million people who self-identify as Arab-American. After September 11, however, everything about being Arab and American suddenly took on political significance. Many Arab-Americans became political activists, forming political coalitions made up of people with connections to many different religions and nations of the Middle East. They organized around antiracism, monitored anti-Arab activity, and brought together neighborhood associations to make demands on local authorities and promote positive images of Arab and Muslim culture, for their children and the broader world. In short, they sought to make the hyphen something less confusing and more conscious and political than the painful and often lonely trial and error process that the writer of this passage, Shams Alwujude, had to go through to recognize that she was both Arab and American.

QUESTIONS TO CONSIDER

1. Do you think that the writer of this passage sees herself as more American or more Yemeni? Use examples from the document to explain your answer.
2. Shams Alwujude says she wants to succeed in her life. What do you think she means by that?
3. What impact do you think racism and prejudice may have had on how Alwujude strikes a balance between being Arab and being American?

My family immigrated to the Southend of Dearborn in the summer of 1972, a year after I was born. My father had a well-paying job working on the assembly line in the Ford Rouge Plant and was able to have us brought close to him. We rented a flat in a house owned by my father's cousin, the same man who always insisted that females should not immigrate to America. In fact, when we did finally come here so that we could live with my father, we left my sister behind. We immigrated to the United States without her. My father also wanted to leave me behind, but my mother would not allow it because I was only a baby.

My sister was eight years old when she was left behind. She was told that we would be back in a year or two and that she should take care of our grandparents until we got back. This was my father and his cousin's idea. They felt that girls should not be raised in the United States, that they were better off in the old country where they could be protected from any and all evils that might be found in the new country's foreign culture and ideas. My mother, when leaving my sister behind, honestly thought that we would be going back to Yemen. Life's circumstances, such as my father losing his job, led to our not being able to go back to Yemen. My mother remained separated from my sister for nine agonizingly long years. It had not been her choice to leave her.

My earliest memory of being aware of my identity is when I was five years old. We had moved to a neighborhood in Detroit that year, out of the safety of the Arab culture of the Southend. We moved into a neighborhood where we were one of only two Arab families. One of our next door neighbors did not appreciate that we had bought the house next to theirs. They made sure to let us know this at every opportunity.

One day, when I was five, I was sitting on the front sidewalk playing with some rocks—an innocent child not knowing what kind of hatred lurked in the world. The teenage girl who lived next door approached me and started calling me a camel jockey. Not only did she call me this, she started cheering, like a cheerleader does, about my being a camel jockey. The cheer she used was a popular cheer called "Firecracker." For the word "firecracker," she substituted the words "camel jockey." I remember sitting on the sidewalk staring at her in awe, not really understanding what she was talking about, but realizing that when she said "camel jockey," she was saying it at me and that it was a very negative word. I also remember sensing her disdain when she looked at me. . . .

My family bought a house in the Southend because many of the people there had the same culture we did. My mother had new neighbors that she could communicate with. We felt embraced by other Arab families who had the same concerns that we did about being in a different culture. Like us, they wanted to be a part of it, but they did not want to give up their own identities. Since this is a free country, there was always the sense that if we did not want to give up some of our traditional Yemeni customs, we did not have to. So my parents sent us into the schools, and I got to go to school because my mother felt it was safe.

The older my brothers and I got, the more we became aware of our dual cultures. One culture was that of television, which, more importantly, we also found in our school. The other culture was that of our home.

When we were in school six to seven hours a day, we were exposed to a curriculum that catered to Christians of European descent. I remember how absurd it was when we Arab Muslim children would sing in the Christmas concert that was done every year (the school was made up of mostly Muslim Arab children) and that the teachers would say "Merry Christmas" to us when we did not even celebrate the holiday. The teachers didn't even ask us if we celebrated it or not. I wondered if they assumed that we did or if they did not care whether we did. Needless to say, it was a very awkward situation where two cultures met and assumed not to notice the differences they had.

After the long days with our teachers who were all, as I recall, ethnically European Christian people, the same kind of people who belonged to the culture that we watched on TV, we went back home. As soon as we walked over the threshold into our house, we walked into Yemen. We would immediately be met by the mother whom we spoke to in Arabic. We would be in a home decorated with pictures of Muslim holy places and handwoven Yemeni *debegs* used to serve Yemeni breads. . . .

In this Yemeni world, I had a certain role to play based on my gender. I was very protected and worried about. Every day before I went off to school, my mother would remind me not to play with boys because they were very bad and had nothing better to do than take advantage of girls and ruin their reputations. I believed her and stayed away from boys. I have never had a male friend in my life, and I am not sure that I could have one, or that I would even want one. I was also often reminded to keep my virginity. I had to be a virgin when I got married or else I might be killed. I took this threat very seriously and became resentful of the opposite sex for having so much power and say over my life and my death.

Besides being a virgin when I got married, I also had to be a good cook and housekeeper. My mother often told me that if I did not learn how to cook and keep house, my husband would divorce me. Because she was sincerely worried that I would be of no use as a wife without these skills, she began training me when I was ten years old, so that by the time I became a teenager, and was old enough to marry, I would be able to cook for my husband and for any amount of guests he might want to entertain, and therefore be a good wife. She taught me to cook traditional Yemeni food and how to serve and clean up by making me serve my brothers. My brothers, being the evil boys they were, would call me "slave" and taunt me for my having to serve them.

As I got older, my mother started asking me to wear the *hijab*, the head scarf that Muslim women wear. When I started wearing it, it was easy since all of the Yemeni women I knew wore it. When I asked what it was about, my mother said that we wear it because we are Muslims, that it is part of our religion. That was as good an explanation as I needed at the time. Later in my life when I was faced with a crisis and was looking for help from God, I had a profound religious experience during which I realized the significance of wearing the *hijab*. I understood my identity as a Muslim woman, and that the *hijab* identified me as one of "the believing women" the Holy Quran talks about. I realized that my ethnic heritage is significant and legitimate and cannot be ignored. It is significant to the extent that those who hate Muslims hate me because I am one, even though they have never met me. I knew and loved who I was historically and became able to see how beautiful people of other cultures were. My recognition of my Yemeni history helps me to know which way I should be heading in my life. I choose to dress like a Muslim so that I may honor my religious beliefs and my identity. I wear my *hijab* and also my *jilbab* (a long robelike dress) in order to feel sacred and in touch with God.

I learned to believe in God and that He would be the only One that I would submit to. In so believing, I had embraced my cultural and ethnic heritage and rejected the Western idea that the less a woman wears the freer she is. I had found true freedom when I found God, and when I found Him I was fully dressed—there is absolutely no greater freedom that can be known (and people who have known God will attest to this) than the freedom one knows when one submits to God and is encompassed by Him. I felt, at the same time, that because I lived in a free country and the Bill of Rights guaranteed my religious freedom, that I was blessed to even make such a decision. I felt that I must be the ideal American. I am a Muslim Yemeni woman who espouses her identity wholeheartedly, but who also cherishes the ideals of freedom. By my very existence in this country, I prove that this is truly a free country because I can be who I am, not who the conformists want me to be. If I am made to submit by assimilation into the dominant culture, then how could this country be called "free"? Certainly many of my beliefs are Muslim, but I also sincerely believe in the ideals that this country was founded on, in the Constitution and in the Bill of Rights, and I do consider myself an American who would fight for the cause of freedom.

When I was a girl, like all other Muslim girls in this world, living in free countries or not, I received proposals of marriage. I remember the first time that I knew someone was proposing to my family. I was about twelve years old. I walked into the house after I had been playing outside. I don't remember why I went inside, but I found my mother on the telephone talking about me. She was saying things like "Yes, I understand, but she is too young"; "I know your family, you are very well respected, you come from an excellent family." My jaw dropped when I heard her say these things. I was petrified. I interrupted her, saying that I was only a child, that I could not get married yet, I had to go to junior high. After my mother finished talking on the phone, she explained to me that it was a man from Ohio who wanted me to become engaged to his son, and that he had no intention of my marrying him right away. My mother kindly said no to him, that I was too young.

A year later, however, my mother gave me a proposal of her own. She had gone to Yemen that year and after she came back, she showed me a picture of her nephew and said that he wanted to be engaged to me. She said that I would not have to marry him until I finished high school. I agreed to the engagement mostly because it meant that I was "taken," it was a guarantee that I could finish high school without worrying about marriage proposals. At age thirteen, I became engaged to my eighteen-year-old cousin whom I had never met or spoken to. We were engaged for four years. When I was seventeen, his mother died after giving birth to one too many babies. Because my fiancé was the oldest son and his mother had left behind a house full of children who needed someone to take care of them, he and his father looked to me to fill her role, but I had other plans. I had not finished high school as was the agreement, and besides that, at this point in my life I did not look at marrying a cousin as something that I wanted to do. Neither was I capable of going to Yemen and instantly becoming the mother of a house full of children or becoming a wife. We broke off the engagement, which then opened the door for others to propose.

Many proposals came. Some were from cousins who wanted to marry me so that I might bring them into the country; others were just from young men who wanted to get married to start a family. I eventually accepted a proposal and got married when I was twenty years old, in 1991. At the time, I was considered an older bride. Most of the weddings then had brides who were still teenagers. I had graduated high school, which was very important to me. I had known girls who were married at young ages and consequently stopped attending school because they had started families. I did not want to do that. I knew that it was important for me to get an education. Marriage could wait, at least until I finished high school.

I remember when I first heard of the man I would later marry. I was preparing my sister's new house for my high school graduation party. My sister's husband told me that there was a man who was interested in marrying me and asked me if I would marry the man. I looked at my brother-in-law wanting to say, "Are you crazy?!" like I always wanted to say to him, but I tried to keep calm and asked him to tell me what the man's name was. He told me and then asked me again if I would marry him. I again kept calm and asked him to tell me more about this man. He said that he drove a taxicab in Detroit and that he also lived there. This information did not satisfy me. I could not make a decision to marry or not, so I asked my brother-in-law to find out more about him.

Eventually, this man who wanted to propose marriage paid a visit to our house and proposed in person. He did not propose to me, he proposed to my family. My family did not see any reason not to like him. After an investigation into his family and their roots, and his reputation, he was deemed an acceptable marriage partner. After he passed my family's tests, it was up to me to decide whether I would marry him or not. I agreed to marry him. I agreed to the marriage for several reasons. I was out of high school. I was tired of living at home and could not leave home unless I got married. I thought that marriage and family life would be much more fulfilling than going to college.

During our engagement of one year, we spoke on the phone about three times, but we never sat together or went out anywhere—not that I wanted to. I wanted to stay away from him as long as possible. I was surprised that I was even allowed to speak to him on the phone. We eventually had the wedding party, which was quickly followed by the wedding night. That was the night my whole life depended on, so I had been brought up to believe. Right before my wedding night, a close female friend of the family had a "chat" with me that I didn't expect to hear. My mother had also tried to "chat" with me, but I ended that "chat" by telling her that I already knew about the birds and bees (I was twenty years old, for heaven's sake!). Anyway, this woman, whose identity I will never reveal, told me that I should keep some frozen chicken's blood with me on my wedding night just in case I wasn't a virgin, and that if I wasn't a virgin, I could use this blood to save the family's honor. I could not believe what I heard. I had no idea people did that.

The wedding night came and went. Nine months after we were married, our son was born. I had never felt such blessing and love than when he was born. God had smiled down upon me and gave me this child who would be a light in my life. My marriage was not a marriage. I tried to "make it work" but it never did. My husband and I separated, then eventually divorced. Afterward, I decided to go back to school so that I could earn a degree that I could use to get a decent, secure job. I found myself having to support myself and my child; I could no longer look to a man to support me.

Even though I was engaged and married in a very Yemeni way, I took to the marriage some beliefs that were American in influence, which might have contributed to my eventual divorce. Because I grew up in America, even though where I grew up was made up of ethnic immigrants, I was influenced by American ideas that belonged to mainstream American culture. I am reminded of this American influence by Yemeni people who call their children who grow up in America, *'eyal imreeka*, which means "children of America."

Older Yemeni women sometimes compare themselves and their former difficult lives in Yemen with the "easy" lives that their daughters have in this country. This makes our existence even more difficult because we do not have it easy. It is not easy to be an identifiable ethnic immigrant. It is not easy to be a Muslim woman who wants to wear the *hijab* and has to deal with people who think of her as being oppressed by it—a piece of fabric. These people never really understand that what truly oppresses Muslim women is that which oppresses all women. It is also not easy to be a Muslim Arab immigrant in this country, because America occasionally makes immigrants feel unwelcome. Besides the pressures of mainstream American culture, *'eyal imreeka* are pressured by the guilt sometimes put on them by their elders, who had to live a more difficult existence. . . .

I feel that it is absolutely necessary for me to succeed in my life in this country. If I don't, all my parents did would have been in vain, even though they had the intention of seeing my brothers succeeding in this country, while all I was supposed to do was get married. Times change, and then so do expectations. God willing, I will remind my son of our story when he is a grown man. It's a shame that people forget what immigrants go through to try to grow roots in a new land. I hope my son will not forget what we went through and that he will use our story as fuel to drive him so that he might fulfill the hopes of his immigrant parents.

45

Homophobia in the Heartland
Dennis W. Shepard

On October 12, 1998, Matthew Shepard, a twenty-one-year-old University of Wyoming student majoring in political science and foreign relations, died from head trauma and internal injuries suffered five days earlier in a gay-bashing incident. Lured into a truck by two men he had met at the campus bar, Shepard believed he was going with them to discuss gay-liberation politics. Once inside the truck, the men told the 5'2", 102-pound Shepard that they were not gay. They robbed, beat, and tied him to a split-rail fence, where he was found eighteen hours later, barely breathing, with a crushed skull and blood covering his face, except those spots where his tears had washed it away. The image of the gentle and delicate Shepard tied to a fence post and left for dead became a national symbol in the fight against intolerance.

The outrage at the attack and the outpouring of sympathy for Shepard's parents suggested how far most of the country had come in its tolerance of sexual minorities. The trial prosecutor sought the death penalty for Shepard's murderers, despite its unpopularity in Wyoming and the pressure exerted on him by the Roman Catholic Church. Across the nation and around the world, people organized tributes and memorial services for Matthew Shepard. President Clinton held a press conference at the White House where he and Judy Shepard, Matthew's mother, spoke out in support of a federal Hate Crimes Prevention Act. Many states have since passed their own hate crimes laws.

There were, however, many reminders that homosexuality still remains controversial and far from universally accepted. At Matthew Shepard's funeral, parishioners of a Kansas City Baptist congregation disrupted the occasion with signs that read "God hates fags" and "No fags in heaven." Though the trial judge disallowed a "gay panic" defense — that one of the killers had been humiliated as a child by homosexual experiences, which compelled him to commit the crime — the compromise defense, that Shepard's sexual advances had triggered a murderous rage, struck a chord with many Americans who believed homosexuality to be immoral and wrong. Additionally, many people objected to the new hate crimes laws, arguing that they create a two-tiered justice system and punish ideas as well as actions.

The following selection comes from a statement by Dennis Shepard, Matthew's father, that he read to the court after the second of his son's killers, Aaron McKinney, received two life sentences without parole.

Dennis W. Shepard, Victim impact statement, November 4, 1999, http://www.gaylawnews.com/ shepardfatherstmt.html (28 November 2002).

QUESTIONS TO CONSIDER

1. Why did this case become so important to so many people?
2. Why do you think Dennis Shepard gave this speech?
3. Do you think hate crimes laws might have prevented the death of Matthew Shepard?

Your Honor, Members of the Jury, Mr. Rerucha,

I would like to begin my statement by addressing the jury. Ladies and gentlemen, a terrible crime was committed in Laramie thirteen months ago. Because of that crime, the reputation of the city of Laramie, the University of Wyoming, and the state of Wyoming became synonymous with gay bashing, hate crimes, and brutality. While some of this reputation may be deserved, it was blown out of proportion by our friends in the media. Yesterday, you, the jury, showed the world that Wyoming and the city of Laramie will not tolerate hate crimes. Yes, this was a hate crime, pure and simple, with the added ingredient of robbery. My son Matthew paid a terrible price to open the eyes of all of us who live in Wyoming, the United States, and the world to the unjust and unnecessary fears, discrimination, and intolerance that members of the gay community face every day. Yesterday's decision by you showed true courage and made a statement. That statement is that Wyoming is the Equality State, that Wyoming will not tolerate discrimination based on sexual orientation, that violence is not the solution. Ladies and gentlemen, you have the respect and admiration of Matthew's family and friends and of countless strangers around the world. Be proud of what you have accomplished. You may have prevented another family from losing a son or daughter.

Your Honor, I would also like to thank you for the dignity and grace with which this trial was conducted. Repeated attempts to distract the court from the true purpose of this trial failed because of your attentiveness, knowledge, and willingness to take a stand and make new law in the area of sexual orientation and the "gay panic" defense. By doing so, you have emphasized that Matthew was a human being with all the rights and responsibilities and protections of any citizen of Wyoming.

Mr. Rerucha took the oath of office as prosecuting attorney to protect the rights of the citizens of Albany County as mandated by the laws of the state of Wyoming, regardless of his personal feelings and beliefs. At no time did Mr. Rerucha make any decision on the outcome of this case without the permission of Judy and me. It was our decision to take this case to trial just as it was our decision to accept the plea bargain today and the earlier plea bargain of Mr. Henderson. A trial was necessary to show that this was a hate crime and not just a robbery gone bad. If we had sought a plea bargain earlier, the facts of this case would not have been known and the question would always be present that we had something to hide. In addition, this trial was necessary to help provide some closure to the citizens of Laramie, Albany County, and the state. . . .

My son Matthew did not look like a winner. After all, he was small for his age—weighing at the most 110 pounds and standing only 5'2" tall. He was rather uncoordinated and wore braces from the age of thirteen until the day he died. However, in his all too brief life, he proved that he was a winner. My son, a gentle, caring soul, proved that he was as tough as, if not tougher than, anyone I have ever heard of or known. On October 6, 1998, my son tried to show the world that he could win again. On October 12, 1998, my first-born son, and my hero, lost. On October 12, 1998, my first-born son, and my hero, died. On October 12, 1998, part of my life, part of my hopes, and part of my dreams died, fifty days before his twenty-second birthday. He died quietly, surrounded by family and friends, with his mother and brother holding his hand. All that I have left now are the memories and the mementos of his existence. I would like to briefly talk about Matt and the impact of his death.

It's hard to put into words how much Matt meant to family and friends and how much they meant to him. Everyone wanted him to succeed because he tried so hard. The spark that he provided to people had to be experienced. He simply made everyone feel better about themselves. Family and friends were his focus. He knew that he always had their support for anything that he wanted to try.

Matt's gift was people. He loved being with people, helping people, and making others feel good. The hope of a better world, free of harassment and discrimination because a person was different, kept him motivated. All his life he felt the stabs of discrimination. Because of that, he was sensitive to other people's feelings. He was naïve to the extent that, regardless of the wrongs people did to him, he still had faith that they would change and become "nice." Matt trusted people, perhaps too much. Violence was not a part of his life until his senior year in high school. He would walk into a fight and try to break it up. He was the perfect negotiator. He could get two people talking to each other again as no one else could.

Matt loved people and he trusted them. He could never understand how one person could hurt another, physically or verbally. They would hurt him and he would give them another chance. This quality of seeing only good gave him friends around the world. He didn't see size, race, intelligence, sex, religion, or the hundred other things that people use to make choices about people. All he saw was the person. All he wanted was to make another person his friend. All he wanted was to make another person feel good. All he wanted was to be accepted as an equal.

What did Matt's friends think of him? Fifteen of his friends from high school in Switzerland, as well as his high school advisor, joined hundreds of others at his memorial services. They left college, fought a blizzard, and came together one more time to say goodbye to Matt. Men and women coming from different countries, cultures, and religions thought enough of my son to drop everything and come to Wyoming—most of them for the first time. That's why this Wyoming country boy wanted to major in foreign relations and languages. He wanted to continue making friends and, at the same time, help others. He wanted to make a difference. Did he? You tell me.

I loved my son and, as can be seen throughout this statement, was proud of him. He was not my gay son. He was my son who happened to be gay. He was a good-looking, intelligent, caring person. There were the usual arguments and, at times, he was a real pain in the butt. I felt the regrets of a father when he realizes that his son is not a star athlete. But it was replaced with a greater pride when I saw him on the stage. The hours that he spent learning his parts, working behind the scenes, and helping others made me realize he was actually an excellent athlete, in a more dynamic way, because of the different types of physical and mental conditioning required by actors. To this day, I have never figured out how he was able to spend all those hours at the theater, during the school year, and still have good grades.

Because my job involved lots of travel, I never had the same give-and-take with Matt that Judy had. Our relationship, at times, was strained. But, whenever he had problems, we talked. For example, he was unsure about revealing to me that he was gay. He was afraid that I would reject him immediately so it took him a while to tell me. By that time, his mother and brother had already been told. One day, he said that he had something to say. I could see that he was nervous so I asked him if everything was all right. Matt took a deep breath and told me that he was gay. Then he waited for my reaction. I still remember his surprise when I said, "Yeah? Okay, but what's the point of this conversation?" Then everything was okay. We went back to being a father and son who loved each other and respected the beliefs of the other. We were father and son, but we were also friends.

How do I talk about the loss that I feel every time I think about Matt? How can I describe the empty pit in my heart and mind when I think about all the problems that were put in Matt's way that he overcame? No one can understand the sense of pride and accomplishment that I felt every time he reached the mountaintop of another obstacle. No one, including myself, will ever know the frustration and agony that others put him through, because he was different. How many people could be given the problems that Matt was presented with and still succeed, as he did? How many people would continue to smile, at least on the outside while crying on the inside, to keep other people from feeling bad?

I now feel very fortunate that I was able to spend some private time with Matt last summer during my vacation from Saudi Arabia. We sat and talked. I told Matt that he was my hero and that he was the toughest man that I had ever known. When I said that I bowed down to him out of respect for his ability to continue to smile and keep a positive attitude during all the trials and tribulations that he had gone through, he just laughed. I also told him how proud I was because of what he had accomplished and what he was trying to accomplish. The last thing I said to Matt was that I loved him and he said he loved me. That was the last private conversation that I ever had with him.

Impact on my life? My life will never be the same. I miss Matt terribly. I think about him all the time—at odd moments when some little thing reminds me of him; when I walk by the refrigerator and see the pictures of him and his brother that we've always kept on the door; at special times of the year like the first day of classes at UW or opening day of sage-chicken hunting. I keep wondering almost the same thing I did when I first saw him in the hospital. What would he have become? How would he have changed his piece of the world to make it better?

Impact on my life? I feel a tremendous sense of guilt. Why wasn't I there when he needed me most? Why didn't I spend more time with him? Why didn't I try to find another type of profession so that I could have been available to spend more time with him as he grew up? What could I have done to be a better father and friend? How do I get an answer to those questions now? The only one who can answer them is Matt. These questions will be with me for the rest of my life. What makes it worse for me is knowing that his mother and brother will have similar unanswered questions. . . .

Matt officially died at 12:53 A.M. on Monday, October 12, 1998, in a hospital in Fort Collins, Colorado. He actually died on the outskirts of Laramie, tied to a fence that Wednesday before when you beat him. You, Mr. McKinney, with your friend Mr. Henderson, killed my son.

By the end of the beating, his body was just trying to survive. You left him out there by himself but he wasn't alone. There were his lifelong friends with him—friends that he had grown up with. You're probably wondering who these friends were. First, he had the beautiful night sky with the same stars and moon that we used to look at through a telescope. Then he had the daylight and the sun to shine on him one more time—one more cool, wonderful autumn day in Wyoming. His last day alive in Wyoming. His last day alive in the state that he always proudly called home. And through it all, he was breathing in, for the last time, the smell of Wyoming sagebrush and the scent of pine trees from the Snowy Range. He heard the wind—the ever-present Wyoming wind—for the last time. He had one more friend with him. One he grew to know through his time in Sunday school and as an acolyte at St. Mark's in Casper as well as through his visits to St. Matthew's in Laramie. He had God. I feel better, knowing that he wasn't alone.

Matt became a symbol—some say a martyr—putting a boy-next-door face on hate crimes. That's fine with me. Matt would be thrilled if his death would help others. On the other hand, your agreement to life without parole has taken yourself out of the spotlight and out of the public eye. It means no drawn-out appeals process, [no] chance of walking away free due to a technicality, and no chance of a lighter sentence due to a "merciful" jury. Best of all, you won't be a symbol. No years of publicity, no chance of a commutation, no nothing—just a miserable future and a more miserable end. It works for me. . . .

Matt's beating, hospitalization, and funeral focused worldwide attention on hate. Good is coming out of evil. People have said, "Enough is enough." You screwed up, Mr. McKinney. You made the world realize that a person's lifestyle is not a reason for discrimination, intolerance, persecution, and violence. This is not the 1920s, '30s, and '40s of Nazi Germany. My son died because of your ignorance and intolerance. I can't bring him back. But I can do my best to see that this never, ever happens to another person or another family again. As I mentioned earlier, my son has become a symbol—a symbol against hate and people like you; a symbol for encouraging respect for individuality, for appreciating that someone is different, for tolerance. I miss my son but I'm proud to be able to say that he is my son. . . .

. . . Every time you celebrate Christmas, a birthday, or the Fourth of July, remember that Matt isn't. Every time that you wake up in that prison cell, remember that you had the opportunity and the ability to stop your actions that night. Every time that you see your cell mate, remember that you had a choice, and now you are living that choice. You robbed me of something very precious, and I will never forgive you for that. Mr. McKinney, I give you life in the memory of one who no longer lives. May you have a long life, and may you thank Matthew every day for it.

Your Honor, Members of the Jury, Mr. Rerucha,
Thank you.

46

The Dot-Com Bubble
Tom Ashbrook

Like the California gold rush of 1849 and the Texas oil strikes of the early twentieth century, the dot-com boom set off a speculative frenzy across the planet. Often referred to as a bubble, where prices rise without regard to the actual value of an investment, the dot-com boom saw investors bidding up stock prices to stratospheric levels based on "mind-share" and "traffic," or number of visits to a Web site, rather than on actual profits.

Young entrepreneurs started Web sites with clever gimmicks, catchy slogans, and memorable acronyms or onomatopoetic domain names, and as with the Texas oil boom of the 1900s, in which formerly valueless land sold for thousands of dollars an acre before any oil had been found, investors worldwide rushed to pay for particularly good domain names and snap up each new initial public offering (IPO) while entrepreneurs "burned" through cash promoting these Web sites and increasing the hype surrounding "the new economy." During the television broadcast of the 2000 Super Bowl, near the height of the boom, seventeen dot-com companies each paid over $2 million for thirty-second commercial advertising spots. By the next year the bubble had burst and the same individuals and companies who had rushed to invest, were stampeding to get out before they lost all their money.

Tom Ashbrook, the author of the following selection, was one of these entrepreneurs. By his own account, neither young nor dynamic, Ashbrook was a successful middle-aged journalist with a family. Although journalists were particularly fearful that the Internet would make newspapers and the brick-and-mortar businesses that sold them obsolete, it was neither fear nor necessity that drove Ashbrook. Like the forty-niners of the California gold rush, Ashbrook also wanted adventure and, like those forty-niners who often left home with the family savings for start-up, he risked everything. Using the time off afforded by a journalism fellowship at Harvard, Ashbrook and a college buddy created a dot-com that did not have a particularly clever gimmick, catchy slogan, or memorable name. Though the dot-com never became a giant like Amazon, Yahoo!, or Dell, it did continue to flourish after the collapse, and Ashbrook wrote a book about using the dot-com boom to resolve his mid-life crisis.

Tom Ashbrook, *The Leap: A Memoir of Love and Madness in the Internet Gold Rush* (Boston: Houghton Mifflin, 2000), 3–5, 20–23, 149–50, 188–89.

QUESTIONS TO CONSIDER

1. How was Tom Ashbrook similar to and different from prospectors who ran off with their family savings to look for gold in California in 1849?
2. What strengths did Tom Ashbrook bring to the dot-com world that younger, more computer-savvy entrepreneurs might not have had?
3. Tom Ashbrook mentions Bill Clinton in his account. What is the connection between Ashbrook's business and the Clinton presidency?

Everything.

That word was in the water lately. It was in the air. It was *ubiquitous*.

Everything to win. Everything to lose. Have everything. Risk everything. Walk away from everything.

And, of course, everything changing. The way we thought and felt and dreamed. Our expectations. The economy. The century. My marriage. The news business. Me. Everything.

It had been almost fifteen years since I first walked into the *Boston Globe* on a bright winter morning with shoes full of snow and a couple of scribbled names in my pocket. The *Globe* was a temple to me then, with its big presses and its brassy editorial voice. It had colorful characters and idealism and prestige and power. It hired me, and it held out the possibility of changing the world. I loved it.

Now things were changing, all right. But the paper didn't seem to have much to do with it, and neither did I. It was the economy, stupid. It was technology I barely understood. And some kind of new world, humming through the telephone lines, that we couldn't touch but was all around us. Changing everything, they said. Everything.

I had always been a heat seeker, but somehow the heat had slipped away from my corner. I was a top editor at the paper now, but what were we editing? And when we went out to report and write, who was honestly panting to read the stuff? We held a management retreat to look into the future, and a somber professor told us that tumbleweeds would blow through the pressroom within a decade. Nobody would bother to pull the last paper from the presses. Nobody would care to read it. When we all laughed, Ted Leonsis, the burly tough guy who would soon be president of America Online, flushed and growled into his microphone from the podium.

We had a simple choice, he said. "Digitize or die."

And I didn't know what he meant.

I would lie awake in bed with Danielle, her leg thrown over mine, and ramble in the night. . . .

I'm restless, Danielle, I would say. I'm crawling out of my skin. You know, at work, people actually sit in the cafeteria and debate whether newspapers will last long enough for us to retire. Maybe I'm paranoid. But the whole place is starting to smell of dinosaur. I didn't get into this business to be a minor priest in a dying religion, Danielle. I got in because it had gusto and life. Because it felt big and urgent and true. And now I don't know. I don't know if I've still got the passion for this. If it's worth it. Everything's changing. It's not what I came for anymore. . . .

And there was something else. My old college pal Rolly Rouse had been calling with a stream of wild ideas lately. I couldn't get used to hearing his voice again. In my mind's eye Rolly was still a skinny kid with a long ponytail and an unplugged electric guitar. . . .

He had written down some ideas, he said, and wanted me to take them home and think about them and tell him what I thought. So I did. And on that day I saw Xanadu beginning to come out into the sunlight.

The packet Rolly gave me was twenty-two pages long, on simple white paper, stapled at the corner. It wasn't really a business plan. Later, we would get to know all about business plans, more than I ever imagined I would know. This document was more basic. It was part business plan, part raw vision. And it was part—a large part—simple fantasy. None of the software and systems it confidently described even existed. There was no explicit mention of the Internet. It was a set of ideas and an impulse. But it was a beginning, and we took it seriously. Why be embarrassed to be beginning?

When Rolly had gone, I sat down on the back steps of the house and took off my sneakers and socks. It was early evening. Sadie was sprawled in the backyard, snapping at the occasional bee buzzing by from our weedy flower garden. I leaned against the warm brick wall of the house and began to read.

BuildingBlocks Software
The Electronic Pattern Book Company
presents
The New Victorian Home

A. Unique Selling Proposition

1. *A New Way to Design Houses*

The New Victorian Home is an "electronic pattern book" on CD-ROM. It is a high-tech, high-touch version of the 19th century architectural pattern book. *(These popular, mass-market publications presented design styles and ideas, practical construction advice, and philosophical notions linking good building to healthy living. Coupled with rising affluence and cost-cutting technological innovations, they helped make possible the profusion of high-style, high-craft "Victorian" houses that homeowners today hold in such high regard.)*

Our pioneering program lets you make choices for yourself before you hire an architect or builder. It helps you to explore the design tradeoffs you think are most important. It zooms quickly from whole houses to building elements and back and highlights relationships between the parts and the whole. . . .

The New Victorian Home is as simple to use as leafing through an interactive magazine and pointing and clicking on what you like. It is a combination of a game, an educational program, and a practical home design tool.

2. *Satisfy the Baby Boomers*

Available in both CD-ROM and applications software versions, The New Victorian Home is designed to appeal to the rising architectural tastes, standards, and construction budgets of the baby boom generation. . . . Affluent "boomers" want houses that are the modern day equivalent of those built during the Victorian Era. . . .

The New Victorian Home helps satisfy the growing demand for customized house design by tapping into the skills, knowledge, and learning capacity of the most important—and most disenfranchised—player in the process: the home buyer or renovator. You choose the building style and details you like best. You identify the attributes (e.g., "a ten-room house with a wraparound porch and large kitchen") and design qualities (e.g., "cute with lots of nooks and crannies") that are most important to you. . . .

3. *First to Market in Its Niche*

Rapid growth in computing power, falling hardware prices, the wide market penetration of the Microsoft Windows graphic interface, and the explosive sales trajectory for CD-ROM players have set the stage for a revolution in how people use computers. It is making possible new ways of organizing, exchanging, and using information.

Our flagship CD-ROM product is designed to create a new market. By being the first to take this approach, BBS hopes to define in our customers' minds a new class of knowledge-building software. . . .

The New Victorian Home is based on a simple premise: that homeowners need a way to sort out their home design options, preferences, priorities, budget constraints, and household conflicts, and to do so effectively. . . .

4. *A Proprietary Open Architecture*

BuildingBlocks Software will create an open graphical knowledge-building architecture for The New Victorian Home. We will create additional titles using the same interactive visual problem-solving environment. We will encourage other companies to create titles using our development platform, which will be a proprietary open architecture.

For example, building products manufacturers will be able to use customized versions of The New Victorian Home to showcase their products and services. This will create opportunities for in-context informational advertising in response to specific or open-ended customer requests. Use of BBS's object-oriented graphical environment on both user and senders' computers will allow fast downloading of complex images and information over standard phone lines. . . .

A mosquito made a pass at my ankle. I slapped it away. I was making a mental list of questions. Object oriented? No idea. Graphical environment? I guessed that meant the interface. Proprietary open architecture? I had an idea what that might mean, but it sounded like an oxymoron. Platform? I thought Microsoft and Bill Gates had a pretty good lock on software platforms, what little I understood of them.

And what was up with all this Victorian stuff? It could be right, but it sounded stuffy.

Still, something here was grabbing me. I liked a handsome house and had seen people struggle to get the home they wanted. I could relate to that. But there was more. Intuitively, this seemed to me like a big potential piece of new economy turf. It was a long way from covering the news, I thought. But this new economy, this digital stuff, might *be* the news of the next century.

I riffled through, looking for the money part. It was the slimmest section of the packet. Barely there. Bone simple. Up to fifty percent of the company would be sold, it asserted, to build a prototype, develop the product, and market it nationally. With no point of comparison, that sounded fine to me.

How big was the market? Well, the United States had 60 million owner-occupied homes, it said, and at any given time, probably half would be interested in home design software that helped them "clarify their preferences and options, have fun, and dream big dreams."

Have fun and dream big dreams. I liked that.

BuildingBlocks modestly assumed it could win a five percent share of the market for such software in its third year, or revenues of over $8 million on the sale of half a million CD-ROMs. But the real goal would be to win half of the market, or ten times that revenue — $80 million — by year three.

Eighty million dollars! Fine! Beautiful! Why not?. . .

[The author goes on to pursue his dot-com dream. At one point he attends a political rally in New Hampshire for aspiring Democratic presidential nominee, Bill Clinton.]

Bill Clinton was hot that night, wowing a huge crowd with his President Elvis routine. He sparkled and emoted and wooed. . . . But it worked. And his theme was the same as every other candidate's we heard that day. The American worker was in trouble and the country had better do something quick.

Each had a different prescription. Clinton's very first thundering promise from the stage was to put an Internet connection in every classroom and public library in the country. On that cold February night, odds were that not one in ten, maybe not one in fifty, people in that gym had ever been on the Internet. But they all cheered wildly when he raised it. This wasn't the race to the moon or victory over Hitler he was talking about. It was the Internet. It was pipes and bandwidth and a little electricity. And they were going wild.

The stupendous bull market of the late '90s had not yet hit its full stride that night, or that season. The decade's earlier recession and economic restructuring were still resonating powerfully. Layoffs — sudden, unpredictable, *white-collar* layoffs — were the nation's fear. A few days later, the *New York Times* launched a massive seven-part series, "The Downsizing of America." The day-one headline: ON THE BATTLEFIELDS OF BUSINESS, MILLIONS OF CASUALTIES. The *Boston Globe* announced plans to lay off forty-one mailroom workers and cut the pay of fourteen top executives.

The Internet was a baby, but it was the future's baby.

Let's go, I was thinking. I'll take the future.

[Ashbrook continues to pursue his dream and at last is ready to leave his job as a journalist at the *Boston Globe*.]

For the op-ed page a few weeks later, my last piece for the *Globe*:

Figure this.

I'm 40. I have three kids, two car payments, one fat mortgage on a house that needs paint, an all-American stack of credit card bills, and I'm quitting my job.

After 15 good years with one good employer, I'm walking away to start a company of my own. I'm taking the leap from the old economy to the new economy. From paper and ink to digital magic. From major corporation to tiny start-up. From automatic deposits, pension plan and 401K statements to big dreams, white knuckles and prayer.

The leap is thrilling. Terrifying, too. It's hard on a marriage and hard to explain to a financial planner. But it feels so right. So free. So full of promise. And somehow, so intimately connected with an American legacy much older than the vanishing 9-to-5 certainties of mid-20th-century work.

Americans are turning entrepreneurial in record numbers. Is anyone surprised? Years of layoffs and corporate "restructuring" have led most of us to weigh our own resources and imagine how we might rely on them. Dreaming is the beginning of doing.

We're told that we'll all have seven or eight careers in the new economy—the fluid, digital, no-guarantees economy that's lapping at everyone's hips by now. Maybe some of us just get tired of waiting to find out what the next career will be. When nothing is forever, why pretend? Maybe now, to leap is to live.

But some part of the urge to jump feels almost genetic, a seed of history and blood just waiting for the climate that calls it up. In all my life, I've never felt closer to the experience of immigrant forebears than I do now. They sailed from old world to new. Now it's my turn.

The new economy is, in its way, like a new continent in our midst. It has its own rough shoreline, its own excited vocabulary, its own rambunctious ethos, heroes and hustlers. It has its staked territories, its uncharted wilderness, its mythical streets paved with gold and its dreams of manifest destiny. Some people go to it voluntarily. Some arrive against their will. Almost all are changed in passage. Human nature isn't upended in the new economy, but human relationships and assumptions and identities surely are. It is a new world. . . .

47

Confronting a Planetary Emergency

Al Gore

What do you do after having held the most powerful position in the world, U.S. president? Ex-presidents usually continue to serve their country in retirement, building presidential libraries, writing books about the challenges they faced in office, acting as elder statesmen for their political party, advising sitting presidents, and supporting charitable causes. But what happens to the also-rans who almost become president, but don't? Most return to posts in Congress, the Senate, or private life and pick up where they left off, usually sadder, wiser, and more famous.

In 2001, former vice president Al Gore fit into neither category. He had won the popular vote in the 2000 presidential election, but lost in the Electoral College because of what many believe was fraud in the Florida election process. Many people believed that Gore had been pushed out by a man who had received fewer votes, but who had "wanted it more." Regardless of the veracity of the claims of electoral fraud, Gore was content neither to retire as an ex–vice president nor to return to ordinary life as an also-ran, who gave it his best shot. Instead, Gore returned to championing the environment, the cause that had made him famous as vice president under Bill Clinton.

One of the first U.S. politicians to realize the dangers of global warming, Al Gore published the book Earth in the Balance *in 1992. The book made the* New York Times *best-seller list and cemented Gore's reputation as America's most important environmentalist. The book called for a "global Marshall Plan" to address a coming environmental catastrophe, but little action was taken by the Clinton administration. By the first years of the twenty-first century, however, global warming had become one of the most important issues to heads of state as well as ordinary people around the world, and the United States was becoming internationally notorious for its rejection of and inaction on key international initiatives on climate change, such as the Kyoto Protocol.*

During this time Gore's new career flourished internationally. He became the global face for a sustainable future, founding an environmentally friendly investment company and advising multinational corporations on the environment. His documentary, An Inconvenient Truth, *won an Academy Award. In 2007, the Swedish Nobel Foundation awarded him and the Intergovernmental Panel on Climate Change its prestigious Peace Prize. Gore's acceptance speech, delivered in Oslo, Norway, on December 10, 2007, constituted a moral call to arms to people around the world to take action on the crisis of global warming.*

Al Gore, Nobel Prize Acceptance Speech, December 10, 2007, Oslo, Norway. http://nobelprize.org.

Questions to Consider

1. What does Gore think are the biggest challenges to saving the environment?
2. What does he advocate that people should do to confront those challenges?
3. Do you find Gore's speech persuasive? What, if any, language and rhetorical devices do you find effective in the speech and why?
4. Some conservatives have dismissed Al Gore's Nobel Peace Prize as an "anti-Bush trophy." What do you think they mean by this phrase?

Your Majesties, Your Royal Highnesses, Honorable members of the Norwegian Nobel Committee, Excellencies, Ladies and gentlemen.

I have a purpose here today. It is a purpose I have tried to serve for many years. I have prayed that God would show me a way to accomplish it.

Sometimes, without warning, the future knocks on our door with a precious and painful vision of what might be. One hundred and nineteen years ago, a wealthy inventor read his own obituary, mistakenly published years before his death. Wrongly believing the inventor had just died, a newspaper printed a harsh judgment of his life's work, unfairly labeling him "The Merchant of Death" because of his invention—dynamite. Shaken by this condemnation, the inventor made a fateful choice to serve the cause of peace.

Seven years later, Alfred Nobel created this prize and the others that bear his name.

Seven years ago tomorrow, I read my own political obituary in a judgment that seemed to me harsh and mistaken—if not premature. But that unwelcome verdict also brought a precious if painful gift: an opportunity to search for fresh new ways to serve my purpose.

Unexpectedly, that quest has brought me here. Even though I fear my words cannot match this moment, I pray what I am feeling in my heart will be communicated clearly enough that those who hear me will say, "We must act."

The distinguished scientists with whom it is the greatest honor of my life to share this award have laid before us a choice between two different futures—a choice that to my ears echoes the words of an ancient prophet: "Life or death, blessings or curses. Therefore, choose life, that both thou and thy seed may live."

We, the human species, are confronting a planetary emergency—a threat to the survival of our civilization that is gathering ominous and destructive potential even as we gather here. But there is hopeful news as well: we have the ability to solve this crisis and avoid the worst—though not all—of its consequences, if we act boldly, decisively and quickly.

However, despite a growing number of honorable exceptions, too many of the world's leaders are still best described in the words Winston Churchill applied to those who ignored Adolf Hitler's threat: "They go on in strange paradox, decided only to be undecided, resolved to be irresolute, adamant for drift, solid for fluidity, all powerful to be impotent."

So today, we dumped another 70 million tons of global-warming pollution into the thin shell of atmosphere surrounding our planet, as if it were an open sewer. And tomorrow, we will dump a slightly larger amount, with the cumulative concentrations now trapping more and more heat from the sun.

As a result, the earth has a fever. And the fever is rising. The experts have told us it is not a passing affliction that will heal by itself. We asked for a second opinion. And a third. And a fourth. And the consistent conclusion, restated with increasing alarm, is that something basic is wrong.

We are what is wrong, and we must make it right.

Last September 21, as the Northern Hemisphere tilted away from the sun, scientists reported with unprecedented distress that the North Polar ice cap is "falling off a cliff." One study estimated that it could be completely gone during summer in less than twenty-two years. Another new study, to be presented by U.S. Navy researchers later this week, warns it could happen in as little as seven years.

Seven years from now.

In the last few months, it has been harder and harder to misinterpret the signs that our world is spinning out of kilter. Major cities in North and South America, Asia and Australia are nearly out of water due to massive droughts and melting glaciers. Desperate farmers are losing their livelihoods. Peoples in the frozen Arctic and on low-lying Pacific islands are planning evacuations of places they have long called home. Unprecedented wildfires have forced a half million people from their homes in one country and caused a national emergency that almost brought down the government in another. Climate refugees have migrated into areas already inhabited by people with different cultures, religions, and traditions, increasing the potential for conflict. Stronger storms in the Pacific and Atlantic have threatened whole cities. Millions have been displaced by massive flooding in South Asia, Mexico, and 18 countries in Africa. As temperature extremes have increased, tens of thousands have lost their lives. We are recklessly burning and clearing our forests and driving more and more species into extinction. The very web of life on which we depend is being ripped and frayed.

We never intended to cause all this destruction, just as Alfred Nobel never intended that dynamite be used for waging war. He had hoped his invention would promote human progress. We shared that same worthy goal when we began burning massive quantities of coal, then oil and methane.

Even in Nobel's time, there were a few warnings of the likely consequences. One of the very first winners of the Prize in chemistry worried that, "We are evaporating our coal mines into the air." After performing 10,000 equations by hand, Svante Arrhenius calculated that the earth's average temperature would increase by many degrees if we doubled the amount of CO_2 in the atmosphere.

Seventy years later, my teacher, Roger Revelle, and his colleague, Dave Keeling, began to precisely document the increasing CO_2 levels day by day.

But unlike most other forms of pollution, CO_2 is invisible, tasteless, and odorless—which has helped keep the truth about what it is doing to our climate out of sight and out of mind. Moreover, the catastrophe now threatening us is unprecedented—and we often confuse the unprecedented with the improbable.

We also find it hard to imagine making the massive changes that are now necessary to solve the crisis. And when large truths are genuinely inconvenient, whole societies can, at least for a time, ignore them. Yet as George Orwell reminds us: "Sooner or later a false belief bumps up against solid reality, usually on a battlefield."

In the years since this prize was first awarded, the entire relationship between humankind and the earth has been radically transformed. And still, we have remained largely oblivious to the impact of our cumulative actions.

Indeed, without realizing it, we have begun to wage war on the earth itself. Now, we and the earth's climate are locked in a relationship familiar to war planners: "Mutually assured destruction."

More than two decades ago, scientists calculated that nuclear war could throw so much debris and smoke into the air that it would block life-giving sunlight from our atmosphere, causing a "nuclear winter." Their eloquent warnings here in Oslo helped galvanize the world's resolve to halt the nuclear arms race.

Now science is warning us that if we do not quickly reduce the global warming pollution that is trapping so much of the heat our planet normally radiates back out of the atmosphere, we are in danger of creating a permanent "carbon summer."

As the American poet Robert Frost wrote, "Some say the world will end in fire; some say in ice." Either, he notes, "would suffice."

But neither need be our fate. It is time to make peace with the planet.

We must quickly mobilize our civilization with the urgency and resolve that has previously been seen only when nations mobilized for war. These prior struggles for survival were won when leaders found words at the 11th hour that released a mighty surge of courage, hope and readiness to sacrifice for a protracted and mortal challenge.

These were not comforting and misleading assurances that the threat was not real or imminent; that it would affect others but not ourselves; that ordinary life might be lived even in the presence of extraordinary threat; that Providence could be trusted to do for us what we would not do for ourselves.

No, these were calls to come to the defense of the common future. They were calls upon the courage, generosity and strength of entire peoples, citizens of every class and condition who were ready to stand against the threat once asked to do so. Our enemies in those times calculated that free people would not rise to the challenge; they were, of course, catastrophically wrong.

Now comes the threat of climate crisis—a threat that is real, rising, imminent, and universal. Once again, it is the 11th hour. The penalties for ignoring this challenge are immense and growing, and at some near point would be unsustainable and unrecoverable. For now we still have the power to choose our fate, and the remaining question is only this: Have we the will to act vigorously and in time, or will we remain imprisoned by a dangerous illusion?

Mahatma Gandhi awakened the largest democracy on earth and forged a shared resolve with what he called "Satyagraha"—or "truth force."

In every land, the truth—once known—has the power to set us free.

Truth also has the power to unite us and bridge the distance between "me" and "we," creating the basis for common effort and shared responsibility.

There is an African proverb that says, "If you want to go quickly, go alone. If you want to go far, go together." We need to go far, quickly.

We must abandon the conceit that individual, isolated, private actions are the answer. They can and do help. But they will not take us far enough without collective action. At the same time, we must ensure that in mobilizing globally, we do not invite the establishment of ideological conformity and a new lock-step "ism."

That means adopting principles, values, laws, and treaties that release creativity and initiative at every level of society in multifold responses originating concurrently and spontaneously.

This new consciousness requires expanding the possibilities inherent in all humanity. The innovators who will devise a new way to harness the sun's energy for pennies or invent an engine that's carbon negative may live in Lagos or Mumbai or Montevideo. We must ensure that entrepreneurs and inventors everywhere on the globe have the chance to change the world.

When we unite for a moral purpose that is manifestly good and true, the spiritual energy unleashed can transform us. The generation that defeated fascism throughout the world in the 1940s found, in rising to meet their awesome challenge, that they had gained the moral authority and long-term vision to launch the Marshall Plan, the United Nations, and a new level of global cooperation and foresight that unified Europe and facilitated the emergence of democracy and prosperity in Germany, Japan, Italy and much of the world. One of their visionary leaders said, "It is time we steered by the stars and not by the lights of every passing ship."

In the last year of that war, you gave the Peace Prize to a man from my hometown of 2000 people, Carthage, Tennessee. Cordell Hull was described by Franklin Roosevelt as the "Father of the United Nations." He was an inspiration and hero to my own father, who followed Hull in the Congress and the U.S. Senate and in his commitment to world peace and global cooperation.

My parents spoke often of Hull, always in tones of reverence and admiration. Eight weeks ago, when you announced this prize, the deepest emotion I felt was when I saw the headline in my hometown paper that simply noted I had won the same prize that Cordell Hull had won. In that moment, I knew what my father and mother would have felt were they alive.

Just as Hull's generation found moral authority in rising to solve the world crisis caused by fascism, so too can we find our greatest opportunity in rising to solve the climate crisis. In the Kanji characters used in both Chinese and Japanese, "crisis" is written with two symbols, the first meaning "danger," the second "opportunity." By facing and removing the danger of the climate crisis, we have the opportunity to gain the moral authority and vision to vastly increase our own capacity to solve other crises that have been too long ignored.

We must understand the connections between the climate crisis and the afflictions of poverty, hunger, HIV-AIDS and other pandemics. As these problems are linked, so too must be their solutions. We must begin by making the common rescue of the global environment the central organizing principle of the world community.

Fifteen years ago, I made that case at the "Earth Summit" in Rio de Janeiro. Ten years ago, I presented it in Kyoto. This week, I will urge the delegates in Bali to adopt a bold mandate for a treaty that establishes a universal global cap on emissions and uses the market in emissions trading to efficiently allocate resources to the most effective opportunities for speedy reductions.

This treaty should be ratified and brought into effect everywhere in the world by the beginning of 2010—two years sooner than presently contemplated. The pace of our response must be accelerated to match the accelerating pace of the crisis itself.

Heads of state should meet early next year to review what was accomplished in Bali and take personal responsibility for addressing this crisis. It is not unreasonable to ask, given the gravity of our circumstances, that these heads of state meet every three months until the treaty is completed.

We also need a moratorium on the construction of any new generating facility that burns coal without the capacity to safely trap and store carbon dioxide.

And most important of all, we need to put a price on carbon—with a CO_2 tax that is then rebated back to the people, progressively, according to the laws of each nation, in ways that shift the burden of taxation from employment to pollution. This is by far the most effective and simplest way to accelerate solutions to this crisis.

The world needs an alliance—especially of those nations that weigh heaviest in the scales where earth is in the balance. I salute Europe and Japan for the steps they've taken in recent years to meet the challenge, and the new government in Australia, which has made solving the climate crisis its first priority.

But the outcome will be decisively influenced by two nations that are now failing to do enough: the United States and China. While India is also growing fast in importance, it should be absolutely clear that it is the two largest CO_2 emitters—most of all, my own country—that will need to make the boldest moves, or stand accountable before history for their failure to act.

Both countries should stop using the other's behavior as an excuse for stalemate and instead develop an agenda for mutual survival in a shared global environment.

These are the last few years of decision, but they can be the first years of a bright and hopeful future if we do what we must. No one should believe a solution will be found without effort, without cost, without change. Let us acknowledge that if we wish to redeem squandered time and speak again with moral authority, then these are the hard truths:

The way ahead is difficult. The outer boundary of what we currently believe is feasible is still far short of what we actually must do. Moreover, between here and there, across the unknown, falls the shadow.

That is just another way of saying that we have to expand the boundaries of what is possible. In the words of the Spanish poet, Antonio Machado, "Pathwalker, there is no path. You must make the path as you walk."

We are standing at the most fateful fork in that path. So I want to end as I began, with a vision of two futures—each a palpable possibility—and with a prayer that we will see with vivid clarity the necessity of choosing between those two futures, and the urgency of making the right choice now.

The great Norwegian playwright, Henrik Ibsen, wrote, "One of these days, the younger generation will come knocking at my door."

The future is knocking at our door right now. Make no mistake, the next generation will ask us one of two questions. Either they will ask: "What were you thinking; why didn't you act?"

Or they will ask instead: "How did you find the moral courage to rise and successfully resolve a crisis that so many said was impossible to solve?"

We have everything we need to get started, save perhaps political will, but political will is a renewable resource.

So let us renew it, and say together: "We have a purpose. We are many. For this purpose we will rise, and we will act."

Acknowledgments (continued from p. ii)

Bracketed numbers indicate selection numbers.

[1] "Victory at Greasy Grass." From *Lakota and Cheyenne: Indian Views of the Great Sioux War, 1876–1877*, edited by Jerome A. Greene. Copyright © 1994 by the University of Oklahoma Press, Norman. Reprinted by permission of the publisher. All Rights Reserved.

[3] "African Americans during Reconstruction." From B. A. Botkin. Ed., *Lay My Burden Down: A Folk History of Slavery*, published by The University of Chicago Press, 1945. Copyright © B. A. Botkin. Reprinted by permission of Curtis Brown, Ltd.

[12] "Antilynching Campaign in Tennessee." Excerpt from *Crusade for Justice: The Autobiography of Ida B. Wells*, edited by Alfreda M. Duster. Copyright © 1970 by The University of Chicago Press. Reprinted by permission of The University of Chicago Press.

[16] "A Bintel Brief." From *A Bintel Brief: Sixty Years of Letters from the Lower East Side to the Jewish Daily Forward*, by Isaac Metzker. Copyright © 1971 by Isaac Metzker. Used with permission of Doubleday, a division of Random House, Inc.

[17] "Letters from the Great Migration, Letters of Negro Migrants of 1916–1918." From *Journal of Negro History*, pp. 177–80. Copyright © by the Association for the Study of Afro-American Life and History. Reprinted by permission of the publishers.

[18] "The Trial of Katie Richards O'Hare." Excerpts from *On Trial: American History through Court Proceedings and Hearings*, Volume 2, by Robert Marcus and Anthony Marcus. Copyright © 1998. By permission of Brandywine Press.

[20] "In Defense of the Bible." From *Monkey Trial: The State of Tennessee vs. John Thomas Scopes* by Sheldon Norman Grebstein. Copyright © 1960 by Sheldon Norman Grebstein. Reprinted by permission.

[21] "An Odd Eulogy for William Jennings Bryan." From "To Expose a Fool," by H. L. Mencken. Originally published in *American Mercury*, October 1925, pp. 158–60. From the H. L. Mencken Collection. Reprinted by permission from the Enoch Pratt Free Library of Baltimore, in accordance with the terms of the will of H. L. Mencken.

[22] "The Harlem Renaissance." Excerpts from "Harlem Literati," "Parties," and "When the Negro Was In Vogue." From *The Big Sea* by Langston Hughes. Copyright © 1940 by Langston Hughes. Renewed © 1968 by Arna Bontemps and George Houtson Bass. Reprinted by permission of Hill & Wang, a division of Farrar, Straus & Giroux, LLC.

[23] "My Fight for Birth Control." Excerpts from *My Fight for Birth Control*, by Margaret Sanger. Copyright © 1931 by Margaret Sanger. Reprinted with permission of Sanger Resources and Management, Inc.

[24] "On the Road during the Great Depression: 'On the Bum.'" Account from *Morey Skaret: Riding the Rails in the 1930s*, the autobiography of Morest L. ("Morey") Skaret. Courtesy of Historylink.org.

[25] "Taking a Stand: The Sit-Down Strikes of the 1930s." "Conditions Before the Strike" and "Sit Down." From *Striking Flint: Genora (Johnson) Dollinger Remembers the 1936-1937 General Motors Sit-Down Strike* by Susan Rosenthal. Copyright © 1996 Susan Rosenthal, L.J. Page Publications. Reprinted by permission of Susan Rosenthal. http://susanrosenthal.com/pamphlets/striking-flint.

[28] "To Use an Atomic Bomb." An interview with the Pilot of the *Enola Gay*, Paul Tibbets, by Studs Terkel, from *The Guardian*, August 6, 2002. "The First American Report on the Bombing of Nagasaki, George Weller" by Studs Terkel. Reprinted by permission of the Tuttle-Mori Agency, Inc. (Tokyo) and Dunow & Carlson Literary Agency (New York) on behalf of Anthony Weller.

[29] "Rosie the Riveter." From *Rosie the Riveter Revisited* by Sherna Berger Gluck. Copyright © 1987 by Sherna Berger Gluck. Reprinted by permission of the author.

[30] "Memories of the Internment Camp." Excerpted from *The Home Front: An Oral History of the War Years, 1941–1945* by Archie Satterfield. Copyright © 1981 by Archie Satterfield. Published by Playboy Press. Reprinted by permission of Dominick Abel Literary Agency, Inc.

[31] "The Bataan Death March." Excerpts from *Death March: The Survivors of Bataan*. Copyright © 1981 by Donald Knox. Reprinted by permission of Houghton Mifflin Harcourt Publishing Company.

[32] "Blacklist: Post–World War II Red Scare." From "Notes on the Blacklist: Lardner." Interview by Barry Strugatz, from *Film Comment*, October 1988, 24, 5. Ring Lardner, Jr. Reprinted by permission of Barry Strugatz.

[34] "Cover-Up and Outcome." Westmoreland excerpt from *A Soldier Reports* by William Westmoreland. Copyright © 1976 by William C. Westmoreland. Reprinted with the permission of Random House. Nixon excerpt from *RN: The Memoirs of Richard M. Nixon* by Richard M. Nixon. Courtesy of Warner Books, Inc., New York, NY. USA.

[36] "Feminism and Consciousness-Raising." From "Consciousness-Raising: A Radical Weapon" by Kathie Sarachild. The complete speech can be found in the Redstockings anthology *Feminist Revolution* (1975, 1978), which is available along with materials on how women's liberation groups are using consciousness raising today from Redstockings Women's Liberation Archives for Action, P.O. Box 744, Stuyvesant Station, New York, NY 10009 or www.redstockings.org. Reprinted by permission of Kathie Sarachild.

[37] "Mississippi Freedom Summer." From *Letters from Mississippi* by Elizabeth Sutherland. Original edition copyright © 1965 and renewed 1993 by Elizabeth Sutherland Martinez. New edition copyright © 2002 by Elizabeth Sutherland Martinez. Reprinted with the permission of Zephyr Press, www.zephyrpress.org.

[38] "The Young Lords." Originally appeared in the the *Village Voice*, March 21, 1995. "La Vida Pura: A Lord of the Barrio" by Pablo Guzman, reprinted in *The Puerto Rican Movement: Voices from the Diaspora* edited by Andres Torres and José E. Velazquez. Copyright © 1998 by Temple University. Used by permission of Temple University Press. All rights reserved.

[39] "An American Hostage in Tehran." From *The Destined Hour: The Hostage Crisis and One Family's Ordeal* by Barbara and Barry Rosen. Copyright © 1982 by Barbara and Barry Rosen, George Feifer, and Richard Bogutski. Used by permission of Doubleday, a division of Random House, Inc.

[40] "Border Crossings." (a) Excerpts from *Mexican Voices/American Dreams: An Oral History of Mexican Immigration to the United States* by Marilyn P. Davis. Copyright © 1990 by Marilyn P. Davis. Reprinted by permission of Henry Holt & Co. LLC (b) Ramón "Tianguis" Pérez, excerpts from *Diary of an Undocumented Immigrant*, translated by Dick J. Reavis. © 1991 Arte Publico Press–University of Houston. Reprinted with permission from the publisher.

[41] "What I Saw at Gitmo." By Gordon Cucullu. From *The Right Approach*, June 30, 2005. Copyright © 2005. Reprinted by permission of Gordon Cucullu.

[42] "What Price Security? The View from Inside Gitmo, Erik Saar et al." Copyright © 2006 by Moazzam Begg and Victoria Brittain. This text originally appeared in *Enemy Combatant: My Imprisonment at Guantánamo, Bagram, and Kandahar* by Moazzam Begg (The New Press, 2006). Reprinted by permission of The New Press. www.thenewpress.com. Jon Snow interviews Moazzam Begg on Channel 4 News on February 24, 2005, "From Kandahar to Bagram to Guantánamo." Amy Goodman interviews Erik Saar, Witness to Interrogations, and James Yee, former Muslim chaplain at Guantánamo Bay, May 22, 2006. http://www.democracynow.org.

[44] "Daughter of America." Excerpt from *Arab Detroit: Margin to Mainstream*, edited by Nabeel Abraham and Andrew Shryock. Copyright © 2000 by Shams Alwujude. Published by Wayne University Press, 2000, pp. 382–90. Reprinted by permission of the Yasmin Mohamed.

[45] "Homophobia in the Heartland." Victim Impact Statement read by Dennis W. Shepard at the sentencing of Aaron J. McKinney, November 4, 1999. Reprinted courtesy of the Matthew Shepard Foundation.

[46] "The Dot-Com Bubble." Excerpts from *The Leap: A Memoir of Love and Madness in the Internet Gold Rush* by Tom Ashbrook. Copyright © 2000 by Tom Ashbrook. Reprinted by permission of Houghton Mifflin Harcourt Publishing Company. All rights reserved.

[47] "Confronting a Planetary Emergency," acceptance speech by Al Gore. © The Nobel Foundation (2007). Nobel Peace Prize, 2007, Oslo, Norway, December 10, 2007. Reprinted by permission of Nobel Media.

isual Portfolios and Documents

e Peopling of the West

[Figure 1] Norwegian Immigrant Family in Dakota Territory, 1898. Library of Congress.
[Figure 2] Benjamin "Pap" Singleton's "Ho for Kansas!" Flyer, 1878. Kansas State Historical Society/The Granger Collection, New York.
[Figure 3] Exodusters Going West, late 1870s. Library of Congress.
[Figure 4] Buffalo Soldiers, 1880s. The Granger Collection, New York.
[Figure 5] Nat Love, 1870s. The Granger Collection, New York.
[Figure 6] Anti-Chinese Campaign ad, 1888. Bancroft Library.
[Figure 7] *Harper's* Cartoon, 1869. Courtesy of HarpWeek.
[Figure 8] Sikh Workers Building the Railroad, 1908. Plumas County Museum, Quincy, CA, PCM 4-1984.
[Figure 10] Indian Children Praying at Phoenix Indian School, 1900. National Archives.

Age of Reform

[3] TR and John Muir in Yosemite, 1903. The Granger Collection, New York.

rban Industrial America

[Figure 1] Alvin Langdon Coburn, Workers, New York, 1910. George Eastman House.
[Figure 2] Alvin Langdon Coburn, Pillars of Smoke, Pittsburgh, 1910. George Eastman House.
[Figure 3] Alvin Langdon Coburn, Skyscrapers, Manhattan, 1910. George Eastman House.
[Figure 4] Jacob A. Riis, An Ancient Police Station Lodger, c. 1898. Museum of the City of New York.
[Figure 5] Jacob A. Riis, Shoemaker in Ludlow Street Cellar, c. 1890. Museum of the City of New York.
[Figure 6] Jacob A. Riis, Baxter Street Court, c. 1890. Museum of the City of New York
[Figure 7] Lewis Wickes Hine, Doffer Girl in New England Mill, 1909. Library of Congress.
[Figure 8] Lewis Wickes Hine, Young Women in Mill, c. 1910. Library of Congress.
[Figure 9] Lewis Wickes Hine, Young Woman outside Mill, c. 1910. Library of Congress.

A New Society

[26] ScotTissue advertisement. *Saturday Evening Post*, September 11, 1926. Brer Rabbit Molasses advertisement, *Ladies Home Journal*, January 1934. Brer Rabbit® is a registered trademark of B & G Foods, Inc.

Contested Boundaries

[34] Street in Levittown. Corbis. Levittown Sales Brochure, 1957. Levittown Historical Society.

Protest Movements of the 1960s and the 1970s

[Figure 1] Sit-in Protesters at Jackson, Mississippi, Lunch Counter, May 28, 1963. Corbis.
[Figure 2] African American Demonstrator Mocked in New Bern, North Carolina, April 19, 1960. Corbis.
[Figure 3] Mario Savio Speaking to Demonstrators Occupying Sproul Hall at the University of California, Berkeley, 1964. AP/Wide World Photos.
[Figure 4] New York Radical Women Protesting the Miss America Contest in 1968. Corbis.
[Figure 5] Armed Members of the Black Panthers, 1969. Bruno Barbey/Magnum Photos.
[Figure 6] Vietnam Veteran Protesting the War, May 1970. Karen Schafer/Corbis.
[Figure 7] Standoff at the Pine Ridge Reservation, 1973. Corbis.
[Figure 8] Mattachine Society Picket Line in Front of the White House, 1965. Kay Tobin Lahusen/New York Public Library.

Between History and Tomorrow

[43] Suspects Handcuffed in the Wake of the Los Angeles Riots. AP/Wide World Photos. Aerial View of Burned-Out Los Angeles, May 1992. AP/Wide World Photos. Cleaning up in South Central, Los Angeles, May 1992. José Ivey/Urban Voyeur.